The Money Shot

THE MONEY SHOT

Trash, Class, and the Making of TV Talk Shows

Laura Grindstaff

The University of Chicago Press

Chicago and London

Laura Grindstaff is assistant professor of sociology at the University of California, Davis.

The University of Chicago Press, Chicago 60637
The University of Chicago Press, Ltd., London
© 2002 by The University of Chicago
All rights reserved. Published 2002
Printed in the United States of America

11 10 09 08 07 06 05 04 03 02   1 2 3 4 5
ISBN: 0-226-30909-6 (cloth)
ISBN: 0-226-30911-8 (paper)

Library of Congress Cataloging-in-Publication Data

Grindstaff, Laura.
      The money shot : trash, class, and the making of TV talk shows / Laura Grindstaff.
        p.   cm.
      Includes bibliographical references and index.
      ISBN 0-226-30909-6 (cloth : alk. paper)—ISBN 0-226-30911-8 (pbk. : alk. paper)
      1. Talk shows—United States. I. Title.

   PN1992.8.T3 G75 2002
   791.45′6—dc21

                                                                                                              2001056891

⊗ The paper used in this publication meets the minimum requirements of the American National Standard for Information Sciences—Permanence of Paper for Printed Library Materials, ANSI Z39.48-1992.

CONTENTS

ACKNOWLEDGMENTS

Many people think of research and writing as solitary activities, but that is rarely, if ever, the case. Ethnographic research in particular is a collaborative process, requiring the help and support of others. First and foremost, I want to thank all the people who participated in this project, especially the producers and guests, without whom none of this would have been possible. People gave very generously of their time, were enthusiastic about my work, and had faith in my ability to represent them fairly and with sensitivity. I hope that I have not disappointed them. Rachel deserves special mention here, for it was she who took me under her wing and sponsored my entry into the inner sanctum of the production process. I benefited not only from her valuable insights and boundless energy but also from her camaraderie and friendship. I must also thank the institutions that provided financial support for the research and writing that led to this book: the Office of the Vice-Provost for Research at the University of Pennsylvania, which awarded me a summer fellowship in 1998; and the Office of the Vice-Chancellor for Research at the University of California, Davis, which provided me with a publications-assistance grant the following year.

Another heartfelt thanks goes out to Judy, Wendy, and Greg, all dear friends who supported me in a different way, putting me up (and putting up with me) on and off for weeks and months at a time while I was doing fieldwork in the cities where they live. Most of all, however, I am indebted to my sister, Kelly Grindstaff, and my husband, Ryken Grattet, each of whom made it possible for me to continue writing after I experienced a crisis in my life that would undoubtedly have made a good talk-show topic. They gave me support and encouragement when I needed it most, and this book is dedicated to them.

A WORD ABOUT NAMES

Ethnographers typically spend many months, even years, in a given research setting. They immerse themselves in a group, organization, culture, or community in order to better understand some social phenomenon from the "inside" perspective of its members. In many cases, especially those in which ethnographers study aspects of their own culture or write about people and places that their readers might recognize, it is standard practice to mask the identity of research subjects and even the research site itself. Consequently, with a few exceptions (noted below), the names of all individuals listed here and as used throughout the text are fictitious. *Diana* and *Randy* are likewise pseudonyms; although they refer to real shows, I have renamed them in order to preserve the anonymity of the people who work there and because, ultimately, the specific identities of these shows is less important than their capacity to illuminate more general insights about the genre. The names of other talk shows mentioned in this book are the actual names of shows that either still exist or did exist at the time I conducted my research.

There are a few exceptions to my use of pseudonyms. On occasion, I use the real names of *Diana* and *Randy* so that readers cannot deduce their identities by process of elimination. I use the real names of talk-show hosts Bertice Berry and Richard Bey since they are public figures and graciously spoke to me as such. The same was true for former talk-show producer and executive Saul Feldman (now a consultant). Three of the "organic experts"— Isaac Cubillos, Lorna Hawkins, and Joyce Ann Brown—wanted their real names used in connection with this book for the same reason that they wanted to participate on talk shows: to publicize a cause in the service of social justice. Finally, Tony West is the real name of an aspiring actor who has been on several different daytime talk shows playing the role of "ordinary" guest. Tony wanted me to use his real name primarily for the exposure.

Production Staff—*Diana*

Host	Diana
Executive producer	Jackie
Supervising producer	Bob
Talent coordinator	Heidi
Talent executive	Florence
Audience warm-up	Alex
Audience coordinator	Harry
Travel coordinator	Lena
Attorney/legal adviser	Kristina
Producers	Jocelyn, Donna, Peggy, Brian, Michelle, Justin
Associate producers	Rachel, Tamara, Susan, Ellen, Kenneth, Doug

Production Staff—*Randy*

Host	Randy
Senior producer	Vanessa
Producers	Sandra, Kelly, Jacob
Associate producers	Mark, Carmen, Angela
Audience coordinator	Latisha

Producers at Other Daytime Talk Shows

Frank, Maggie, Louise, Doris, Joe, Tyler

Other Television-Industry Personnel

Bertice Berry (host), Richard Bey (host), Saul Feldman (former executive producer), a director of daytime programming (major network), a vice president of
programming (major network), market research analysts

Talk-Show Guests—"Ordinary"

On *Diana:*   Jane ("Child Custody Battles")
         Helen ("Rape: When It's Someone You Know")
         Nancy ("Abusive Relationships")
         Cora ("Secret Loves")
         Bonnie ("Believe It or Not!")
         Charlotte and Vince ("Busted for Bigamy")

On *Randy:*   Winona, Jack ("Mom, Why Did You Abuse Me?")
         Barb, Joanne ("I Want to Confront That Guest!")
         Lori ("Why Can't We Get Along?")
         Pam and Len ("My Mom Needs Help!")
         Sharon, Colleen, Ben, Tina, and Andy ("Provide or
          Step Aside!")

On Other Shows: Tony and Ingrid (multiple shows about cheating on
          your mate)
         Ramón, Cheri, and April (*Sally Jessy*, "My Daughter's
          Out of Control!")
         Melissa (*Geraldo*, "Men Who Measure Up")
         Katherine (*Ricki Lake*, "I Can't Live without a Man!")
         Anitra (*Jenny Jones*, "Dysfunctional Families")
         Fran (*Oprah*, "Casanova Con Men")
         Charlotte, Keisha, and Vince (*Montel* show about
          bigamy)
         Wayne and Brittany (*Montel* show about hypnotism)
         Sonny and Jordan (*Jerry Springer*, "Teen Prostitutes")

Talk-Show Guests—"Experts"

Professional experts: Richard, Connie, Rebecca, Grace, Rita, James,
         Rhoda, Lilian, Jeremy

"Organic" experts: Abby, Grant, Nathan, Isaac Cubillos, Lorna
         Hawkins, Joyce Anne Brown

Setting the Stage

"Hello Diana. This is Carrie, from Cedar Rapids, Iowa. I'm calling in regards to the show you're advertising on the TV there about 'Toxic Relationships.' About people who are always putting you down. Well, I reunited with my biological father back in 1990, and, I don't know, it seems like everything I do just isn't good enough for him. I do a lot for my father; I try to do all the things a good daughter is supposed to do. But he just doesn't—"

At this point the caller began to cry, and the tape beeped, cutting her off before she had time to leave her telephone number. I sighed and adjusted my headphones more comfortably around my ears. The producers would never have phoned her back, anyway; her story wasn't unusual or dramatic enough. She did cry easily, however, and that was in her favor. Transcribing the 800 line was one of my least favorite jobs as an intern. As much as I sympathized with the people who called in—the majority of them women—it was tedious, recording this endless litany of heartache and complaint. Callers rambled on and on, and they never seemed to get to the point. Sighing again, I cued the tape to the next call.

1

"Hi Diana. I'm calling about the upcoming Mother's Day make-over show—"

I cut her off there and fast-forwarded to the next call. The producers had more than enough potential makeover candidates.

"Hello. My name is Carlos. I'm seventeen years old. You were asking about 'Runaway Gay Teens.' I'm gay, and I went to a club one night, and a man, he, uh, he raped me and one of my friends by gunpoint. And if I would've turned him in, my parents would've found out I'm gay. So I ran away to Orlando and, uh, went into prostitution. And my parents are having a really hard time with it . . . they're really religious and stuff, and I just want to be who I am, and I, I really need to talk to somebody about it. And I would love more than anything to be on your show, Diana. 'Cause you're the best. My telephone number is—"

I was poised to write down the number when suddenly I felt a sharp tap on my right shoulder. I hit the pause button on the tape recorder and turned around.

"Here, the name tags are ready. Run them down to the dressing rooms, and then stay there because the first guests are due to arrive any minute—I'll be along as soon as I can."

The order came from Heidi, the talent coordinator, who was rifling through a stack of consent forms. Her face was flushed and her voice full of tension. Pushing back from the table, I tossed my headphones aside, grabbed my clipboard, and left the bustling production office for Stage 12 on the other side of the studio lot. Outside, the sun was blinding as it bounced off the metal siding of the surrounding buildings, and the ever-present din of construction rose faintly in the distance.

Within minutes I was at the stage, an immense warehouse containing more offices, dressing rooms, a lounge and kitchen area, the "green room," a control booth, editing suites, and a huge set with seating for roughly two hundred audience members. This is where *The Diana Show* is taped, one of a dozen or so daytime talk shows produced in the United States, and one of two produced at Zenith Studios.[1] At the sight of a stretch limousine parked at the rear entrance, my heart sank: at least one guest had already arrived. I took the stairs two at a time and went inside, greeted by a blast of cold air and the distant shouts of George, the stage manager, who was complaining about the position of the overhead floodlights. A large, dark-haired woman I didn't recognize sat alone on one of the couches in the lounge clutching her purse—one of the guests, very pale, and clearly ner-

---

1. As noted earlier, *Diana* is a pseudonym. So is Zenith Studios.

vous. The first show today was about childhood sexual abuse, and, on the basis of the script that I photocopied for the producers, I guessed that this was Karen, a young woman repeatedly molested by an uncle.

"You must be Karen, our guest of honor." I smiled warmly and extended my hand, introducing myself as an intern and Heidi's assistant.

I took Karen first to one of the dressing rooms, fixing her name tag to the metal plate on the door just below the gold star, then to the green room, which was equipped with couches, a television monitor, and an assortment of catered foods. By this time Heidi had arrived, along with the two producers for today's show and most of the technical crew and support staff. People rushed back and forth, readying equipment and attending to last-minute details. The studio audience was filing in; I could hear the comedian doing his warm-up routine every time the outer door to the set swung open ("Why is it that when a man talks dirty to a woman it's sexual harassment but when a woman talks dirty to a man it's three dollars a minute?"). The remaining guests were also arriving, including an incest survivor, a boy abused by his baby-sitter, a convicted pedophile, and a psychologist/expert. Heidi gave me explicit instructions to keep the pedophile as far from the other guests as possible until taping began to avoid any friction. This proved easy enough, as the man stayed in his dressing room with the door closed until called by the wardrobe personnel to get his hair and makeup done.

While Heidi made the rounds securing written consent from the guests for their participation, the stage manager wired them for sound, and the producers prepared them for key questions that Diana, the host, would ask on the air. The "ordinary" guests who were neither experts nor celebrities always needed a little extra reassurance before going on television for the first time, and, in this particular interaction, the producers made a special effort to position them as experts, too, of a sort—experts on their own personal experience. I knew the routine by heart:

"Just relax, you'll do fine. This is your life, you've lived it, so there are no wrong answers. Just tell it like it is, straight from the heart. Don't hold back on those emotions because this is your big chance to show millions of people you really care about this issue. And don't be shy—this is *your* show, so if you have something to say, jump right in there. Now, when Diana asks you to describe the first time your husband beat you, what are you going to say?"

Finally, the executive producer, supervising producer, and director appeared backstage at the same time Diana herself emerged from her dressing room. Taping would begin in fifteen minutes. Diana said a few words of welcome to each guest, then went out to greet the audience. I raced back across the lot to the production offices for the third time that afternoon to retrieve a set of photographs that had to be scanned and prepared for use later in the show. The office was just as busy as before since there would be a second taping later in the day and two more tomorrow. I delivered the photos to the graphics department and took my seat in the control booth above the set just as the director started the countdown. The room was cool and dark, illuminated primarily by the double row of television monitors in the far wall above the editing console. The soundboard looked like a miniature city block sprinkled with neon lights. It was my job to answer the phones in the booth so that those working there were not disturbed during the taping. For me, it was the most interesting of all my duties as an intern because I got to witness two performances at once: that of the host and guests onstage and that of the production staff around me.

"Cold open—no music, no applause!" the director shouted. "Three! Two! One! *Roll tape!*" The camera was tight on the first guest, Karen, a victim of childhood molestation, who spoke of the abuse that she suffered as a child every holiday when her uncle came to visit. Her voice was high and clear, with a faint Southern accent. Diana, the show's host, prodded for more details, and Karen obliged, tears welling up in her big brown eyes. I could feel the tension rise in the control booth; we were simultaneously horrified by her suffering, incredulous that she would discuss it on national television, and elated that she was doing so with such visible emotion— especially with the November ratings sweeps just around the corner. When the woman broke into sobs describing the time her uncle "shared" her with a friend, the look of triumph on the producer's face told me that this show was indeed a "sweeper." The segment ended with the introductory credit sequence accompanied by the trademark *Diana* music, and then the director cut to a commercial. As soon as the stage manager gave the "clear" signal, the silence in the booth gave way to the buzz of conversation.

When taping resumed a few minutes later, eight-year-old Troy described how his baby-sitter forced him to perform various sex acts over a period of several years, threatening to kill him if he ever told anyone. Troy's mother begged parents to be ever vigilant when trusting the care of their children to others. "What happened to us could happen to you too!" she said, dabbing delicately at the corners of her eyes with a tissue. Because they were African American, Troy and his mother satisfied the show's mandate for "diversity" on the panel. In a different way, so did the next guest to appear, a convicted child molester out of jail on parole. White, well dressed, and in his early thirties, he was, Diana announced, participating in a radical new therapy that brought perpetrators and victims together in direct confrontation.

"What's so radical about that?" the script supervisor sneered from his seat beside the director. "Talk shows have been doing it for years!"

No sooner had the molester taken his seat than audience members, roused by the testimony of the first three guests, began to denounce him as sick and perverted. A short, gray-haired, elderly woman stood up and called him a messenger of the devil. I wondered aloud at the man's decision to appear on the show. The sound technician sitting next to me simply shook his head in disgust—whether at the pedophile, at the show for giving him a platform, or at the behavior of the audience, I couldn't tell. The phone at my elbow rang; I put the caller on hold until the commercial break.

The next guest waiting in the wings was Margaret, the incest survivor. I knew that the two producers for today's topic had disagreed about whether to lead with Margaret or with Karen. Margaret's sexual history was more sensational because she had been raped repeatedly by her father and then again by her first boyfriend, but Karen was more emotional during the preinterview ("fresh" and "raw," as the producers put it) and thus promised a better performance. At the eleventh hour, they decided to use Karen up front to draw the audience in and bring Margaret on later as a success story and role model for other survivors since she now runs a women's political-advocacy organization in San Francisco. Margaret was also, apparently, lesbian, for the host read the following tease off the prompter before breaking to another commercial: "Up next is a woman whose history of sexual abuse by the men in her life caused her to give up on guys altogether! Don't go away!"

This was Margaret's cue to walk onstage. We waited for what seemed like minutes, but she didn't appear in the monitors. Suddenly, the director took off his headset and turned to the supervising producer.

"Bob, we've got problems. That Margaret lady got mad and took off. Just threw down her wireless and took off. Jackie is going crazy down there on the floor; you better see what's going on."

Bob sprang to his feet, disentangling himself from his own headset as he rushed out the door, cursing under his breath. I sat for a few minutes not knowing quite what to do. I turned to the technician. Had this ever happened before? He said no, not to his knowledge, and asked me to pass him the sports section of the paper. I glanced over at the others in the room. The sound man and chyron operator were discussing the show's desperate need for better, high-tech equipment, while the assistant director and script supervisor debated the merits of fake versus real Christmas trees.

The director was yelling at somebody on the phone. Taking a chance that the other line wouldn't ring, I slipped away and headed down to the set to see what more I could learn.

The camera operators and various other technical staff had gathered at the edge of the stage. Diana was standing in front facing the audience, explaining that the delay in production was due to a technical problem with the sound system. The producer and associate producer for today's topic were nowhere to be seen, nor was the executive producer or supervising producer. I learned from a stagehand that all four were outside in the parking lot with Margaret. It took them almost an hour to figure out why she was upset and persuade her to return. It seems that, when Margaret heard Diana introduce her as a woman whose history of sexual abuse caused her to "turn gay," she bolted because she felt that the description was silly and untrue. She insisted that the topic of the show was childhood sexual abuse, not lesbianism, and that the matter of her sexual orientation was not open for discussion on the air—she had made that very clear to the producers. At this point the executive producer apologized for the mistake, blaming it on miscommunication between the associate producer, who conducted the original preinterview, and the producer, who wrote the final script. They promised to rewrite Margaret's introduction and tape it again.

Meanwhile, back in the booth, the crew was getting irritable. There was another show after this one, and we were hours behind schedule— after Margaret, there was still the expert psychologist to get through. I knew that it would be quite late before I left the lot. Just as I was picking up the phone to cancel my evening dinner plans, Heidi rang on the other line. She was sending another intern to relieve me in the booth because she wanted my help backstage with the changeover; the guests for the second show were starting to arrive, and we had to clear the dressing rooms for them. Ordinarily, when guests overlapped, we would put the overflow in portable trailers outside, but, because the second show featured "industry people," we couldn't do that. The topic was "Former Child Stars: The High Price of Fame" (back in the production office it was known as "Hollywood Has-Beens"). Heidi was anxious and stressed. Celebrities, even B-grade celebrities willing to appear on a daytime talk show, did not like to wait around. All five guests were former child stars from 1960s television sitcoms, three still eking out a living as actors, the other two having left the industry for jobs in the "real" world. All had been negatively affected by early fame. Overall, the show went smoothly; the producers relied heavily on visual elements such as photographs and old sitcom footage to vary the pace and keep audience members engaged. It was almost 10 P.M. when the last guest was thanked and the last limousine pulled away from Stage 12.

"In every way save one this was a typical tape day at *Diana*," I wrote in my journal later that night. "The pace backstage was frantic, the tension high." As usual, the first show was more emotionally charged than the second because the host found it too draining to do two "heavy" shows back-to-back. The exception to business as usual was Margaret's rebellion, for, although producers believe that the probability of unforeseen or unexpected events increases when "ordinary" people are onstage, the production of daytime talk shows, including the performances of ordinary people, is remarkably predictable and routine. Most of the time.

The following day, while at lunch with some of the staff, I asked them about the incident with Margaret.

"First of all," said Donna, the producer in charge of the taping, "it's a lot of raw nerves when you have a group of survivors sitting next to a pedophile. It's a time bomb waiting to go." Second, she continued, Margaret had been leery of participating from the very beginning because she recently had a bad experience on another daytime talk show: the producers had led her to believe that the topic was about "turning your life around" when, in fact, they were setting up a confrontation with her homophobic ex-husband.

"So she came in with a major chip on her shoulder," said Donna. "She was expecting some sort of ambush or setup, you know, some sort of confrontation." And who could blame her, Donna concluded, given the garbage that other talk shows are producing and the sleazy way they treat their guests? Everyone at the table nodded their agreement. *Diana* was considered a "class act" with a "clean" reputation, appealing primarily to middle-class women.

"One of the best things about working at *Diana*," said Rachel, an associate producer and one of my key informants, "is that I never have to do anything I find personally objectionable." She hesitated for a second and then added, "Well, almost never. I mean, I wouldn't want to work on a really trashy show where the goal was to produce sensational television whatever it took."

Again, heads around the table bobbed up and down. "I was at a show like that for a year," another producer volunteered. "It was the worst year of my life. It was horrible." The consensus was that shows geared toward conflict and confrontation had changed the character of daytime talk for the worse. Whereas talk shows used to tackle serious issues in a more or less dignified manner, now they were more raucous and theatrical, with "sleazy" topics and younger, less-educated guests. That is, whereas talk shows used to be "classy," now they were "trashy." I was to hear this lament again and again in various guises during the season that I interned at *Diana*. It was pretty much the same lament about daytime talk shows that I read in the newspaper, and I remember thinking to myself (not for the first time) as I walked back to the production offices after lunch that, rather than construct an image of "that kind of show" from the outside, I should go take a look for myself.

About a year later I did just that when I started interning at another talk show that I'll call *Randy*. Aimed at a younger, more gender-mixed demographic than *Diana*, *Randy* made no pretense about being classy. Topics were chosen for their titillating and incendiary qualities and focused primarily on interpersonal conflict. As I heard Randy himself say many times to his staff, "This is a show about relationships and conflict, about the drama of human conflict. This is not a show where you pull out a notebook and take down information." It didn't take me long to understand what he meant and to see how the emphasis on "drama" affected the work behind the scenes in ways both obvious and subtle. My clearest glimpse into the backstage relations between producers and guests came one day when Mark, one of the associate producers whom I had gotten to know, invited me to shadow him during the taping of one of his shows. Mark was an affable, easygoing man in his late twenties. He could use my help, he said, since they were going to simulate a homeless shelter on the set and might need an extra pair of arms to carry props. Titled "Provide or Step Aside!" the show was about women who disapproved of a family member's mate. It featured only one story and one set of guests, which was somewhat unusual since most talk shows, *Randy* included, tended to stack the panel with multiple stories, each with a different set of guests.

Colleen, a twenty-year-old housewife and mother of two, had called the 800 line because her sixteen-year-old sister, Tina, had recently married a man twice her age and was now living with him in a homeless shelter. Colleen wanted to confront Tina's husband on the air for being an inadequate provider. She also wanted Tina to leave him and go live with their older sister, Sharon, who was to appear on the show with an extra plane ticket—paid for by the show—and an ultimatum: leave the husband, and go live with her, or lose the goodwill of the family. Sharon's presence on the show was to be a surprise because Tina had not seen her in more than a year. In fact, before she was contacted by the producers, Sharon had no idea that Tina was even homeless. For their part, Tina and her husband knew only that this was a show about "homeless couples" trying to make ends meet.

I arrived early at the studio, not wanting to appear ungrateful for this opportunity to help out backstage (assisting producers on the set was not a typical activity for *Randy* interns). The office manager was circulating a memo that listed the green rooms in use for that day. Below the list was a postscript that stated in bold, block letters: PLEASE DO NOT DISCUSS THE SHOW TOPICS OUT LOUD WITH ANYONE. NO EXCEPTIONS! Mark was still in a meeting, so I joined a small cadre of production assistants—also known as "PAs"—lugging mattresses and bedding from the service elevator to the stage. The floodlights had not yet been turned on, and the temperature was a chilly fifty-two degrees. Whereas the set at *Diana* was large, with "Town and Country" decor, comfortable padded chairs in the audience, and wall-to-wall carpeting, the *Randy* set was smaller and more sparsely decorated: the backdrop to the stage consisted of plain beige paneling with the word *Randy* written in large, masculine script across one side, and the space for the audience was filled with metal folding chairs. Overhead, on the catwalk, a member of the crew was tinkering with a temperamental lighting fixture. He was almost invisible, dwarfed by the huge cables and wires that snaked the length of the ceiling.

Heading back to the production office, I fell into step behind a producer and one of her guests from another taping, a show titled "Why Can't We Get Along?" They took the hallway at a fast clip, heels clicking sharply on the linoleum. The guest was a pale young woman in her early twenties wearing a very short skirt and heavy makeup.

"You're the first one on," the producer was saying, "so we're relying on you to make an impact, to make sure viewers out there don't get bored and change the channel—you gotta talk about the stripping right off the bat, OK? Don't take forever to get it out. Say what you came here to say. And, whatever you do, do it *big*. This is national television, remember, and my ass is on the line."

Mark was just emerging from the executive producer's office. His face was grim, and I knew that this meant a last-minute problem involving one or more of the guests. Last night, Tina and her husband, Andy, were discovered by the police sleeping in their car in a residential neighborhood. Then the couple had been detained at the downtown police station because Andy had refused to respond when questioned about his relationship to the young girl.

"I got some soft money approved from accounting," he told me. "A PA is on her way down there right now to bail them out."

Meanwhile, Colleen, her husband, Ben, and the other sister, Sharon, had arrived and were all waiting together in Green Room 2. Mark and I entered just as the producer, Kelly, was leaving. She handed Mark the guests' legal documentation, which included birth certificates as well as driver's and marriage licenses. Everything checked out, she said, and they had all signed consent forms guaranteeing the authenticity of their identities and stories. Kelly was a slight, dark-skinned woman with a no-nonsense attitude. Mark told me that he liked working with her because it allowed him to play the "good cop" with guests: while she demanded strict compliance and refused to make exceptions or entertain special requests, he was friendly and sympathetic, a division of labor that ultimately made him more influential with particularly difficult or demanding guests. This strategy had proved useful only yesterday during the taping of an episode on white supremacy, in which one of the guests, a member of the KKK, picked a fight with a black man sitting in the front row of the audience. The bodyguards intervened, but the guest attacked again as soon as they released him. Because Mark had listened to the KKK guest with a sympathetic ear earlier in the green room and had thus established a personal bond with him, Mark was eventually able to calm him down when no one else could.

I took a seat on one of the couches at the back of the room while Mark turned his attention to Colleen, Ben, and Sharon. They sat around a small table littered with coffee cups and half-eaten bagels, talking among themselves. They seemed pretty relaxed considering that they were about to make their debut on national TV.

"OK you guys, I just want to go over a few things," Mark said. "Nobody is chewing gum, right? Good. Now, when you're out there onstage, be careful not to giggle or fool around during the commercial breaks because it looks strange to the audience if you're crying or angry one minute and happy the next. We don't want people thinking, 'Hey, what's up? Are these guys actors or something?' OK?"

Colleen interrupted him. "Don't you worry. I was mad at Andy before I got here, I'm mad at Andy now, I'll be mad at him during the show, and I'll be mad at him after the show."

Mark said, "OK, good. Now, I know the producer already talked to you about your stories and all, but I just want to go over a couple of points again. The most important thing is that you speak your mind. Show us your feelings. Don't be afraid to take charge, OK?" He stood up and rearranged a couple of chairs in the room to simulate the stage. "Like, for example, Colleen, when you walk onstage and Tina is sitting there, grab her hand, let her know you care, tell her you only want what's best for her. 'Tina, you're only sixteen years old, you're just a baby! What are you doing living with this man in a homeless shelter? You need to be in school. You deserve better than him.'"

Sharon, the older sister, interrupted at that point and said, "Don't call her a baby. She hates that, and she won't listen to you."

Mark replied, "OK, well, you don't have to use those words exactly, but, you know, talk about how she's still young, how she's got her whole life ahead of her, and she's sleeping in a car for God's sake!"

All three guests were from a small town in the Midwest, and neither Colleen nor Ben had ever been on a plane before. Ben, a rather quiet, shy man, was a welder and frequently out of work. He and Colleen have two small children. As for Sharon, she'd left home at a young age and was living on her own in Arizona. As the women chatted, they kept looking over at Mark to see if he was paying attention. Sharon asked when the show would air, lamenting that her unruly red hair would look awful on camera. All of them were wearing dress clothes provided by the show's wardrobe department. I leafed through the few pages of script that Mark had given me—a much less elaborate kind of document than producers at *Diana* were required to write.

At that point, we were interrupted by a knock on the door. One of the production assistants pulled Mark aside and whispered that the guests we'd been waiting for—Tina and Andy—had arrived and were sequestered in Green Room 1 with the producer. They would be ready for Mark in about ten minutes. Mark excused himself, and I followed him back to the production offices. Earlier in the day, he had done a computer search for facts about homelessness to use during the show but wasn't happy with what he'd found. He asked me if I knew any professors who studied homelessness, and, when I said yes, he told me to get in contact with them while he went to see how things on the set were progressing. I telephoned a friend who quoted me half a dozen or so statistics about homelessness and the lack of affordable housing in the United States. Mark chose three and had the chyron operator in the control booth type them in to the character generator. Later, I was asked to find the number of the National Coalition for the Homeless so that they could flash that on the screen as well. (As it turned out, neither the facts nor the telephone number was used during the taping—although possibly they would be inserted later during the final edit, either along with the credits or as transitions in and out of commercial breaks.)

Mark then went to greet Tina and Andy, the homeless couple. He told them that it was important for them to hold fast to their convictions throughout the show, not to lose their energy or to lose sight of why they were here—to defend themselves and their love for each other.

"Don't let Colleen and Ben get the last word," Mark warned. "You've got a good relationship, and you love one another. That's all that matters, and that's what you have to let everyone know." To Tina he said, "You need to tell Colleen that you're not a baby anymore. Don't be afraid to look her right in the eye. Say, 'Girlfriend, we're sisters, and I love you, but this is my life, and you can't tell me how to live it, so just lay off.'"

Tina gave an uncomfortable laugh. With her soft brown curls and cherubic face, she looked much younger than her sixteen years. "I don't say *girlfriend*; I don't talk like that," she said.

"Of course, say it in your own way," Mark agreed. "The important thing is not to hold back on your feelings." Addressing them both, he said, "I'm giving you the license to express yourself. Don't be afraid to butt in, interrupt, do whatever it takes to get your point across—don't wait for the host to call on you, and don't let anyone push you around. *You* are the star of this show."

As the taping drew near, the pace got more frantic. Mark ran a couple of photographs to the graphics department to be scanned into the computer and sent me to his office for the consent form that Tina's parents had signed allowing her to marry Andy before she was of legal age. I then ran to wardrobe for extra clothes to pile in one corner of the stage so that the "shelter" would look more lived-in. On the floor where the front row of the audience would normally be was a park bench strewn with old newspapers and debris. The show began with Randy, the host, sitting on the bench between Tina and Andy.

Colleen, Ben, and Sharon watched from the control room. Mark was there with them in order, in his words, to "keep them pumped up" and to help them identify points to respond to when it was their turn to go out onstage. Both Colleen and Sharon began crying the moment they saw their sister pictured in the monitors. They cursed Andy for marrying a mere child and then failing to provide a home for her.

Colleen took the stage at the beginning of the second segment. As she waited nervously in the wings, the producer came running over and said, "OK, now, this is it, this is the intervention, this is where the intervention begins."

Initially, Colleen was alone onstage with Tina, and then, in the third segment, the producers reintroduced Andy. The two sisters cried a great deal, although I noticed that Colleen stopped long enough to yell periodically at Andy and to check her makeup during every commercial break. Tina wept almost continually throughout the entire taping, her face growing increasingly red and blotchy. She missed her family and her friends, but she loved Andy, she said. When one of the audience members called him a "sicko pedophile," she ran off the set and had to be coaxed back on by Randy himself. The security personnel were clustered in one corner watching the show on a monitor, and some of them were crying, too.

Back in the control room, Mark reminded Sharon that she must talk directly to Tina and get to the point. They were running out of time, and, if nothing else, she had to say, "Here's a plane ticket, come home with me." Sharon was very nervous. As she stood waiting in the wings for her cue, she kept wiping the palms of her hands on her skirt. Finally, Randy announced to the audience that there was another family member waiting to speak with Tina: her older sister, Sharon. Sharon then rounded the corner and met Tina's gaze. I would not have thought it possible for the younger girl to sob any harder, but the sight of her older sister produced a fresh flood of tears. Sharon was more quiet and subdued onstage than was Colleen, who was clearly enjoying the spotlight. Toward the end of the segment, the arguing between Colleen and Andy escalated, and the audience, emboldened, taunted Andy with increasingly derogatory comments, but there was no physical confrontation between him and Colleen, and time ran out before Colleen's husband, Ben, could be introduced. Just before the show ended, when everyone was yelling at everyone else and Tina was still sobbing, tears streaming down her face, Randy made her an offer. He said that, if she went to Arizona with her older sister, he would put her up in her own apartment until Andy got back on his feet and was able to provide for her—in the meantime, she would enroll in school. This brought the audience to its feet, everyone clapping and cheering, "Randy! Randy! Randy!" Quite a publicity stunt, I thought, although I did not doubt that he would keep his word.

Backstage immediately after the show, the guests were fairly quiet. They weren't separated in green rooms as before but sat together in a lounge adjacent to the production offices. Tina retreated to an inner changing room, where she continued to sob uncontrollably. Andy attempted to console her. Then things began to heat up again as Colleen joined them, followed by Ben, and pretty soon I heard yelling and the crash of an overturned chair. The cameraman and bodyguard ran in at the same time. The latter threatened Ben with bodily injury unless he behaved himself; the former got it all on tape. Ben retreated meekly to the lounge, and, minutes later, Andy followed, but the three sisters stayed in the changing room, and I could hear Tina crying on and on. Apparently, she was trying to make up her mind what to do—stay with her husband, or go to Arizona with Sharon. Meanwhile, the producer was attempting to herd everyone into limousines so they wouldn't miss their flights; I could tell that she was torn between needing to get everyone out of there and wanting to let the cameraman film the drama. First Tina decided to stay with Andy, then she said she was going with Sharon, then she changed her mind again and chose Andy.

Finally, the whole lot of them were herded down the elevators to the cars waiting outside. The camera was running right up until the elevator doors slid shut. The last thing I overheard, the executive producer told Mark to contact a camera crew in Arizona and put them on standby at the airport there—just in case Tina changed her mind yet again and decided at the last minute to go with Sharon. "Make sure you get somebody who's used a camera before," she snapped. She was a tall, thin woman, with piercing brown eyes and an imposing demeanor. She was used to be being obeyed.

I went back to the production office, my head spinning. I was grateful for my afternoon assignment to the audience department, where the main task was to book the studio audience over the phone when people called to request free tickets. About an hour prior to the second show, Latisha, the audience coordinator, appeared at the door, panic-stricken: several large groups had failed to show up for the taping, and the audience was too "thin." So I grabbed my coat and joined several other interns who had been ordered to give away tickets on the street. Like the others, I found myself instinctively avoiding middle-class businessmen in suits and targeting instead women shoppers and groups of teenagers hanging about. I had the most luck with tourists standing outside the lobby of the nearby Hilton.

It was late in the evening when, exhausted, I finally went home and long after midnight before I finished writing about the day's events.

To do a great talk show, you need two things: lies and breasts. And if they both relate, you've got a killer show. In other words, you need deception because that's a form of drama, and then you need that dramatic Perry Mason moment when the lie is exposed. And you need cleavage, you know, sex. You have to be able to imagine sex; you have to be able to feel it. This is nothing new because if you watch any successful television show, you'll see it. All the great ones have those two elements, lies and breasts. That's all you need.

— SAUL FELDMAN, former television executive
and talk-show producer

CHAPTER ONE

Airing Dirty Laundry

Mind over Matter: Talking Heads and Talking Bodies on Television

I spent more than a year "behind the scenes" at *Diana* and *Randy*, two nationally televised daytime talk shows produced in the United States. Besides working as a production assistant and intern, I took copious notes, conducted lengthy interviews, and sat in the studio audience during the taping of countless episodes, both at these shows and at others around the country. This book is an ethnographic account of that experience. It is also an account of how daytime talk shows both challenge and reinscribe long-standing hierarchies between "high" and "low" culture, expert and ordinary knowledge, and the ways in which these hierarchies are related to social—especially class—inequality.

A close cousin of "reality television," daytime talk shows typically feature a host, a panel of "ordinary" guests, and a participatory studio audience. Phil Donahue is generally credited with pioneering the genre in the
late 1960s, and, for almost twenty years, his was the only nationally syndicated program of its kind. By 1988, however, *Donahue* had been joined by
Sally Jessy Raphael, *Oprah*, and *Geraldo*, and, by early the following decade,
there were more than a dozen different shows on the air watched by millions of viewers worldwide. Although many of the newcomers didn't last
more than a season or two and some of the veteran hosts like Donahue and
Geraldo have retired, the genre retains a strong foothold in the daytime
schedule. Traditionally geared toward women, talk shows cover a wide
range of topics, from sexual abuse, weight loss, and interracial adoption to
gay parenting, marital infidelity, and prostitution. They take the backstage
of everyday life and put it up front, onstage, making public events of personal experience. And, despite the fact that talk shows routinely incorporate experts as well as the occasional celebrity guest, "ordinary people" are
the real stars and experts of the show.

Excepting this emphasis on ordinary people, the assembly of daytime
talk could be said to parallel the assembly of late-night celebrity talk shows
or more serious discussions of news and public affairs among experts. Stardom and expertise in these contexts is no less constructed than is ordinariness (see Tuchman 1974). All three types of programming are concerned
with generating lively interaction, which is partly a function of guests' performative potential and partly a function of their strategic combination. All
talk-show producers aim for diverse or opposing viewpoints to maximize
interest or the potential for conflict, and they also want panelists who are
outgoing, energetic, opinionated, and capable of speaking in sound bites.
Since this kind of talk doesn't come naturally to the inexperienced guest, a
certain amount of practice and coaching is required, for experts and
celebrities no less than for ordinary people. The chief difference seems to
be that daytime talk shows substitute ordinary people for these other kinds
of guests.

Yet daytime talk reinforces the distinctions between the categories
ordinary, *expert*, and *celebrity* even while seeming to challenge them, for
ordinary people are expected to yield a type of dramatic performance quite
different from that of professors, politicians, Hollywood stars, or other
elites. *Ordinary* thus means something very specific in relation to daytime
talk. It does not necessarily mean "average," "typical," or "representative of
the population in general." Indeed, like the subjects of most media accounts, talk-show guests are often chosen for their unique rather than their

typical qualities. *Ordinary* means that guests are not *experts* or *celebrities* in the conventional sense of those terms. Their claim to stardom and expertise is rooted in different criteria.

There are several related issues at work here. The first is what ordinary people talk about and where the source of their authority lies. Ordinary people on talk shows discuss mostly personal matters pertaining to sexuality, identity, interpersonal relationships, family conflict, and victimization or abuse, and their expertise stems from firsthand experience rather than formal educational or professional credentials. (Recall the backstage coaching of guests described earlier: "Now, when Diana asks you to describe the first time your husband beat you, what are you going to say?") Rarely are ordinary women and men invited on daytime talk shows to discuss politics, law, or current affairs, unless their personal experience with the political or legal system—as a victim of sexual assault or gang violence, for example—makes them self-taught experts in these areas. This focus on the backstage of people's lives is often perceived negatively by critics as "airing dirty laundry" (literally) because it brings into the public arena what they believe ought to remain private. Airing dirty laundry is not associated exclusively with ordinary people on daytime talk shows since experts and celebrities occasionally discuss personal issues on television and since journalists are quick to air private scandal in ostensibly public cases (witness the enthusiastic reporting of President Clinton's affair with Monica Lewinsky). Yet airing dirty laundry is still largely coded as *ordinary* even when famous people are involved because, more often than not, it serves to prove just how ordinary—how like the rest of us—they are (see Meyrowitz 1985).

Another issue in comparing ordinary people on daytime talk shows with experts and celebrities elsewhere on television is not just what they talk about but how. ("Tell it like it is, straight from the heart. Don't hold back on those emotions because this is your big chance to show millions of people you really care about this issue. . . . If you're happy, show us *how* happy; if you're sad, show us *how* sad; if you're angry, show us *how* angry. . . . Jump right in there, don't wait for the host to call on you, and don't let the other guests push you around. . . .") Ordinary people are expected not just to discuss personal matters but to do so in a particular way. They're expected to deliver what I call, borrowing from film pornography, the "money shot" of the talk-show text: joy, sorrow, rage, or remorse expressed in visible, bodily terms. It is the moment when tears well up in a woman's eyes and her voice catches in sadness and pain as she describes having lost her child to a preventable disease; when a man tells his girlfriend that he's

been sleeping with another woman and her jaw drops in rage and disbelief;
when members of the studio audience lose their composure as they listen
to a victim recount the lurid details of a crime. These moments have become the hallmark of the genre, central to its claim to authenticity as well
as to its negative reputation. According to producers, the more emotional
and volatile the guests and audience members, the more "real" (and the
more "ordinary") they are.

There is, of course, a long tradition of describing "low" culture using
such feminized sexual terms as *sleazy, cheap, loose,* and *easy* (see Bourdieu
1984; Petro 1986; Fiske 1989). I employ the pornography metaphor not to
condemn talk shows but to highlight why both discourses are disparaged
in the first place. Most obvious is the unacceptability of exposing one's private parts in public. Like pornography, daytime talk is a narrative of explicit revelation in which people "get down and dirty" and "bare it all" for the
pleasure, fascination, or repulsion of viewers. Like the orgasmic cum shot
of pornographic films, the money shot of talk shows makes visible the precise moment of letting go, of losing control, of surrendering to the body
and its "animal" emotions. It is the loss of the "civilized" self that occurs
when the body transcends social and cultural control, revealing human
behavior in its "raw" rather than its "cooked" form. To draw on a phrase
used by Fiske (1989) in another context, it is the breakdown of culture into
nature.

As with the issue of airing dirty laundry, there is common ground
here with other media, especially other forms of talk on television. "Serious" political debates among experts, for example, may entail shouting,
finger-pointing, and other displays of less-than-civil discourse. Likewise,
when celebrities and other public figures give interviews, the "best" are
those in which the celebrity expresses visible emotion. Most media texts, in
fact, are organized around moments of dramatic revelation and emotional
intensity—organized, that is, around some version of the money shot.
Print journalists recognize certain colorful or dramatic quotes as "ringers,"
while reporters for supermarket tabloids actually refer to them as "good
money quotes" (Bird 1992). What makes talk shows unique, and what helps
distinguish different shows within the genre, is the *kind* of money shot that
people deliver (hard-core or soft-core, tasteful or vulgar), what it's in response to, and who delivers it.

Daytime talk shows thus share many of the conventions governing
other forms of media but invert some key hierarchies: they privilege ordinary people over experts and celebrities, and, related to this, they encourage heightened emotional displays over (or alongside) more rational dis-

cussion or debate. In other words, daytime talk tends to subordinate the talking head of experts to the talking body of "the masses" such that what is said—the talk itself—is often the least important part of any given show. What matters is bodily evidence of a guest's emotional investment in the issue that the talk supposedly addresses. What matters is the money shot, and virtually all production efforts—choosing topics; finding, interviewing, and rehearsing guests; coaching audience members—are geared toward maximizing the probability of its display. Expert and celebrity guests, on the other hand, are understood to be more distanced and dignified participants whose private lives are, generally speaking, off-limits to public scrutiny. The genre is thus a kind of machine for producing ordinariness, where ordinariness is associated with emotion (the body) and expertness with reason (the mind), the former a signifier of the private world of personal relations, the latter a signifier of the larger universe of social relations.

Generally speaking, what makes the genre distinctive is also what tends to compromise its respectability in the eyes of media critics. Tania Modleski (1982) once wrote that there was no surer way to denigrate a cultural object or practice than to invoke a comparison to soap opera, but, these days, her observation applies more aptly to daytime talk shows. Never held in particularly high regard, the genre came under increasing attack during the mid-1990s, when the number of shows more than doubled and the resulting competition for ratings prompted a general shift to a more sensational or tabloid style of programming. Topics with a social or policy dimension such as gang violence, sexual harassment, and child abuse gave way to more purely personal issues such as love triangles, mother-daughter conflicts, and family feuds. At the same time, guests—always predominantly female but now increasingly black, queer, and working class—were encouraged to abandon politeness and restraint for more raucous, carnivalesque performances. At the height of this trend occurred an incident known among journalists as the "*Jenny Jones* murder," in which one talk-show guest shot and killed a fellow panelist several days after taping an episode on *Jenny Jones*, ostensibly because of information revealed during the taping.[1]

1. More specifically, during the taping of an episode devoted to "secret crushes," a gay man, Scott Amedure, confessed to having a crush on Jonathan Schmitz, another male guest on the show that day. Schmitz, who is heterosexual, allegedly had been expecting a female admirer. Three days later, he shot and killed Amedure, claiming to have been unbearably humiliated by the surprise confession. Schmitz was convicted of second degree murder in 1996, and, in a later civil trial, Warner Brothers—which owns the *Jenny Jones* show—was found negligent and fined $25 million. The jury verdict is currently on appeal before the Michigan Court of Appeals.

While controversy over daytime talk did not begin or end with this incident, the murder functioned as a kind of flash point, igniting a fresh wave of condemnation. Thereafter, and despite the diversity of programming within the genre, daytime talk has been framed as a "social problem" with deleterious or harmful effects and denounced as tasteless, crude, and pornographic. Described variously as "the popular culture version of the red-light district" (Bennett 1996, B9), "a trashy forum for trashy people to act trashy" (Jarvis 1994, 7), and "a vast, scary wasteland where the dregs of society . . . become stars for 15 minutes" (Linda Stasi quoted in Kurtz 1996, 67), talk shows have inspired endless comparisons to garbage cans, toilets, brothels, crack houses, and carnival freak shows. Producers are routinely characterized as "pimps" and "pushers," while guests suffer any number of unflattering put-downs from "freaks of the week" and "nuts and sluts" to "trailer trash," "perverts," and "uneducated lazy scum."

Although some critics are reportedly worried that producers deliber-

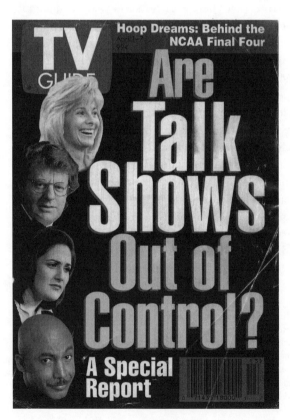

Figure 1. Cover of *TV Guide* magazine, April 1–7, 1995. Reprinted with permission from News America Publications, Inc., publisher of *TV Guide* magazine. Copyright Vol. 43, No. 13, 1995, News America Publications, Inc.

Figure 2. Cartoon by Gary Brookins. Originally published in the *Richmond Times-Dispatch,* 1995. Reprinted with permission of Gary Brookins.

ately mislead or deceive guests in order to secure their participation, the larger concern seems to be the willingness of people to laugh, shout, cry, and bicker about personal matters in the apparent *absence* of deception since such behaviors are said to epitomize the degradation of American culture. According to the media scholar Vicki Abt, disclosing one's personal secrets on television is like "defecating in public" (Abt quoted in Kaplan 1995, 12). Abt and others claim, moreover, that, in making entertainment of the problems and transgressions of real people, talk shows blur the line separating fact from fiction, normalize deviant behavior, and desensitize viewers to genuine suffering (Kaminer 1993; Heaton and Wilson 1995; Kurtz 1996; Abt and Mustazza 1997).[2] In the words of the critic Howard Kurtz, "By parading the sickest, the weirdest, the most painfully afflicted before an audience of millions, these shows bombard us with sleaze to the point of numbness" (1996, 63). Even politicians joined the fray, staging several "talk summits" to debate the ethics of talk-show production and to urge

2. According to Rössler and Brosius (2001, 144), in Germany, where the number of daytime talk shows climbed to a dozen in 1999, the response of critics has been similar, talk shows being regarded as highly personalized and emotional programs that depict bizarre behavior and social deviance; include bad language, fighting, and confrontations as means of problem resolution; leave most conflicts unresolved; are mainly oriented toward issues of sexuality; and present the exception as ordinary, thereby distorting reality and desensitizing viewers to the misfortunes of others.

Figure 3. Cartoon by Jeff Stahler. Originally published in the *Cincinnati Post,* 1995. Reprinted with permission of Newspaper Enterprise Association, Inc.

Americans to "just say no" to trash TV. The pressure was effective: many hosts and executive producers subsequently vowed to tone down their shows. *Oprah* dropped conflict-based topics entirely and began a regime of moral and spiritual uplift, while Geraldo Rivera created a "Bill of Rights and Responsibilities" to help encourage more ethical production practices.[3]

Not everyone agrees that talk shows are trashy, however. As Gamson (1998) points out in his book about talk shows and sexual nonconformity, where detractors see "freaks" and "trash," defenders tend to see "have-nots" and "common folks." Although vastly outnumbered, the latter focus on the redeeming as well as the problematic qualities of the genre, arguing that, flawed as they are, talk shows grant visibility to people and issues normally excluded from television and, in the process, offer a refreshing, commonsense counterpoint to the more elite authority of experts and officials. Defenders also point out the important influence on daytime talk shows

3. Geraldo's "Bill of Rights and Responsibilities" guaranteed, among other things, that guests would always be fully informed about the nature of their participation, that producers would accentuate the positive aspects of topics rather than dwelling on the negative and bizarre, that onstage violence would no longer be tolerated, and that counselors, therapists, and trained professionals would play a more prominent role vis-à-vis ordinary guests. Interestingly, German broadcasters recently agreed on a similar, voluntary code of conduct for daytime talk shows produced in that country. Consisting of nine different commitments, the code is intended to discourage extreme topics, promote more positive outcomes to conflicts, and establish a baseline level of dignity and respect (see Rössler and Brosius 2001).

"TALK SHOWS: DO THEY DISTORT REALITY?
WE'LL ASK THESE THREE MORBIDLY SWEATY SERIAL KILLERS WITH OVERBITES ON THE NEXT *Springer*."

Figure 4. Cartoon by Jim Borgman. Originally published in the *Cincinnati Enquirer,* 1995. Reprinted with special permission of King Features Syndicate.

of the social movements of the 1960s and 1970s, especially feminism, in terms of topics addressed and the privileged role accorded emotion and personal experience in what counts as "legitimate" knowledge and "acceptable" public discourse (Carpignano et al. 1990; Masciarotte 1991; Squire 1994). Talk-show hosts themselves have defended the genre on similar grounds.[4]

There are thus two kinds of talk at stake here: the talk on the shows and the talk of scholars and critics about that talk. Probably the single most common way of disparaging the genre is to invoke the metaphor of cultural refuse, or *trash*. *Trash*, of course, has specific class connotations in the United States, having long been used as a pejorative term to describe poor, rural whites of Southern origin. A euphemism for a conception of lower class–ness related but not reducible to socioeconomic status, *trash* is a cultural designation signifying a host of indulgences that "respectable" people supposedly eschew. As such, it helps secure for more-privileged whites a sense of moral and aesthetic superiority (see Bettie 1995; Wray and Newitz

---

4. When I first began studying talk shows, I started a small library of press clippings, magazine articles, and TV news reports on the subject. Then, when I interned at *Randy*, the publicist on staff allowed me access to the show's own collection of material, which documented virtually every occasion in which daytime talk shows were discussed or mentioned in the media, both print and electronic. By my estimation, detractors outnumber defenders by a ratio of roughly ten to one.

Figure 5. Cartoon by Jeff Stahler. Originally published in the *Cincinnati Post,* 1994. Reprinted with permission of Newspaper Enterprise Association, Inc.

1997). With reference to media texts, the label *trashy* tends to be employed interchangeably with *tabloid*, meaning "sensational," "vulgar," or "excessive," and appears to function in an analogous manner, enabling the more-elite media—especially the establishment news press—to distance themselves from their trashy talk-show kin.

This sort of boundary work among media professionals is nothing new. Indeed, the attack on daytime talk shows, which intensified as the genre grew increasingly sensational, can be viewed as part of an ongoing struggle for distinction between the elite and popular media that goes back to the very origins of journalism.[5] What is interesting about this in the wake of the 1990s boom and the general shift to tabloid fare is the reproduction of a classy/trashy binarism internal to the genre itself. On the classy end of the continuum are shows like *Oprah* or *Diana*, which have retained an overall serious focus and tend to be more restrained in style and execution. Confessional rather than confrontational, soft-core rather than hard-core, *Diana* is a forum largely for, and about, middle-class white women, and it aims for a "feminine" money shot—one based on heartache or joy rather than conflict and anger. While branded embarrassing or melodramatic compared to more "rational" forms of talk, *Diana* nevertheless taps into (indeed, is a product of) an increasingly legitimate

5. Sparks and Tulloch (2000) provide a good historical overview of this struggle.

contemporary discourse about the therapeutic benefits of emotional expressiveness (see Lowney 1999).

Closer to the trashy end of the continuum are shows like *Randy*, *Jenny Jones*, and *Ricki Lake*, which focus on people's interpersonal conflicts in the service of generating "lively" on-air confrontation. Relatively hard-core (and "masculine") by contrast, these shows tend to feature a more ethnically diverse cast of working-class women and men and attract younger, more gender-mixed audiences. At the outer edge of the continuum is *Jerry Springer*, at the time of this writing the most popular talk show on the air. Just at the point when other shows were toning down the performances of guests in response to negative publicity, *Springer* dropped all pretense of rational discussion (along with, not coincidentally, the participation of experts) and began to encourage ever more volatile behavior among guests. On and off during the show's stormy history, this behavior has centered around explicit physical confrontation; at its most extreme, brawling guests would have to be pried apart by well-muscled bouncers. Even in its tamer moments, "talk" on *Springer* has consisted almost entirely of body language, its emotional expressiveness a breach of taken-for-granted norms that transgresses acceptable therapeutic limits.

Not surprisingly, both Springer and his show have been the subject of innumerable news reports, commentaries, and exposés. The Chicago police have threatened to arrest guests for assault, media-watchdog organizations have called for national boycotts, and Springer himself has been hauled before Congress—all of which has no doubt increased the show's popularity, especially among its younger viewers. Going hard-core at this particular juncture was a shrewd marketing decision because it clearly distinguished *Springer* from its competitors, just as Oprah Winfrey's much-lauded decision to take the "high road" several years earlier was successful in part because virtually every other talk show was moving in the opposite direction. As the 1990s drew to a close, these two shows, one trashy, the other classy, were the two top-rated talk shows on the air.

Although the classy/trashy distinction tends to obscure the extent to which most shows are a blend of both as well as the fact that even the classy shows are trashy in comparison to more elite forms of media, it does, nevertheless, foreground some of the genre's different, even contradictory, influences. Daytime talk shows are the offspring of mixed parentage: they combine a middle-class, public-service model of talk that emphasizes discussion, information, and advice with the more lowbrow conventions of tabloid journalism that emphasize drama and spectacle in the presentation of odd or sensational content (see Munson 1993; Shattuc

1997; Gamson 1998). These, in turn, stem from different—and differently classed—historical antecedents: the coffeehouse, the salon, or the town-hall meeting, on the one hand, and gossip, folktales, the dime museum, and the carnival sideshow, on the other. Hence Gamson's (1998) characterization of daytime talk as a two-headed monster, one head "respectable," the other "vulgar." Add to this mix the therapeutic, confessional style pioneered by Oprah Winfrey—a kind of "third head," if you will—which reflects the influence of popular psychology, the witnessing traditions of religious revivals, and the consciousness-raising methods of analysis popularized by second-wave feminism (Squire 1994; Shattuc 1997; Lowney 1999). Themselves the products of complex historical developments, these influences do not map neatly onto either the public-sphere (classy) or tabloid (trashy) models of journalism, although their focus on emotion and personal experience clearly aligns them with popular rather than elite culture and with traditionally feminine rather than masculine modes of knowledge.

The latter half of the 1990s, when I conducted most of my fieldwork, proved to be a crucial moment in the overall trajectory of talk-show programming. During this period, daytime talk was louder, brasher, more controversial, and more emotional than ever before or since. It was, in effect, the money shot of the genre's history to date, with the *Jenny Jones* murder standing as its most visible signifier. The murder thrust talk shows into the national spotlight and intensified the pressure on them to clean up their act. Talk shows as a whole stood trial, the murder providing scholars and critics with a fresh opportunity to reassert a long-standing narrative about the dangers of tabloid media. And, while much of the news coverage focused on the perceived manipulation of guests by producers (producers were accused of luring guests onto shows under false pretenses and then "ambushing" them with an unpleasant surprise), the larger issue at stake was the role, nature, and acceptability of the money shot, for it is in the service of eliciting the money shot that producers orchestrate surprise encounters in the first place. The subsequent controversy over the level of physical confrontation on *Jerry Springer* was likewise a controversy about what kind of money shot is acceptable and what the bounds and limits of the genre ought to be.[6] How far will the media go in pandering to people's

6. This redrawing of boundaries was well illustrated by the outcry among journalists in May 1997 when Jerry Springer was hired to do occasional news commentary for a local Chicago news station. A ratings ploy if ever there was one, the station's decision to incorporate a representative of the "trashy" media into the sacred space of legitimate journalism generated such ire among establishment media professionals that Springer resigned only a few days later.

voyeuristic desires, critics wonder? Is there no aspect of one's personal life too private or sacred for public consumption? Will people do anything to get on TV? Not surprisingly, the recent spate of primetime reality programs like *Survivor* and *Big Brother* have prompted similar concerns, although without the same heightened degree of disdain.

Class and Cultural Hierarchy

All these interrelated elements discussed so far—that daytime talk prefers ordinary people over experts or celebrities; that these ordinary people talk about things, and behave in ways, that experts and celebrities typically do not; that this behavior often privileges the body over the mind and private over public life; and that, as a result, talk shows are a much-maligned form of popular culture disdained by cultural critics—have led me to focus on some particular issues and aims in the course of writing this book.

In the most general terms, I use talk-show production as a lens to examine the production of cultural hierarchy in the United States and the relation of that hierarchy to social—especially class—inequality. Of course, talk shows do not purport to be a discourse explicitly about class. Scholars generally agree that, compared to race, gender, and sexuality, class does not constitute a central category of identity or consciousness in the United States, that most Americans—save for the very rich or the very poor—do not think of themselves as occupying particular class locations outside a vague, amorphous middle (see Pakulski and Waters 1996; De-Mott 1990). Television entertainment has generally helped perpetuate this state of affairs by underrepresenting the experiences of working-class and poor people, making them an exception to the "norm" of upward mobility (Butsch 1992; Jhally and Lewis 1992). When working-class characters do appear, they tend to be of the Archie Bunker/Homer Simpson mold, which is by now anachronistic, industrial blue-collar work having given way to part-time, low-wage service jobs filled largely by white women and people of color.[7] Filled, that is, by the people who populate the world of daytime talk shows.

---

7. Bettie (1995, 132–33) summarizes nicely the changing face of U.S. labor and class formations: "In 1959, 60 percent of those employed worked in the production of goods and 40 percent in services. By 1985, only 26 percent produced goods while service occupations increased to 74 percent. . . . Researchers estimate that between 1988 and 2000 the total

Yet class status—and representations of class status—can be expressed in ways other than through one's relation to the site of economic production. Class, especially in the context of television, is also a performance, a social script involving, among other things, language use, mannerisms, and dress (see Bourdieu 1984; Bettie 2000). In Bettie's (2000, 11) words, "Class can be conceptualized as performative in that there is no [innate or] interior difference that is being expressed; rather, institutionalized class inequality creates class subjects who perform, or display, differences in cultural capital." In the case of daytime talk shows, these differences organize around norms of emotional and bodily restraint. What is the process by which the media mediate these norms in relation to so-called ordinary people, especially members of disadvantaged groups? Talk shows clearly produce ordinariness as something both similar to yet distinct from professional stardom and expertise, and they do so by translating taken-for-granted, class-based assumptions about both ordinary and expert guests into dramatic performances onstage.

I am further interested in the conflicts and tensions that arise as the result of this translation. In the case of daytime talk shows, there is a struggle between producers (acting on behalf of institutional interests) and talk-show guests, both ordinary and expert, who may have wholly other agendas and desires. Such conflict is often dramatic, and it became a focal point of my interviews. There is also a more diffuse but pervasive tension between elite and popular knowledge, between the expertise of professionals and the expertise of ordinary people. On television, the tension around who gets to "own" expertise is played out at multiple, overlapping levels: between the respectable and the tabloid media, between classy and trashy talk shows, between expert and ordinary guests within any given show, and even between different kinds of experts.

In their work on talk television and public debate, Livingstone and Lunt (1994) suggest that the historic growth of audience-discussion programs (including daytime talk shows) signals a move from elite to more participatory social arrangements and represents a challenge to traditional expertise fueled by public ambivalence about forms of knowledge that are increasingly rationalized, specialized, and divorced from ordinary understanding. In promoting personal experience over more distanced, scientific, or abstract discussion, such programs in a very real sense seek to

---

number of jobs in the US will [have increased] by 18 million; 16.6 million of these will be in service industries and the bulk of those will be 'bad jobs' characterized by few skills, low pay, and poor job security."

revalue lay knowledge vis-à-vis professional expertise. Consequently, experts are marginal participants whose legitimacy is circumscribed by the genre's valuation of lay knowledge; to be heard and taken seriously in the talk-show context (and, arguably, American culture more generally), one must speak in terms of emotion and personal experience. Not surprisingly, some experts—notably counselors and therapists—are better able and/or more willing to do this than others. Best suited to the genre are the guests I call, borrowing from Shattuc (1997), *organic experts,* typically grassroots community activists who belong to, and work on behalf of, marginalized or disenfranchised constituencies. Like professional experts, they are spokespersons for established groups, organizations, or institutions; like ordinary people, their expertise stems from firsthand personal experience.

The contentious relation between elite and popular knowledge is in turn part and parcel of the larger struggle for cultural distinction: the elevation of high over low culture. As various scholars have noted, it is not the specific content of the categories *high* and *low* that matters here—since these change from one historical period to another—so much as the fact that a categorical distinction exists. The emergence of cultural hierarchy in the United States long predates the rise of television talk shows and has depended in crucial ways on equating distance from, and control over, the body and its emotions with rationality, civility, and "good taste" (see Bourdieu 1984; Levine 1988; Kasson 1990). Put simply, what belongs to the realm of the body is denigrated, and certain classes or groups of people are perceived to be more closely ("naturally") aligned with it than others. This is not a matter of having or not having bodies. Clearly, we all have bodies—men as much as women, light-skinned peoples as much as dark-skinned peoples, heterosexuals as much as homosexuals, social and cultural elites as much as the working classes. The issue is how one's embodiedness is perceived and valued, how its specific features get signified in the complex registers of social discourse.

The racialization of people of color along the nature/culture axis is a dramatic example: Western discourses on race have constructed Africa and Asia as signs of savagery and dark skin more generally as a sign of nature and physicality (see Torgovnik 1991; Goldberg 1993; Omi and Winant 1995). "Improper" bodies are also linked in a complex chain of associations to gender and social class. To quote Bourdieu (1984, 490), "The antithesis between culture and bodily pleasure (or nature) is rooted in the opposition between the cultivated bourgeoisie and 'the people,' the imaginary site of uncultivated nature, barbarously wallowing in pure enjoyment." The working classes are said to live "close to the ground," be unrefined ("coarse") in manner and speech and visceral in their pleasures and tastes. These attributes are doubly stigmatizing for working-class women since they violate not only the codes of bourgeois respectability but also the very codes of femininity itself. Despite the fact that women as a group have tended to occupy the nature side of the nature/culture divide, gender and class intersect such that the "higher" standards of refinement and cultivation associated with elites partly define the standards of "ideal" femininity as well—an ideal that working-class women by definition fail to measure up to.

On one hand, then, daytime talk shows clearly reproduce cultural stereotypes by positioning ordinary people—especially women, people of color, and the white working classes—as somehow closer to nature and more obviously (i.e., negatively) embodied than elite white men. At the same time, talk shows are a forum to which groups without a lot of power and resources have regular and institutional access, one that addresses issues considered too "private" or "offensive" for the more respectable media. This coincidence—offensive conduct and marginalized individuals—warrants serious inquiry. It is not simply that one leads to the other because such individuals are "naturally" less respectable or even because their relative powerlessness leaves them vulnerable to exploitation by the media, although this latter explanation is surely part of the story. It is also that accepted definitions of *trashy* and *offensive* contribute to the marginalization of guests in the first place insofar as these definitions reflect middle-class assumptions about appropriate public conduct and legitimate public discourse and insofar as they obscure the class privilege associated with keeping one's private life off-limits to public scrutiny.

Further complicating the picture is the fact that talk-show guests contribute in significant ways and with varying degrees of freedom to their own representation. As someone with previous training in television, I knew even before setting foot backstage that the simplicity of the format—real people telling real stories—was deceptive, that the appearance of a panelist onstage was the result of intense effort and collaboration among many diverse production elements, including the guests themselves. Consequently, I was suspicious of viewing guests as many critics did: as dupes complicit in their own degradation or hapless victims manipulated by producers into making intimate disclosures on camera. Not only did I doubt the accuracy of this view, I was bothered by its paternalistic tone. As Stuart Hall (1981) observed some years ago, intellectuals and other cultural elites might feel right and justified about denouncing the culture industry, but to assume concurrently that the people who engage with it must themselves be debased by this engagement or else suffering from false consciousness is not an adequate accounting of social relations or of the economic and political circumstances that underpin them.

This is not to suggest that everything "the people" do is in their best interests or cause for celebration (setting aside for the moment just who *the people* are and what their *best interests* might be). This too is an inadequate accounting of social relations and one that reproduces the same attitude of paternalism toward the working classes, except that the critic or scholar lauds rather than denigrates what they do. But one can decry the oppressive aspects of commercial culture and still take seriously Hall's point that what we call *popular culture* involves a continuous and unequal struggle between forces of domination, points of resistance, and everything in between. This struggle is particularly complicated (and particularly unequal) in highly mass-mediated, postindustrial societies like the United States in which popular culture—the culture of "the people"—is increasingly fashioned from the products of commercial capital and depends on commercial consumption for its expression. In such a context, as de Certeau (1984) has so aptly demonstrated, the desires of marginalized groups may manifest themselves not so much through their own products as through their *ways of using* products that originate elsewhere, products imposed on them by a dominant economic order.

The purpose of virtually all television entertainment (and television news as well) is to commodify audiences and sell them to advertisers for profit. Thus, when it comes to daytime talk shows, Gamson (1998) is right to insist that exploitation is the starting point rather than the conclusion of analysis. One can reject the elitism implied in metaphors of talk as trash *and* be suspicious of the reverse claim that talk shows are democracy in action. The question is not whether daytime talk is trashy or classy, and not whether it "gives voice" to marginalized people, on the one hand, or reproduces their marginalization, on the other, but how and why the two hands come together in this context, and, consequently, what kind of voice they allow. Whatever the particular circumstances of a guest's participation, this voice will never be "free" of the media's influence, not only because producers have more power than guests do to set the agenda and terms of debate, but also because, as Hebdige (1979) insists, the typical members of a subordinate class culture always partly contest and partly agree with dominant definitions—including mass-mediated definitions—of who and what they are. This is precisely how hegemony works. If it were otherwise, then popular culture would not be so popular. And, if popular culture were not so popular, it would be easier to dismiss or ignore.

What's a Nice Girl Like You Doing in a Place Like That?

Academics are typically purveyors of high rather than low culture. In the overall cultural hierarchy, the academy occupies a similarly elevated status relative to the mass media as the establishment news press does to daytime talk shows (and for similar reasons: it is considered to be more disembodied and objective, and it plays to a more elite, educated audience). However, this has not stopped academics from *studying* low culture (especially from a distance), and I am certainly not alone in taking daytime talk as the subject of serious intellectual inquiry. As talk shows began replacing soap operas on the daytime dial, they attracted the attention of media scholars representing diverse theoretical perspectives and methodologies.[8] Yet very little of the resulting research examines daytime talk shows ethnographically, from the "inside" perspective of producers and guests, and with an eye toward understanding how the norms and practices of the production process itself shape and inform the talk show as text. This book does just that, relying primarily on interviews and participant observation in the field. It is informed by a tradition of ethnographic research in the United States that presumes that understanding *how* media texts are put together—how they *work*—helps us understand not only the meaning and significance of those texts but also the culture in which they are embedded.[9] As Becker (1982) reminds us, the production of cultural forms results from collective action, from the activity of networks of people whose cooperation at various levels and stages yields a final result: a painting, a photograph, a quilt, a jazz performance, a film, or a television talk show. Often, the story of how cultural objects come into existence—how diverse actions are coordinated, how decisions are made, how conflicts are mediated, how norms and conventions are challenged, followed, or ignored—is as interesting and revealing as the object itself, for ways of talking about the production of popular culture are simultaneously ways of talking about society and social relations.

An ethnographic approach typically attempts to understand the workings of a community or a cultural object through direct contact, sus-

8. A working list of these scholars would include the following: Carbaugh (1988); Carpignano et al. (1990); Masciarotte (1991); Mellencamp (1992); Munson (1993); Abt and Seesholtz (1994); Livingstone and Lunt (1994); Nelson and Robinson (1994); Squire (1994); Priest and Dominick (1994); Heaton and Wilson (1995); Peck (1994, 1995); Priest (1995); Abt and Mustazza (1997); Shattuc (1997); Gamson (1998); Lowney (1999).

9. See Powdermaker (1951); Tuchman (1978); Fishman (1980); Becker (1982); Gitlin (1983); Bacon-Smith (1992); Bird (1992).

tained immersion, and attention to detail in combination with a focus on larger cultural patterns or social structures. It aims for a fruitful dialectic between experience and interpretation, a continuous tacking back and forth between what James Clifford (1988, 34) describes as the *inside* and *outside* of events: "On the one hand grasping the sense of specific activities and events empathetically, on the other hand stepping back to situate these meanings in wider contexts." The focus on individuals in their natural set-ting—of which the researcher is inevitably a part—also makes available for scholarly engagement the sense that people make of their own lives and activities in a way that few other methods do. Thus, just as daytime talk shows differ from many other forms of television in that they give ordinary people the opportunity to contribute to their own narrativization (albeit in a highly circumscribed and limited manner), ethnography affords ordinary people a similar opportunity in an academic context with different limita-tions and constraints. At its best, ethnography evokes a world that is dense, richly textured and nuanced, one that treats people as participating subjects and not just passive objects of research. This approach does not assume that research subjects necessarily have the best or most accurate insights about institutional processes or other social phenomena, nor does it deny that large-scale structural forces shape and constrain individual behavior, often in unconscious ways. But it does take people's experience in the world as a valuable source of data, and it recognizes that how people think about cul-tural forms, respond to them, and reject or accept them is a large part of what these forms are. To paraphrase Geertz (1973), human behavior must be attended to, and with some exactness, because it is through the flow of human interaction that cultural forms find articulation.

In my own case, I set out to investigate the complex world of daytime talk shows, the norms and practices that circumscribe its production, as well as the ways in which participants themselves make sense of the genre. I wanted to understand the process by which experts and ordinary people are transformed into mass entertainment, including how topics and guests are chosen, how a show is put together and carried off, and the nature of the relationship between producers and guests. Consequently, I spent the 1995-96 television season working as an intern and researcher at *Diana* and an additional three months after that at *Randy*, both nationally televised shows. At the time of this writing, both are still on the air. I did not origi-nally plan to take on more than one site, nor did I target a particular type of talk show; instead, I went where the requirements of the internship matched my own interests and qualifications and where the producers were agreeable to my presence. Academics are no less concerned with a balanced story than are journalists, however, and, after my stint at *Diana*, I sought experience on a show representing the trashy end of the continuum. I entered both sites through established internship programs and so took advantage of an existing institutional arrangement between the television industry and the academy rather than attempting to negotiate special access through a sponsor or gatekeeper. Once inside, I explained my research goals and agenda and secured formal interviews with the production staff.[10]

The two shows differed in terms of topics and guests as well as the production staff behind the scenes: *Diana* blended social issues and current affairs with lighthearted, personal topics; relied more heavily on experts; had a predominantly white, middle-class female audience; and featured mostly middle- and lower-middle-class white women as guests (by my own calculation, approximately 65 percent of the guests were female and 90 percent white). Most of the production staff were middle-class, college-ducated white women in their late twenties and thirties. On *Randy*, the staff was also largely female, middle class, and college educated, although considerably smaller (in terms of numbers), younger, and with greater representation of African Americans, especially at the lower levels. Topics were almost entirely geared toward interpersonal conflict, and the audience was younger, roughly equally divided by gender, and more ethnically diverse than that at *Diana*, although still predominantly white. Judging from their dress, manner, speech, and occupations, *Randy* guests were overwhelmingly working or lower class. Women constituted slightly less than 60 percent of all guests, people of color (of whom the vast majority were African American) roughly one-fifth.

Despite the differences between shows, the work behind the scenes was similar in many ways. My duties as an intern included transcribing the 800 line for viewer comments and responses to on-air plugs soliciting guests, booking the studio audience, opening fan mail, assisting production staff on the set with guests, answering the phones in the control booth during taping, running errands for producers, contacting former guests about the upcoming air dates for their shows, and occasionally preinterviewing potential guests. During my last few weeks at *Diana*, one of the producers was unexpectedly called out of town, and I stepped in to help her partner put together the final two shows of the season. This meant researching the topics, finding and interviewing guests, learning how to write and edit the script, and attending daily production meetings. Likewise, in my last days

---

10. For a more detailed discussion of my entry into the field as well as other aspects of the fieldwork, see the epilogue.

at *Randy*, I was fortunate to have access to producer-guest interactions above and beyond that of a typical intern when one of the associate producers allowed me to shadow him during the production of several shows.

During the course of my fieldwork at *Diana* and *Randy*, I observed hundreds of shows on a wide range of topics: forbidden relationships, compulsive lying, medical mishaps, roommate problems, interracial romance, cross-dressing, sibling rivalry, marital infidelity, promiscuity, mother-daughter conflicts, child-custody battles, sexual assault, teenage runaways, drug addiction, drunk driving, dating disasters, makeovers, celebrity look-alikes, and family feuds. I was both a talk-show intern and a field researcher in this context. I worked long hours, performed a great many menial as well as interesting tasks, and developed close working relationships with specific individuals. The fieldwork, like the work of producing itself, exacted a certain amount of emotional labor: it was variously exciting, boring, stressful, frustrating, depressing, and rewarding. I took copious field notes and struggled to make sense intellectually of my own experiences as well as the experiences of those around me.

In addition to interning at *Diana* and *Randy*, I attended the live taping of more than two dozen talk shows around the country over a three-year period. On two separate occasions after a taping, I volunteered (along with other audience members) to take part in an informal focus-group session with producers, designed to assess what audiences like and dislike about talk shows. I also conducted roughly eighty in-depth interviews, spanning the years between 1994 and 2000, with producers, other talk-show staff, talk-show hosts, and talk-show guests (both ordinary and expert). The people I interviewed were sometimes the same ones I worked with or met on *Diana* and *Randy*, sometimes individuals referred to me by my contacts at these shows. A few guests I interviewed because they responded to an ad I had placed in the newspaper or because they were known by people in my own circle of friends and acquaintances. With the few exceptions noted (see "A Word about Names"), I have changed the names of my informants to help protect their privacy and to set them at ease—a standard practice in field research. The different talk shows represented by the range of individuals with whom I spoke is considerable. They include (in alphabetical order) *Bertice Berry, Charles Perez, Danny, Donahue, Gabrielle, Geraldo, Jane Whitney, Jenny Jones, Jerry Springer, Leeza, Marilu, Maury Povich, The Mo Show, Montel Williams, Oprah, The Other Side, Richard Bey, Ricki Lake, Rolanda, Sally Jessy Raphael, Shirley!* and *Susan Powter.*

By and large, people were interested in my project and generous in sharing their thoughts and feelings about the genre. Although securing interviews was a challenge (producers were often too harried to spend time with me apart from the work we did together, while guests, for different reasons, lead harried lives of their own), the same energy and gregariousness that make people "good" producers and "good" talk-show guests generally make them "good" research subjects. Guests were particularly forthcoming since the very things that drew them to the genre—wanting to right a wrong, champion a cause, complain about an injustice, or simply get external validation for their views—also drew them to me. Sometimes, what guests wanted to complain about was their experience on the show itself, and for these people I served the same function in relation to talk shows as the shows themselves did in relation to whatever personal problems the guests originally went on television to discuss. In fact, producers and guests both tended to use their interview with me as an occasion to express frustration or dissatisfaction, either with one another or with the production process more generally.

Ordinary People and Media Discourse

For producers, putting together a talk show is, above all else, *work*. Hard work. Talk shows may be trashy; they are certainly much maligned. But trash is just as, if not more, difficult to produce as more respectable kinds of television. According to one veteran executive, "Talk shows are probably the toughest gig in the business." Indeed, talk shows are trashy in reputation and difficult to produce for some of the same reasons: because ordinary people are by definition not media-savvy professionals and because their ordinariness is associated with emotional expressiveness rather than emotional restraint. The two qualities are related to one another, and their combination makes the performances of ordinary guests less predictable and, hence, more difficult to routinize on a daily basis. This, in turn, creates a strong tension between scriptedness and spontaneity that producers must actively negotiate. As one producer said to me about working with ordinary people, "Sometimes you get gold that you didn't expect to get, and sometimes the show just goes in the toilet because they can't deliver. That's exactly what it means to deal with real people, with Joe Average American."

Moreover, because of the connection between ordinariness and emotion, working with ordinary people exacts a certain amount of "emotional labor" (Hochschild 1983) from producers. That is, producing an authentic money shot requires emotion work on the part of producers backstage, just as delivering it requires emotion work of a different sort from guests on-stage. Day after day, show after show, in dealing with people who are feuding with their in-laws, cheating on their spouses, or going through an acrimonious divorce, producers must treat emotion—their own as well as that of guests—in a routine and businesslike way, as just another element of the production process. Drawing on Marx, Hochschild calls emotion work of this sort *alienated labor* because one's feelings are externalized and separated from the self; they become objects to be managed and manipulated. Whether producers succeed in their efforts to elicit the money shot through emotion management depends largely on the collaboration of guests, who, interestingly, also objectify or externalize their emotions to varying degrees. Guests understand the premium placed on performativity in this context, and most are quite adept at manipulating their own emotions, much as professional actors are (a small subset of guests are, in fact, aspiring actors hoping that a talk-show appearance will help launch a professional career). As we shall see, producers generally try to avoid guests of this sort because a performance that appears fake or disingenuous undermines the very qualities of authenticity and spontaneity that distinguish ordinary guests from experts and celebrities in the first place.

For their part, ordinary guests do not orient toward their performances on daytime talk shows as work. For them, appearing on national television is unique and exciting, usually a once-in-a-lifetime event. Whereas producers consider one show to be much like another, guests naturally invest their own performances with a special significance. They have specific motivations for appearing, they want something that they think the show can provide, and they have specific expectations about how the show will provide it. The relation of any individual guest to the production process is thus strategic and opportunistic rather than routine, even though the place of ordinary people in the genre more generally is not. It is this opportunistic quality that appears most opaque to critics, who cannot seem to fathom why anyone in her right mind would go on a talk show. But there are many reasons why people who are not normally considered experts or celebrities are willing to participate—or, more accurately, ordinary guests have many ways of explaining their participation. Interestingly, just as there are classy and trashy shows, with classy and trashy topics and guests, there are classy and trashy reasons for participating. Not surprisingly, the more those reasons diverge from the reasons that experts give for going on television—that is, the more they privilege the body over the mind, the more they have to do with "mere exposure," with simply wanting to be on TV rather than championing a cause or educating the public—the trashier they are considered to be.

Whatever their individual reasons, and regardless of whether they actually accomplish their goals, guests' motives for participating cannot be understood outside a larger social context characterized by inequality of access to media representation and the fundamental validation that such representation seemingly guarantees. The mass media are generally recognized as a significant social force, central to the orchestration of everyday life and consciousness. They select what is important to know about the world and frame how we ought to know it. Consequently, media coverage or exposure serves a powerful legitimating function in our culture not only for experts, celebrities, politicians, and activists of various sorts (see Molotch and Lester 1974; Molotch 1979; Gitlin 1980) but for ordinary people as well. Yet, unlike these other groups, ordinary people categorically and by definition exist largely outside the official channels and established routines of newsmaking and the entertainment industry. This outsider status has implications for why and how people gain entry as well as how the media mediate them. The fact that ordinary people are by definition *not* experts or celebrities in the conventional sense also alters the established routines of media production in ways that are both obvious and subtle. It affects the terms of the relationship between producer and guest and the work that each must do; it influences the kind of performance that a guest is expected and encouraged to give; and, in the end, for good or bad, it challenges the historic exclusion of "just folks" from the very categories *expert* and *celebrity* in the first place.

This book no doubt represents only a small fraction of what I learned and experienced as a fieldworker behind the scenes. Just as producers may spend considerable time with guests but put only a tiny portion of their story onstage, ethnography by necessity selects and excludes. Like all research methods, it seeks order in chaos and imposes a certain coherence on the messiness of life that bears the imprint of the method itself as much as the social relations under examination. There are many other ways to study popular culture than the one I have chosen and many things to say about daytime talk shows that I do not say. This book is not a content or textual analysis of talk-show programming. It is not a Foucauldian critique of the confessional impulses of guests or a theoretical inquiry about the voyeuristic predilections of viewers. Nor does it seek to explain the rise of therapeutic discourse in American culture. Most notably, although I did conduct roughly two dozen interviews with talk-show viewers before beginning my fieldwork, this book does not balance a focus on production with an equally systematic focus on reception, except insofar as the results of industry research about audiences (along with producers' personal beliefs and assumptions about audiences) influence the work of producers behind the scenes.[11]

All these issues are relevant to the study of daytime talk shows, although not all are equally amenable to ethnographic inquiry. Fortunately, they have been taken up most competently by other scholars. My contribution is to examine daytime talk as a form of popular culture that, quite literally, "produces" ordinary people for mass consumption. In doing so, it gives voice to individuals normally positioned outside the regular machinery of the television industry. But these individuals speak only in certain ways, only under certain conditions, and only according to certain rules. What kind of voice is this? How is it conceived, scripted, and produced? What is it saying—not only about daytime talk shows, but about mass media and American culture more generally?

My fieldwork taught me a great deal about these things. But it also taught me something about sociology and the ethnographic enterprise. In fact, one of my most surprising discoveries was that, in many ways, fieldwork mirrors the methods of talk-show production: while producers transform real-life experiences into entertainment, ethnographers transform

---

11. Qualitative "reception studies" of television consumption are difficult to execute for various complicated reasons, one of the most significant being the private and dispersed nature of this consumption (see Radway 1988). Livingstone and Lunt (1994), Shattuc (1997), and Gamson (1998) all devoted some portion of their research on daytime talk shows to studying viewers, but, in each case, this was the weakest part, as samples were small and not representative of viewers in general. As mentioned, I, too, conducted a number of interviews with talk-show viewers when I first started researching the genre and before beginning my fieldwork—roughly two dozen with people who watched at least four talk shows per week. Because I was working in an academic context, most of my interviewees were college students, although I also spoke with eight nonstudents living in my community who responded to an advertisement I ran in the local paper. Then there were the countless casual conversations that I had with fellow members of the studio audience when I started attending live tapings, many of whom also claimed to be regular viewers at home. But these encounters were fairly opportunistic and could not compare in scope or accuracy to the formal market research (both qualitative and quantitative) routinely commissioned by executives at *Diana* and *Randy* and discussed every few months at production meetings. It seemed pointless for me as an individual scholar with limited time and resources to gather information about audiences when professional market-research companies were better equipped to do so. In any event, I was less interested in why people watch talk shows (or, rather, in the reasons that they give for watching) than in why producers and television executives thought that people were watching and how, if at all, this information was incorporated into the production process itself.

them into research. Both attend to the ordinary details of everyday life, emphasize personal experience as a source of knowledge, and take real people as data while still framing the account with an "expert" voice. Sociologists and talk-show producers share the additional tendency to "study down," that is, target people with less power or privilege. Although they typically have different motivations for doing so—sociologists may desire social change and producers commercial gain—in each case the penchant for deviant or marginal subject matter is partly structural, because of greater access to social subordinates, and because marginalized groups themselves may have few other options for representation. Consequently, this book is motivated by a desire to ask, What can I as a scholar teach others about daytime talk shows? as well as, What can the study of daytime talk shows teach scholars about themselves and about their place of privilege in the cultural hierarchy that talk shows both challenge and sustain?

The year I worked at Sally *was the worst year of my life. You were constantly living in fear of, "We've gotta have these guests first, if it's breaking news we've gotta get them, and if we don't get them we've gotta explain to our boss why we couldn't talk them into it." Also, with regular people, they have to deliver the goods in act 1. I mean, right off the top of the show, if they're not crying or screaming or emoting in some incredible way, you felt tremendously inadequate, like, "Ugh, I'm a failure, my show's a failure."*

—A DIANA PRODUCER, formerly
with *Sally Jessy Raphael*

The Genre Goes Hard-Core:
A Brief History of Talk Shows
and the Money Shot

Every Thursday evening during my tenure at *Diana*, a few members of the technical crew and production staff would sit relaxing in the main lounge backstage after taping was done for the day. On one such occasion, a lighting technician named Zack, a man in his late thirties who had been with the show for about two years, told the story of how he almost got fired. At every taping, he was responsible for bringing the house lights down during the commercial breaks between segments, giving the panelists and audience members respite from the heat generated by the lights. It was pretty tedious work, and he took to watching other television shows on the small monitor at his workstation while the taping was in progress. One afternoon, Diana was conducting an interview onstage with a B-list celebrity (one of her relatively rare celebrity-guest shows), and Zack was watching an episode of *Geraldo* at the same time. He grew more and more engrossed as the *Geraldo* guest talked about being stalked and eventually kidnapped and held hostage by a psychotic coworker. Just as the guest was about to relay the details of her dramatic escape, Geraldo turned to the camera and said, "Don't go away, we'll be right back," thus signaling the transition to a commercial break. Automatically, and without a moment's hesitation, Zack turned off the bright, overhead stage lights—on Diana and her celebrity interviewee, in the middle of their conversation while the cameras were still rolling! Because the entire segment had to be retaped, the slip cost the show several thousand dollars, it cost Diana the ill will of the celebrity, and it almost cost Zack his job.

Zack's story illustrates not so much that people get easily distracted when performing tedious work (although this may well be true) but that hearing ordinary people talk about their real-life experiences can be compelling and engrossing for viewers. Indeed, the attempt to highlight shared experience or lived reality has been one of the guiding principles of news and documentary production since the advent of television itself and, before that, cinema. Of course, how and why lived reality is represented vary considerably across time, mediums, and genres and, in the case of commercial television, cannot be separated from shifts and changes in the political economy of the industry itself. Until the late 1980s, the participation of ordinary people on television was limited mostly to brief appearances in news reports or to game shows, quiz shows, game/talk hybrids, and the long-running *Candid Camera*. Ordinary people also got occasional exposure on television documentaries, including *An American Family*, a twelve-part PBS series that aired during the early 1970s, considered the inspiration for the contemporary MTV series *The Real World*.[1] Then, as the

---

1. To produce *An American Family*, Craig Gilbert and his crew spent fourteen hours a day for seven months documenting the activities of a "typical" American family in their natural setting, in an attempt to show life "as it really is" with as little intervention or manipulation on the part of the filmmakers as possible (see Gilbert 1988a, 1988b). Gilbert chose the Loud family of Santa Barbara. As he wrote in his proposal, "if you could stay with a family, any family, for a long enough period of time, something interesting would be revealed about why men and women in their various roles were having such a difficult time in the America of the early seventies" (1988b, 289). *The Real World* emerged on the scene in 1992, amid a host of other reality-based programs, and is still going strong after nine seasons. It airs in half-hour installments on MTV and features half a dozen young people chosen by producers from among thousands of eager applicants to live, work, and play together under one roof while cameras document their lives. Unlike *An American Family*, which

dominance of the three original networks began to crumble under federal deregulation policies and increased competition from cable and satellite technologies, along came "reality programming," which, together with the new spate of daytime talk shows, gave ordinary people visibility on television like never before. Most of these early shows—*Cops, Hard Copy, A Current Affair, America's Most Wanted*—were considered lowbrow, tabloid fare, but, just as there are high and low distinctions within other genres, there is an elite side to reality programming, too. *The Real World, Road Rules, Survivor,* and *Big Brother,* for example, are primetime, not daytime, shows, have big budgets and slick production values, and feature ordinary people who are, for the most part, young, hip, attractive, and middle class. Generally speaking, daytime talk shows differ from these other forms (high and low alike) in that they employ an interactional rather than an observational mode of representation and are situated within a studio rather than in a real-world context.

Other scholars have provided comprehensive accounts of the origins of daytime talk shows (Munson 1993; Shattuc 1997) as well as of the critical response to the genre in the rest of the media (Munson 1993; Gamson 1998). I do not intend to reproduce those histories here. Rather, I outline briefly the participation of ordinary people on television, highlight some of the recent developments in daytime talk more specifically, and relate these developments to the work of producers behind the scenes. Talk shows typically air every day for an hour, which means that producers handle roughly two hundred shows (two hundred hours of television) every season. And, while, unlike dramas and sitcoms, talk shows do not require elaborate scripts, sets, costumes, or rehearsals, they do require producers routinely to elicit dramatic performances from people who are not media-savvy professionals. In the words of a *Randy* producer, "It's a huge challenge to take normal people and turn them into a hometown celebrity because they have no television experience. All they have is their life."

---

adhered strictly to the principles of direct cinema and allowed no interaction between the family members and camera or crew, *The Real World* intercuts observational footage of the participants with interviews conducted by the show's producers, and participants even have special "confessional" moments in front of the camera in which to carry on their own "private" conversations with the audience (see Marsh 2000). A recent imitator is *Big Brother,* which is similar in concept but, à la *Survivor,* is also part game show in that participants gradually vote each other out of the house—with the help of viewers, who can watch the residents full-time on the Internet. The person left in the house at the end is the "winner" and collects a cash prize. Meanwhile, a host conducts in-studio interviews with "expert" commentators as well as friends and family members of participants.

Talk Shows and Ordinary People: Historical Roots

As a broad generic category, the talk show is one of the oldest and most durable electronic-media forms with roots dating back to the early days of radio. Radio programs of the 1930s and 1940s such as *The People's Platform*, *Vox Pop*, and *The Voice of Experience* typically featured some combination of host, expert, and "average citizen" conversing before a live studio audience, and, by the early 1960s, interactive call-in shows had become a regular fixture of radio's daytime schedule (Munson 1993).[2] While most call-in shows maintained a political focus and were geared primarily toward older, affluent men, in the 1970s the talk-radio industry launched a new type of show directed at women and younger audiences, one featuring light, humorous conversations about male-female relationships. Informally known as *topless radio*—and denounced as smut by the Federal Communications Commission—this shift marked the beginning of the genre's intensely interpersonal focus now standard on *Oprah* et al. and on countless call-in radio sex-therapy and sex-advice programs (Munson 1993, 48–49).

On television, the talk show has traditionally been devoted to either light entertainment, with comedy, skits, music, and celebrity guests, or more serious discussion of news and public affairs among experts (Rose 1985). Although audience participation was a fundamental component of the short-lived *America's Town Meeting* (a public-affairs show that originated in radio), it was primarily on game/talk hybrids that ordinary people played more than a peripheral role. Two such hybrid programs from the 1950s were *Queen for a Day* and *Strike It Rich*, both cited as precursors of contemporary daytime talk shows because they featured individuals willing to step forward and relate their woeful life stories on camera in exchange for prizes such as refrigerators and washing machines.[3]

The vast majority of talk television aimed at women, however,

---

2. Of these programs, *The Voice of Experience* came closest to prefiguring the contemporary daytime talk show in that it was hosted by a social worker who conducted sessions on the air with prostitutes and other hardship cases (Munson 1993, 27).

3. On *Queen for a Day*, e.g., women who provided the most harrowing tales of personal tragedy and hardship were voted queen by the studio audience and awarded a prize (Munson 1993; Priest 1995). *Strike It Rich* was similar but did not last as long on the air; according to Priest (1995, 6), the show's producers came under considerable fire from health and welfare officials for luring the country's destitute to New York City, where they sometimes waited for weeks in the hopes of winning money and gifts on the air. A third game/talk hybrid was called *Stand Up and Be Counted*. Less focused on tragedy and misfortune, it dealt with the personal dilemma of an average woman, chosen from letters submitted by viewers (see Munson 1993, 54–55).

consisted mostly of chitchat between hosts and celebrity guests, along with light entertainment, cooking demonstrations, and household tips. It was not until *The Phil Donahue Show* debuted in 1967 that the concept *homemaker entertainment* underwent a radical shift. As Rose (1985) observes, *Donahue* broke down the formal barriers of existing talk-show models, eliminating conventions such as the host's desk and the opening monologue that tended to impede discussion. Guests—ordinary people as well as celebrities, experts, and politicians—sat onstage as Donahue roamed the audience with a microphone soliciting comments and questions; viewers at home could also phone in and speak with guests on the air.[4] The formal innovation was both a cause and a consequence of changes in content as well. "*Donahue* became a forum for exploring every issue in society, particularly the diversity of sexual lifestyles, in an open manner not previously attempted by any daytime talk show" (Rose 1985, 338). Donahue made everyday life controversial, a matter of discussion and debate, and he did so by giving prominence to marginal or stigmatized cultures. He also blended the personal and political in a more or less conscious nod to the emerging feminist movement, hosting shows on midwifery, birth control, lesbian mothers, and "alternative" marital arrangements alongside heated debates between known political rivals. By the late 1970s, *Donahue* was more popular than either the *Today Show* or *Good Morning America* and had a rating higher than the *Tonight Show* (Shattuc 1997). Although its popularity waned over time, the show ran for almost thirty years, until Donahue retired from daytime talk in 1996.

Although Donahue may be best remembered for his treatment of sociopolitical issues, his show had tabloid elements as well. Its mixture of seriousness and sensationalism was a product of specific historical developments. As Shattuc (1997) reminds us, *Donahue* came of age during the protest culture of the early 1970s, when social and political consensus was fragmenting, and when, related to this, the old model of "objective" journalism was giving way to a more active, mediated, and personalized style of reporting. By the early 1980s, TV stations were looking for broader audiences and cheaper forms of public-affairs programming in the light of early

---

4. According to Rose (1985, 338), "Donahue was a probing interviewer who placed great emphasis on letting his studio audience (99 percent of which were women) ask the questions." In his autobiography, Donahue himself reveals that audience participation developed somewhat by accident when women began asking good questions and offering astute comments during commercial breaks. At some point, both host and executive producer realized that integrating the off-camera interaction would make for a better, more interesting show (Donahue & Co. 1979).

competition from cable, and the networks responded by mixing news and entertainment in a more obvious and dramatic fashion—a strategy that had proved lucrative for local news and the tabloids (Shattuc 1997; Hallin 1994). According to Hallin (1994), by the mid-1980s, the network news had adopted the more subjective language of tabloid journalism and began presenting the journalist less as an objective or neutral expert and more as an "ordinary guy" who shared the concerns and emotions of the audience. In the decade that followed, technological developments coupled with federal deregulation began to undermine the dominance of the three original networks and created new patterns of production and distribution that further encouraged the tabloid trend in news and also prompted the rise of reality-based programming (see Raphael 1997).[5]

Thus, as Shattuc (1997) notes, daytime talk shows do not represent a sudden tabloidization of the "serious" traditions of network news and public affairs. Rather, talk shows came of age at the same time that news itself was taking on an entertainment orientation and increasingly being narrativized around character identification. Both are part of a continuum of general changes in programming designed to generate greater profit by appealing to broader audiences. It was in this context that *Sally Jessy Raphael*, *Oprah*, and *Geraldo* emerged in the late 1980s, shows that mimicked *Donahue*'s format but tailored it to a more personal and emotional style (signified in part by the hosts' use of first rather than last names). While the two shows hosted by women focused largely on romantic and family relationships within a therapeutic context, *Geraldo* typically dealt with crime or scandal and was modeled after the muckraking, investigative tradition of the tabloid news.

By the mid-1990s, there were roughly two dozen different daytime talk shows on the air, and this proliferation refigured the genre in key ways. Most obvious was a shift to more sensational topics as new shows struggled to distinguish themselves from one another and gain a foothold in the

5. Specifically, the privatization of the satellite industry, the rise of cable and VCRs (and now digital systems), the success of new networks like FOX and USA, and the expansion of first-run syndication throughout the 1980s all helped undermine the dominance of the three original networks by fragmenting audiences and requiring distributors to compete for increasingly smaller advertising shares. Many production companies, both in-house and off-network, responded by reducing production and labor costs in order to maximize profits. Daytime talk shows and other reality shows are attractive from an economic standpoint because, unlike dramas, sitcoms, and soap operas, they do not employ writers or actors, they do not use elaborate sets or costumes, and they often do not hire unionized crews. Indeed, the format pioneered by *Donahue* almost thirty years ago remains a tremendously successful daytime advertising vehicle and lucrative investment—for production companies and

market. According to former executive producer Saul Feldman, the shift meant that, when industry executives were faced with a choice about what to air, they increasingly opted for topics such as "Moms Who Prostitute Their Daughters" or "Women Who Marry Their Rapists" rather than something more conventional like "Should White Families Adopt Black Children?" "That's not to say producers couldn't get heat and sizzle out of the adoption topic," he insisted, "but these days people are expecting sleaze and soap opera. They are looking to be shocked." A former *Geraldo* producer made a similar point when he said that talk shows have always gone after sensational, confrontational stories but that the sudden proliferation pushed programming to a different register: "When the industry transformed into this giant beast of eighteen, nineteen, twenty shows, then all bets were off. You know, the ante was up to get those guests in those chairs and make something happen."

Related to the shift in content, then, was a shift in style, in the performances that guests were expected to give, and in the orchestration of these performances behind the scenes. Generally speaking, shows became faster, louder, more visual, and, in the words of one producer, "full of attitude." The number of guests onstage at any one time doubled, particularly on shows targeting younger audiences. Such shows also adopted a younger point of view: whereas *Sally Jessy Raphael* might air "Are Your Kids Having Sex in the House?" *Ricki Lake* would air "My Parents Won't Let Me Have Sex in the House!" Producers also began to rely on surprise encounters and conflict in order to elicit an ever more dramatic money shot: someone abandoned as a child is reunited with her birth mother; a woman reveals to her husband of ten years that she used to be a man; a child molester is confronted by the angry parents of his victims. As Feldman observed, "Because of how salacious and sleazy these shows became, if a woman on a talk show said, 'My husband is having an affair,' you immediately expected that she would be confronted with the mistress, that there would be an opportunity for the wife and mistress to have a go at it."

---

network affiliates, but especially for the first-run syndicators (see Heaton and Wilson 1995; Shattuc 1997, 50–54). As Shattuc (1997) explains, syndicated programs are sold, licensed, or distributed to network affiliates in more than one market for nonnetwork broadcast. Unlike syndicated network reruns (*Roseanne, Seinfeld, The Simpsons*), first-run syndicated programs like daytime talk shows are original shows produced by a syndication company (or a production company formed by the host) and then sold to local network affiliates; the rights to these programs are owned by the syndicator, not the network affiliate or the production company. Multimedia, Tribune, Viacom, and King World Productions are examples of syndication companies.

Giving wives and mistresses the opportunity to "have a go at it" thus created the informal subcategory of daytime talk show known among industry insiders variously as *confrontalk*, *tabloid talk*, or *talk theater*, shows that stood in contrast to the older, more "respectable" prototype created by *Donahue*. According to the head of daytime programming at NBC, "These shows ambush guests, and viewers watch them for pure entertainment value, for the conflict and fighting and what have you. People don't necessarily believe the guests or situations are real, but they watch. These shows are rating well."

In some ways, this type of programming combines the genre's more conventional focus on interpersonal and family relationships with the surprise element of Allen Funt's popular *Candid Camera* series of the 1950s and 1960s, where guests were deliberately provoked into transgressing, or almost transgressing, social codes out of anger or frustration (see Ross 1989), and where the money shot depended on the unveiling of a secret. Confrontalk also bears the legacy of *The Morton Downey Jr. Show*, a late-night audience-participation program that aired briefly in the late 1980s, the televisual equivalent of the abrasive, politically conservative "shock-talk" phenomenon in radio best exemplified today by Howard Stern. *Downey* violated every convention of accepted talk-show protocol at the time. Cruz (1990, 156) describes the program as "part witch-hunt, part carnival," a "no-emotions-or-expletives-barred format" in which arguments quickly escalated to "sheer hollering matches" and the host himself deliberately maneuvered his topics and guests "in order to verbally demolish them."

Downey's confrontational style found its way into daytime talk via the more politically progressive Geraldo Rivera, who came to the genre from a career as an investigative reporter for the tabloid newsmagazine *20/20*. No stranger to conflict, Rivera made television history in 1988 when he sustained a broken nose during a brawl that erupted on the set of his show. The particular episode that day—"Teen Hatemongers"—pitted a group of white-supremacist youths against black activist Roy Innis. The fight on *Geraldo* spread beyond the panelists to include the host and members of the studio audience: a chair flew through the air, someone's fist connected with Geraldo's nose, blood spurted, the television studio got trashed. Virtually every producer I interviewed over the age of thirty-five mentioned this incident at some point in our conversation, usually with a mixture of admiration and chagrin; the broken nose was a pivotal moment in talk-show history but not one that they wholeheartedly embraced.

Geraldo's broken nose was significant for two reasons. First, it momentarily positioned the host as spectacle right along with his guests, part of the presentation of emotions that hosts normally only guide and elicit. In this sense, it was similar to Oprah Winfrey's shocking, and reportedly spontaneous, admission during an episode on child abuse that she, too, like the ordinary panelists onstage that day, had been sexually abused as a child (she made another "spontaneous" on-air admission about cocaine use some years later). Such events confirm the genre's promise of real, unscripted television while blurring the boundaries between ordinary people and experts or celebrities—this time, however, instead of ordinary people gaining celebrity status through intimate disclosures and emotional displays, celebrities engage in these same behaviors to show just how ordinary they can be. Winfrey's frequent references to her own struggles with weight loss also perform this function, as do Jenny Jones's self-referential shows about the dangers to women of breast-implant surgery.

Second, and perhaps more important, the broken nose foreshadowed the development of a new kind of money shot, a tabloid, "masculine" version based on anger and aggression rather than on empathy and tears. As Acland (1995) observes, so neatly did the theatrics of the brawl on *Geraldo* fit the emerging demands of the genre that not only did Rivera proceed with the show but he immediately taped two more, the blood on his face and shirt dramatic testimony of his commitment to "real" controversy and conflict. Even the kinder, gentler hosts grew more confrontational. *Sally Jessy Raphael*, for example, reportedly aired the first "ambush" show about cheating husbands in 1990 and the first family feud a year after that (Stasio 1995). By the mid-1990s, conflict had been routinized to the point where many of the producers I interviewed compared daytime talk to gladiatorial combat or other sporting contests, a common metaphor used in the popular press as well. Saul Feldman called daytime talk "professional wrestling of the '90s" and admitted, only half jokingly, that, as an executive producer, he was more than once tempted to put the host in a referee's uniform. The supervising producer at *Diana* used exactly the same analogy during our interview, suggesting that "the body slam that used to come from Bruno Samartino or George Animal Steel is now the emotional slam from the bitter ex-girlfriend."[6]

These changes have foregrounded and made visible the genre's connections to lowbrow traditions of entertainment and leisure, to the

6. At least one daytime talk show positioned itself as a deliberate parody of this development. Taped in New Jersey, *Richard Bey* coupled the standard talk-show focus on sexuality and intimate relationships with the theatrical aspects of *American Gladiators:* disgruntled guests faced off in water-balloon contests or confronted one another in a makeshift mud pit positioned to the side of the stage (I found that sitting in the front row at *Richard*

"uncivilized" body of popular culture rather than the classical body of high- or middlebrow culture. Whereas the rational, public-service model of talk epitomized by *Donahue* recalls the historic lyceum, town hall, or salon, the current generation of shows has more in common with the tabloid media, the carnival freak show, and, as I will argue later, the nineteenth-century minstrel show. The most obvious of these historical influences is the tabloid press, which survives today in both print and electronic forms. Producers themselves make frequent reference to tabloid journalism when discussing talk shows, and there appears to be some crossover between the two worlds: a *Jerry Springer* producer I interviewed was formerly a reporter for the *Star*, while another interviewee had recently moved from *Ricki Lake* to the *National Enquirer*.

These venues have their roots in the socially conscious "yellow journalism" of the nineteenth century (Shattuc 1997; Bird 1992). Exemplified by early newspapers such as the *Sun* and Joseph Pulitzer's *New York World*, yellow journalism targeted a growing urban population that was poor and semiliterate and combined a simple, colorful style with a populist emphasis on the injustices done to the average working man.[7] The tabloid press as we know it today emerged out of this context, applying the same graphic, sensory style to more "entertaining" stories of crime, murder, and scandal. As with daytime talk shows, different papers occupy different niches in the genre: the *Enquirer* and the *Star* focus almost entirely on celebrity gossip, the *Sun* and the *Weekly World News* favor bizarre human-interest features about "ordinary" people ("I've Been Married to an Alien for Ten Years!" "Woman Turns into Dog after Diet of Pet Food!"), and the *Examiner* and the *Globe* straddle both ordinary and celebrity worlds (Bird 1992).[8]

Bey was much like sitting in the front row at Sea World). Obesity was a frequent topic and food a common device in rituals of torture or punishment. On one episode about sexual infidelity, the cheating boyfriend was tied to the "Wheel of Torture" and spun around while his girlfriend poured hot fudge over him. The show made liberal use of props and sound effects, and Bey himself occasionally appeared on the set wearing an umpire's uniform or some other costume.

7. Pulitzer is credited with the first use of photographs, illustrations, and bold headlines as well as the invention of the sports page, the woman's page, and the advice column.

8. The *National Enquirer* was the first of the contemporary supermarket tabloids and was developed by Generoso Pope in the late 1950s. According to Bird (1992), Pope experimented with various themes for the paper before settling on gore, then built its circulation up to 1 million "on stories of horrific murders and accidents, with a sprinkling of unexplained mysteries, unusual human-interest tales, vicious celebrity gossip, and—somewhat incongruously—occasional pictures of cute animals and children" (25).

Although their language is vivid and titillating, the tabloids tend to emphasize a narrow repertoire of conventional moral themes, such as the importance of children and good parenting, the sanctity of marriage, the in-
evitability of fate, the dangers of excess, and the power of love. Contrary to
stereotype, there is little gore in current-day publications and, unlike talk
shows, little explicit sexuality. More common is what Bird (1992, 50) describes as an "odd emotional blend of sideshow prurience and maternal
compassion," best illustrated by the stock-in-trade stories about two-
headed babies or Siamese twins.

The same sensationalist impulse that characterized the development
of the tabloid press was institutionalized during roughly the same historical period in two other forms of entertainment: "true-confession" romance
magazines aimed at young, working-class women and the circus sideshow
and dime museum, popular with working- and middle-class audiences from
the late nineteenth century through the mid-twentieth. Founded in 1919
(and still in existence today), the true-confession genre has been virtually
ignored in discussions of talk shows, despite striking similarities. The chief
feature of these magazines—which sport such titles as *True Story*, *True
Love*, *True Romance*, and *Secrets*—are "real-life" accounts of misfortune and
abuse, commonly sexual assault, narrated by a young heroine in the first
person. On the front covers are color photos of wholesome, attractive girls,
accompanied by headlines that sound remarkably like the topics of daytime
talk shows: "My Doctor Made Me His Sex Slave," "Raped by the Boy Next
Door," "I Sent My Own Father to Prison," "One Week after Our Wedding, I Slept with Another Man," "My Little Girl's Three Words: He
Hurts Me." As with talk shows, there is an emphasis on truth and authenticity (the confessions are promoted as "a mirror of life") and an attempt to foster a participatory consumer base. Editors invite both commentary from readers about the stories and heroines and readers' own
first-person accounts of misfortune, which may deal with subjects like
abortion, premarital sex, and adultery as well as rape and sexual assault.
In taking this approach, founders Bernarr and Mary Macfadden specifically set out to target young women and girls passed over by conventional middlebrow magazines. According to one editor in chief, the
women who read confessional magazines "will never be the avid readers
of text books or the patients of psychiatrists . . . they read very little that is
not written in conversational language . . . their interests are almost entirely in people . . . the abstract is seldom discussed" (quoted in Downes
2000, 4).

More widely recognized by scholars, critics, and producers are the links between daytime talk shows and carnival freak shows. As Gamson (1998) notes, key elements of sideshow entertainment—the barkers, the sensational promotional strategies, the exhibition of anomalous beings and behaviors to a half-believing audience—are re-created quite plainly in contemporary talk shows (see also Dennett 1996; Lowney 1999).[9] For most critics, the comparison is not a point of flattery, serving as it does to highlight the moral bankruptcy of both discourses (like talk shows, freak shows were said to cater to the lowest common denominator, capitalize on people's base, voyeuristic instincts, and exploit the less fortunate for profit). There are also interesting parallels in production practices between freak shows and talk shows, including tensions surrounding the authenticity of performances. Just as producers distinguish between guests who are "real" and those who are faking their stories, those on the inside of the exhibiting business distinguished between genuine freaks (those who either were born with physical anomalies or acquired unusual attributes) and fakes or frauds—what insiders called *gaffed freaks*—people who merely pretended to have such anomalies or attributes (Bogdan 1996). Yet, as with talk-show guests, *every* exhibit was in some sense a fraud because, like ordinariness, freakishness was a matter not only of real, "natural" characteristics but also of how those characteristics were constructed and narrativized for exhibition. Much like television executives today, sideshow promoters knew that packaging was as important as content and that the "accurate" story of those exhibited could always be "worked on" to produce a more appealing freak (Bogdan 1996). Toward this end, showmen employed a highly stylized set of codes and procedures from promotional pamphlets and lectures to artful costuming, staging, and choreography. At the same time, they attempted to legitimate and make real the theatrical presentation of unusual bodies by aping the trappings of science, using the word *museum* in the title of their shows, and referring to freak-show lecturers as *professor* or *doctor* (in this manner, the lecturer assumed a role analogous to the expert on daytime talk shows). As Rosemarie Thomson (1996) points out, as a consequence of these production efforts, when people flocked to the dime museum or circus

9. The press has also made much of the comparison between talk shows and freak shows. An essay in *Time* magazine, e.g., describes freak shows as places where "scores of anonymous wretches abused themselves grotesquely for the amusement and amazement of paying customers" and daytime talk shows as their direct, mainstream descendant, "a virtual round-the-clock pageant of geeks inviting the contempt of viewers without even the old quiz-show promises of kitchen ranges or living-room furniture" (Andersen 1993, 94).

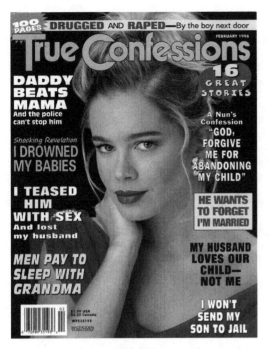

Figure 6. Cover of *True Confessions* romance magazine, February 1998. Courtesy Sterling/Macfadden Partnership, Inc.

sideshow, what they witnessed was as much a freak of culture as a freak of nature.[10]

The general slide from seriousness to sensationalism that exposed the genre's lowbrow roots and raised the ire of critics and intellectuals also generated considerable controversy among industry professionals themselves. The vast majority of producers with whom I spoke lamented the

10. Although talk shows are often compared to freak shows for less-than-flattering reasons, it is interesting to note that *freak* was not a term of derision until well into the twentieth century, when the medicalization of the body rendered illegitimate the theatrical presentation of physical anomalies and the shows became dissociated from respectable society (Thomson 1996; Bogdan 1996). According to Bogdan, as the power and dominance of the professions increased in the twentieth century, people with mental and physical anomalies came under the control of professionals, and many were secluded from the public, their conditions contained or treated behind closed doors. Moreover, the rise of science and medicine was part of a larger modernizing process in which standardization—of goods, of services, of people—helped produce and reinforce the concept of a normative, unmarked body and decreased the tolerance for human physical variation. Bogdan argues that, in an urbanizing, industrializing society with no social security, discrimination in employment, and strained personal relations, most sideshow performers did not become exhibits for the small financial benefit or fleeting fame but to find refuge in a world where others were similarly situated.

Figure 7. Sideshow at the circus, Klamath Falls, Oregon. Photograph by Russell Lee. Date unknown. Farm Security Administration, Office of War Information Photograph Collection, Library of Congress. Courtesy Library of Congress.

trend; *Diana* staffers invariably expressed relief that they did not have to produce, in the words of one producer, "the nasty catfight screaming-match trailer-trash stuff" that other shows were airing, while those at *Randy* made clear distinctions between their work lives and their personal ethics or pointed out the ways in which the respectable media was also manipulative and inflammatory.

During this period, then, classy/trashy emerged as a primary axis of distinction between shows, and it figured centrally in the efforts of executives and producers at *Diana* and *Randy* to establish both an identity and a set of backstage strategies and practices consistent with that identity. For example, the executive producer at *Diana* described that show as being "classy and respectable, but with a bit of an edge." "We're not one of those sleazy, tabloid talk shows," she said. "We don't ambush people, and we're not overly confrontational. But we're not afraid to push the envelope a little either, as long as we do it tastefully. Any talk show can do a racy topic—you know, like cross-dressing or lesbian mothers. What makes the difference is the *way* you handle it."

In avoiding overt conflict and confrontation and opting instead for more subtle performances, *Diana* constructs its identity in deliberate opposition to "those sleazy, tabloid talk shows." All the producers on staff mentioned the show's "higher" approach as important to both their job satisfaction and their sense of personal ethics.

"I think it's possible to have a great dynamic on the show and even have it be somewhat confrontational," Rachel said to me one evening as we left the stage together after a particularly hectic taping. "But there has to be a higher purpose to people's stories, some larger element. Otherwise, it just becomes, you know, like, 'Here's a big sore filled with pus, here's another one, and here's another one.'" She then made a comparison to pornography: "It's like pornography in that some people find it more interesting to watch if women have some clothing on because total nakedness can actually be a turnoff. And that's how I feel about it if you were to just line up a bunch of grotesque, horrible stories. I mean, what's the point of that?"

Most critics of daytime talk would agree that there is little point or educational value to such a confrontation. But talk shows like *Randy* do not aim to educate, at least not in any conventional sense. Rather, they orchestrate emotional encounters on television in order to capitalize on the visual immediacy of the medium. "Total nakedness" is precisely what the show aims to produce. As Randy himself told me, "This isn't an educational show other than what you learn by seeing how people relate to one another." At the time, we were sitting in his office, a spacious room containing an enormous polished desk dotted with stacks of paper and a photograph of a girl I presumed was a daughter or a niece. He apologized for wolfing down a bagel as we spoke, but he had not had time to eat breakfast before coming to work.

"Sometimes," he said between bites, "what even the producers don't realize is the subject, what we're discussing that day, is the least important thing about the show. The subject is merely a vehicle to get people to engage one another in all forms of interaction. So it doesn't much matter— you can run the same subject five days in a row and have five great shows because the people are different. We see their personalities; we see how they react. You know, that's what fascinates us."

Every show, then, has its identity, despite how similar to one another the various shows might appear to those unfamiliar with the genre, and these differences have consequences for the work that producers do: eliciting conflict at *Randy* requires different strategies than does eliciting tears at *Diana*. The assumption of industry professionals is that differences among shows are designed to appeal to the tastes and preferences of different viewer demographics, and the emergence of shows like *Randy* or *Ricki Lake* marked an attempt to draw in a previously untapped market composed of younger viewers, male viewers, and what industry insiders call the *ethnic demographic*—meaning African Americans and Latinos. According to a supervising producer interviewed by Gamson (1998), this process of discovering "new" audiences was really more reactive than proactive, less a matter of trying to find the right formula for the right demographic than simply letting guests speak in their own way to their own constituencies. According to the supervising producer, guests were not told how to behave onstage; they just naturally incorporated preexisting cultural practices into their perform-ances. Thus, the African American gesture known as *talk to the hand* (which is short for *talk to the hand because the face doesn't understand*), now a common gesture among guests, did not originate on talk shows; it originated "some-where in the street, somewhere in urban life" (Gamson 1998, 64).

Ricki Lake was the first of the new wave of shows to make it big. Fore-shadowing the later success of *Jerry Springer*, its ratings began to rival *Oprah*'s among younger viewers after only two seasons. According to *Spin* magazine, not only did Lake's executive producer aim to take the *Donahue* format and "age it down," but he also made "an upfront appeal to black au-diences, with the expectation that people of color would tune in to see their own, while the white kids would come along because black = street = hip" (Schone 1996, 69). Other considerations aside, this was a sound marketing decision since industry research has long revealed a connection between television consumption and race and class: people of color and those with lower incomes tend to watch more hours of television, especially more hours of daytime television, than do whites or those with high incomes. One market-research analyst I interviewed put it this way: "The ethnic de-mographic watches a lot more television, so if you're doing a show that's not appealing to that particular demographic, it's going to hurt your over-all daytime audience. You don't want to target them *exclusively*, but you do want to target them *inclusively*." This same individual said that Oprah's rat-ings had dropped in part because she had lost touch with this audience — viewers perceived that she had become "a rich woman with her trainer and her cook and the whole bit" and consequently was no longer "one of us." Setting aside for now the question of why appealing to younger, low-income, and/or "ethnic" viewers should coincide with an increased em-phasis on conflict and sensationalism, it is worth taking a short detour at this point to discuss the matter of talk-show audiences since, without audi-ences to sell to advertisers, there would be no talk shows for producers to produce or for critics to criticize.

Stand Up and Be Counted: Talk-Show Audiences

While talk shows are invariably acknowledged to be popular, estimates of the actual number of people who watch daytime talk shows are difficult to come by, in part because figures are typically tabulated for individual shows, rather than for the genre as a whole, and they can vary widely depending on whether they reflect a yearly average, a monthly average, or the viewership for a particular episode or whether they reflect local or national markets, different figures reflecting different measurement techniques. Numbers will also vary by age and gender, which are the two primary subcategories of interest to advertisers. Saul Feldman estimates that roughly 30 million viewers watch talk shows on a daily basis, which is consistent with Lowney's (1999) observation that between 3 and 6 million households watch each of the seven top-rated shows. For much of the 1990s, *Oprah* was undisputed queen of the genre with a daily viewership of approximately 15 million,[11] and, although their audiences were considerably smaller, *Donahue*, *Sally Jessy*, and *Geraldo* also rated consistently well in the early half of the decade, followed by relative newcomers *Jenny Jones*, *Montel Williams*, and *Maury Povich*. At the peak of the boom, however, shows across the board had to compete for increasingly smaller advertising shares, and, according to one marketing researcher I interviewed, most of the new ones could not survive, garnering daily audiences of 2 million or less. The chief exceptions here were *Ricki Lake* and, after an initial slump, *Jerry Springer*, which, in February of 1999, was reported to have 8.5 million viewers, 1 million more than *Oprah*.[12] There is big money behind these numbers. Heaton and Wilson (1995) report that, in 1992, *Oprah* earned $157 million in revenues, *Donahue* an estimated $90 million, and *Sally Jessy Raphael* $60 million.

Industry insiders argue that the home viewing audience is more than two-thirds women, although this figure drops for shows like *Ricki Lake* or *Jerry Springer*, which have succeeded in attracting a more gender-mixed audience (the publicist at *Jerry Springer* says that roughly half the show's viewing audience is male). Different shows target different age ranges: *Oprah* and *Leeza*, for example, target women aged eighteen to fifty-four,

---

11. Squire (1994) estimates the number of daily *Oprah* viewers to be 20 million, Shattuc (1997) 15 million. Some of the discrepancy here can be explained by the different time periods measured. Also, it is important to bear in mind that the figures quoted by scholars and journalists often derive from press packets or conversations with publicists, which may be selective, presenting the show in the best possible light (e.g., press packets often report the ratings only for "sweeps" months, when the figures are higher than average).

12. This figure comes from a FOX television news report, and it is not clear whether it reflects a yearly average, a monthly average (February is a sweeps month), or the difference between shows on the day of the report. Nor does it distinguish differences within the gross category *viewer*: if you consider only female viewers or only viewers over thirty-five, *Oprah* would get a higher rating than *Jerry Springer*.

while *Maury Povich* aims for the over-fifty crowd, and *Ricki Lake* and *Jenny Jones* target mostly people under thirty-five. As mentioned above, the younger, more confrontational shows also tend to attract working-class and ethnic audiences; while the audience for *Oprah* is predominantly white and middle class (Peck 1994), *Springer* is reportedly popular among black and Latino viewers, college students, and blue-collar workers.[13] Despite the range, producers and executives retain a concept of the typical talk-show viewer, assumed to be a housewife with a ninth-grade education in a lower socioeconomic bracket (Shattuc 1997). This is certainly consistent with what I heard from producers at *Diana* and *Randy*, who would describe viewers as "your average housewife," "people who are home during the day, such as mothers, housewives, and the unemployed," or "Mrs. Middle-America," which typically meant married with children, living in a small town in the Midwest on a modest income. It is also consistent with the products and services advertised alongside the shows, which include diet pills, weight-loss clinics, personal-injury lawyers, "affordable" medical and dental care, kitchen appliances, discount furniture, cosmetics, personal hygiene products, and cleaning supplies.

Yet, as Shattuc (1997) points out, industry researchers do not really know the viewers they are presumably measuring any more than advertisers do. "The concept of a knowable audience of women," she writes, "is ultimately a fiction used by producers and advertisers to support their self-ascribed ability to attract specific audiences for specific products. . . . From this perspective, the female audience is a self-perpetuating industry construct that needs no real women" (48). According to Shattuc's sources, "women demographics," especially women in the eighteen to forty-nine age range, remain the single most important category of viewers for daytime programmers both because they constitute the largest percentage of habitual viewers of television during the day and because purchasing household goods is still perceived to be primarily a woman's responsibility. As these factors change, however, so do the daytime demographics, and the targeting of younger, gender-mixed audiences by some of the newer talk shows is evidence that old assumptions about the daytime audience are breaking down.

Producers often have specific ideas about who viewers are and why they are watching, and there are market-research techniques such as phone

13. This information derives from "A Look at the Week Ahead" (1998) and was confirmed by the show's publicist.

surveys and focus-group interviews that attempt to obtain more qualitative information about viewers. The three most common reasons for watching daytime talk shows given by producers are the same as those most frequently cited by journalists and media critics writing about talk shows in the press: (1) people identify with, or want information about, the problem or issue being discussed; (2) people like hearing about the problems of others because it makes them feel better about their own lives ("My marriage isn't perfect, but at least it's not as bad as *that*"); and (3) people are drawn to watch guests say and do things that they themselves would never say or do on national television—the *freak-show gawk factor*, as it is known among producers. As the audience coordinator at *Diana* put it, "People are drawn to the soap-opera aspect of talk shows. They can't believe that such things go on in real life, that they have been invited, in the privacy of their own homes, to participate in someone else's dysfunction."

Producers forge these conceptions of the audience partly on the basis of their own assumptions about audiences (which stem from conversations with coworkers and from the rest of the media) and partly on the results of market research or other, less systematic forms of feedback such as viewer phone calls and fan mail. At *Diana*, producers are briefed about the latest focus-group research findings in production meetings, while *Randy* producers paid little attention to anything but ratings, which rose steadily along with the level of conflict among guests. (*Randy* producers knew that their audience was looking to be entertained, and they assumed that it was primarily the freak-show gawk factor that drew viewers in. As one producer put it, "It's just human nature to love gossip and to want to glimpse the dirt of other peoples' lives.") Generally speaking, various forms of qualitative market research are perceived by television executives as an important but approximate tool for getting to know the tastes and preferences of the viewing audience. This knowledge enables the show to tailor an identity consistent with those preferences more precisely, in the process (it is hoped) boosting ratings and attracting advertisers.

Focus-group interviews can be quite comprehensive, involving questions both about the genre as a whole and about specific shows and also about the details of specific episodes as well as about hosts, topics, and production strategies. Then there are random phone surveys of self-identified viewers and other measures called *TV-quotients* (TV-Qs), which are essentially indices of a show's likability: respondents indicate their level of familiarity with a given show and then rate how much they like it on a five-point scale. Some research firms also conduct experimental sessions in which viewers watch a show and turn dials back and forth in response to things they like and dislike. Yet qualitative research of any sort is always acknowledged to be but one factor in the overall decision-making process and will by itself rarely prompt a major change in production. As the vice president for programming at NBC put it, "Research is used only as an indication, plain and simple. This business is not cut and dry. There's still a little bit of magic, there's still a little bit of luck involved, and timing. So we don't make decisions, we assist in making decisions." According to this same executive, one thing that qualitative research has consistently shown is that viewer preferences have become increasingly topic rather than host driven: while viewers tend to have favorite shows or favorite hosts, they will change the channel and see what else is on if they don't like the topic for that day. So, whether a show commissions phone surveys or focus-group interviews, the idea is to determine its substantive strengths and play those up while weeding out the topics and elements that viewers consistently dislike. "It's like taking an apple and cutting the bad part away so that what you have left is all the sweet stuff," he said.

Another important dimension of the audience for daytime talk shows is the people who attend live tapings. Producers like to claim that the studio audience is representative of, or a proxy for, viewers at home, but this is rarely the case since the studio audience is typically composed of tourists, school or church groups, college students, the unemployed, the elderly, and sometimes groups of people who have a particular stake or interest in the topic addressed that day. Audiences tended to be older at *Diana* than *Randy*, less ethnically diverse, and more heavily female (whereas women consistently outnumbered men by roughly two to one at *Diana*, at *Randy* men typically outnumbered women by a slight margin).[14] Aside from the fact that they represent somewhat different demographics, however, the main difference between viewers at home and members of the studio audience is that the latter can participate in the performance in a way that home viewers cannot, and their reasons for attending may differ as a

14. Official demographic data on studio audiences are virtually nonexistent. Even Livingstone and Lunt's (1994) exhaustive study of audience-discussion programs in the United States and Britain focused on guests and home viewers, but not members of the studio audience specifically. While at *Diana*, I was granted permission to administer short surveys to audience members, asking people's age, gender, race, occupation, and place of residence, but the response rate was too low to be of any use (of those who did respond, most were white, female, over fifty, retired homemakers, and living within a ninety-mile radius of the studio).

result. I sat through live tapings of more than two dozen different talk shows in Los Angeles, Santa Monica, New York, New Jersey, and Chicago, and the participatory aspect, the chance to be seen and heard on camera, was undeniably a source of great enjoyment for audience members.

Most talk shows aim to create a festive, energetic environment well before taping even begins. *Diana* is fairly typical in that it employs a comedian to warm up the audience, whereas, at *Randy*, the stage manager (and sometimes the senior producer) does this along with his other tasks. (The host may also do all or part of the warm-up routine, as was the case at both *Richard Bey* and *Jerry Springer*.) Invariably, the pretaping warm-up involves telling jokes ("Your mamma is so dumb she thinks Taco Bell is a Mexican phone company") and keeping up a steady stream of idle banter with audience members: where are you from, are you married, do you have any kids, who's your favorite celebrity? Shows geared toward younger audiences pipe loud rap music over the sound system and award prizes such as T-shirts, coffee mugs, or fanny packs to audience members who tell jokes of their own or who volunteer to sing or dance onstage. As the comedian at *Jenny Jones* put it, "This is the preshow show starring *you*— the audience!"

More than once, I was struck by the talent displayed in these impromptu performances and by the fact that it was mostly young people— and disproportionately young people of color—who volunteered. At the *Jenny Jones* taping, the comedian asked how many of us wanted to be in show business, and roughly one-third of the people in the room raised their hands; at *Ricki Lake*, *half* the room responded affirmatively to the same question. Some portion of audience members had usually attended tapings before, and there were always a few individuals who seemed well-known to the production staff and crew. Perhaps what "regulars" knew that others did not was that, on occasion, producers would canvas the studio audience for potential guests for their upcoming shows. The day that I attended a taping at *Leeza*, for example, the person who prepped the audience was seeking potential guests for upcoming shows on single people who fear that they will never find a mate, parents who think that their teens need makeovers, people with strange phobias, and people with unusual names (Ben Dover, Warren Peace, Crystal Ball). Interns ran through the audience handing out blue index cards to individuals who might qualify for any of these categories. Some shows also solicit topic ideas from audience members, and, at one show I attended, the senior producer invited audience members to meet with her at a designated time and place to discuss their ideas in person.[15]

The main purpose of the warm-up, however, is not to recruit potential guests but to energize the audience, to make people feel an integral part of the action and crucial to the success of the taping. "You can make or break this show," audience members are told. "Get involved! Ask questions! Remember, you represent all those viewers out there who can't ask questions for themselves. You represent America!" The staffer leading the warm-up goes over the proper procedure for asking questions or making comments on the air ("Stand up tall, speak into the mike, and don't ramble!"), has people practice clapping and booing, and instructs them in the finer points of audience etiquette, which forbids wearing ball caps, chewing gum, responding to beepers or cell phones, mugging for the camera, or speaking without being called on but encourages "big reactions" to the events onstage.

All this is common procedure across shows. But there are also subtle and not-so-subtle differences within the genre in terms of how audience members are expected to behave, for, while all talk shows want energy, emotion, and enthusiasm, the audience, like the topics and guests, must be consistent with the identity of the individual show. As Gamson (1998) has noted, when programs began targeting a younger demographic, they brought onto the set and into the studio audience people with different interests, different rules about talking, and a different relation to television. As a consequence, the taken-for-granted norms of audience conduct began to change.

Studio audiences thus do their part in reflecting the classy/trashy divide, with the classier shows demanding more restrained and "civilized" behavior. At *Donahue*, for example, which used to tape at the Rockefeller Center in New York, we were told by the executive producer to be supportive of the guests onstage and to voice our opinions in a respectful manner. We were supposed to greet Phil and the guests warmly when it was time for them to walk onstage—"just as you would greet guests arriving for a party at your house, only with more emotion." The executive producer also warned us not to clap before and after commercial breaks because you never knew what you were clapping for—it could be an ad for feminine-

---

15. Of course, the actual percentage of guests or topics culled from the studio audience is quite low. I know that producers at *Diana* perused the index cards submitted by audience members infrequently and only as a last resort after exhausting their regular channels and sources. They often allocated this task to an intern, with instructions to "give a yell if anything jumps out at you."

hygiene products or a public-service announcement about AIDS. Photographs were permitted during the taping, she said, "but be discreet, and maintain a sense of decorum; don't go chasing Phil down the aisle yelling, 'Yo Phil!'" (I recall thinking that there was very little chance of anyone chasing Phil down the aisle as the majority of the folks seated around me were over forty and conservatively dressed.) No need for bouncers or metal detectors here.

This contrasts starkly with shows such as *Ricki Lake, Jenny Jones*, or *Jerry Springer*, where, like the guests onstage, audience members are encouraged to "let go," the bigger the better. At these shows, audiences provide running commentary (groaning, gasping, hissing, booing) to events onstage and clap wildly going in and out of commercial breaks. This can be disconcerting, depending on what is happening to guests. At my first *Springer* taping, for example, which was uncharacteristically serious, a young girl was sobbing onstage, pleading with her stepfather to stop supplying her mother with drugs when suddenly we cut to a commercial and the audience was up on its feet, clapping and cheering. At another taping I attended titled "You're Busted!" each time a new guest was ambushed with surprising information, the audience cheered, and, when a fight erupted, they gave the "ambushee" a standing ovation. Under these circumstances, people seemingly can be very cruel, standing up to chastise guests or make mean-spirited and insulting remarks, particularly if a panelist is overweight, physically unattractive, or not heterosexual (which, on *Springer*, is much of the time). Thus, at trashy shows, the raucousness of guests onstage is reproduced at the level of the studio audience and may even involve physical as well as emotional expressiveness. Before Springer toned down his show, members of the audience—particularly young men—would occasionally charge the stage and get drawn into fights with guests. I also learned from a security guard at *Ricki Lake* that audience members have been known to fight with one another, either during the taping itself or as they stand in line waiting for admittance. *Circus-like* was the term employed most often by the producers and guests I interviewed to describe this sort of atmosphere. On occasion, the studio audience may even provide a more spectacular show than the guests. I recall clearly a particular moment during a *Randy* taping when I noticed a panelist onstage staring in disbelief at the people in the audience. The expression on his face was unmistakable. In an odd turn of the tables, he was wondering, "Who are these freaks? Why would any self-respecting person behave this way on television?"

Earlier, I spoke of the similarities between talk shows and freak shows as well as between talk shows and the tabloid press, but the participatory, performative quality of studio audiences also links the genre to historic forms of working-class entertainment like vaudeville, cabaret, and, especially, early-nineteenth-century theater. By all accounts, audiences in the early nineteenth century were anything but orderly and reverential (see Levine 1988; Kasson 1990). They treated concert halls, theaters, and opera houses not as sacred precincts but as places of entertainment where they could express their opinions freely and interact with the performers. According to Levine (1988, 68), "The theater was one of those houses of refuge in the nineteenth century where the normative restrictions of the society were relaxed and both players and audience were allowed to 'act out themselves' with much less inner and outer restraint than prevailed in society." Levine tells us that the gap between the stage and the pit, which today we treat as a boundary separating two worlds, was then perceived as an archway inviting participation. Audiences would sing along and recite out loud lines of familiar dialogue. They clapped and shouted their approval, booed and hissed their disapproval, interrupted the show to demand encores of favorite scenes, and occasionally threw food at the stage. Not surprisingly, social elites of the period complained about this "illbred" and "uncivilized" behavior, much as scholars and critics today complain about "trashy" talk-show audiences and guests. Such complaints about audiences were hardly trivial, for they reflected a much broader set of concerns about standards of bodily conduct and emotional control during a period when the character of America's cultural life and the definition of the public realm were undergoing fundamental transformations.[16]

Of course, talk-show audiences differ from nineteenth-century theatergoers in important ways, and it is unwise to overstate the parallels. Back then, there was no "warm-up person" to rehearse questions and comments, tell people how to react, or lead those reactions from the sidelines. Back then, of course, there was no such thing as TV. But the larger participatory desire on the part of audiences was likely much the same, as I will elaborate

16. With industrialization, urbanization, and immigration came increasing cultural heterogeneity, including class and ethnic diversity. According to Levine (1988), the response of elites was a tripartite one: to retreat into their own private spaces whenever possible (hence the emergence of separate institutions of "high" culture, accompanied by a separation of audiences by class); to transform public spaces by rules, systems of taste, and canons of behavior of their own choosing; and to convert the masses so that their modes of behavior and cultural predilections emulated those of elites. Generally speaking, the more public the space, the more self-monitoring one's behavior, and, despite reverse stereotypes of high culture as artificial and pretentious, rising standards of restraint eventually spread to more popular entertainments such as minstrel shows, cabaret, vaudeville, amusement parks, and the cinema (Kasson 1990; Levine 1988; see also Peiss 1986).

later on. Just as nineteenth-century theatergoers blurred the line between actor and audience, making the spectator in some measure part of the action and part of the scene, giving "big reactions" or asking a question on camera positions those attending a live taping as participants, the "supporting cast" for the players onstage.

Defining Ordinariness

For producers at both *Diana* and *Randy*, the shift from seriousness to sensationalism and the battle for ratings made more difficult what was already a challenging process: putting ordinary, everyday people on television. The hours are long, the pace grueling, the stress level high, and the pay (for all but the senior people and top executives) much lower than for comparable jobs in primetime. Like most kinds of work in the television industry, there is little or no job security since contracts tend to be short term and dependent on the success of the show. Producers feel this lack of security acutely because the ultimate responsibility for the success or failure of any given episode lies most heavily with them. And, while virtually all staffers from the top of the workplace hierarchy to the bottom feel pulled in multiple directions at once, as if they are performing single-handedly what is really a job for four or five people, producers especially have to be jacks-of-all-trades: journalist, salesperson, therapist, travel agent, tour guide, and sometimes referee all rolled into one.

Compounding this problem is the frantic pace of production. Although I was merely a tourist for a brief spell in this world that others inhabited on a more permanent basis, every day walking into the production offices at *Diana* or *Randy* I felt the tension that producers later spoke of at length in interviews: the constant crank-it-out daily grind of putting together show after show under the pressure of deadlines and the stiff competition for ratings. "A treadmill you can't jump off," was the way one producer described the work. It was this very environment that made the unpaid labor of interns essential and thus created the structural opportunity for my own insertion behind the scenes.

Many producers work seventy-hour weeks and take their jobs home with them. A twenty-five-year-old *Randy* staffer who was promoted to producer while I was interning there said that the new title meant more money but did not change her hectic schedule much. For her, the pace was all consuming: "I look around here and wonder, What's going to happen to me when I'm fifty? Am I going to be in a loony bin? Because this job, it's crazy.

Producers are as wacko as the guests for doing this stuff!" At twenty-eight, an associate producer at *Diana* already feels burned out. "Honestly Laura," she said to me one day as we were leaving the studio together, "some days I walk into the office—I swear I can't talk to one more potential guest, and I'm pretty young to have that feeling. I think, why am I doing this? I can't do it anymore." An associate producer at *Sally Jessy* felt much the same way about the frenzied pace but was unable to normalize or adjust to it. After only six months she quit. As she explained to me later on the phone, "I never saw my family. I spent every holiday, every weekend nailed to my desk. I was literally putting in twelve to fifteen hours every single day—I worked through the flu, I worked through bronchitis. I was exhausted, you know? And finally I'd just had enough."

To some degree, these complaints are common to television production generally, especially daily programming like news and public affairs. Some of the producers I worked with and interviewed had in fact come to daytime talk from jobs in news organizations. They made the switch because they wanted to work in entertainment television and saw talk shows as a stepping-stone to more lucrative careers in primetime, either behind the camera as writers and producers or, more rarely, in front of the camera as "talent." But prior media experience does not necessarily prepare one for working on a talk show, where the normal pressures of television production are complicated by the genre's focus on ordinary people and, more important, by the ways in which ordinariness gets constructed in this context.

At the most fundamental level, *ordinary people* means "real people"— "just folks," individuals who lack expert or celebrity status and are not media-savvy professionals. On the one hand, this ordinariness, and the real-life topics associated with it, can be a source of pleasure and satisfaction for producers and other staff members. A *Diana* producer, formerly with *Oprah*, described ordinary guests as "the salt of the earth. They're funny, they're joyous, they're sad, they're full of pain, they're touching, they're *real*." Producers spoke of using the power and glamour of television for exploring issues that they found personally interesting or important (more often the case at *Diana* than at *Randy*, given the different aims and identities of the two shows) and of learning about problems and injustices that otherwise would have remained invisible to them. Many also found meeting guests, hearing their stories, showing them a good time, and, in some cases, changing their lives personally rewarding. They spoke of reuniting long-lost loves or adopted children separated from their birth parents, introducing young fans to their favorite soap star or sports idol, sending a drug-addicted teenager to rehab at the expense of the show, or giving grandma the makeover of her life. At *Diana*, producers displayed on their desks and bulletin boards thank-you cards from guests expressing gratitude for shows that helped or touched them in some way. Ellen remarked that her job at *Diana* always reminded her of the 1970s television series *Fantasy Island.* "Here are these people, they're in Middle America, this is the biggest thing thats ever happened to them. They're jumping on a plane, coming out here, we give 'em fifteen minutes of fame, a nice hotel and stuff . . . and then, you know, we send 'em off in limos like we're Mr. Rourke in *Fantasy Island*, going, 'Good-bye, my friends, that's it! Your fantasy's over! Go home!'"

On the other hand, the very ordinariness that producers find pleasurable or rewarding is also the source of their greatest frustration, rendering more challenging their work behind the scenes. There are several layers or dimensions of ordinariness at issue here. The first is what might be called *first-order ordinariness*, which results from simply being an outsider to the production apparatus, from a lack of professional training and media experience. Ordinary people are by definition not experts or celebrities, yet they are being asked to perform as both and conform to the codes of television in the process, a set of taken-for-granted expectations that producers understand but ordinary guests may not. For instance, if a person has never before been on camera, she will not naturally know to speak in sound bites, reveal the punch line at the beginning (not the end) of her story, or consider her emotions as production elements to be managed and manipulated by others.

Offstage, too, guests do all sorts of things that frustrate or annoy producers simply because appearing on national television is not part of their daily routine. Unlike celebrities, ordinary people do not have agents, publicists, or personal assistants to handle their schedules and juggle their competing obligations. Thus, an associate producer at *Diana* did a show on the high school sweethearts of celebrities and got a phone call at five in the morning from Farrah Fawcett's ex-boyfriend who was ready to cancel because he could not find a kennel to house his ailing dog. Another producer got a frantic call after midnight from a guest who could not decide what to wear on camera and wanted the producer's advice about the beige suit versus the navy dress. Such incidents can lead producers and staffers to infantilize guests, to look on them as petulant children in need of constant attention and reassurance. Rachel made this explicit when she referred to the guests on her most recent show as "a bunch of giant babies" who think that "the whole world revolves around them" and who have "no awareness of what it takes to put a show together." The travel coordinator—the person on staff who books airfare, hotel accommodations, and limousine transportation for guests and their entourages, typically between forty and fifty people every week—would no doubt agree. Lena, the travel coordinator at *Diana*, told me countless stories about getting paged at all hours by people who had misplaced their tickets, missed their flights, lost their luggage, wanted to change their departure or arrival times, or simply could not remember where they were supposed to go or when they were supposed to get there. She described herself as the "umbilical cord" between guests and the show because she is the one they contact if problems arise. "I'm on call twenty-four hours a day," she said. "It's ridiculous. I'm like, you know, trying to have a life, maybe even have a date—I'll, like, be on a date in an intimate moment with somebody and suddenly, Beep! beep! beep! My pager goes off, and I'm, like, oh my God, what *now?*"

The challenges associated with first-order ordinariness are then exacerbated and amplified by the conflation of ordinariness with emotional expressiveness. Emotional expressiveness—the capacity to convey, on camera, raw, real emotion—is the ordinary guest's greatest form of cultural capital, the element most desired and anticipated, yet, in the final analysis, the one producers perceive to be most beyond their control no matter how much or little they prepare. As the supervising producer at *Diana* observed, "Raw reaction is a great thing. When someone tells you a true story in a compelling manner and it's in that emotional and raw form—that's really something. That's what it's all about. But it's not something you plan; it's never going to be that kind of expected behavior."

Giving raw reaction—delivering an authentic money shot—is precisely what makes ordinary guests real people. It is what distinguishes them from contrasting categories of guests, both experts, who are routine, if marginal, participants on daytime talk, and celebrities, who appear more rarely. Although producers did not speak of the distinction between guests in terms of the money shot, without exception they agreed that, while you looked to ordinary people for personal revelations and emotional drama, celebrities and experts serve a different purpose and deliver different kinds of performances. As we shall see in chapter 7, experts are there primarily to lend respectability to the topic, and, in the case of psychologist experts, to dispense a few words of advice—a practice that allows producers to claim to be helping guests. They are crucial to the genre's structure, but, because they are not featured performers, they are not crucial to the success or failure of any given episode, and, as a consequence, they command only minimal attention from producers.

Celebrities, by contrast, on the rare occasion that they deign to appear on a daytime talk show, are very much featured performers and must be handled with considerable delicacy. Far more than experts, celebrities constitute an elite class in American culture (see Gamson 1994), and, despite the fact that they go on talk shows precisely to construct themselves as regular folk, they provide not only respectability but an aura of specialness akin to royalty. Rachel, in fact, compared working with celebrities to "being around the queen of England" because there was always a coterie of agents and assistants to deal with and because of the big egos involved. ("It's like walking on eggshells—these people are really temperamental, and you can offend them without knowing how you did it.") Most producers, however, felt that, despite their egos, celebrities were "a piece of cake" compared to ordinary people because, as Jocelyn put it, "Celebrities are pros. They know what they're doing. You know that they're going to be great on the air—it's their job."

The trade-off is that celebrities do not provide the money shot, or at least not the right *kind* of money shot. Again to quote Jocelyn, "The one thing that you don't get from [celebrities] that you get from real people is they're not going to be as honest or emotional with you, they're not going to divulge secrets necessarily." Thus, while producers sometimes disagreed about which category of guest is more enjoyable to work with or difficult to handle, they were unanimous in their belief that the *nature* of the performance is different for each, that celebrities do not give of themselves the way ordinary people do. Some complained that celebrities dictate so many limitations that they make it nigh impossible to have a good show. Rachel, for example, said that she understood them not wanting to get "too personal and appear out of control," but, on the other hand, "you can get so restrictive that it's hard to do anything interesting. It's like, How's the weather in Hollywood, now that we have nothing to talk about?"

Justin, another *Diana* producer, characterized the difference between ordinary people and celebrities in terms of rigid versus permeable boundaries. "With celebrities, there are boundaries," he said. "You have to keep a certain distance *because* they're celebrities. There are more layers to go through, and the whole process is just more formal." While acknowledging that real people have egos too and can at times be just as imperious or reserved as Hollywood stars, Justin agreed that, on the whole, ordinary people are more casual and less guarded than celebrities: "Celebrities are not going to cough up a bunch of stuff. They don't give you that real human drama." All this was something that Florence, the "talent executive," knew very well since her main job at *Diana* was to book celebrities for the show and to ensure that they have a good experience. She told me that dealing with celebrities on a regular basis required three things: knowing how to stroke their egos, knowing what boundaries one could and could not cross, and knowing that celebrities don't *do* topics, they *are* the topic. As she put it, "If we're going to get celebrities to come on the show, they're not going to come on and talk about whether they were sexually abused, raped, or whatever. You know what I'm saying? You don't go to Barbra Streisand and ask her to talk about not getting along with her mother. And you don't ask her to share the stage with a dozen other people talking about that stuff either."

In other words, the more powerful a person, the more sacred their boundaries, the less they reveal about themselves in public, and the more they control the conditions of the revealing. Certainly, Powdermaker (1951) found this to be true of celebrities in the course of doing fieldwork on the Hollywood film industry. Celebrities, and to a lesser extent experts, typically have more status, power, and prestige than ordinary people, and, for this reason, they are not expected, as Justin put it, to "cough up a bunch of stuff" the way ordinary people are. They do not—or only rarely and with great fanfare—disclose intimate or private information, admit to personal failures and transgressions, or bicker with friends and family on national television. Even when politicians or other high-status figures reveal aspects of their personal lives in public (or have aspects of their personal lives revealed by others, as with the highly publicized affair between Bill Clinton and Monica Lewinsky), such revelations often function to position them as ordinary folk just like everybody else. Thus, the fact that ordinary guests on talk shows do these things as a matter of generic expectation helps secure and reinforce their status as ordinary people—and often, not just any ordinary people, but ordinary people of a particular class. The more dramatic the emotional outburst or physical display—the louder the yelling, the harder the sobbing, the more vicious the conflict or confrontation—the lower the class (and the less like celebrities and experts) they are perceived to be. Not surprisingly, celebrity guests were rare on *Randy* compared to *Diana*, *Randy* being the trashier show. Similarly, when Oprah Winfrey decided to separate from the pack and take the high road, she devoted herself more and more to celebrity-based topics. Generally speaking, when celebrities do appear on daytime talk shows, they are usually former child stars, motivational speakers, or soap actors drawn from the B and C ranks. A-list celebrities do the late-night circuits and would never be caught dead on a daytime talk show.[17]

Ordinary guests on daytime talk shows are thus distinguished from expert and celebrity guests by their lesser status, their lack of specialized media training, and their higher level of emotional expressiveness, all of which make their performances more challenging for producers to orchestrate. On top of this, guests are also likely experiencing some personal problem or crisis—which is why they respond to plugs in the first place and why producers find their stories compelling. As in the culture at large, *realness* or *ordinariness* on a daytime talk show more commonly signifies misfortune or disadvantage than prosperity or privilege. Paradoxically, this construction of ordinariness helps maximize the probability of emotional expressiveness but at the same time exacerbates the unpredictability associated with it because the very things that make people willing and desirable guests also make their lives difficult and their participation problematic—from a production as well as an ethical standpoint. Sandra, a *Randy* producer, made this point as we sat talking in her office while she waited for an unconfirmed guest to return her phone calls: "Basically, we're booking these ordinary people who have problems in their life. So not only are they ordinary people, but they're not the most *reliable* ordinary people."

By way of an example, Sandra described a particularly volatile show that she produced on multiple-personality disorder in which a girl with an alleged fifteen personalities was confronting her mother on the air because she believed that the mother was the source of the problem: "There was a fear that, because this girl had multiple personalities, she might become her two-year-old self and not talk at all. Instead of that, she became her angry

---

17. According to Florence, A-list celebrities are "household names," actors such as Brad Pitt or Julia Roberts, well-known by everyone. As she put it, "Unless you've been in a coma for several years, you pretty much know who these people are." In the heat of producing a topic, however, producers at *Diana* sometimes overlook the celebrity hierarchy and naively request an A-list guest. Florence then has to gently redirect their sights toward a more practical choice. Actors from daytime soap operas are a favorite since soaps draw on a melodramatic aesthetic, emphasize emotional expressiveness, are geared primarily toward a female audience, and are denigrated by critics, thus having much in common with daytime talk shows. More important, soap actors are not generally household names and may be willing to appear on a daytime talk show, either alone or alongside a few carefully chosen ordinary guests. A common scenario is for producers to arrange a "surprise" meeting on-stage between a soap star and an adoring young fan. The money shot here is a heartwarming display of unbridled joy and enthusiasm on the part of the fan, accompanied, it is hoped, by a few well-timed tears, while the celebrity appears duly flattered and gracious, perhaps even genuinely touched, but invariably more emotionally restrained.

adult self and just went nuts! This one scene is just like the best television moment you'll ever see. It was so powerful and real. But she could have been, like, totally silent and withdrawn. It was just a wild card because there was so much emotion there. It was a wild card, and we got lucky."

Getting lucky here of course means obtaining the money shot, and, as this comment from Sandra suggests, the inability of producers to control guests completely or predict their behavior with 100 percent accuracy is a function not just of the fact that ordinary equals nonprofessional equals emotion but of the difficult life circumstances that many guests endure. While I was with *Diana*, a similar type of show aired on Munchausen syndrome, a condition in which people deliberately harm themselves or a loved one in a desperate plea for sympathy and attention. The producer for the show described it as "touch and go from the beginning . . . it was just the most exhausting ordeal—because these people are mentally ill. They're paranoid. And they're pathological. And yet you still have to try to understand them, relate to them, in order to get them to come on and say whatever it is you want them to say."

Setting aside for now the ethical implications of putting someone with a genuine psychiatric disorder on television (something producers could not do easily without the cooperation of mental-health professionals), such guests are only the extreme end of a range of nonexpert, noncelebrity guests who are simultaneously attractive to producers because of their potential and willingness to execute the "right" kind of performance and difficult to incorporate into the production process for precisely the same reason. Guests may be battling cancer or AIDS; they may be homeless or the victims of crime; they may be feuding with their in-laws, cheating on their spouses, or going through an acrimonious divorce. Given that television is strongly elite centered, guests who are simply poor or lower class—who belong to a category of people with no regular access to the national media unless they become a serial killer or sprout two heads—are also difficult from the perspective of producers. One *Randy* producer estimated that 80 percent of her guests have never before been on an airplane, let alone on television. Some are living in poverty, some are addicted to drugs, some are in trouble with the law. Twice at *Randy*, and once at *Diana*, I saw shows canceled at the last minute because a key guest was arrested and jailed and thus unable to make the taping, and the same thing happened at *Maury Povich* while I was talking with a producer there. All the communication between producers and guests prior to taping occurs by phone, yet, if a guest is destitute or institutionalized, she may not have a home, let alone a telephone. According to Joe, a former producer at *Geraldo* and *Ricki*

Lake, "When you're dealing with the lower economic strata, you're dealing with people who—they have no sense of commitment, for one thing, you know, their lives are in disarray because they have no sense of commitment, at least some of them. They don't appreciate for a moment that a national television show with a multimillion dollar budget etc. etc. is counting on them to come forth." Other producers were more charitable in their comments but still agreed that lower-class guests often required "serious babysitting"—meaning that they were high maintenance, in need of considerable energy, time, and attention.

Complicating the picture still further is the emphasis on surprise and confrontation. At *Randy*, producers deliberately minimize their pretaping contact with unsuspecting guests in order to avoid giving away too much information and ruining the surprise, but this lack of contact then means that they often have a poor sense of the guest as a performer. Consequently, as Sandra observed, surprise shows can be the most nerve-racking because the main element—the reaction to the surprise—remains, in a sense, unproduced: "You can't prepare the person properly because they don't even know why they're here. So you can't say, 'Remember to say this,' or, 'Remember to say that' . . . all you can do is say, 'Whatever happens, you've got to be emotional.'"

The biggest challenge associated with confrontational topics is not so much getting guests to deliver dramatic performances, however. After all, if two people hate each other and you fan their mutual enmity and then put them together on the same stage in a context that actively encourages emotional expressiveness, the outcome is really not all that uncertain. Rather, the challenge is keeping guests committed to participating—an issue that I address in more detail later. With such topics, the sense of uncertainty and instability experienced by producers inheres less in the actual performances of guests onstage than in the producer-guest relations that lead up to the performance. This was especially obvious to *Randy* producers like Mark who had prior experience on other, "nicer" shows. Mark told me that, at his old job, he could count on guests showing up but that, at *Randy*, "people get suspicious, they worry we're going to bring up something negative, and, yeah, that *is* what we want to bring up! So it's not easy keeping that balance together until show time." Virtually every *Randy* staffer I spoke with confirmed this observation, noting that the trend toward confrontation (and the subsequent condemnation of the genre in the rest of the media) has made potential guests wary of participating and that this in turn has generated a certain level of instability behind the scenes. As Sandra put it, "You get a lot of people who say, 'I'm definitely coming.' So you do their hotel and limo reservations, and you spend a lot of time talking to them. And then the day the plane's leaving they say, 'I'm not coming.' That happens all the time."

Not surprisingly, the end result of this multilayered construction of ordinariness is a heightened sense of unpredictability for producers, above and beyond the degree of unpredictability that might be said to character-ize the production of documentary television more generally. Although producers and other staff members do a great deal of preparatory work to mitigate against unforeseen developments, they still feel at the mercy of what they see as the genre's inherent tension between scriptedness and spontaneity and thus often experience the work as volatile and unstable de-spite the fact that, as we shall see, it is also highly routinized. According to Doug, an associate producer at *Diana*, "The bottom line is that, no matter what you do, even if you're doing everything right, things can still totally backfire. Because the blessing and curse of talk shows is that they're spon-taneous. They involve real people, and you never know what's going to happen. They're real people, and ultimately you can't control them."

To summarize, working with ordinary people on daytime talk shows poses unique challenges for producers because of the unpredictability as-sumed to stem from ordinary people's lack of professional media training, from the association of ordinariness with emotional expressiveness, and from the things that producers do to ensure its display onstage, such as tar-get guests experiencing a problem or crisis and emphasize conflict and confrontation between guests. Like other forms of media, talk shows are interested in ordinary people only insofar as, paradoxically, they do or say extraordinary things, and, while nothing guarantees the money shot, the choice of topics and careful orchestration of people and events behind the scenes increases the probability that guests will perform (and emote) in the appropriate way. As Tamara put it, "You love those moments when the audience is genuinely shocked for a second or the guest gets really emo-tional. But, you know, people don't cry on cue. They cry because they get to that place, emotionally. They come here ready to get to that emotional level. And that's not just a total accident, that's part of producing."

How, exactly, do producers help ordinary people get to that emo-tional level? Where do guests come from, and how are they prepared for their roles? In the world of daytime talk, "good television" requires that the money shot be genuine and spontaneous and at the same time consistently produced. How is this delicate balancing act accomplished?

Producing in a sense is like putting a wedding together. In order for it to be a successful wedding, everything has to be right, everything from the bride and the groom have to show up, to how the place settings look on the table, to the music, and to the organization, and to the flow of things. Did you remember about parking? Did you remember that the groom's mother-in-law-to-be needs a wheelchair? And who's going to rent the wheelchair? What about MSG in the Chinese food? You have to plan out everything. And then you have to execute it, you have to make sure that people know what to say and how to say it, and that the energy's right. Any little thing can throw it off and screw it up. . . . So you have to be very detail oriented, and yet you also have to remember, "Oh my God, in doing all the logistics, I'm trying to put together an entertaining show."

—Doug, associate producer at *Diana*

CHAPTER THREE

Talk as Work: Routinizing the Production Process

The Beat Territory

Anyone who has planned a wedding—or organized a conference, staged a play, or thrown a large dinner party—can probably relate at some level to the complex orchestration of events required to produce a daytime talk show. Just as the wedding ceremony or conference or dinner party itself often belies all the preparatory work behind the scenes, talk shows look deceptively simple: decide on a topic, find some guests, put them on a stage, ask them some questions, and let the cameras roll. But there is more to producing the money shot than that, just as there is more to a wedding than saying "I do." Producers strive to elicit the money shot because they require visible evidence of a guest's emotional state. At the same time, because any one producer has only five or six days to prepare for a show, producers must make these seemingly spontaneous and unpredictable moments predictable and routine. As Tuchman (1973) notes, organizations routinize tasks whenever possible in order to facilitate the control of work. Routinization would seem especially important—albeit especially challenging—when the work involves the intentional orchestration of emotional or volatile situations. Thus, producers employ a variety of strategies and practices to streamline the difficult process of putting ordinary people on television. In doing so, they draw largely on the codes and conventions of journalism as well as the production of late-night talk shows.

While the parallels to late-night talk are, perhaps, more obvious (daytime talk merely replacing celebrity guests with ordinary people), the production of daytime talk is also systematically organized behind the scenes much like the production of news. Certainly, in a physical sense, talk-show offices resemble newsrooms, with producers sitting in cubicles behind desks piled high with papers, files, and clippings as well as an assortment of coffee cups and disposable food containers. Messages scribbled on Post-it notes sprout from every available surface: bulletin boards, filing cabinets, telephones. While producers use computers for researching stories and writing scripts, telephones are the lifeblood of the business. They ring constantly, and producers spend the better part of every day on the phone, their voices blending to form a steady drone of background noise punctuated occasionally by a loud exclamation or peal of laughter. In general, there is an air of hustle and bustle in this space that can take on a frantic, abrasive edge in the hours just prior to a scheduled taping.

There are other, more significant parallels to news gathering. Fishman (1980) has detailed the ways in which journalists must rely on routine sources and established information channels in order to produce fresh news daily under the pressure of deadlines, even when the news consists of unpredictable or unexpected events like accidents, emergencies, or natural disasters. This means accessing a few key nodal points within the vast expanse of their beat territory where information is already concentrated (files, records, meetings, press conferences, expert sources, etc.) and then repackaging that information according to the mandates of the news organization. The world of daytime talk is similarly organized, despite the often makeshift, seat-of-the-pants appearance of the programs. As one *Randy* producer put it, "People seem to think we pull guests right off the street like a dogcatcher picking up strays, but that's not the way it happens."

When producers look for topics, or when they book guests for a given show, they, like journalists, seek out strategic nodal points that serve as stable loci of information. Like reporters, talk-show producers have beat territories that they survey on a regular basis for possible story ideas—mostly magazines, newspapers, trade publications, and other television programs. Informally, these beats are classified by type of publication or program (the "tabloid beat," "hard-news beat," "woman's-magazine beat," "soap-opera beat," etc.), and, from these preconstituted sites, producers come up with ideas that they pitch to the executive producer in production meetings. Just as with news gathering, there exist a potentially infinite number of available stories. In actual practice, however, talk-show topics do not come from just anywhere but are reflexively constituted with reference to other mass-media texts, including other daytime talk shows. Indeed, producers rely "internally" on other media for their material even more than most journalists do, and in this they have something in common with the tabloid writers studied by Bird (1992). Producers will unabashedly take a news item or an idea from elsewhere and personalize it, making it "friendly" to a talk-show audience, or they will take a topic from another talk show and put a different twist or spin on it. "There are no original topics left in this business," one *Diana* staffer confided. "It's all just variations on a theme. I've done a dozen shows on mother-daughter conflicts alone."

The heavy reliance on other media as well as on certain core scripts within the genre illustrates another observation made by Tuchman in her studies of both news gathering and late-night TV talk: variability in raw data impedes routinization. Thus, the recycling of topics (and, to some degree, guests) on daytime talk shows is not just about—or even primarily about—laziness or producers' lack of imagination but rather about generic expectations and the structural demands of the workplace, which together encourage a relatively narrow range of material. As Bird (1992) also found with the journalists who write for supermarket tabloids, "creativity" or "originality" in such a context is less about unearthing new material and more about combining and recombining information into familiar patterns, adhering to the conventions of the medium. The same holds true for the production of late-night talk, which, like its daytime variant, aims for "spontaneous" performances within an overall scripted context. Looking at the careful planning and choreographing of host-guest and guest-guest interactions as well as the topics of conversation, Tuchman (1974) argues that, while industry professionals cannot predict with accuracy what topics or guests will be popular (and therefore successful), such shows strive for predictability under conditions of uncertainty by employing formulas and "typifications" that have generated high ratings in the past.

Producers and executives of daytime talk do likewise. At *Diana*, the topics that consistently rated well were dubbed *evergreens* by Jackie, the executive producer, and it was a term well-known by the rest of the staff. On the particular day that I interviewed her, there were two such topics listed in blue marker on the big board above the conference table: "Sexy Twins" and "Captured on Video."

"People are fascinated with certain things," she told me. "We have done more triplet, quintuplet, twins, sibling shows—they tend to rate extremely well. Makeover shows, if they're done the right way. Reunion shows. Weight-loss shows. Stuff caught on videotape. I mean, there's a reason why all these talk shows do the same topics—they do 'em because they work. They're the bread-and-butter topics that producers do again and again. I call them *evergreens*. I'll say, 'It's an evergreen, it will work, we just have to figure out a different way to do it.'"

Not surprisingly, producers were often unable explicitly to articulate the criteria that guided their choice of topics. As Becker (1982) observes, people find it difficult to verbalize the general principles according to which they make decisions or even to give any reasons for their decisions at all. Instead, they resort to such noncommunicative statements as, "It looked good to me," "It worked," or "I just know." Indeed, the first thing that many producers said when I asked how they knew a good topic from a bad one or a topic that would work from one that would not was, "Instinct," or, "It's an innate feeling." According to Jackie, "When I say, 'It's an evergreen, it will work,' it's a gut feeling that tells me that. It comes from years of doing it and seeing how it rates, and then you just know."

Instinct, then, is often a code word for experience or a kind of knowledge so taken for granted that it appears natural and inevitable. But producers are in fact guided by some specific considerations, each of which presumes its own taken-for-granted stock of knowledge. In choosing topics, they ask themselves, Will it appeal to the target demographic? If it has been done before, does it have a fresh angle? [1] Can real people be found to talk about it? Most important, is it visual? This last question is really about the money shot because, by *visual*, producers mean "emotional" or "volatile." Does the topic involve controversy, conflict, or confrontation? If not, where will the drama come from? Getting the guest to emote is the

---

1. Finding a fresh angle or novel twist is key, given the repetition of topics. Consider Rachel's description of a novel twist on a tried-and-true topic, "Dating Disasters": "There has to be something unique to a topic; there has to be a twist to it. Like, this show I'm doing right now called 'Dating Disasters.' This woman married a guy who got a sex-change operation to become a woman, and they're still in love and still married—only as lesbians! I mean, good grief! If you have that story and the people want to come on, what's to figure out?"

bottom line, and it cannot be left to chance. In this sense, talk shows face a dilemma diametrically opposite to that of organizations like funeral homes and hospital emergency rooms, potentially volatile settings where the goal of routinization is to minimize rather than maximize emotional displays.

Another consideration is whether the topic and intensity of emotional expression are consistent with the image of the host and the talk show itself, for, despite their seeming homogeneity, there are significant differences between shows. As we have seen, each has a unique identity, and it is the job of the executive producer to ensure that the topics, the guests, and the way both are scripted and produced support and reaffirm this identity. At *Randy*, for example, because the specific subject matter of any given show is relatively unimportant, serving primarily as a vehicle for provoking an emotional response from guests, topics are less varied than they are at *Diana*, limited primarily to conflict situations. As one *Randy* producer put it, "It's really simple: we book conflict. Conflict is the main ingredient, and topics without it just don't have any bearing for the show." During my first week interning at *Randy*, the topics listed on the board in the executive producer's office included "I Hate My Mother," "Stop Selling Sex," "Back Off My Lover," "I Want to Confront That Guest," "My Man Wears a Dress," and "It's Her . . . or Me!" The topics for the following week reprised the same themes: "Wives Confront Cheating Husbands," "Real-Life Soap Operas," "Dump Your Mate," "Transvestite Makeovers," and "Sexual Conflicts." *Randy* thus has a stock repertoire of stories that get recycled over and over, and producers there spend relatively little time and energy trying to come up with original ideas.

At both *Randy* and *Diana*, staffers attend daily production meetings to go over the details of shows currently under development. *Diana* producers attend additional meetings every week where they pitch new show ideas to the executive and supervising producers. These meetings are held in the executive producer's office around a large oval conference table. On the wall behind the table is an enormous white message board, with the titles of upcoming shows written across the top in blue and the names of guests listed in the vertical spaces underneath (red marker for confirmed or booked, green marker for potential or unconfirmed). The meetings usually last about an hour and often have a festive air about them, with people joking and laughing or sometimes getting into debates about the issues that a topic raises. In the pitch meetings that I attended while assisting with the production of a show titled "Teens with HIV," I noticed that much of the humor is self-reflexive: producers make fun of the genre, the guests, and their own pursuit of the money shot. For example, Michelle was dubbed producer of the week for using *horrifying, heart wrenching,* and *humiliating* in the same sentence when pitching a show idea, while Doug got a round of applause for imitating his office mate reaching orgasm while on the phone with a guest because the story was so juicy. Judging from its specific content, the joking was primarily a commentary on the sleazy, tabloid topics associated with trashy shows like *Randy* rather than those typically produced at *Diana*.

"Eat your hearts out," Brian announced breezily to his coworkers on one occasion when it was his turn to give a progress report. "I found a drug-addicted, overeating, bisexual Satanist."

"That's nothing," Susan replied, dismissing him with a wave of her hand. "I just booked a transvestite stripper with multiple personalities and panic disorder who's being stalked by three of her other personalities! They're articulate, energetic, emotional, and—get this—a total bargain: all four agreed to share the same limo!"

While I laughed with the others, I also noticed that at least some of the topics listed on the board that day were not so very unlike those airing on the shows being mocked: "Pet-Custody Battles," "Addicted to Soaps," "Wedding Scams," "Agoraphobia," "Teens with HIV," "Sexual Anorexia," "Fling Reunions," "Dates from Hell," "Forbidden Relationships," and "Miracle Plastic Surgery." And, while *Diana* producers might avoid orchestrating fights and confrontations, they are no less interested in the money shot. Part of selling a story during a pitch meeting is convincing one's boss that good guests are available to tell it, and, all joking aside, invariably when describing a guest producers will emphasize his or her potential for emotional display. "This guest is going to be great," said Jocelyn, who was producing a show about battered women. "She's not afraid to talk, and she's really emotional—she broke down three times on the phone."

At most talk shows, if producers consistently handle the same type of topic, they will find themselves occupying niches much like journalists who cover beats. At *Diana*, the main distinction is between *light* and *heavy*, similar to Tuchman's (1978) distinction between *soft* and *hard* news. Tamara was someone who typically produced light fare like "Babe Brothers" or "Miracle Makeovers," while Donna was known as a producer of heavy subjects such as sexual assault, incest, drunk driving, domestic abuse, homelessness, or anorexia. At *Randy*, the most general distinction was between topics that revealed secrets (known as ambush shows) and those that did not; finer distinctions were then made according to the nature of the conflict involved. Some producers did almost nothing else but marital

disputes, while others consistently did family feuds, mother-daughter conflicts, or sexual rivalries. Producers recognize that, on the one hand, it requires less work to produce the same type of show because it reduces variability in the production process. This is also why journalists cover the
same beat territory and why university professors publish multiple articles
based on the same set of data or develop and teach the same classes year
after year with only minor alterations. On the other hand, producers sometimes dislike being slotted into niches, partly because they find it limiting, and partly because it intensifies the burnout factor. As Donna put it,
"I know that I get a lot of the heavy topics, the gut-wrenching emotional
stuff, and most of the time I don't mind that, but I definitely want to mix
it up a little bit. You can't keep doing this for seventeen years without mixing it up."

Going Hunting

Once producers have been assigned a show topic, the next step is to find
ordinary people to represent it. Saul Feldman compares the process of
finding guests to tracking down game: "You are going out there tracking
guests, bringing guests back, recalcitrant guests especially. You're going
hunting." This process, too, must be highly routinized, given the sheer
numbers of guests involved. On some shows, and with some topics, the
challenge is simply to find someone—anyone—willing to come on the
show. On other occasions, the issue is slightly different: of all these willing
people, who will make the best guest?

   Like the search for topics, producers rely on a number of routine
channels for finding guests to be on a panel, the specific channel being determined largely by the topic. For serious, current-affairs, or social-issue-
oriented subjects, producers can search on-line databases like Lexis-Nexus
that cross-reference stories and sources from a vast network of local and
national media, or they can target existing groups and organizations—
channels routinely used by journalists as well. As Fishman (1980) notes, not
only are media organizations themselves bureaucratically structured, but so
is the rest of society, and it is precisely this knowledge that allows journalists to detect and report events in routine ways. The institutional character
of society provides media professionals with a preexisting map of relevant
knowledge holders for any given topic. Thus, producers go to the Screen
Actors Guild or various publicity agencies when seeking celebrity guests
and organizations such as Alcoholics Anonymous, Stop AIDS Now, or the

local rape crisis center when seeking the participation of experts, typically counselors and therapists. These experts then put producers in contact with selected ordinary people, often their own clients.

For example, when I helped produce "Teens with HIV" at *Diana*, my first assignment was to compile a list of all the HIV/AIDS organizations in the area and then use their experts as conduits to locate potential ordinary guests, in this case, HIV-positive teenagers. Once I finally had someone in a supervisory position on the telephone, I then had to convince her to help me, and I did this by emphasizing the positive reputation of the show, the social significance or educational value of the topic, and the fact that guests and audience members alike would benefit from the guest's participation— the same things that producers emphasize when dealing directly with guests themselves. If people hesitate, you find out what their concerns are and try to dispel them. If they impose conditions, attempt to meet them. Perhaps they want to have their organization listed in the credits, to accompany the guest to the taping, or to be the expert voice on the panel. As with ordinary guests, some experts do not need much persuading: they know and like the show, they think that the topic is important, or cooperating fulfills an agenda of their own.

Even for topics less clearly oriented toward social issues—agoraphobia, multiple-personality disorder, or alopecia areata (female baldness)— experts will put producers in touch with their clients, although in a more roundabout manner. Justin described the process of finding guests suffering from Munchausen syndrome, whose victims do strange and even pathological things in a desperate bid for attention.

"You start with a clinic or a mental hospital, and, you know, the doctor or psychiatrist will say, 'Oh my God, I could never give you the name of a client, that's unethical. But why don't you call so-and-so.' And you call that person, and they're like, 'Well, I don't know, but why don't you call so-and-so.' And that's how it happens. You never get a guest right off the bat, but, if you're persistent, eventually you get something."

On rare occasions, entire panels are booked by calling a single organization or agency, as was the case for a *Diana* show on female stalkers. All the guests on that show were affiliated in one way or another with the organization Take Back Your Life—three were victims, one was a reformed ex-stalker, and one was an expert who led the organization's counseling program.

Experts are thus important to the genre as much for their connections to ordinary people as for their expertise, and the fact that doctors and therapists have a client base is one reason that talk shows draw more heavily from psychology and psychiatry than from sociology. Even when experts are brought into the process as panelists, they are typically onstage only during the last segment of a show to mediate between hostile parties or lend an air of professional legitimacy. Sometimes, they are seated in the audience and not onstage at all. Former host Bertice Berry put her experts in the audience as a matter of course, explaining, "It was a visual thing we did to suggest that everybody is on the same level, experts aren't the only ones with answers." Daytime talk is rarely a satisfactory forum for experts, as many of the expert guests I interviewed will attest. In part, this reflects the deep-seated belief among media professionals in the superior efficacy of individual, personal narrative over distanced intellectual analysis for both educating and entertaining mass audiences. Producers firmly believe that, if a show is to play an educational role, it will be the result of real people talking about their personal experience, not experts talking about their research. "Experts are beside the point," Rachel informed me bluntly. "Although we might get the show idea from their book or whatever and they lend an umbrella of credence to what our guests are saying, they're beside the point."

Actually, in addition to putting producers in contact with ordinary people and "lending an umbrella of credence" to their testimony, experts contribute to shows in invisible ways they rarely get credit for, the most common being the information that they provide over the phone in an initial preinterview, which can help producers structure their shows or formulate the right questions to ask of the guests on the air. This was clearly the case for the expert who appeared on a *Diana* show about date rape. Although she sat in the audience and spoke for only a moment, she noticed that much of what she might have said had she been allowed more time was addressed by the ordinary guests on the panel, all young rape survivors. "The girls did a marvelous job," she said. "Most of what I thought was important to talk about they covered, so I didn't have to do it. You know, I don't care *who* says it; let's just get it said." After a brief pause, she suggested that perhaps producers were right, perhaps it was more effective for audiences to get information this way. "If it's an ordinary person onstage, Middle America kind of turns in their chair and goes, 'Oh my God! Come here, Angel, sit down, and look at this!' And then they're going to get education, whereas maybe someone like me comes along and they're like, 'Oh, boring, time to go get a glass of water.'"

At *Diana*, close to half of all ordinary guests (and certainly the vast majority of expert guests) are found by either phoning groups and organizations or perusing already-existing media, both bureaucratic channels and

nodal points that limit the parameters of daytime talk, like the news, in systematic ways. The largest proportion of ordinary guests, however, especially on shows like *Randy*, come from plugs, brief advertisements for upcoming topics that air at the end of every show ("Are you constantly using
food as a substitute for sex? Do you refuse to date outside your race? Does
your mom act younger than you do? Call us at. . . ."). Having emerged as a
regular feature of the genre only since the early 1990s, plugs are used for
topics that do not necessarily have an organizational base and that otherwise would not appear in the media and are thus difficult or impossible to
book through conventional news-gathering mechanisms. For example,
makeover shows are standard fare on *Diana*, yet, as one producer there explained, "There is no center for makeover candidates, no group or club or
whatever to call. So, instead of going to the guest, the guest comes to us."

Plugs thus create a bureaucratically organized site for locating ordinary people where none existed before. As an intern, I logged thousands of
phone calls from viewers responding to on-air plugs about forbidden relationships, compulsive lying, medical mishaps, roommate problems, interracial romance, cross-dressing, sibling rivalry, infidelity, promiscuity, dating disasters, love triangles, family feuds, and reunions of various sorts,
among other topics. Transcribing these calls was undoubtedly one of the
most tedious and yet crucial of duties because the 800 line was the initial
point of entry for many potential guests: if they did not pass through this
screening process, they had little chance of appearing on the show. Invariably, the plugs on *Diana* that drew the largest responses were those in
which the gains to participants were clear and immediate—makeovers, for
instance, or reunions with long-lost loved ones. On *Randy*, there was less
variation: most plugs were asking people to confront a friend or family
member about a past wrong or injustice, and there was never a shortage of
callers willing to do so.

Not surprisingly, perhaps, plug topics have the reputation among
industry insiders as being the most trashy, not only because they target
people outside official organizations and media circles, but also because
these people are embroiled in personal conflicts that do not carry the same
weight or legitimacy as "serious" social issues. Not coincidentally, such
guests tend to be younger, poorer, less well educated, and, although still
predominantly white, more often black or Latino than the ordinary people
recruited for more serious topics. This is certainly consistent with Gamson's (1998) observation that, as the vulgar head of the genre gained visibility, it did so by both representing and exploiting previously marginal or
invisible class cultures. In his words, "The new recruiting practice meant a

very non-*Donahue*, even non-*Oprah*, pool of guests, drawn not so much from predominantly white, middle-class organizational and personal networks as from the population of viewers" (60). Indeed, the emergence of plugs is perceived by industry insiders to be both a cause and a consequence of the genre's "downward" slide, and plug topics are typically behind comments about the inappropriateness of *certain kinds of people* airing their dirty laundry in public.

One producer at *Maury Povich* made no attempt to hide his disdain for the type of guest that plug topics attract: "When it comes to doing conflict shows, shows that require plugs, those are definitely all people who are low income, don't have a job, you know, they're, uh—white trash, I really can't put it any other way. They're very uneducated people who just want their fifteen minutes of fame." They must also be at least occasional viewers of daytime talk because one must be watching a show in order to respond to a plug. Plugs thus reward fans or insiders for their loyalty while at the same time compromising their integrity in the eyes of producers and critics. Plugs are also considered cop-outs by some industry professionals because, in giving ordinary people direct access and thereby bypassing official organizations and expert contacts, they require little investigative work on the part of producers. In fact, advertising for one's sources is about as far from the respected tradition of investigative journalism as one can get. It is partly for this reason, and because *Diana* defines itself in opposition to the sleazy, tabloid brand of talk show, that the supervising producer there actively discouraged producers from relying too heavily on plugs to book their shows, stressing instead the importance of maintaining connections with expert sources as well as more informal networks of contacts. In his view, the thicker the Rolodex, the better the producer. Conversely, at *Randy*, which *is* one of those sleazy tabloid talk shows and does not pretend otherwise, producers rely almost exclusively on plugs, bypassing expert sources altogether—even when booking topics that might very well have an organizational base.

While plugs and official organizations (including the experts associated with them) are the two major channels for locating potential guests, they are by no means the only ones. Producers will occasionally find guests by sifting through letters and fan mail, which interns or production assistants organize according to topic, or by canvassing the studio audience during tapings—methods that, like plugs, reward insiders for their participation. More commonly, producers at both shows rely on their own informal networks and contacts, much as journalists and other media professionals do. Sometimes, these are family and friends, sometimes former guests with whom producers have maintained a friendly relationship, sometimes staffers at other talk shows. Often, once producers find one suitable guest, that person serves as the stepping-stone or conduit to others connected to the story—typically close friends or family members. In this way, certain ordinary guests perform much the same function as experts who refer producers to their clients or colleagues. Colleen, one of the young women described in the opening pages of this book, played this role on the *Randy* show about homeless couples, serving as the liaison between producers and the other participants involved. April was another such guest; she persuaded her daughter and the girl's legal guardian to appear on a *Sally Jessy* show about mother-daughter conflicts. Producers even flew her to New York a day ahead of the other guests in order to work more closely with her. An associate producer at *Randy* aptly call guests like Colleen and April *ringleaders*.

Ringleaders typically call the show responding to a plug. At *Randy*, owing to the nature of the topics, if they prove unwilling to help recruit others involved in the conflict, producers will drop the story entirely. "The most important thing when you are first pursuing a story is the willingness of the person who called in to the show to get those other guests to come on," a producer there told me. If they are willing and the story goes forward, key guests have more power than other guests in their negotiations with producers because, if they change their minds and back out, the others may withdraw their support too. This was true at *Diana* as at *Randy*, as Rachel discovered when producing a show about a summer boot camp for juvenile offenders. I was interviewing Heidi, the talent coordinator, in her office when Rachel appeared at the door flustered and out of breath.

"Excuse me for interrupting," she apologized, "but I have a quick question. I have this guest from hell—she is trying to drag, like, eleven people along with her to the show, and most of them have nothing whatsoever to do with the topic. It's just—I don't even want to go into all the details, but the bottom line—"

Heidi interrupted. "Which show is this?"

"'Death in the Desert,'" Rachel replied, "but it's going to be 'Death Backstage' because I'm going to kill this woman."

We all laughed. Rachel and Heidi then discussed the logistics of arranging VIP seating in the audience for all the extra people as well as babysitting for their children. Rachel lamented that all this would inflate the show's budget considerably.

"If this woman wasn't so critical to getting other guests on the show, I would—"

Again Heidi interrupted. "Which one is she?"

"The one who helped us get two exclusive interviews that are a really big deal. We can't lose her because—" Rachel glanced over at me, and I could tell that she was talking now as much for my benefit as Heidi's. "It's like a domino effect. If one person pulls out, the others will panic and wonder why she is withdrawing, and they may pull out, too."

There is yet a final way that producers secure guests, one considered less legitimate than the rest and, therefore, less frequently acknowledged and discussed. When in a bind, producers have been known to rely on "stringers," freelance bookers who provide them with made-to-order guests in exchange for money. Berkman (1995) reports that many guests procured by stringers are actually aspiring actors willing to assume fake identities and that stringers essentially act as informal talent agents,[2] but one of my interviewees, Joe, a retired producer formerly with *Geraldo* and *Ricki Lake*, contested this framing. He told me that a stringer is simply any person who is paid to find guests and that the guests aren't necessarily actors lying or assuming false identities—some are real enough. But certain guests exist outside a producer's normal network of contacts and thus are not easily accessed by producers without outside help, usually because of class and race differences.

"Stringers are used for certain kinds of shows," Joe said. "You know, if producers are doing 'Girls Who Dress Like Sluts,' and the phone logs come up empty, they'll pay a stringer $500 and say, 'Find me five girls.' That happens all the time. 'Cause, to be perfectly blunt, these lily-white producers out of these preppy little schools, they wouldn't know the first thing about going to the inner city and finding guests. Do you think some twenty-three-year-old Polly Purebred is riding around Watts or, like, you know, the South Bronx looking for heroin addicts and prostitutes? Forget it!"

As far as I know, producers at *Diana* did not use stringers, although several producers at *Randy* and others I spoke to from *Geraldo*, *Ricki Lake*, *Sally Jessy*, and *Jerry Springer* admitted to using them on occasion. This is certainly consistent with the image of *Diana* as classy and of *Randy* as trashy and the consequent necessity of *Randy* producers to seek out nonexpert sources and contacts. But the distinction between stringers and other, more legitimate sources is a fine one. Whereas stringers are paid outright for their services, experts, key guests, and a producer's own circle of acquaintances are not; whereas stringers track down drug addicts, prosti-

2. I take up the issue of fake guests and professional ordinary guests again in chapter 5.

tutes, and "girls who dress like sluts," experts call on their clients, and key guests call on their friends and family. In all cases, however, because of structural constraints and the pressure of deadlines, producers seek the help of others to book their shows, and sometimes the distinction between a stringer and a friend or acquaintance is blurry indeed. For example, Carmen (from *Randy*) told me that she knew a group of women who lived near the television studio, some of them former guests, on whom she could always count for leads. She described them as "very gregarious," "very friendly," and as having "hoards of acquaintances and friends." "So, if we run into trouble, I call them up and say, 'Listen, I'm looking for a cheater. Do you know somebody who's cheating on their mate that would want to reveal it on TV?' And they're like, 'Oh yeah, give me half an hour, and I'll call you back!'"

Thus, *Randy* producers have thick Rolodexes too. It's just that the names that they contain are not necessarily those of professional experts.

The Blind Date

Various formal and informal mechanisms exist in order to streamline the difficult process of locating the kind of ordinary people that producers need—those willing to talk about their personal problems, hardships, or transgressions on national television. What is more challenging to routinize, of course, is the actual performances of guests once they have been found. Producers of late-night talk have long recognized that casual conversation is as performative as an entirely scripted affair and that "being oneself is itself a constructed activity" (Tuchman 1974, 126), especially when one does it on national television. Celebrities rely on their acting skills to "play" themselves, and ordinary guests on daytime talk shows do exactly the same thing. Since the latter are not professionals, however, producers spend a great deal of time and energy preparing them for their roles. Producers seek to ensure that guests will not be boring, freeze in front of the camera, or fail to show up altogether, and the first step toward this end is an extensive preinterview over the phone, sometimes referred to by producers as *the blind date* because they claim to know immediately whether the guest is good and the relationship worth pursuing.

As Rachel put it, "I usually know within two or three minutes. I know that fast. Because they immediately go into a story, and they start using all these really vivid examples, and they have a lot of energy. You know, you have to keep interrupting them because you can't get a word in edgewise." Tamara agreed. "You can tell immediately if someone is a good guest. A good guest is someone with energy who can articulate their story well."

The criteria that producers employ in determining the potential of a guest are actually little different than those used by interns and production assistants when making decisions about which phone messages to flag as promising and which to ignore. Does the person have an interesting or unusual story? Can he or she tell it in a compelling manner? Is the person expressive or emotional? Other indices are physical appearance (as Rachel put it, "Do they not, like, weigh five hundred pounds and have acne?") and a person's willingness to reveal specifically personal information. According to Jocelyn, a good guest is not only energetic and articulate but also honest and forthcoming. "They divulge to me things I never even would ask them to divulge, but they do; they're like really honest to the point of no discretion, sometimes. That makes a great guest." Virtually every producer at *Diana* said something similar, although a few also admitted that, on occasion, they initially misjudged a guest. Susan described a woman whose daughter ran away from home and remained missing for seventeen months. Despite the fact that she had a promising story, Susan almost passed her over because she was too reserved on the phone. "Then she started to talk to me a little bit more, and eventually she broke down, and I was like, 'Well, maybe she will work out after all.'"

On *Randy*, because a good performance is defined more narrowly in terms of conflict, a person's ability to talk is judged in combination with the potential for creating an argument or confrontation onstage. As Carmen explained, "When we're looking for good stories, we look for people who are going to be pissed off. You know, this is their last hope to confront someone. Or this is their only chance to come clean on something. It's not like we're dealing with, 'Oh dear, my neighbor rolled over my lawn with a tire.' This is bigger stuff." But, while there is never a shortage of calls from people embroiled in conflict situations, not all are equally promising. "I don't know the number of people I talk to in a day when I'm booking a show," Carmen continued, "but you feel like you make two hundred calls trying to find a handful of guests who will be good, and you can still come up empty-handed." One dilemma is that the majority of *Randy* callers are young adults (people between eighteen and twenty-five), yet producers prefer somewhat older guests (people in their thirties) because they have more life experience and are more likely to be emotionally invested in their relationships. From a production standpoint, all else being equal, it is better to expose a cheater who has been married for ten years than one who's been dating for six months. All else is rarely equal, however, because older guests are generally more reserved than younger ones, and emotional expressiveness trumps all other criteria. "The bottom line is, the person has to show emotion. If a girl is cheating on her boyfriend and he says to me, 'Oh, OK, thanks for letting me know,' then we can't use him. We want people to care about what they're going to hear. We want people who will bust out, go crazy, you know, be verbal *and* physical."

On both *Randy* and *Diana*, an additional challenge in the search for guests given the growth of the genre (and the accompanying pressure to deliver the money shot) is to find ordinary people who are "real," that is, people without prior media experience whose stories are authentic and whose emotions are genuinely expressed. While some so-called ordinary guests are actually actors playing roles and are thus similar to the gaffed freaks mentioned earlier who faked their physical anomalies, more commonly the challenge facing producers is not to distinguish fake from real guests but to find people who are "fresh" or "raw" to the process and, consequently, less guarded with their emotions. "Because there are so many talk shows," Donna said, "you have to be careful that you're not all going after the same people, or that they have not done other shows, because I think that actually comes across on television."

Likewise, Tamara distinguished between real guests and those who are media savvy, having been on other talk shows before: "The real people—the truly real people—probably never called into a talk show before, but they see a plug on the air that touches them, and they respond. Or you find them through someone you know, or whatever. . . . Then there's the kind of guest who's very savvy, they have a story everybody wants, and they—they treat you like a talent agency. That kind of guest I dislike, and it's not just personal: they don't make for good television. Their experience shows through. You know, they might as well be celebrities."

Not surprisingly, producers' need for people who are simultaneously inexperienced yet capable of emoting on cue is shared by other industry professionals whose work also involves putting "real life" on television. In Marsh's (2000) behind-the-scenes account of MTV's *The Real World*, for example, the criteria for choosing participants described by the casting director mirrors the criteria employed by talk-show producers. According to Marsh, the director looks for young people who "pop out at her," by which she means kids who have strong opinions and a good sense of humor and who are "communicative" yet "spontaneous" on camera. Participants also have to be willing to "give a full story" and "not be afraid to tell the embarrassing parts." Actors are the number one red flag in the screening process since the point is to find young people who will open up and "be themselves" rather than "hide behind a role." The dilemma here, according to Marsh, is that, while the applicant pool has grown larger over the years—the 1999 casting call alone occasioned thirty-five thousand audition tapes—finding the "right" teenagers has grown harder because applicants are increasingly savvy about the qualities staffers are looking for. *Real World* staffers face a paradox: given the mandate for authenticity, the ideal kids for the show are those unfamiliar with it, but the vast majority of applicants have not only grown up watching the show on television but applied to be on it in the first place because achieving celebrity status is their ultimate goal.

Talk-show producers face a similar challenge in that they desire "truly real people," but this realness is gradually being compromised by the number of shows on the air and by the increasing likelihood that some proportion of guests are responding to plugs simply to get on television. The naïveté that drives producers crazy and makes their job more difficult is also considered a key ingredient for a successful, compelling show. At the same time, the proliferation of talk shows over the last several years—in combination with structural pressures to recycle topics and guests—increases a producer's chances of getting people who are, in fact, savvy to the process.

Aside from the kind of savvy guest mentioned by Donna and Tamara—people like John Wayne Bobbitt or Monica Lewinsky who used to be "just folks" until something extraordinary happened to thrust them into the media spotlight—there are also ordinary people who deliberately use talk shows to gain television exposure by responding to plugs that do not necessarily fit their situation. Sometimes called *professional ordinary guests*, they do not necessarily lie about their stories, but they may exaggerate or twist the details to better suit the topic, and they may lie to producers about having been on other shows. A producer I interviewed at *Maury Povich* called such guests *talk-show sluts* because they're "easy": they'll do or say anything to be on a talk show. I met two professional guests my very first day at *Diana*, a couple named Don and Janet who had been on so many other talk shows that they were recognized instantly by members of the studio audience. In general, however, guests of this type are more common on shows like *Randy* since they enter the process primarily through plugs and tend to be from the younger end of the spectrum.

The most extreme version of the professional ordinary guest is the aspiring actor whose story is an outright fabrication. Virtually every producer I spoke to had been duped by a guest at one time or another, and incidents of talk-show fraud occasionally appear in the news. The most infamous case occurred in the early spring of 1995 when three members of a Canadian comedy troupe fooled the entire staff at *Jerry Springer* by posing as guests on an episode titled "Honey, Have I Got a Secret for You." (On the show, a man revealed to his wife that he was having an affair with their teenage baby-sitter, and, when the baby-sitter appeared, the wife began sobbing so uncontrollably that she had to be led off the stage.) Several days after the taping, they revealed to the *Toronto Star* that their performance was a hoax (see Belcher 1995). More commonly, teenage guests on some of the newer shows geared toward younger audiences fake their stories just to get away with the deception. Joe estimated that, during the two years that he worked at *Ricki Lake*, upwards of 30 percent of the guests were lying. "It got so bad," he said, "they had to hire a full-time fact checker." Increasingly, then, the search for ordinary people who are real also means the search for people who are truthful.[3]

Producers at both *Diana* and *Randy* placed a high priority on authenticity, insisting that fake guests were rare on most shows, primarily the result of laziness or bad instincts (as a *Randy* producer put it, "This is where the killer instinct comes in. Guests who are lying just give you that feeling that something is wrong"). On the other hand, the lines between truth, exaggeration, and lying—like that separating legitimate from illegitimate sources—are rarely neat and distinct, and producers expect—indeed, actively encourage—a certain "heightening" of reality. Consequently, when Rachel was producing a show on bisexuality and a coworker voiced suspicions that the lead guest was really gay, not bisexual, Rachel responded, "Well, sexuality can be a fluid thing, people go through different phases, maybe that person—I mean, I have no way to crawl inside that person's head. If he or she is claiming to be bisexual, I'm going to have to trust that; I can't follow them around with a camera, you know? And I hate to admit it, but, as long as they can produce good television, I won't ask too many questions."

Maintenance Work

Once a guest has been deemed a competent performer over the phone— that is, someone with an authentic story who promises to deliver the money shot—producers have frequent follow-up conversations to iron out

---

3. For a more detailed account of fake guests, see chapter 5. For a general discussion of the issues of authenticity and realness on talk shows, see chapter 8.

the exact details of the narrative and to get a sense of how the show will unfold on the air. Typically, they talk to other people to corroborate facts or get additional information, and they gather supporting visuals such as letters, photographs, or videotape. If there are medical, legal, or criminal elements to the story, producers might also speak with the person's doctor, lawyer, or probation officer. Depending on the show's focus, producers may, like journalists, do some background research to gather facts and statistical data. Along with the interviews, this research usually informs the questions that producers prepare for the host, and a succinct summary of it may appear as a series of "bullet points" flashed on the screen during taping. Meanwhile, the travel coordinator will have been in contact with the guest about flight and limousine arrangements. This brief but intense series of communications begins the process of drawing guests into the production sphere. It is a more decisive phase than guests typically realize because the more interaction they have with producers and other staff, the greater their investment in the show and the higher the probability of their compliance onstage. The process is something like boarding a fast-moving train: you can refuse to buy a ticket and take the trip, but, once you get on board and the train picks up speed, it's hard to get off or change direction.

Because talk shows deal with sensitive or emotional topics, perhaps the most crucial task that producers face at this stage is judging how much "maintenance work" guests require, both to keep them committed to participating and to extract from them the best possible performance.

"It's always a kind of dance," Rachel mused. We were talking in her office after everyone else had gone home for the day. I had stayed late to finish writing thank-you notes to the guests from last week's shows, and Rachel was catching up on some paperwork. "You have to be really careful how fast and hard you push people because you want [the emotion] to come out on the show and not in the preinterview and you don't want them so overwrought that they back out." By way of example, she mentioned a show that she was working on about kids who inhale aerosols to get high. One of the families involved had a son who had died from doing this. Although the other producer was impatient to get the full details from family members, Rachel deliberately held back, explaining, "I didn't push real hard with them yet. Because I could feel on the phone the edge of their emotion. You know, if I'd gotten them a week or two ago to burst into tears on the phone with me, they're going to have all this wrenching, painful, stirred-up stuff to deal with, and they're going to back out. I don't want to put them through that a week before the show and then lose them on top of it."

How much attention, and what kind of attention, a guest requires in the days before taping depends on the topic and the individual guest. If a story involves revealing a secret or a surprise, the producer will try to minimize contact with the guest to avoid answering questions that might compromise the surprise. When anger is the desired emotion rather than sorrow, the producer may want to stoke the fire occasionally rather than leave guests alone—or, if the anger is already at the surface, the challenge may lie in reining them in. Regardless of the specific situation, producers recognize that there is a fine line between overpreparing guests and providing adequate guidance. As a *Diana* producer once said to a guest who was nervous and wanted to rehearse his answers, "It's not a good thing to rehearse what you're going to say word for word because, when you get out there, you will sound distant, you will sound detached, and we don't want that. That's not good for you, and it's not good for us." The mandate for spontaneity, however, exists in tension with another equally important one: getting guests to condense their stories and speak concisely, homing in on the important elements first—in other words, getting guests to tell their stories in sound bites, following the conventional pyramid structure employed by journalists. This is largely what follow-up conversations with guests are designed to do and is something that producers continue to stress backstage and in the green room right up until the moment of taping.

According to the same *Diana* producer just quoted, "People aren't naturally inclined to speak in ways that translate well on TV, so you've got to work with them. A lot of people, they'll talk forever because this is their pet issue. But you have to narrow everything down to a few basic points because otherwise people lose their focus. They have to say stuff in the right order, and in a nutshell, what's going on, so viewers will be interested."

Rachel's description of this aspect of the work was characteristically detailed and colorful. At the time of our conversation, she had just finished a show titled "Miracle Success Stories."

"You want guests to be fresh and spontaneous," she conceded, "but the other reality is, if they take ten minutes to answer something, it's not going to work. So I help them get to the point. I help them understand they have to start with the highlight of the answer and, once they hit that, they can digress all they want. You know, if the highlight of the story is that they found Jesus, I say to them, start with, 'I'm here today because I found Jesus.' And *then* you can go back and say, 'I was living on welfare in the gutter as a wino, and went through all these horrible things because I lost my job and my car and my house in a fire, and da da da da da da.' You know? Say what you found and *then* how you got there. Don't build up to a point. And, with some people, that takes a lot of work, a lot of conversations, because they want to tell you every little detail way on back to their childhood and their high school prom."

Since producers presumably choose guests in the first place largely on the basis of how talkative they are, it is not surprising that guests need help condensing their stories. Producers see this work not as altering or transforming the guest's account but rather as focusing or streamlining it, and they consistently mentioned the sense of gratification that they felt backstage when guests told their stories as coached. Helping guests "get to the point" is simultaneously one of the most important dimensions of producing and one of the most difficult things for guests to learn. At both *Randy* and *Diana*, the challenge of speaking in sound bites was often compounded for guests dealing with issues such as alcoholism or child abuse because, on the one hand, an adequate understanding of their situation may require substantial elaboration and, on the other hand, one serious problem or dysfunction in their life was often connected to others.

Maintenance work also helps producers determine the best combination of guests for the panel. *Balance*—another concept familiar to journalists and other media professionals—is key. Journalists are typically concerned with representing "both sides" of an issue; in the twin interests of fairness and drama, they choose sources or interview subjects with opposing viewpoints, the more diametrically opposed the better. Producers of late-night talk are also concerned with creating dynamic interaction, with assembling a panel of guests who complement or play off one another in predictable ways, although not necessarily through opposition or conflict. As staff members in Tuchman's (1974, 129) study observed, "A 'good program' is more than a composite of individual guests, just as a successful dinner party is more than a collection of individual diners and good food. Both involve an undefinable spirit, a process of 'hitting it off' that makes 'guesting' enjoyable." Marsh (2000) suggests that a similar ethos governs the selection of participants for *The Real World*. Although producers deny casting for specific types, the lineup for any given season typically includes one gay kid, one African American, and at least one "hyperactive, troubled extrovert" (75).[4]

4. According to Marsh (2000), the 2000 season lineup boasted the following cast of characters: the Sassy Woman of Color, the Hardworking Black Guy, the Gay Guy, the White Guy, the Southern Belle, the Alternative Christian, and the Naive Mormon.

For their part, producers of daytime talk often combine general journalistic concerns about conflict and balance with more specific considerations about interactional dynamics and "diversity" among panelists. For example, at *Diana*, when I helped put together "Teens with HIV," the producers gave me explicit instructions to aim for a panel that was varied in terms of race, gender, sexual orientation, and method of contracting the virus—even though the majority of the individuals referred to me by expert contacts were young gay men who had acquired the virus through unprotected sex. The producers said that this sort of balance—which existed on the show but not in real life—was crucial for reaching a mainstream audience. They wanted to avoid doing, as they put it, "a gay show," and they also wanted to avoid sending the message that only gay youths need worry about infection. Producers implicitly assumed that a panel that was diverse along the dimensions listed above would elicit a diverse set of narratives and make for good interaction onstage. Thus, the white, heterosexual girl from Seattle had a different story to tell than the gay, Latino teenager from East Los Angeles, whose story in turn was different from that of the white hemophiliac adopted by two gay men from the Midwest.

Along with the choice of topic and careful screening of guests, decisions about the combination of guests on the panel have consequences for the success or failure of the money shot. In one of our very first interviews, Rachel described to me the guests whom she and her partner had booked for a highly emotional (and therefore successful) show on drunk driving.

The first guest was the survivor of a drunk-driving crash and the subject of a recent made-for-TV documentary (she kicked off the show because she was, according to Rachel, "an easy cry" with "fantastic visuals"). Next were a father and son from the Midwest, chosen because the son was serving a prison sentence for a drinking-and-driving fatality (ironically, his own brother had been killed by a drunk driver just a few years earlier, devastating the entire family). Then came a representative from MADD (Mothers Against Drunk Driving), followed by a local politician who was proposing some kind of new legislation.

According to Rachel, it turned out to be "an amazing show," largely due to the father-son interview. Emotionally reserved during the preinterview, they broke down unexpectedly onstage, an event that Rachel attributed largely to timing and their placement in the lineup: "It was just unbelievable. They both started sobbing, father and son, and he put his arm around his dad—and I was like, 'Oh my God, oh my God, oh my God!'"

This is what you go for! We had no idea he would do that! You know, they were just an amazing, amazing interview. We ended up doing two segments on them. And, you know, I don't know if they would have reacted so well if we made them talk first or if we waited until the end to bring them on. I think timing had a lot to do with it." Rachel had similar success with "Teens with HIV" when it taped, also because the particular choice and combination of guests helped draw out the inherent emotionality of the topic.[5]

It is precisely to increase the likelihood of emotional display—to make the money shot more probable and predictable—that, on many shows, *balance* is consistently conceived of in oppositional terms. As Mark put it during our interview at *Randy*, "You can be guaranteed fireworks when you have two people who disagree and both feel 100 percent right about their stance." The fireworks are most spectacular, of course, when generated by anger rather than some other, softer emotion. "As long as there's anger there," Sandra told me, "as long as you have these people who are pumped up about something, then you know your show will turn out OK. Because if you can really feel the anger, then it almost doesn't matter what they say. They can say stuff in the wrong order or whatever, and it's still interesting to watch."

On *Randy*, having a diverse guest list typically means securing as many parties involved in a dispute as possible. If a woman is cheating on her husband, you bring the lover as well as the husband on the show. If the lover is female and/or related to the husband, all the better. And, if both the husband and the wife are cheating on each other with the same person, you have a guaranteed "sweeper."

Of course, sometimes producers do not achieve the kind of diversity that they desire. On a *Randy* show about racism, producers were looking for someone to confront a white supremacist from the KKK—a man who had been a guest several times before. They had originally planned a twist: to confront the racist guest with a member of his own organization. And their initial choice was the grand dragon of the KKK, who had complained in numerous letters and phone calls that the Klan members habitually

---

5. The show opened with each of the teenagers giving testimony about what contracting HIV meant to them. The first guest discussed how, at eighteen, he felt "cheated out of life," while the youngest, the fourteen-year-old hemophiliac, read out loud a poem he had written for his dad, poetry being the first way in which he had begun to communicate his anger and despair. The poem reduced the entire room to tears and set the tone for the following segments, which included testimony from the panelists' family members and friends.

appearing on the show were always too extreme and not truly representative of the organization. But the grand dragon failed to show up. So, at the
last minute, they replaced him with a black woman, an entirely predictable
move. "We didn't go after a black woman initially," said Mark, "because
that's what you'd expect." That the black woman replaced the grand
dragon did not change the underlying dynamic of conflict, but it made for
a less interesting, more predictable show.

Mechanisms of Persuasion

The primary purpose of the preinterview and the other extensive preparatory work is to solidify a structure for the show, identify the participants,
narrow their stories down to manageable bits, and determine how these
various bits will come together onstage in a visually compelling way. Again,
this is not so different from assembling a late-night talk show or producing
a serious talk show devoted to news and public affairs. But, given the different topics discussed by ordinary people and the performances expected
of them, the producers of daytime talk face certain challenges that the staff
of these other types of talk shows do not.

Given the reputation of the genre, one of the biggest challenges is
convincing people who may be reluctant to participate that it is in their best
interests to do so or that their disclosures will serve some higher purpose.
Doug, one of the associate producers at *Diana*, made this point in a roundabout way during our interview.

"Producing is sort of like making a salad," he said. "Once you have all
the lettuce in the bowl, you say, 'What else do I put in there? How do I
make it special and different from every other salad?' But the frustrating
part is getting that first head of lettuce." By this, he meant booking the
guests. "Getting that first head of lettuce is difficult because you might have
to do a show where people don't necessarily want to be a part of it, where
you need them more than they need you." This describes well the show
that Doug was currently working on, about couples who argue over
finances. One of his potential guests was poised to divorce his wife over this
issue, and he plain out said to Doug, "Why the hell would I want to come
on a show and air my dirty laundry and tell everybody that I'm cheap?"

Like making a salad, producing a show requires some basic ingredi-
ents, and, with a talk show, ordinary guests are the foundation on which
everything else is built. But many potential guests rightly perceive that the
television industry is driven by financial rather than ethical concerns, and

they question the motives of producers as well as the wisdom of their own participation. As we shall see in later chapters, people express reluctance for a variety of reasons, some related to the specific topic, and some related to the genre more generally. Booking guests was especially difficult in the immediate aftermath of the highly publicized *Jenny Jones* murder. According to a production assistant at *Maury Povich*, "For about two weeks there, all they wanted to know was, 'Am I going to get killed after the show?'"

In general, the more sensitive the issue, and the greater the potential for embarrassment or exposure, the more wary is the guest, and the more difficult is the show to book. "Picture a mother coming on national TV and saying, 'Yes, I poisoned my child because I was dying for attention,'" Justin said, referring to the show that he had produced on Munchausen syndrome. "You know? No one is going to want to come on and do that because that is just the most despicable act imaginable. And so it was just the most exhausting process, convincing these guests." *Randy* producers knew the feeling only too well since guests on confrontational shows are also generally wary and those involved in surprises are the most reluctant of all. "It's amazing we can still get people to do surprises," Sandra admitted, "because they see on TV, you know, a guy's girlfriend turns out to be a man or something, so they're scared, a lot of people. They're, like, 'No way are you surprising me! I've seen some of the surprises on your show!'"

The reluctance on the part of guests means that producers become skilled salespeople with keen perceptions and finely honed methods of persuasion.[6] They learn how to push the right buttons, and they work hard to develop a personal relationship with guests to allay their fears and misgivings. According to Justin, key to pushing the right buttons is the ability to read guests, to figure out what they are afraid of or what they really want. At the same time, "You try to personalize the situation as much as possible; you make them feel like you're their friend, that you're there to help them, and that they can trust you. Whatever the issue, you take their side."[7]

6. Producers often make comparisons to sales or telemarketing, for it was generally understood that you have to be prepared to hear a lot of noes in the course of getting a few yeses. Tyler, formerly with *Jerry Springer*, had in fact once been a telemarketer.

7. This was precisely the strategy that Justin used when booking the cousin of the Menendez brothers after the man initially refused. (Eric and Lyle Menendez were accused and ultimately convicted of murdering their wealthy parents for the inheritance money. I spoke with Justin prior to the second trial and subsequent guilty verdict and just after O. J. Simpson was accused of murdering Nicole Brown Simpson and Ronald Goldman.) As Justin described it, "I had to figure out what was going to press this guy's buttons, what would spark some passion. So I said to him, 'You know what? This whole thing with O. J. is overshadowing the Menendez brothers, and Eric and Lyle are being forgotten. I bet people

Because they work in pairs, producers may also play a version of "good cop/bad cop" with guests, where the "good" producer promises certain favors or agrees to certain conditions in order to secure their participation and then blames the other, "bad" producer when the favors fail to materialize or the conditions are not met. They think of these practices not as deceptive or manipulative necessarily but as essential—even obligatory—job skills.

Depending on the specific situation, producers may appeal to a person's self-interest ("Coming on the show may be your last chance to reconcile with your sister"), altruism ("If sharing your story can help protect even *one* child, your daughter will not have died in vain"), sense of justice ("After what your boyfriend did to you, he deserves whatever he's got coming to him"), or personal vanity ("We can make you look like a million bucks"). They may emphasize the cathartic or therapeutic aspects of disclosure or, if guests fear retaliation, point out that a public forum is safer than a private one. Producers may arrange for day care, offer money in the form of "lost wages" or per diem stipends, or stress the excitement and glamour of being on TV, in some cases playing on guests' acting or modeling aspirations or their desire to meet the celebrity host. This is a once-in-a-lifetime experience, producers tell guests; you'll be able to talk about it for the rest of your lives. Joe said that producers in New York would buy guests tickets to Broadway shows and that he even knew of a case where a producer arranged to have a guest's trailer home moved: "This one woman they wanted on the show, her husband was showing up at night with a shotgun, so, you know, the talk show paid for the trailer to be moved, to make her feel more secure and to convince her to do the show."

A former staffer at *Jerry Springer* said that producers there routinely promised makeovers, expensive haircuts, and even dental work. As she explained, "For some people, that's pretty frickin' exciting because they don't get those things done at home. You know, their neighbor cuts their hair, or their mother, or their sister." Even more exciting to guests is the lure of air travel and a paid vacation. According to Mark, "The vast majority of people who call in, I mean, we're lucky if they've ever been on a plane

---

in Ohio think Eric and Lyle are sitting pretty in Beverly Hills when in reality they're sitting in prison. You should come on our show and talk about that, remind people what they're going through and how unfair it is.' And you know what? He totally went for that. Because I was totally taking the side of Eric and Lyle—which I do anyway."

before, you know, so they're anxious to come here and stay in a hotel and all that."

Not surprisingly, in conflict situations, the easiest guest to book is the wronged party, the most difficult the person being confronted. While most talk shows now have official policies forbidding producers to lie—producers cannot tell a guest that the show is about one thing when it is really about something else, nor are they supposed to lure guests onstage under false pretenses—they are nonetheless adept at withholding the full details of a given situation, choosing their words carefully to frame an issue in a particular light, or emphasizing only the benefits of participating. Thus, producers can avoid lying and still not be completely forthright with guests. When booking confrontation shows at *Randy*, for example, producers specifically avoid using the word *confront*. "We don't say to a guest, 'Your sister wants to confront you,'" Angela told me. "We say, 'I've been speaking to your sister, and she told me, you know, that you two have had some problems in the past, and she'd like to come on our show to try to, you know, talk out the issues.'"

On rare occasions, producers find themselves persuading guests *not* to participate if making the sale conflicts strongly with their own sense of personal ethics. Several producers related incidents where they felt that, while a guest's appearance was in the best interests of the show (in terms of ratings and profitability), it was not in the best interests of the would-be guest. In these cases, the producers felt obligated to protect the individual in question from his or her own impulse to participate. A *Ricki Lake* producer, for example, told me about a woman who called in wanting to confess to her husband that she had prostituted herself because they were poor and needed the money. The producer felt badly for the woman and instructed her, "Don't ever tell him; you can just keep that to yourself. You know, you did it for the good of your family." Likewise, when staffers at *Maury Povich* were producing a "fling reunion" show (reuniting people who had had one-night stands), a woman called wanting to surprise her ex-lover on the air with the child whom he had helped conceive during the night they spent together. But, because the man had no inkling of the child's existence and now had a wife and family of his own, the producer in charge considered the story too exploitative, both for the child and for the man's current family.

These examples are the exception rather than the rule, however. Producers hardly ever suggest to guests that their personal disclosures might have negative consequences. Rather, producers emphasize the therapeutic and otherwise positive dimensions—how a guest's disclosure will benefit others, how much better it will make her feel. Whatever problem, secret, or concern the guest has, and whatever else producers say or do to secure his or her participation, they rarely miss the chance to insist that talking about it will help.

The Dropout

The more difficult people are to persuade, the greater the likelihood they will change their minds. Even people who respond to plugs—essentially volunteering to participate—may reconsider their initial impulse if the topic involves conflict or the revelation of sensitive or incriminating information. Several producers mentioned last-minute cancellations—or *dropouts*, as they are sometimes called—as absolutely the most frustrating aspect of the job. Jocelyn said that she faced this problem all the time when she was producing at *Sally Jessy Raphael:* "Not only did I work around the clock and have no social life, on top of that you had people calling your home over the weekend, 'Mah sistah doesn't think ah should do your show, so ah'm not gonna do it' [adopting an exaggerated southern accent]. And so you had people not getting on the planes right before your show. Leaving you high and dry, panicking, what the hell am I going to do?"

"It was just the most vexing, frustrating, annoying part of it," Joe agreed. "I'd book my show Friday, and check my voice mail Saturday night, and half the guests had canceled. So I'd stop whatever I was doing—I mean, I literally walked out of restaurants in between my appetizer and my main course—and go back to work from a pay phone. It was just hateful."

"What was the typical reason a guest would cancel?" I asked.

"Because someone in the next trailer talked them out of it, saying they were a fool to air their dirty laundry. That's typically what would happen. Sometimes, too, I think guests begin to realize that saying disparaging things about someone on the phone is not the same as confronting them in person. The death knell was when you let them sit and think about it over the weekend."

Last-minute cancellations have consequences aside from the headaches that they cause just prior to taping. First, it is largely to compensate for possible cancellations that producers consistently overbook their shows, going after six, eight, even ten guests for a panel when there is realistically time for only three or four. This was one of the most common complaints among guests, especially experts: that a forum allowing for only the most rudimentary kind of intervention or advocacy to begin with was further compromised by the number of voices competing to be heard.[8] In general, the more volatile the topic, the greater the pressure to overbook. As Donna observed in relation to the teen-runaway show that she produced at *Diana:* "That one drove me totally and completely nuts because we were never on solid ground. Because, even if you get a commitment from them, nine times out of ten the kids won't show up, and you have no way of contacting them, they're runaways, they don't have homes. So that day I seriously overbooked myself just to make sure that, if some of them dropped, I still had a show."

Second, in an effort to discourage cancellations, many producers—especially at shows like *Randy*—wait until the last possible minute to book guests embroiled in crises or conflicts so that they have little time to reconsider or press for more information. One veteran of the business, formerly with *Jerry Springer,* told me that he used to book his most explosive shows the very night before taping. Joe said that producers at *Geraldo* and *Ricki Lake* would do the same thing, even though it would drive the executive producers (EPs) crazy. "The EPs, you know, they'd want to see the show locked down a week ahead of time so they could list the topic in *TV Guide,* but, practically speaking, that was impossible because the guests would be long gone by then." Thus, sensitive or controversial topics increase the likelihood of cancellations, which leads producers to overbook their shows and minimize contact with guests, which in turn weakens the sense of obligation that guests feel toward producers, ultimately leading to more cancellations.

If a guest has initially agreed and then reconsiders, producers often stress the obligations of the informal contract, promise special treatment, offer money, threaten, wheedle, cajole, claim that their job is at stake ("If you don't show up, I'll lose my job"), or, if the story is big enough, fly halfway across the country in order to beg in person. I have seen producers send messages to guests via pizza delivery boys or send roses, fruit baskets, or other, more expensive gifts. When guests show up at the studio but then start waffling backstage or in the green room, the host himself or herself may intervene. According to Joe, "Every host in the business has been on their knees pleading to get some gas-station attendant to come onstage and talk about the fact that he dresses up like Popeye or something."

8. Chapters 6 and 7 explore this issue more fully.

Alternatively, producers can simply get angry at guests. Frank, an associate producer at *Maury Povich*, said he knew staffers who literally screamed at guests over the phone, saying, "You better get on that plane right now! There's no way in hell I'm going to go to my boss with my tail between my legs and tell him my main guest isn't coming because they got scared! Get on that fucking plane!" And the amazing thing, according to Frank, is that guests comply. "Not only that," he said, "they respect you more for it, and they suddenly become your best friend."

Sometimes, of course, there is nothing that producers can do, and it is precisely to prevent this unhappy situation that producers stress the importance of knowing when to cut your losses, stop pushing a reluctant guest, and move on to somebody else—a luxury that producers at *Diana* could afford more often than could those at *Randy*.

"Unless I'm very desperate, I don't push a guest," Rachel told me, her voice emphatic. "If someone really can't handle it and doesn't want to be here, I usually drop 'em like a hot potato and go on because it's so nerve-racking to keep going back and forth, and it's not worth it in the end. If a guest wants to bail and you feel that they've been hesitant all along, you should let them bail—because they're going to anyway, bottom line."

Every single *Diana* producer with whom I spoke agreed that, in the end, the most successful mechanism for securing the participation and compliance of guests is not to deceive, bribe, cajole, or threaten them but to establish a trusting relationship, albeit a short-lived one. A relationship creates a sense of mutual obligation that helps ensure both parties keep their end of the bargain. "I do everything I can to create a bond with people, to obligate them to come to the show," Tamara said. "I talk to them frequently. Every day if I can. And I know that Lena is going to phone them to arrange their travel. A lot of times they're sending us photos. And, on top of that, I've gotten their social security number, I know their home address. We've talked about some very personal things. So you're crossing a certain line with them, of intimacy. You know, all these little things add up."

While not impossible, building relationships with guests is more difficult on shows like *Randy*, where the volatile nature of the topics and the shorter lead time foreclose the possibility of establishing strong bonds with guests, which in turn means that producers and guests have a weaker sense of responsibility toward one another. This is not to suggest that producers and guests do not form relationships at *Randy* and other trashy talk shows. For example, Tyler, a former *Jerry Springer* producer, made a big point of meeting her guests at the hotel the moment they arrive in town. You cannot wait until show time to meet your guests, she told me. "It's part of selling them on doing the show. Nothing works better in sales than being face-to-face." So she—or her associate producer—would be there at the hotel when the limousine arrived from the airport. She helped the guests carry their bags and get checked in, made sure that they had food vouchers, that they were, in her words, "All tucked in and cozy." You just cannot accomplish the same goal by sitting in your office, she said. It was only because she and her associate producer had done this face-to-face work with guests that Tyler was able to salvage one of her best shows from certain disaster the night before the taping. The show was "Mom, Will You Marry Me?" about a man who wanted to marry his own mother. The entire wedding party had arrived when the star guest—the mom—announced that she had changed her mind and would not go through with the taping. Tyler, her associate producer, the senior producer, and the head of security then spent the rest of the night in the hotel convincing the woman to reconsider. According to Tyler, "Ultimately, it was her relationship with [the associate producer] that saved the day. It ended up that we had to play good cop/bad cop. I was the bad cop. The guests all hated me. I was not allowed to be near them. But they just adored my partner. And, in the end, they did it for him." The show went forward as planned.

Saul Feldman believes that, at bottom, the exact nature of the relationship between producer and guest is less important than the mere fact that a relationship exists. This is because, in his view, people crave attention and rarely get it, and thus it is the attention from producers that best explains a guest's compliance. People are suckers for attention, he said; as a result, they put up with a lot in relationships, whether a talk show or a marriage. In his words, "If I pay attention to you, I can get you to do almost anything. It's an extreme statement I'm making, but it's true. If I pay attention to you, if I listen to you for hours and hours and I say I'm going to fly you in, put you in a hotel, give you a per diem, give you the opportunity to tell your story—I don't care who you are, I don't care if you're terribly educated, terribly wealthy, or very, very poor and ignorant—as soon as someone is willing to listen to your story, you feel you have an advocate there."

I really could not disagree with this observation. The fact that people are "suckers for attention" was probably the reason that producers and guests alike agreed to talk with me and be interviewed and why some of them gave very generously of their time on an ongoing basis. Clearly, both producers and guests on daytime talk shows experience a certain amount of frustration in their respective roles, and, as Powdermaker (1951) noted in her research on the Hollywood film industry, frustrated people love to talk.

But frustration or dissatisfaction is not the heart of the matter. In Powder-maker's words, "The most important reason for being able to get data is one that underlies success in any field work [or talk-show production]: all human beings love to talk about themselves and are flattered at having their opinions taken seriously" (6). This was as true for producers and their in-teractions with guests as it was for me and my interactions with producers.

To summarize, producing a daytime talk show is work, much of it similar to that performed by other media professionals, some of it unique to the genre. Like journalists of various sorts, producers face the relentless pres-sure of deadlines and, consequently, need a ready stock of material, stable sources of information, and ways of routinizing the participation of guests. They rely self-referentially on other media when choosing topics, and, when an organizational base exists for these topics, they seek out experts and spokespersons from established institutions for access to information or guests. Otherwise, they create their own base, relying primarily on plugs. In this sense producers, like reporters, see the world as bureaucrati-cally organized. Yet the focus on ordinary people in combination with the performative nature of the genre (the *show* aspect of the talk show) makes the production of daytime talk quite different from news gathering and even from the production of other forms of talk on television. Not only must guests be outgoing and expressive, but they must be willing to employ those qualities in the service of discussing controversial or taboo subjects, disclosing unusual or titillating experiences, or hashing out interpersonal conflicts. Finding the right guests is no easy task, and, once having found them, producers must develop a framework for their stories, shape their talk to fit the frame, allay their fears or misgivings, and keep them inter-ested in participating. To reduce uncertainty and help guarantee an emo-tional performance, producers prioritize conflict and strive for the type and combination of guests that will maximize it. Despite the routine pro-cedures and all the preparatory work behind the scenes, however, putting ordinary people on television always entails a certain risk, an element of unpredictability, an expectation of the unexpected. And at no time are pro-ducers and guests alike more aware of this tension than on the day of tap-ing itself.

You're not asking guests to fake their emotions, but you're giving them the license to express their emotions, so they know when they're on television they don't have to sit with their hands in their laps and monitor what they say. If they cuss in their normal life, cuss on our show. You know, "Don't hold back in terms of your emotion." And by telling them that, I think they realize we want them to be expressive. . . . I always tell 'em, "It's like going to church. Being a guest is like going to church. If the spirit overwhelms you, just jump up out of your seat and release it!"

—MARK, a *Randy* producer

CHAPTER FOUR

Talk as Show (a Show of Emotion)

Mining for Diamonds

In the last chapter, I quoted Doug, a *Diana* producer, comparing producing a talk show to planning a wedding and making a salad. His colleague, Rachel, used another metaphor that I also found compelling. She once told me that producing a talk show was like mining for diamonds or working a giant siphon with a tiny opening at the bottom that everything must filter through. You end up with a lot of waste material, she said, because only a tiny portion of what you sift through actually gets used. "But you have to have that huge pool of resources to get those nuggets."

With daytime talk shows, the drop that comes out at the end, the nugget or diamond that is mined from the surrounding material, is the money shot: concrete, physical evidence of real, raw emotion. As we have seen, the foundation for the money shot is laid long before a guest actually shows up at the studio. Producers have an easier time leading guests to the emotional brink if the topic is sensitive or volatile to begin with, if the guest feels strongly about it, if the guest is being surprised, or if producers have found others with an opposing viewpoint to challenge him or her on the air. Given these conditions, coaxing a dramatic performance from guests may not seem so difficult, but producers experience this aspect of their job as one of the, if not *the*, most unpredictable—and hence stressful—aspects of the job, for, no matter how much they work with guests, they can never be sure that someone who is good on the phone or in the green room will also be good onstage. As Tuchman (1974, 122) so aptly observes, "Try as one might, one cannot accomplish an interaction for someone else."

Although it rarely happens, producers live in constant fear that guests will become tongue-tied, fail to express emotion, not disclose the most important information first, get the story mixed up or confused, go into too much detail, or lose focus and go off on a tangent. Other things being equal, however, it is better to have a guest wander and digress than give simple yes or no answers, for, when guests get nervous, they may shut down, becoming quiet and reserved. The most extreme version of this is what one producer calls the *Cindy Brady disease*, referring to a particular episode of *The Brady Bunch* in which the Brady children appear on live television. When it is her turn to perform, the youngest sibling, Cindy, gets stage fright and is unable to speak. As Ellen explained it, "Even though we prep the guests right before the show, sometimes they choke, sometimes they freeze up, sometimes they get the Cindy Brady disease. Like, I had this one woman, she didn't say a single word the whole time, it was like watching paint dry. It would have been funny if it hadn't been so frustrating." When I asked what she did in a situation like that, she replied, "You just try and skip over the person, and, yeah, you're disappointed, but that's life, and they're real people—you can't expect any more from them."

Actually, producers can and do expect more from guests because the Cindy Brady disease is relatively rare—and likely more memorable for this reason. Indeed, after first complaining about the unreliability of real-people guests, producers invariably expressed surprise that they perform as consistently, and as consistently well, as they do. Jocelyn, a ten-year veteran of the business, put it best when she said, "I don't know if you've ever been on TV, but it's an intimidating experience. And I'm always amazed—

amazed—that these little people from their trailer parks don't totally freak out on camera more often and deliver, you know, one- and two-word answers. But the majority of the time they don't."

On the one hand, then, producers perceive the ultimate success or failure of a show to lie beyond their control because it rests with the unpredictable performances of ordinary people; on the other hand, they also recognize that a good performance is largely a matter of careful producing—otherwise, why bother screening guests, interviewing them, and otherwise preparing them for their roles? ("People don't cry on cue. They cry because they get to that place, emotionally. They come here ready to get to that emotional level. And that's not just a total accident, that's part of producing.") Producing is why the behavior of guests on any given show is remarkably consistent with the identity of that show and why guests' behavior will change if the mandate of the show changes. After the *Jenny Jones* murder, for example, many daytime talk shows toned down the level of conflict in response to public pressure. Likewise, in the spring of 1999 when the Chicago police threatened to show up on the set of *Jerry Springer* during tapings and arrest feuding guests for assault and battery, guests "miraculously" stopped fighting. At bottom, it is the *perceived* unpredictability of ordinary people, the *potential* for guests to freeze or clam up, that looms largest in the minds of producers.

This perception means that all the energy expended on guests in the days prior to taping a show is intensified the day of the taping itself, for this is when the presentational or theatrical aspects of the genre are foregrounded and the backstage efforts of producers come to fruition onstage. It is a day of tension and anxiety as well as excitement and drama—for staff and guests alike. There is simply a different feeling in the air when you walk into the production offices, a kind of electricity or energy that is almost palpable. At both *Diana* and *Randy*, producers are on edge, making final adjustments to the script and snapping at their associates to tie up any loose ends. They are well dressed, usually in black, like they are about to attend a grand opening or formal dinner engagement. At some point there is a brief production meeting to go over the use of any videotape packages, stills, or live satellite hookups. Small crises erupt: Guest 2 overslept and missed his flight, so he has to be moved to a later segment, and that means that Guests 3 and 4 can't mention his affair until after his wife joins him onstage. Guest 5 has to stop at the pharmacy on the way from the airport to the studio because she forgot her medication, Guest 6 has changed her mind about coming altogether because she found out that her sister-in-law will also be on the show, and Guest 7 is in tears because the flight attendant spilled coffee on her best suit and anything else will make her look fat on television.

When the guests begin to arrive, the tension in the air thickens perceptibly. At *Diana*, each guest or set of guests has a private dressing room or trailer complete with name tag and gold star on the door. If the rooms are still in use from a previous taping (there are two, sometimes three tapings per day), guests wait in the green room until the changeover is complete. At *Randy*, guests go directly to the green room or other areas reserved for the same purpose, and, because the topics typically deal with confrontations and surprises, producers take great pains to keep people separated backstage. Memos circulate warning staff and crew not to discuss the topic with *anybody*. Mentioning the name of a guest out loud is also taboo since, as producers never tire of telling production assistants and interns, their voices dropping to a whisper, *"You never know who might be listening."*

Surprises at *Diana* are orchestrated almost exclusively around reunions (with children given up for adoption, with long-lost friends or family members, with one's first love) or shows where fans get to meet their favorite sports star, actor, or idol. In either case, the segregation of guests prior to taping is key to maintaining the surprise and thus provoking an authentic display of emotion onstage. While producers and other staff usually manage this without mishap, sometimes the surprise is revealed prematurely. Heidi recalled such an occasion at *Diana* involving weight-loss guru Richard Simmons and a young female fan: "Somehow, the girl ventured back to the green room by herself and saw a tease on the monitor saying, 'Coming up, Richard Simmons!' So she found out, and the surprise was ruined." To prevent this sort of thing at *Randy*, I was sometimes asked to "baby-sit" guests in one of the makeshift dressing rooms used when both green rooms were full (I have since heard producers refer to these rooms as *holding pens*). This meant keeping an eye on guests to ensure that they did not go wandering around the set. Only guests on the same side of an issue would be housed together in the same room—for example, only the cheaters if the show was about cheating on your mate or only the victims if the show was about rape or childhood sexual abuse. On the occasions when I was called on to watch over guests, I was instructed to say nothing about the show and, if asked a direct question, respond with, "I don't know, I'm only an intern." If guests grew restless, I would attempt to make small talk, asking where they lived and worked and whether they were fans of the show.

Generally speaking, however, there was precious little time for conversation, especially when shows featured more than six or eight panelists or involved children, animals, or (very rarely) special events such as cooking demonstrations or musical performances. Even for average, run-of-the-mill shows with no special frills, the hours prior to taping are hectic. Despite specific instructions from producers, guests often arrive wearing clothing inappropriate for television, either because it violates accepted convention (horizontal stripes and plain white do not "translate" on camera and are forbidden) or because it is just too casual (jeans, T-shirts, flannel). These guests receive a visit from a staffer in wardrobe and are outfitted with clothes rented by the show. As we shall see, sometimes at *Randy* outfitting guests proved a production in itself, as producers and guests often differed in their taste and guests resented what they perceived to be producers' attempts to change them. Guests also have their hair and makeup done, and this, too, can be a source of tension if guests are unhappy with, or dislike, the results. Meanwhile, the stage manager wires them for sound, and the talent coordinator or a production assistant obtains written consent for their participation, along with a signed statement guaranteeing the authenticity of their story. Eventually, the audience files in, while the technical crew and support staff rush back and forth, readying equipment and attending to last-minute details. After all this is complete, the most important remaining task is for someone on staff to warm up the studio audience and for producers to prep the guests.

Fluffing

The goal of backstage prepping and coaching is twofold. First, producers go over story content one last time, reminding guests of key points and the order in which to make them—for, despite the fact that producers routinely tell guests, "Relax, this is *your* life, you've lived it, so there are no wrong answers," they nevertheless prefer those answers to be structured in a particular way.[1] In addition to content, the *what* of guests' stories, producers are concerned with form and style, the *how* of those stories. Thus, the second goal of backstage coaching is to "work the guest," to prepare him or her emotionally for what is about to transpire.

1. I was reminded of the difficulty that some guests have in adhering to this structure listening to Peggy prep her lead guest for a *Diana* show on "Toxic People." The guest's marriage was falling apart, and, in the green room just before taping, Peggy pretended to be the host, asking him, "So tell me, what are your gripes with your wife?" The man then

As we have seen, producers approach different guests in different ways, depending on whether the desired performance is soft- or hard-core. If the topic involves a tragedy such as illness or death, producers are gentle and solicitous. They thank the guest repeatedly for coming on the show and acknowledge his or her bravery. It's OK to cry on the air, they say, offering tissue; Diana will be there for you. As Doug observed, "You don't crack jokes. You approach the person in a certain way and in a certain mode." This mode is clearly different if the guest is an angry wife waiting to confront her husband for running off with a sixteen-year-old girl. "In that case," according to Angela, you generally just reinforce for the person why they're here. You remind them, 'You're here because your husband left you for this young girl and you want to give the bastard a piece of your mind.' With a topic like that, you know, that's usually all it takes to get them going."

As always, producers urge guests to "cut loose" and "let it all out." "Whatever the emotion," they say, "give it to us *big*." Cheerleading of this sort often continues during the taping itself, when producers run over to guests from the sidelines to whisper a few hurried words between segments. ("She's making you look like a real jerk! Are you going to let her get away with that? Remember what you told me on the phone? Well, tell her that now!") They acknowledge that such practices result in a certain amount of exaggeration on the part of guests, but, from their point of view at least, there is a distinction between exaggeration and lying, and the former does not compromise the authenticity of a person's story. "You want their emotions to be exaggerated," Angela conceded. "After all, this is television. But the facts of the story, what actually happened, can't be a lie."

Coaching guests backstage increases the probability of obtaining the preferred outcome onstage, and in this sense it has a number of parallels: the locker-room pep talk before the big game or the process by which

---

began talking in abstract terms about how all marriages have their little annoyances and irritations. "Hey, stop!" Peggy cut him off, annoyed herself. "By now we're on to the next segment, and you have not said one specific thing. You told me on the phone that your wife doesn't listen to you, that she puts you down, she argues with you—so, when Diana asks, 'What are your gripes?' give her the gripes!" Sandra faced a similar situation at *Randy* when prepping a guest for a show titled "Mom, Stop Prostituting Me!" The girl was clearly nervous, and, when Sandra asked, "What are you going to say when Randy asks about your mom?" she launched into a detailed description of her unhappy childhood, how she felt abandoned and unloved. "Wait!" Sandra stopped her. "Start off with, 'My mom prostitutes me. My mom beats me.' You know, you've got to tell Randy and the audience first what is going on *now*, why you're even on this show. You can't wait until the last segment and say, 'Oh, by the way, I'm mad at my mom because she prostituted me.'"

actors psych themselves up for a dramatic performance. Method acting, popularized by Russian director Konstantin Stanislavsky, has particular relevance here in that it strives for authenticity and realness by having actors experience, as fully and deeply as possible, the feelings and emotions of the characters they play—and they do so by tapping into their own emotional reservoirs, revisiting past emotional experiences.

The most fitting comparison in my opinion, however, takes us back to pornography. Prepping guests for an emotional performance is not unlike preparing male porn stars for a sex scene: it gets them all "hot and bothered" so that they can go out there and "show wood." With porn films, there is even a person—typically a young woman—employed on the set for this very purpose; she's called *the fluffer* (see Faludi 1995). Just as the fluffer arouses the actor to increase the probability of the money shot, producers "fluff" guests to increase the chance that they too will climax in the appropriate way. As with the male stars of pornographic films, sometimes talk-show guests can show wood, sometimes they can't. Most of the time, however—I'd say 90 percent of the time—guests can. Indeed, my guess is that producers have a far greater success rate than do fluffers.

Significantly, guests are not the only ones expected to show wood during a taping. At the same time as producers are in dressing rooms or green rooms preparing guests for their roles, someone on staff is on the set preparing audience members for theirs, and this process, too, entails a certain amount of fluffing to encourage emotional expressiveness. The studio audience is an integral part of the genre, yet audience members are no less ordinary than are guests. Hence, the selection, coaching, and rehearsing of audience members performs much the same function as the selection, coaching, and rehearsing of guests: to minimize uncertainty and ensure a lively performance.

While the studio audience at any given show is composed mainly of people who live in the city where the show is taped or are there vacationing, sometimes the audience coordinator will seek out specific groups of people with a vested interest in the topic. At *Diana*, for example, when we taped "Teens with HIV," the audience coordinator arranged to bus in a group from a local AIDS organization, and I recall another occasion when I was asked to canvass the audience queue for volunteers to attend an upcoming show called "Blondes Have More Fun." Producers wanted one or two dark-haired "confederates" seated in the audience who would challenge the views of the panelists. More commonly, producers "pepper" the audience with individuals they preinterviewed but did not end up choosing as guests, people who obviously have a connection to, and a stake in, the subject matter at hand. Such practices do not guarantee fireworks and drama, but they help because they locate the potential for dramatic inter-action in the strategic juxtaposition of participants rather than (or in addi-tion to) individual performative competence.

It also helps if audience members know the proper procedure for ask-ing questions and if producers have a sense of what questions might be asked during the taping, for audience members are subject to the same pyramid structure when posing questions as guests are when answering them, and, if they cannot get to the point or stay on track, they derail the focus of the show. Alex, the comedian who does audience warm-up at *Diana*, has people rehearse the procedure in advance, and he sometimes screens potential questions during the breaks between segments. A less ac-ceptable practice is deliberately planting questions in the audience. Al-though this is discouraged by industry executives and, depending on the show, may be grounds for dismissal, Alex said that some talk shows do it routinely, and he admitted to planting questions himself on rare occasions, at the request of producers.

"If a producer comes to me, you know, and says, 'Look, I really need to hit this point,' I'll go out in the audience and say, 'You know what, you're all asking really good questions, but doesn't anybody want to know why she stopped talking to her brother when she turned thirteen? I want to ask that question myself, but I can't, so will somebody ask it for me?' And somebody will. I seldom do that, though—it's highly looked down on."

Although "highly looked down on," screening and planting questions in the audience, like coaching and cheerleading guests, is generally per-ceived by staffers as a necessary precautionary measure. As Alex put it, "People might think, 'Wow, that's really staged,' and the fact of it is I really encourage the audience to come up with their own questions. And 99 per-cent of the time they do. But every once in a while—I mean, it's not staged, we just have to get a sense of how the show's going to run."

Even more important than the specific questions or comments that audience members contribute, however, is the overall atmosphere that they provide, and the chief task of the audience warm-up is to raise the energy level in the room and get people in the mood to participate. While there are clear differences between shows in terms of just how lively the audience is supposed to be—just how much wood they are supposed to show—the basic procedure for fluffing is similar across the genre and, within a given talk show, across topics.

As discussed in chapter 2, a festive mood is generated well before tap-ing even begins. Music is piped over the PA system, the warm-up person cracks jokes, and audience members are awarded prizes for answering trivia questions or singing and dancing onstage. They practice oohing, aahing, and clapping furiously. During the taping itself, the warm-up person will often lead these reactions from the sidelines, and, during the breaks, it is not uncommon for a producer to chastise audience members for being too quiet or polite, much as they chastise guests. "Don't hold back on your emotions," they warn. "You'll get ulcers!" Like guests, audience members are told over and over, "Express yourself! This is your moment of glory! You represent America!" At *Ricki Lake*, the audience coordinator divided the room in two and had each side try to outshout the other. At another show, when a technical delay kept the entire audience waiting in a small room outside the studio for almost two hours, a staffer named Betty had people practice "guest walk-ons," bursting out from a pair of nearby restrooms into the waiting crowd as if from backstage onto the set. "Pretend you're a guest on the show," Betty said. "Let loose! Show a little attitude!"

Showing Wood

In the actual staging of a show, producers follow the same pyramid structure that they urge on audience members and guests. The most important guest always goes on first, setting the tone and framework for subsequent events (in a conflict situation, this person is typically the heroine of the story, the person who feels victimized by a past wrong or injustice). *Important* does not necessarily mean that the guest has the most sensational story; it often means that she is the most energetic and the best talker and thus the one most likely to hold viewers' interest and prevent them from changing the channel. When *Diana* producers did a show about date rape, for example, they debated back and forth about whom to lead with: the woman repeatedly raped, stabbed, and left for dead or the woman raped once by her best friend. Ultimately, they decided to go with the second woman because she was a better storyteller, even though the story itself was less sensational. Sometimes producers will switch guests at the last minute depending on what transpires in the green room. If Guest 3 proves more excitable and easier to fluff, producers may bump Guest 1 and put Guest 3 in her place. (In the words of Kenneth, a *Diana* producer formerly with *Oprah*, "Maybe the guest you thought would go last is PMSing or whatever, but all of a sudden she's really emotional about her kid being killed by gang members. Dammit, start with her!") The same need for flexibility holds true during the taping itself: a guest may go off in a direction that producers did not anticipate, or a particular interaction may prove so emotional that they have to let the segment run longer than planned. Producers recognize that a given show's success or failure depends in large measure on their ability to make these snap decisions. For some, it is the most exciting aspect of the job.[2]

At *Randy*, if a given guest surprises producers with an unexpectedly dramatic performance and they realize that that person should have been their lead-in only after he or she is onstage, they can change and reorder the show after the fact through careful editing. As Mark explained it, "If the last person in the lineup gets onstage and they're just, like, phenomenal, you didn't know they had that in 'em to bust out like that, depending on the circumstances, you might be able to kind of reorder the show. Because that's the rule, that's what we're told: 'Lead with your most explosive story.'"

Conversely, *Randy* guests who do *not* perform well onstage can redeem themselves in the green room after the taping is over. In order to capitalize on the frequency with which emotions generated during taping spill over to backstage interactions, *Randy* and a number of other talk shows have begun incorporating behind-the-scenes footage, using it either as a coda to the episode or as brief "teasers" advertising events yet to come. Guests are filmed walking on- and offstage, down the corridors from the green rooms to the set, and, most important, in green rooms afterward, where they continue to hash out whatever conflict erupted earlier. These scenes can sometimes be as volatile as the taping proper, partly because emotions and adrenaline are running high, and partly because the theatrical aspects of the taping that some guests find inhibiting—the stage, lights, and audience—are absent from the green-room context. I witnessed these secondary performances often enough myself when assisting the mobile camera operator or when helping the production assistants retrieve borrowed shoes and clothing from guests.

Generally speaking, of course, producers know before the cameras roll which guests are good, what they will say, and how events will unfold. Most of the time, the taping goes according to plan. Occasionally, however,

---

2. Tamara, a producer at *Diana*, certainly thought so: "The fun part is to be out there on the floor the day of the show, you and the executive producer and the host, judging where the show is going, on the fly. Because—although generally you stick to your format—you've got to be able to change things. And some shows you will change a lot throughout; you'll say, 'Let this go long, dump that, move that!' That's when it really gets exciting."

things do happen that producers cannot foresee or control, and these events—all the more memorable for being relatively rare—become part of the lore that shapes how producers think and talk about their work. Guests can get cold feet and drop out; they can get nervous on camera and forget their training; they can get angry and walk off the set. Guests might be willing but unable to make the taping, having fallen ill, had an accident, gotten arrested. Someone in the audience could have an epileptic seizure and unwittingly diffuse the emotion onstage (this happened once at *Diana*) or ask an irrelevant question that derails the focus of the show. Sometimes, as Joe discovered, guests resolve their differences in transit and ruin the show before it even begins. "I couldn't believe it," he told me. "This couple, they were, you know, fighting like cats and dogs twenty-four hours earlier, and then they arrive all lovey-dovey. They're like, 'Oh, everything is fine now, we're going to keep the baby, and, you know, I'm never going to hit her again. We made up at thirty thousand feet.' I was like, 'Oh shit, come on, you're kidding me.'"[3]

In such cases, producers do not get the money shot that they plan for and have every reason to expect. That these scenarios are the exception rather than the rule is due not only to the extensive fluffing that guests undergo just prior to taping. It also has to do with the previously mentioned fact that, in recruiting guests already embroiled in conflicts or crises, producers are capitalizing on a certain level of dramatic tension inherent in the situation. ("You can be guaranteed fireworks when you have two people who disagree and both feel 100 percent right.") Joe confirmed this point when we were talking about the consistency with which fistfights break out on the set of many shows. Although he denied ever having witnessed a situation in which a producer specifically instructed a guest to punch another guest, he said that if producers are doing their jobs correctly, they don't *have* to give explicit instructions: "You know that if you have some guy who's been abusive and what sets him off is referring to his

---

3. Much the same thing happened to Mark during the very first show that he ever produced at *Randy*. The show featured a gang leader who was cheating on his girlfriend with dozens of other women and the girlfriend who was coming on the show to confront him about it. As Mark described it, the woman was really angry, really going to confront the boyfriend and say, "Either marry me and stop cheating around, or get the hell out of my life." That was supposed to be her ultimatum to him. Mark rolled his eyes in memory of what occurred next. "And then she got here, and I don't know what happened, if they had a great night together in the hotel or what, but she was all [adopting a soft, amorous voice], 'I know you've cheated around on me honey, and I just want you to stop with all that and commit to me,' and she was, like, real soft about it. And it was a bad show because of that."

illegitimate son Ted, and then you tell Sarah Lou to mention Ted in the third segment—you know what I mean? It doesn't take a brain surgeon to figure out the rest."

Another reason why guests so consistently come through for producers is that talk-show guests, especially those responding to plugs, tend to be talk-show viewers as well. And people who watch talk shows have in some sense already been coached and trained for their roles. They are familiar with the codes of the genre, they know what is expected of them, they know what producers want, and they know how to deliver the goods. Producers' concerns about ordinary people as competent performers is thus often misplaced, something Randy himself recognized and mentioned during our interview.

"In a sense, we're all experts on television," he said, "because there is very little else we do in life as consistently as watch television. More people know the words to the *Brady Bunch* song than to the national anthem. So we say they [the ordinary guests] are not professionals, but we're a nation of experts when it comes to television." Saul Feldman agreed: "If you watch talk shows, you pretty much know what the producer is looking for. You may not be completely cognizant, but, subliminally, viscerally, you know. You sense that you've gotta be a good talker, that you've gotta have a dramatic story, that you've gotta point fingers, express outrage, things of that sort. Television has taught an entire generation, millions and millions of people, mostly women eighteen to thirty-four, how to act on a talk show."

Yet a final reason why guests so consistently go out there and show wood has to do with the performative context of the taping itself. To be sure, some guests find the stage, the lights, the cameras, and the studio audience inhibiting. But for most ordinary guests these elements provide the proper set of cues for achieving that heightened emotional state that producers have been soliciting all along. As White (1993) has observed, acting is a social ceremony, not simply an individual act—even, I would argue, when one is acting out real life (see also Goffman 1959). Ordinary people are playing themselves, but they are doing so on national television before a live studio audience and millions of viewers amid all the trappings of conventional theatrical performance. This immediate setting, in combination with certain other aspects of their induction into the world of television— the air travel, the limousine, the five-star hotel, the backstage sessions in makeup and wardrobe—serve to construct a total experience for guests that simultaneously emphasizes the distinction between ordinary and celebrity (actor) statuses and invites ordinary people to cross the boundary and inhabit the celebrity role. Consequently, guests experience a difference between their normal, everyday self and their self onstage, and, despite their lack of professional training, they respond to the staged environment much as real actors do: they "turn on" and perform. At shows like *Randy*, producers want guests to be angry and confrontational, so they are. At *Diana*, guests are expected to be emotional in different (more "dignified") ways, so they are.

The behavior of studio audiences illustrates a similar point. Like guests, audience members tend to be talk-show viewers who know how to behave, have been fluffed in advance, and respond positively to the overall theatrical context. Audiences stand up and chastise guests, ask questions and make comments, and comply with requests to give big reactions— oohing and aahing, clapping and booing, expressing exaggerated approval and disapproval—not because these are natural or spontaneous responses necessarily, or because audience members are especially ill-mannered, mean-spirited, or cruel, but because, in this particular setting, acting this way is the right thing to do.

Acting this way is the right thing to do if you want to be part of the action and part of the scene. In particular, it is the right thing to do if you want to be on television. Indeed, any audience member knows that the bigger the reaction and the more expressive the behavior, the more likely you are to attract the camera. And getting on camera is highly desirable, especially for the younger set; it is one of the main reasons and chief rewards for attending a live taping. I noticed time and again that audience members strive to sit near the front of the stage or on the aisle because, given the spatial arrangement of most studios, the former location increases the chance of getting targeted for a reaction shot and the latter increases the chance of getting chosen by the host to ask a question.[4] When people do get singled out to speak, they often receive a congratulatory high five afterward from the man or woman sitting beside them. Teenage girls check their hair and makeup at every commercial break, and the warm-up person deliberately uses the desire for television exposure to discourage unwanted behavior, warning us that the cameras will avoid those sections of

---

4. Generally speaking, where you sit in the studio is determined by your initial place in the queue. At *Sally Jessy*, I was at the front of the line and was then seated on the aisle in the center section, four rows back from the stage—clearly a strategic position. But, because there was an empty space beside me, I got moved to a single seat in the back, and two women (who had come to the taping together) were seated there instead. They were thrilled to have the spot; I could read it in their faces. Both immediately pulled compacts from their purses and began reapplying lipstick.

the audience in which anyone waves, makes faces, or shouts out unsolicited comments.

Television exposure makes audience members feel important, part of the celebrity machine. Yet, like the guests themselves, audience members find themselves in a highly structured context that limits their participation in key ways. There is an implicit script to follow, and, if they want to get involved and play a role, they must more or less follow the script. In this I am reminded of the Ehrenreich, Hess, and Jacobs essay on the phenomenon known as *Beatlemania*. Rather than interpret the screaming and fainting of young Beatles fans as pathological mob behavior (as did most media critics at the time), the authors ask us to consider the ways in which Beatlemania provided a space for adolescent girls both to express sexual desire safely (i.e., without actually having to have sex and therefore compromising their virtue) and to take center stage in a society that systematically denied them a voice. Despite the fact that Beatlemania was consistent with the mass marketing of rock and roll as *the* legitimate arena of teen expression and, more insidiously, with the stereotype of the hysterical, out-of-control female fan, it was nevertheless a way for these girls actively to *participate* in mass culture and to gain some modicum of public visibility. In the words of Ehrenreich, Hess, and Jacobs (1992, 105), "When the screams drowned out the music, as they invariably did, then it was the fans, and not the band, who were the show."

It is precisely to get on television that many audience members ask questions during the taping itself and why their questions and comments are as predictable and formulaic as they are. Queries by audience members are so predictable, in fact, that before I attended my first taping, I wondered whether there existed some explicit rule limiting what people could say. ("You there in the red, were you abused as a child?" "To the man on the end who can't keep his thing in his pants, were you born in a barn?" "Girl, you got to get some self-respect!") Scholars have noted that such remarks function much the same way a Greek chorus does. More often than not, the so-called transgressive behavior of guests prompts responses from audience members that reinscribe conventional moral boundaries (see Shattuc 1997; Lowney 1999). Audiences inevitably preach sexual restraint, marital fidelity, parental self-sacrifice, and respect for others, including racial and ethnic tolerance. But people draw on the same narrow, familiar repertoire of queries and comments not so much because they share common moral beliefs as because the content of what they say matters less than the mere fact that they are saying it. People want to be part of the show, and a good many are less interested in the response to the question than in asking something, anything, on camera. A shared moral code is simply the ready-made repertoire from which they draw to accomplish this goal.

Herbst (1995) observed a comparable phenomenon with callers who participate in talk-radio programs. At some level, what both sets of participants illustrate is Carey's (1989) distinction between *ritual* and *transmission* models of communication.[5] Whereas a transmission model suggests that people engage with media in order to transmit opinions and disseminate specific information, a ritual model suggests a more diffuse desire to engage in dialogue, get involved, and seek a place in an imagined public. As Herbst (1995, 272) puts it, "It is the act of coming together (electronically) for the distinct purpose of communication, even more than the substance of dialogue itself, that makes this sort of participation unique and meaningful." As we shall see in the following chapters, a similar distinction between transmission and ritual modes could be said to characterize the respective participation of experts and ordinary guests.

Managing the Heart: Talk Shows and Emotional Labor

Once the taping itself is complete, guests retreat backstage while audience members either file out of the studio or remain seated, either to provide additional reaction shots for the camera (inserted at appropriate moments later in the editing process) or to serve as a backdrop for the host as he or she does "promos" for upcoming shows. By this time, most everyone is tired: host, producers, technical crew, and audience members. The overhead lights are very hot, the seats uncomfortable, and, although actual air time is only forty-two minutes, tapings can take several hours. Producers in particular want to go home and get enough rest before they have to start the whole process again. There is a well-known saying among industry insiders that goes, "Bring 'em in by limo, send 'em home by cab," and it summarizes well the changed attitude of producers toward guests once the show is over and guests have delivered the goods. At this point, producers are not concerned about establishing rapport with guests, accommodating

5. According to Carey (1989, 18), "A ritual view of communication is directed not toward the extension of messages in space, but the maintenance of society in time; not the act of imparting information but the representation of shared beliefs." If the transmission model posits the relay of messages across geographic boundaries for the purposes of control, the ritual model is more akin to "the sacred ceremony that draws persons together in fellowship and commonality."

their requests, or coaxing them to the brink of emotional readiness; rather, they are concerned with bringing guests down to earth and getting them out the door.

By contrast, the guests are still energized from having been on national television, the majority of them for the first time. Many guests experience the same postperformance high familiar to actors, musicians, entertainers, and others who perform in public. At *Diana*, guests would linger in the green room or dressing rooms, prolonging the experience, chatting excitedly with each other and the staff, while impatient limo drivers smoked cigarettes outside. Guests always received complementary fanny packs, coffee mugs, or T-shirts (the same items awarded to audience members during the pretaping warm-up), and some asked to keep the name tag attached to their dressing-room door.

On the rare occasion at *Diana* when a show featured a celebrity or a

Figure 8. Live tapings of *The Phil Donahue Show* and *The Jerry Springer Show*. *Top:* The author asks a question on the air. *Bottom:* Host Jerry Springer talks to one of his guests, with audience members looking on. Author's collection.

group of professional performers, the sheer number of accompanying aids, assistants, and support staff made for a festive, if somewhat chaotic, atmosphere. Such was the case at the very first taping I assisted with, which featured a group of female impersonators from a swanky Hollywood club. Only occasionally at *Diana* was the postperformance atmosphere negative or hostile. I recall a show titled "People and Pet Makeovers" where a woman was extremely upset afterward because during the taping a dog groomer shaved her purebred Chow to make it look like a lion. She insisted that she had explicitly forbidden producers to allow this, and Diana herself emerged from her dressing room to apologize. Another time, with a show about gangs called "Caught in the Crossfire," one of the guests—a woman whose son was killed by a gang member—got so riled by an argument with an audience member that she picked a fight afterward with the friend who had accompanied her to the taping.

At *Randy* and other conflict-based shows, hostile posttaping emotions were more common. Joe said that he used to dread dealing with his guests at *Geraldo*. "Too often, the guests would go back to the green room feeling savaged, just beside themselves with anger. Like, 'You didn't tell me that was what this was going to be about,' you know, or, 'I wasn't prepared for it to happen that way.' Sometimes it got so bad I had to send one of my assistants in there to talk to them because I just couldn't face them myself." Thus, emotions generated onstage can spill over to backstage interactions, and producers find themselves placating disgruntled or angry guests, comforting those who are distraught or upset, or even—with the help of bodyguards and security personnel—breaking up fistfights.

It is important to note, however, that a conflict situation onstage where one or more guests are seemingly attacked or humiliated does not always make for postperformance hostility. What a talk show dedicated to the display of real, unscripted emotion will *not* reveal in its backstage footage are the occasions when guests who are angry and volatile during the taping appear friendly enough afterward. One of the experts I interviewed, a psychologist who had appeared on dozens of shows, remarked on the total turnaround in guests' behavior with astonishment. "It never ceases to amaze me," she said. "At the end of the show, these people, like, they just came from the war zone—and they're not even affected. People [in the audience] have stood up and called them disgusting, immoral, unethical. And at the end they just want an autographed photo of the host! They're hugging everyone, you know, like it was nothing!"

I witnessed the same phenomenon many times at *Randy*. Given that producers target people in crisis, it might well be the case that what happens to guests onstage is nothing compared to other, more traumatic events in their lives and that they therefore appear undisturbed by having been accosted, reprimanded, or ridiculed. But guests can also do an about-face either because they are not genuinely angry in the first place or, more probably, because their anger is secondary to some other, larger reason for participating—the attraction of appearing on national television, for instance. That guests are willing to broker their conflicts or crises in exchange for the experience of being a guest—regardless of what happens to them in that role—tells us something about the power that national media exposure holds over people who are rarely granted it. At the same time, the fact that guests are one way with each other during the taping and then another way afterward does not mean that they are fabricating their stories or faking their emotions; rather, it further reinforces the point that producers, capitalizing on preexisting conditions, have engineered a performative space that encourages certain kinds of expressive behavior and that ordinary people are more competent performers than producers and critics give them credit for.

The whole process of putting together and executing a talk show illustrates that, when producers are producing and guests are guesting, much of the time they are engaged in a highly routinized form of what has been called *emotion work* (Hochschild 1983). The performance at the end of all the planning and preparation is the result of jointly produced emotional labor. As with the relation of doctor to distraught patient, funeral director to bereaved client, or flight attendant to disgruntled passenger, the relation of producer to guest is such that producers manage their own emotions—either pretending to care about guests or trying not to care too much—so that they can better manage the emotions of guests themselves. The key difference between producing and many other occupations involving emotion management, of course, is that, on a talk show, emotion is not something to be discouraged or downplayed so that one can carry on with the task at hand. On a talk show, eliciting emotion *is* the task at hand. Either way—as Hochschild (1983, 49) observes—emotion work in commercial contexts differs from emotion work in private contexts because, when institutions are involved, "various elements of acting are taken away from the individual and replaced by institutional mechanisms . . . many people and objects, arranged according to institutional rule and custom, together accomplish the act."

At *Diana*, most of the emotion work that producers do with guests occurs prior to tape day. Producers spend much of their time and energy talking with guests, fine-tuning their stories, and generally making them feel comfortable. In the process, producers have to know how to read people—when to push them emotionally and when to back off. ("I didn't push real hard with them yet. Because I could feel on the phone the edge of their emotion. You know, if I'd gotten them a week or two ago to burst into tears on the phone with me, they're going to have all this wrenching, painful, stirred-up stuff to deal with, and they're going to back out.") The work for *Randy* producers is similar to some extent, but, because the emphasis on confrontation often requires them to minimize pretaping contact with certain guests, they tend to do more emotion work on the actual day of taping, not only in terms of prepping guests backstage ("Don't be shy, show him how you really feel!"), which may or may not involve an investment of genuine emotion on their part, but also in terms of managing and diffusing the emotional energy generated by the taping itself. At both shows, producers also expend considerable effort convincing guests that they will benefit in some way from participating. As we have seen, producers are consummate salespeople. They know how to push the right buttons, and they work hard to develop a personal relationship with guests. ("You try to personalize the situation as much as possible; you make them feel like you're their friend . . . and that they can trust you.")

A key dimension of this emotional labor, indeed, a precondition of its accomplishment, is the ability of producers to orient toward people in various stages of crisis or conflict objectively, that is, as objects or elements of the production process. Producers deal day in and day out with heavy, emotional subject matter, but, with a mandate to crank out two hundred shows a year, they simply cannot afford to sympathize with every hard-luck story that comes across their desk. In a manner similar to the workers studied by Hochschild (1983), producers find themselves performing emotional labor while simultaneously struggling to distance themselves from its emotional effects, to make it just another aspect of the job.

Heidi, the talent coordinator at *Diana*, remarked on the emotional burdens of producing when discussing a show titled "Women with AIDS": "These women were just so neat; they were really just nice people. I was backstage with their kids [during the taping], and it was heartbreaking for me. Here these moms are onstage talking about how they're going to die and what's going to happen to their kids, and I'm sitting back there practically bawling. I don't know how the producers handle it, working with this sort of thing all the time."

To some extent, the status differences between producers and guests, especially at shows like *Randy*, help preclude the formation of emotional attachments. Even if producers do not feel detached from their guests personally and can identify with their problems or conflicts as Heidi did, distance is created by the fact that guests are performing emotion while producers are merely orchestrating it. Few producers express a willingness to appear on a daytime talk show themselves, unless in a professional capacity as an expert, and this unwillingness to do the very things that they demand of their guests cannot help but sustain a certain distinction between them.

More significantly, however, the pace of production, in combination with the sheer volume of guests, functions to discourage strong emotional bonding. Like the staff of a hospital emergency room or those who work in public-health and -welfare occupations, producers are so overtaxed on a daily basis that they have little choice but to orient toward other people's tragedies and transgressions in a businesslike way. Thus, Rachel can speak approvingly of a guest as "an easy cry" or of a father and son breaking down onstage as an "amazing interview," while Sandra considers an incest survivor raging out of control at her mother in front of millions of viewers "one of the best television moments you'll ever see." It is this same attitude that allowed a *Maury Povich* producer to say matter-of-factly while describing a show called "Death Caught on Tape," "My first guest was a skydiver who collided with a friend of his while skydiving, and both his [the guest's] legs were cut off in midair. His friend died in the accident. It was great, it was beautiful."

Another important dimension of producers' emotional labor is the fact that they must leave their real emotional lives at home in order to concentrate on managing emotion at work. Producers cannot let their *own* personal troubles or crises interfere with their ability to make entertainment out of the troubles and crises of guests. They have to sound upbeat and sincere with guests, like there is no one else they would rather be talking to, no matter what is going on in their life or what emotion they might be feeling at the time. According to Tyler, a former *Springer* producer, "You just have to shut out everything, you have to weed out exhaustion and stress, and emotion of any sort, from your personal life. Anyone who deals with a mass amount of people has to be able to do that. You broke up with your boyfriend? Oh fuckin' well, you know, anyone who came to the office and cried into the phone to their boyfriend didn't last very long. Like, last year my associate producer found out his girl was cheating on him. He was devastated, but he wouldn't even talk to her about it until the season ended. Because he had to still come in every day and sound like he was a happy guy who was glad to be doing what he was doing. That's how extreme it has to be."

Ironically, then, getting guests to talk about their personal lives and express genuine emotion means that producers themselves must deliberately refrain from doing either (at *Randy*, the senior producer would occasionally call her underlings on the phone as they worked in the next room, just to monitor their attitude and demeanor when they answered the call). Of course, producers are not alone in performing this kind of emotion management. As Tyler said, "Anyone who deals with a mass amount of people has to be able to do that." Hochschild (1983) estimates that more than one-third of all workers in the United States hold jobs that require emotional labor of one sort or another; that is, they hold jobs in which human feeling is systematically subject to commodification and corporate control. As she puts it, "Those who perform emotion work in the course of giving service are like those who perform physical labor in the course of making things: both are subject to mass production." Both are also subject to alienation, in the classic Marxist sense, for, "when the thing to be engineered, mass-produced, and subjected to speedup and slowdown is a smile, a mood, a feeling, or a relationship, it comes to belong more to the organization and less to the self" (198).

When a mood, feeling, or relationship belongs more to the organization and less to the self, producers and others involved in emotion work must cultivate or work on feeling in ways that respond to particular organizational demands. They become actors whose roles are scripted by the exigencies of their work. Of course, we all do a certain amount of acting in both public (onstage) and private (backstage) contexts. But not all acting is the same. Hochschild distinguishes between *surface acting*, which occurs when we try to change how we outwardly appear to others (the put-on sneer, the posed shrug, the controlled sigh), and *deep acting*, which occurs when the display of emotion "naturally" results from working on feeling. A person is deep acting, she says, when "[he or she] does not try to *seem* happy or sad but rather expresses spontaneously, as [Stanislavsky] urged, a real feeling that has been self-induced" (1983, 35). In both cases, the person may consider the emotion in question the result of conscious mental work, but, with surface acting, it feels *put on*, while, with deep acting, it feels *genuinely expressed*. Thus, winning a client's trust or allaying a guest's misgivings can be done either by surface acting—seeming to be more empathetic—or by the deep act of becoming more empathetic, which, as Hochschild notes, makes the acting of "seeming" unnecessary. The ability to engage in deep acting depends as much on the conditions of work as on the individual worker: when emotional labor is highly professionalized and well remunerated, as it is for, say, therapists in private practice, genuine compassion may well be a good deal easier to muster.

Although they are often cast in the role of counselor or therapist, producers are more comparable to salesmen or flight attendants in that producers may want to do deep acting and claim the emotion as their own, but cannot pull it off under speedup conditions, and so fall back on surface acting. This was the case for Tyler, the *Springer* producer quoted above. The catch-22 of surface acting is that, while it protects producers emotionally, it can appear phony or disingenuous to guests and thus jeopardize the sale. When I asked Tyler about this dilemma, she said, "Well, you just have to work at it. Like, I tell my guests, 'I can't wait to meet you in person!' And you of course have to make it seem genuine. You have to make it seem like it's the first time you ever said that to anybody in your life. Is that inauthentic? Is that syrupy sweet? Maybe. Sometimes. But it's all part of trying to influence them to come on the show."

For Tyler, who claimed to enjoy her job and to be genuinely interested in her guests, her emotional labor was not necessarily incompatible with how she really felt. Other producers experience the disjuncture between how they must behave and how they feel more acutely and rely consciously on surface acting to bridge the gap. As a *Maury Povich* producer told me, "I make friends with all my guests before the show, you know, but really I could care less about most of them. It's just—people just *like* me. That's what I'm good at, making people like me and coming across as a real nice guy."[6]

Generally speaking, *Diana* producers found it more challenging and difficult than did those at *Randy* to keep their emotion work on the surface and distance themselves from guests and their problems, even if they were more or less successful at leaving their own personal troubles at home. Some switched from producing to other positions on staff or left the business altogether because they found the emotion work, in combination with

6. In some ways, Hochschild's notion of deep vs. surface acting is similar to Scheff's (1977) discussion of emotional "underdistancing" and "overdistancing" in relation to drama and ritual. Scheff argues that successful rituals are the result of participants having achieved the proper emotional distance: if someone is underdistanced, he or she is too emotionally involved in the performance, is simply overwhelmed by emotion, and does not experience or receive the ritual correctly. By contrast, someone who is overdistanced is not emotionally involved enough. These concepts are relevant to both guests and producers, guests because they perform onstage for audiences, producers because they perform offstage for guests. Overdistancing makes producers appear phony and disingenuous, while underdistancing can leave them emotionally distraught and may even jeopardize their ability to work.

other aspects of the job, too burdensome or draining. Alex is a perfect example. He started at *Diana* as an associate producer but took a reduction in pay in order to do the audience warm-up act instead.

"I found producing too gut-wrenching," he admitted. "I just didn't have the thick skin or whatever it is other producers seem to have. I'll never forget this one show—this lady's child was abducted right out of the home. Her pain was so great that it tore me up into pieces and I had to walk out of the studio halfway through the show because I was so emotional."

Almost every producer I interviewed mentioned how odd they found the brief spurts of emotional intimacy with guests, how disconcerting to be so completely immersed and involved in another person's private world—often the most personal, intimate aspects of it—only to sever the connection once the guest leaves the studio. "They share so much of themselves with you," Susan observed. "It's weird how you develop a relationship so close to somebody and then it's just gone."

Of course, sometimes producers maintain a longer relationship with guests, especially if they believe that the person will prove a useful contact for future shows, and occasionally they will sustain the connection even when there is no professional gain to themselves. This was case for both Susan, who goes dancing now and then with a pair of brothers she met on a show about "Sexy Twins," and Ellen, who still converses on the phone every other Sunday with an elderly woman whose daughter died of anorexia. But, by and large, once the show is over, so is the relationship with guests. As Brian, another *Diana* producer, explained it, "Some guests really stay with you for a while, you want so badly for their lives to be better, and so you call, and you keep up—or they call you. But it's hard, you know. It's time-consuming—you just can't do that with every guest. You can't let yourself care about every single person."

I well understood Brian's point after months of transcribing the 800-line calls from viewers responding to plugs. At first, I found this work very disturbing. People—mostly women—would talk at length about getting divorced, being abandoned by spouses or lovers, losing a child to illness or accident, fighting with their in-laws, putting on weight that would not come off, or being cheated, duped, conned, or swindled. Sometimes the voices were bitter and complaining; sometimes they would crack with emotion, and the person would break down completely in the middle of a sentence. Often people would ignore the topic being plugged altogether and simply ask for things, as if talk shows were a kind of substitute social service or as if calling a talk show were like buying a weekly lottery ticket. And, while many of the requests were self-centered or unreasonable (a honeymoon cruise to Hawaii, a second face-lift and nose job, dinner at an expensive restaurant with Tom Cruise), sometimes all that people wanted were basic necessities: a working hot-water heater before the winter set in; a park where their children could play safely, removed from drug deals and gunfire; one day's respite from the constant demands of job and family.

Initially, listening to these calls day after day, I felt depressed, awash in an endless sea of despair and complaint that I hadn't the wherewithal to change. But it did not take long for the sense of helplessness to give way to indifference and even, at times, amusement. Like the other interns, I began to attend to the person's grammar and diction rather than the story itself, and, when one of us heard a particularly funny, horrific, or outrageous call, we would pass our headphones around so that the others could listen too. We began to keep a running list of "top-ten" calls, ranking people's stories like judges at a sporting event. At the time, it did not seem callous or cruel. It seemed the only way to stay sane and carry on with work.

Producers, too, recognize that their very survival on the job depends in part on distancing themselves from both the guests and their stories, no matter how sad, disturbing, or depressing. "It was really hard working with that mother whose daughter ran away from home," conceded Donna. "It's hard to prep a guest who doesn't know whether her daughter is living or dead—especially when doing this show is maybe her only shot at finding the girl. But, at the same time, you have to tell yourself, 'This is just one story; this stuff happens all the time.' I mean, you do what you can for the people you bring on the show, but you can't hold yourself personally responsible for the world's problems."

Of all the producers I interviewed, Tamara was perhaps the most conflicted about how to manage her own emotional involvement and where to draw the line with guests. When we spoke, she had just finished producing a reunion show titled "Why I Gave Up My Child." "Everybody had a hard-luck story, basically. Every person I interviewed cried, and I would hang up the phone and feel lousy. I just felt terrible. I was crying, too. I talked to like thirty people over the weekend, and I'm, like, 'I can't do this anymore. Why am I doing this?'"

"The thing is," she continued, "I could immediately tell who would be good on the show and who wouldn't, but, you know, when people tell you stories like that, you can't just blow them off. I mean, you have to talk to them. You have to be compassionate. But I also have to draw a line between being a human being and just doing my job because I can't get so emotionally involved and still do this."

I came to understand this tension myself, albeit on a smaller scale, when I helped produce "Teens with HIV." One of my tasks was to find a couple of mothers to sit in the audience and say a few words about losing a young son or daughter to AIDS. Through an organization called P-FLAG (Parents and Friends of Lesbians and Gays), I eventually found Molly and Liz, both women in their sixties. I talked with them at length on the phone, and they told me in loving detail about their sons who had recently died— gay men, politically active, and in their mid-thirties. Both women became tearful while we spoke. Clearly, the loss was still very raw for them. Yet, at the same time, they were eager for the opportunity to educate the public about AIDS and thus carry on their sons' political activism. Early in the development of the show, the producers were hungry for guests and thought that Molly and Liz might prove useful, especially since both women were well-spoken and displayed considerable emotion on the phone. Later on, however, after several main panelists were booked, the producers changed their minds and told me to cancel the two women—they wanted to keep the show focused on teenagers, and they already had enough "gay material." So I was in a position similar to the one described by Tamara. After establishing a relationship with these women, I couldn't, in her words, "just blow them off." I couldn't just say, "That's a real tearjerker, but, for our purposes, your son was too old when he died, and, besides that, he was gay." Making those calls to Molly and Liz was one of the hardest things I had to do as an intern.

These examples illustrate that, when producers deal with emotional topics, they must nurture a certain disjuncture or dissociation between feeling and the display of feeling, and the degree to which they succeed can be conceptualized in terms of surface and deep acting. As a precaution against burnout, experienced producers do what experienced flight attendants and salesmen do: they find a point along the continuum that allows them to maintain a clear separation of self from role, to define for themselves when their deep or surface acting is their own and when it is part of the commercial show. This is not to suggest that there is some real or authentic self that lies beneath acting, untouched by the performative requirements of social interaction. Rather, producers' capacity to handle the emotional exigencies of their work successfully depends on their *perception* of a difference between a real and an acting self, especially on shows like *Diana* where the line is tenuous and more difficult to draw.

The emotional labor required of producers in securing emotional displays from guests leaves them wondering two things: How much longer can I do this? and, *Should* I be doing this at all? For some producers, helping people is part of what makes the work worth it, but this is not always the outcome, even at a classy show like *Diana*, and producers sometimes question the ethical implications of putting ordinary people with all their problems and conflicts on television. Again, Tamara had something to say about this in relation to the reunion show. The show featured women who had given up their children for adoption thirty to forty years ago, and, when she was booking potential guests, Tamara was in contact either with mothers who wanted to find their children or with adult children who wanted to find their mothers. According to Tamara, the latter scenario meant trying to persuade the mother in question to come out of hiding because, in some cases, even the woman's own friends and family did not know that she had once given up a child for adoption.

"So here I was," Tamara said, "basically playing psychiatrist, saying, you know, 'This will be a really good thing for you, to be reunited with your child.' And you know what? I don't know if it's a good thing. I don't know the mental stability of these people I'm talking to. I really don't. But it was Sunday, and I had a show to tape on Tuesday, and I still had—you know, major things were not in place. So I was just, you know, really—"

She hesitated, and I finished her sentence—"in a tough spot."

"Yeah. Yeah. I mean, the show turned out *really* good, and the guests were pleased with it and everything. But it was hellish because I felt like, 'What am I doing here?' These are major, major dilemmas in people's lives that I'm playing with. You know, these are not minor problems."

Randy producers were even more likely to experience feelings of guilt and confront ethical questions about the legitimacy of their work. They generally did not have the luxury of believing, as *Diana* producers sometimes did, that they were helping guests resolve their problems or educating the public about an important issue. For Mark, this struggle was most pronounced when he first moved to *Randy* from another daytime talk show *not* oriented toward conflict. At that other show, he never experienced feelings of guilt, but, at *Randy*, things were different.

"The first show I did here," he said, "had to do with cheating or something like that. I went home that night and thought, 'Wow, we just ruined this guy's life.' You know, here he is, he finds out that his girlfriend is cheating on him, and he's just devastated. It was pretty heavy stuff. But then I'm thinking, you know, he's got to find out sooner or later. I mean, not that we're playing God or anything, but the guy does have a right to know his woman is sleeping around on him."

"But he doesn't necessarily need to find out on national television," I said.

"Right. But he was told, 'Your girlfriend has something she wants to tell you,' and, if he says, 'Is it good, or is it bad?' you say, 'I can't tell you that; it's going to be a surprise.'"

Clearly, producers find ways of coming to terms with aspects of the work that they find unethical or personally troublesome. Many acknowledge that there is a fine line between exploitation and ethical conduct, but the feeling is that, as long as they do not lie to a guest, as long as the guest knows the range of possibilities when a surprise or confrontation is involved, as long as the guest signs the consent form, they cannot be held responsible when guests become angry or upset with the outcome. Some producers, like Mark, said that it was better for people to know sooner rather than later about a transgression or an infidelity and that letting your anger out was preferable to holding it in. Others pointed out that, since guests are typically viewers responding to plugs, they know what the show is like and are not so easily duped or victimized. As Sandra said about *Randy*, "People watch our show, and they know it's about conflict, and yet they still come on." A former *Geraldo* staffer said much the same thing about that show: "Tricking a *Geraldo* guest into doing the show is like tricking someone into swimming. If they've ever seen water before, they know they're going to get wet." More or less successful at distancing themselves emotionally from guests and separating self from role, producers at trashy shows tend to deny personal accountability—not because they are atypically unfeeling or insensitive, but because the constraints of the workplace demand it. "You have to be able to go home at night and leave it all behind and not feel guilt; you have to be able to not take it personally," Tyler said. "If you feel guilty about anything you do here, you don't belong."

Doing What Comes Naturally: Class, Status, and Feeling

The emotional labor that producers expend behind the scenes—all the talking and persuading, the sympathizing and assuaging, the struggles with burnout, detachment, overinvolvement, and guilt—has a counterpart: the emotional performances of guests. These performances are the payoff for the show, and the emotion work that they require from guests is different in key ways from that performed by producers, quite apart from the fact that, unlike producers, guests do not do such emotion work for a living. While the emotional labor of producers is largely hidden from the public, directed toward others, and highly routinized, the performances of guests are visible and are (for the guests) anything but routine. Moreover, if, in the end, producers must nurture a certain dissociation between feeling and the display of feeling, a separation of an acting from a nonacting self, guests are asked to do precisely the opposite: to collapse the distinction between self and role. Guests are supposed to signify realness, ordinariness, and authenticity. At some point, all the instruction about how to feel must give way to real feeling. In effect, guests are supposed to do deep acting so deeply that they do not appear to be acting at all. Thus, if the art of deep acting enables us to make feelings into instruments that we can use, as Hochschild insists, then guests are being asked to master this art while disavowing its instrumentality. They are expected to *embody* emotion, not just perform it—or else perform it so well that audiences cannot tell the difference between the two.

There is a paradox here, however. Generally speaking, the more dramatic the money shot, the more acute the distinction between "being" and "performing" threatens to become for guests. Ironically, while the money shot is presumed to signify authenticity (the more emotional the outburst, the more real the guest), the demand for ever more volatile performances can lead to a level of exaggeration or caricature such that guests experience a sense of *inauthenticity*, or heightened distance, between self and role. In other words, increasing levels of sensationalism encourage even real guests to put on an act. At the same time, it opens up an opportunity space for the successful infiltration of fake guests. This is because exaggerated, larger-than-life portrayals are easier for amateurs to perform than are subtly drawn ones and also because assuming a false role is more easily done for highly personal topics (meddling mothers-in-law or cheating mates) than for more serious social issues (gay parenting or sexual harassment). In addition, the more bizarre or freakish the topic, the more difficult it is to find real people to talk about it, and the more pressure producers are under to look the other way when confronted with a suspicious (i.e., potentially fraudulent) situation. This was essentially the same dilemma faced at the turn of the twentieth century by freak-show exhibitors, who, over time and as competition increased, resorted to using "gaffs" rather than lose audiences to the more sensational exhibits of competing shows (Bogdan 1988).

But not all guests on the trashy end of the continuum are faking their stories. The majority are not. The genre's overall shift to more tabloid fare, part and parcel of the larger tabloid trend in news and current affairs, not only increased the infiltration of tricksters assuming the role of ordnary guests but also increased the participation of "just folks" who are ordinary in ways consistent with producers' need for heightened emotional expressiveness. In other words, it attracted largely working-class folks with modest incomes and educations, people who, for whatever reasons and in response to whatever persuasive arguments, are willing to bare it all on national television.

As I have emphasized, *Diana* prides itself on being a "nice" talk show, one of the few that remain in an era of intense competition for ratings. *Classy* is its niche identity, and it deliberately cultivates this identity by choosing certain kinds of topics and guests and by deliberately rejecting many of the practices that other shows embrace. Virtually every *Diana* producer made distinctions between *their* guests and those at shows like *Randy*; whereas *Diana* guests share their experiences about important social issues, "those guests" air their dirty laundry. Those other shows deal with the lowest common denominator, the lower class, the down-and-out, and the trailer trash. "Let's face it," Peggy said. "More educated people are less likely to vent their innermost insecurities on TV. You rarely see, like, an upscale *Jerry Springer* guest." Peggy's coworker Brian likewise described the guests on shows like *Randy* as "low class, trashy people" who were naturally inclined toward physical violence. In his words, "They're white trash, black trash, Hispanic—any kind of, like, lower-caliber people, poor people. Physical violence is such a routine part of their lives, they don't need much incentive to yell and scream and all that stuff. It's, like, they fight all the time, and they're half drunk, I don't think you'd even need to offer them money to do it."

The relation between class and emotional expressiveness here is built on the assumption that working- or lower-class people are "naturally" inclined to bicker and fight or disclose the intimate details of their lives. It is not the class status of guests per se that producers disdain; it is their willingness to display their private parts in public and to deliver a hard-core version of the money shot. This is what separates classy from trashy folks rather than simply social status, wealth, or education. At the same time, class and trash are easily conflated because the majority of guests producers see fighting with their in-laws or confronting an unfaithful mate *are* poor or working class. As Peggy said, you rarely see an upscale *Jerry Springer* guest.

The problem, however, is that producers believe that "those kind of people" are attracted to "that kind of display," rather than seeing "that kind of display" as partly an expression of the television industry's assumptions about "those kind of people." In other words, they see the displays themselves as a direct expression of class difference rather than one also mediated by the needs and dictates of the production process. In claiming that guests' behavior onstage is simply an extension of their behavior at home, producers conveniently fail to account for their own production efforts.

They are self-conscious about (and disdainful of) the lower-class status of certain guests, but they seem unaware of the role that the genre itself plays in constructing the lower class as something for which it is difficult to feel anything *but* disdain. Here is another similarity to carnival freak shows, for, as Thomson (1996) points out, often what made people freakish was not (or not only) their physical anomalies but rather the sexist, racist, or xenophobic presentation of their difference by promoters (see also Bogdan 1996).

Interestingly, producers are somewhat more careful about the class images that they construct when people of color are involved. *Randy*, for example, has an informal policy that prohibits producers from including more than one "minority story" per episode. That is, on any given *Randy* show, only one story—one set of guests out of the four or five sets used to illustrate a particular topic—can feature people of color. This is to avoid charges of racism, to avoid suggesting that it is mainly people of color who behave this way, thus contributing further to the problem of negative racial stereotyping in the media. As one *Randy* producer, who is white, said to me, "I would feel very irresponsible if the entire panel was black. You know, here one guest is a prostitute, another one is a pimp, another one is cheating on her lover, and another one has got six girlfriends—and they're all black." Doris, a former *Springer* producer, said that staffers there, too, made a conscious effort to limit the type of black guest allowed on the show and that she personally felt very strongly about this, being African American herself: "Not everybody who is black is a homeboy, you know. We're not all crack heads and dope dealers. Some of us are educated. And so I would tell people like that who called in, you know, I would tell 'em straight up, 'Listen, forget it. I am not bringing no Jherri Curl mouthful-of-gold-teeth dope-dealer pimp-daddy-lookin' type on this show."

This is no idle concern, for content analyses reveal that, along with women and young adults, African Americans are overrepresented on daytime talk shows compared to their overall numbers in the population. Whereas blacks make up 13 percent of the U.S. population and women 52 percent, these groups constitute 18 and 63 percent of talk-show guests, respectively (Greenberg and Smith 1995).[7] This is problematic insofar as talk shows target guests who are, or appear to be, lower class and thus

7. Whites have proportional representation on talks shows (constituting roughly 75 percent of both talk-show guests and the U.S. population as a whole), Latinos are underrepresented (constituting 5 percent of talk-show guests and 10 percent of the population), and Asian Americans are virtually absent. These figures come from Greenberg and Smith's (1995) content analysis of 111 episodes from the eleven top Nielsen-rated talk shows.

contribute to the common perception that blackness and poverty automatically go together. People of color in the United States *are* overrepresented among the poor, but commonsense understandings of race and class often exaggerate the relation, setting up a race-class binary where white equals middle class equals suburban, and black (and brown) equals lower class equals urban (see Bettie 1995). As Doris is well aware, not only does this formulation perpetuate negative stereotypes of African Americans, but it also renders invisible entire categories of people, including middle-class blacks like herself. Of course, in absolute terms, lower-class whites far outnumber blacks as talk-show guests, no doubt also out of proportion to their actual representation. But the category *poor white* (and its counterpart, *white trash*) does not evoke the same concern about negative racial typing because it is not the dominant representation of whiteness in the culture. It is an exception to the rule, running counter to the positive conflation of whiteness with wealth. Hence, images of white people acting trashy are less loaded, politically speaking, than are images of people of color acting trashy—at least in the eyes of media professionals.

The issue here is not the race or income level of guests per se but the relation of class and trash. ("They're white trash, black trash, Hispanic— any kind of, like, low-caliber people.") Producers do not, on the whole, give much thought to their own role in reproducing negative class stereotypes and have limited ways of thinking about the difference between guests at *Diana* and those at other shows. Nevertheless, they are right that a difference exists. While many of the *Diana* guests I spoke to both formally and informally had well-paying jobs and identified as middle class, *Randy* guests typically did not. Roughly one-third of the *Randy* guests I interviewed, for example, were on welfare, and all the rest but one had low-level service or retail jobs with annual incomes ranging from $10,000 to $30,000. On more than one occasion when I attempted to contact a guest a second or third time for additional information, I found that the telephone had been disconnected or was no longer in service. Two people did not have phones; one made all her calls from a neighbor's house, and the other used the phone at work (he was a server at McDonald's). While none of the producers or executives I spoke to could tell me of any industry research on the class status of talk-show guests, they uniformly agreed that ordinary guests on most shows tend to be "of a particular type."

"The trailer-park joke is not far from the truth," Saul Feldman told me. "Not that they necessarily live in trailer parks, but a lot of these people lead very transient lives. I would say [their education level] is high school for the most part, people who are semiskilled. It's the crowd that would have been on an assembly line in a major manufacturing plant before all those jobs disappeared. It's a particular type because it satisfies—because we watch these things and it's almost like, 'Gee, at least I'm not that bad off.'"

Producers at *Randy* agreed that the majority of their guests were lower class, employed in either blue-collar or service jobs, if they were employed at all. According to Mark, those who do work typically have to get permission from their boss to take time off, or they have to find someone to cover their shift. "So you figure they're working at a store or a restaurant or something like that. You know, I haven't talked to an engineer yet." Carmen likewise acknowledged, "It's true, we're not getting the CEO of some major company and his wife talking about, like, their affairs." She shifted in her chair and lit another cigarette. "A lot of our guests are not necessarily working during the day, and usually they do have, uh, lower incomes." But, she added, a person's lack of material wealth should not determine their value or worth, any more than their taste in clothes or their perceived level of physical attractiveness. "I don't think it's a fair judgment to say, like, 'Oh, they all live in trailer parks, they're white trash,' or, 'How tacky, she's got dyed blonde hair, and he's got no teeth.' Well, maybe they can't afford it, these people, you know, all of them don't go to the dentist regularly, they don't go shopping at Saks Fifth Avenue, but their concerns are still the same as anyone else's."

Their concerns are the same as anyone else's. Strictly speaking, of course, this is not true since poor people have many concerns that rich people do not, and vice versa. But Carmen's point is well taken in that producers do not deliberately seek out working-class guests; they seek out people who are deviant or transgressive, are suffering heartache and tragedy, or are experiencing problems or conflicts. Middle- and upper-class folks too are frequently deviant and transgressive, experience heartache and tragedy, and have problems and conflicts. They are simply more reluctant to reveal these aspects of their lives on national television, and this reluctance is part of what constitutes their upper class–ness. So, by choosing certain kinds of topics and particular ways of framing them, talk shows create a natural constituency of potential guests who just "happen" to be lower class. As Tyler said about her work at *Jerry Springer*, "We have a viewer-based show, so, in terms of booking guests, we can only deal with what comes in to us over the [phone lines]. We don't have a huge spectrum to work with, you know. We don't get wealthy people calling us up to get on the show. We have to take what comes in to us and go from there."

As we leave the world of producers and enter the world of guests, it is important to remember that "going from there" involves a process of transformation, the transformation of ordinary people (the "raw" materials) into ordinary guests (the "cooked" product). It is also important to remember that the mandate to emphasize personal experience and emotional expressiveness on daytime talk shows has implications not only for the ordinary guest but for the expert guest as well. This mandate both changes the nature of expert participation and further increases the marginal status of expert guests within the genre. Experts generally do not want to do emotion work or discuss their private lives on television. Their expertise is in part predicated on bracketing off emotion and personal experience, on having a more distanced and abstract relation to knowledge. Even emotion experts such as professional psychologists or therapists—the most ubiquitous category of expert on talk shows—are emotion *managers* rather than emotion *expressors*. Like producers, they manage and make sense of the emotions of guests from a position of professional distance; as a general rule, they do not get teary eyed or angry themselves. Thus, as talk shows became increasingly focused on issues of sexual intimacy and on emotional and physical expressiveness, they became less and less hospitable to the exercise of professional expertise, especially academic or intellectual expertise. This is but a more extreme version of the structural opposition between academics and television more generally. Television has been aptly dubbed *the feeling medium*, but the last thing that most intellectuals want to do on TV is feel.

I wanted to be able to speak out, to talk a little bit about the injustice that had taken place. Because basically my boyfriend—you know, he seemed so wonderful, Prince Charming, nobody could believe he beat up his girlfriend. It was the whole typical abusive situation. And if I was going to be involved in this issue of, uh, battered women's syndrome, then why not? [Daytime talk] would be a good arena for me to get into, even though I didn't really have any experience with it.

—NANCY, guest on *Diana* ("Abusive Relationships")

I went on the show because my girlfriend said, "If you get national attention to your case, maybe your sister will leave you alone." Because my sister kept kidnapping my daughter, and my daughter would go willingly 'cause she had lots of money to lure her with. My daughter was constantly disappearing, and my sister was always behind it, and I almost went crazy. At that time, my daughter was very much against me and secretive and trying to play my sister and I against one another, to manipulate things so she could get what she wanted. And before that she was in two foster homes—so it was a big mess.

—ANITRA, guest on *Jenny Jones* ("Dysfunctional Families")

I go on talk shows for the practice, basically. Because I want to be an actor. . . . You know, what am I going to do, start out as an extra? Be in the background of some scene for, like, five seconds? Forget it. I'd rather be right in front, in everyone's living room, primetime three o'clock. I've been on all the three-o'clock shows.

—TONY WEST, a fake guest on multiple daytime talk shows

CHAPTER FIVE

The Other Side of the Camera:
Motives and Misgivings

When friends and colleagues learned that I was studying daytime talk shows, invariably one of the first questions they asked was, "Why do people go on those shows?" As the epigraphs to this chapter make clear, there are various reasons for appearing on a daytime talk show, depending on the topic, and depending on the guest. What is less clear are the ways in which the motivations themselves are embedded in a larger web of interpersonal and social relations and how talk shows can serve as a vehicle for accomplishing a diverse range of goals and desires.

Up to now, I have discussed the production of talk shows largely from the perspective of producers and their work behind the scenes. Here, I shift ground and discuss the process from the perspective of guests, focusing not only on their motivations for participating but also on their experiences on- and offstage, their struggles with producers (and other guests), and, most important perhaps, their confrontation with the norms and conventions of the production process. I focus on ordinary people in this chapter and the next, while in chapter 7 I examine the experiences of experts. Both categories of guest orient toward the genre differently than do producers, and, just as producers sometimes find guests and their concerns to be a source of anger, amusement, frustration, or contempt, guests may feel the same way about producers and the production process itself. They come to the situation with their own set of expectations about how the show works, what it can do for them, and what their emotional labor is really all about.

During the year that I interned at *Diana* and the three months that I spent at *Randy*, I was able to meet and talk with countless guests, both expert and ordinary. At *Diana*, especially, there were opportunities for informal conversation since one of my jobs was to assist Heidi, the talent coordinator, on the set during tapings. This meant greeting guests on their arrival, showing them to their dressing rooms and the green room, getting them food and coffee or tea, and generally seeing to their needs. My access to *Randy* guests was more limited because I spent less time at *Randy*, because intern duties are structured differently there, and because the show's focus on surprises and confrontations makes for a more chaotic atmosphere backstage, with less time for developing personal relationships. After tapings were over, however, I would sometimes run into guests at the hotel directly across the street from the studio. Many guests stayed there, and this was where I often took breaks from work or went for a bite to eat at the end of the day. If I saw participants from the show pass through the lobby or restaurant, I would approach them to explain my research and either speak with them there or arrange a conversation over the phone at some later date.

Although my selection of guests was determined largely by my access to them rather than a scientific sampling procedure, in the end the thirty with whom I conducted formal interviews reflected the larger population of talk-show guests fairly closely: 70 percent were female, 80 percent white, 10 percent African American, and 5 percent Latino; roughly half were under age thirty, half over.[1] My discussion of these guests is hardly exhaustive.

1. In a content analysis of 111 episodes from the eleven top Nielsen-rated talk shows, Greenberg and Smith (1995) found that 63 percent of the guests were female, 61 percent were under thirty years of age, 75 percent were white, 18 percent were African American, and 5 percent were Hispanic. The authors report that the demographic profile of

Rather, I relate key dimensions of their stories, actions, and experiences and, in the process, paint a portrait of talk-show guests that is, I hope, richer and more complex than the one provided by the shows themselves.

Second Thoughts: Misgivings and Motivations

Every single one of the guests I met had a problem, crisis, or conflict that producers believed would make for a compelling show. In most cases, the guests thought so too because most entered the talk-show arena by responding to plugs or by being recruited by someone who had responded to a plug. The rest tended to enter through the two other major conduits for recruiting guests: other media and established groups and organizations. Katherine was one of the few guests who was recruited not through a plug, a media source, or an established organization but rather through a producer's informal network of contacts. She and her friend Marie went on *Ricki Lake* because Marie knew a producer there who called one day in a panic looking for attractive female guests to be on a show titled "I Can't Live without a Man!" Marie then approached Katherine, and the two agreed to be guests largely as a favor to the producer.

Few of the guests I interviewed had prior experience on a talk show or any other form of media, although some had done, or were slated to do, "updates" (in which the show revisits the same topic with the same guests in order to track their "progress"). Several *Diana* guests did not even watch talk shows. By and large, ordinary guests who did have extensive media experience either were aspiring actors using talk shows as a way of breaking into the entertainment industry or were involved in unusual stories that had been picked up by the larger news community. Thus, Charlotte, a *Diana* guest, also appeared on *Montel Williams* and *Geraldo* as well as a host of other news and current-affairs programs because her husband was apprehended by the police for bigamy. The only nonexpert guest I interviewed with more talk-show appearances than Charlotte was Tony West, an entertainer, musician, and aspiring actor living in West Hollywood. He and his girlfriend went on seven different daytime talk shows in order to get on-camera acting experience.

---

talk-show guests mirrors that of talk-show viewers and loosely approximates the actual U.S. population, which is 52 percent female, 74 percent white, 12 percent African American, and 10 percent Hispanic. Compared to their numbers in the actual population, women and African Americans are overrepresented on daytime talk shows, while Hispanics are underrepresented (Asian Americans are virtually absent on daytime talk shows).

Given the relative inexperience of most guests, and given the reputation of the genre, I made a point of asking guests whether they had misgivings or reservations about appearing on a daytime talk show. *Diana* guests often said that they had no reservations about *that* show but that they would not have gone on most others, and this was consistent with what I heard in countless informal conversations with *Diana* guests backstage. Cora, for one, was grateful that *Diana* was "not like *Ricki Lake* and all them trashy shows with all those people causing a bunch of heartache and cussin' each other out." Likewise, Fran, a guest on an *Oprah* show about con artists, said she was nervous about appearing on national television but trusted Oprah "not to do anything sleazy." Charlotte had no qualms about going on *Montel* or the other shows to talk about having been duped by a bigamist. She felt wronged and saw the media as a way to turn a bad situation to her advantage. A number of *Randy* guests—Jack, Sharon, Lori, and Joanne among them—also said that they had few or no reservations or misgivings, as did Jordan, a *Jerry Springer* guest.

Some guests did have specific concerns and hesitations, however. Helen, the date-rape survivor on *Diana*, said that her first instinct was to decline the invitation to participate because she had never watched *Diana* and thought talk shows were "really cheesy" and "manipulative." Nancy, who had been abused and raped by her boyfriend, appeared on a *Diana* show about athletes and domestic violence. Her concerns were primarily family related, as her parents were prominent citizens in a small town and were still dealing with the emotional aftermath of her rape trial. Bonnie, invited on *Diana* (and later *Jenny Jones*) to talk about her near-death experience, was afraid that the show would mock the notion of paranormal phenomena and trivialize her story. Vince, arrested for bigamy, was concerned that his talk-show appearances might hurt rather than help his pending legal case. Sonny was apprehensive about accompanying her daughter on a *Jerry Springer* show about teen prostitution because she knew that the show could get "pretty wild" and that Jordan was hot tempered and easily provoked. Pam, a *Randy* guest, said that most of her concerns stemmed from the fact that producers were evasive on the phone, giving her only vague information about the topic, the other guests, and the nature of her own participation. At the time, Pam was addicted to drugs and in an abusive relationship; the show was titled "My Mom Needs Help!" and featured Pam, her ex-husband, her abusive boyfriend, and two of her six children. Barb, a *Randy* guest who was confronting her ex-boyfriend about his past infidelities, said that she was afraid that he would make her angry enough to lose control and start swearing, or worse, and that this would embarrass her mother and set a bad example for her four-year-old son.

Despite their misgivings, guests participate because they have accompanying motivations and desires that supersede their concerns. Many of the guests I met over the course of my fieldwork fit the typology constructed by Patricia Priest (1995) in her analysis of thirty guests from the *Donahue* show. Focusing specifically on "sexual deviants" (individuals positioned as sexually different or marginal in some way), she identified four different categories of guests. "Evangelicals" were motivated by the twin desires to educate a national audience about discrimination and to communicate to others in a similar situation that they were not alone (guests here might include transsexuals, gay men who adopt children, or couples who practice group sex). "Moths" are guests who are attracted to the razzle-dazzle of the television industry and yearn for their fifteen minutes of fame. "Plaintiffs" are guests who step forward to plead their case against someone who has victimized them. "Marketers" are those who seize the chance to publicize a book or hawk a business venture.

Not everyone I interviewed fit this typology—in part because I examined a wider range of guests across a wider range of shows. Also, guests' motivations are typically mixed, their decision to participate the result of multiple influences. Some guests find it difficult to articulate a clear motivation; others find that their reasons shift or change over time. Reasons can be somewhat capricious or tangential to the topic, as when Charlotte chose *Montel* among all the shows competing for her story because she had a "crush" on the host, or they can be more clearly calculated, as when Vince, Charlotte's ex-husband, agreed to appear on the same show because he wanted to counter the negative portrait that he knew Charlotte and the other wives would paint of him. Guests may feel very strongly about participating, or they may give in to the persuasive arguments of a producer, family member, or friend—either because they are reluctant to disappoint someone close to them or because the arguments employed resonate at some level with their own beliefs and inclinations.

On classy shows like *Diana*, the reasons most commonly cited by guests and the arguments most commonly used to persuade them are both linked to agendas for advocacy or education rather than self-promotion or personal gain. Helen, for example, was persuaded to go on *Diana* to talk about date rape by the director of the women's center at her college. A producer had initially contacted the director, and the director in turn phoned Helen, insisting that the show would be a good opportunity for Helen to "get the word out" about rape-education policies on campus. Helen discovered that public universities receiving federal funding were required by law to follow certain guidelines about rape education and prevention but that many—her own included—were *not* in compliance. "And so this was my big campaign," Helen told me, "blowing the whistle on university officials and getting them moving on fixing that." Since Helen herself had never watched *Diana*, she asked some of her friends about the show, and one of them assured her that it was "up there among the noncheesy ones." This helped reassure her, although, in the end, it was the director of the center who convinced her to go on the show.

Jane was persuaded by a similar sort of argument when she expressed hesitation about participating on a *Diana* show about child-custody battles. She was contacted by a producer through an organization called the Family Equity Coalition and went on the show hoping both to educate other women about the gender inequities of child-custody law and to publicize her specific case (at the time, she was trying to raise money for her legal expenses). In her initial preinterview, the producer emphasized all the people who would be touched by Jane's story and insisted that Jane had a "moral obligation" to warn other women that "even smart people can get screwed over by the legal system." "She appealed to me in a way that really made sense to me," Jane said. "Because, before this happened to me, I never in my wildest dreams would have imagined it was possible." Nancy, too, saw the *Diana* show as an opportunity to educate the public—in her case, about domestic violence. She had been abused by a high-profile athlete, and producers knew of her because the story had already been covered by *Sports Illustrated*. "Battered women's syndrome is something I feel strongly about," she told me, "and, if I was going to be involved in this issue, then why not? I mean, I figured this would be a good arena for me to get into."

Some guests, then—those motivated by a desire to educate the public or champion a social issue—are like the "evangelicals" described by Priest (1995). They have been galvanized or politicized by a particular experience, have acquired a certain amount of knowledge and expertise in the process, and are invested in passing that knowledge on to others. Such guests often have expectations much like those of experts and actually function on a show much as experts do. They prioritize the transmission over ritual model of communication (see Carey 1989), seeing talk shows as a unique opportunity to educate people on a mass scale otherwise not available to them. Of course, for a certain subset of these guests—those whose personal experience with an issue has led them to write a book or start a business—the desire for public advocacy or education can dovetail nicely with what is more clearly an agenda of self-promotion. Thus, Bonnie went on *Diana* (and two other talk shows), partly to enlighten others about paranormal phenomena, but also to promote her book about near-death experience, while Rodney, a female-to-male transsexual, went on *Diana* with his wife and three children both to discuss the challenges of being transsexual in a heterosexual society and to publicize his book about transsexual families. Such guests were relatively uncommon at *Diana* since writing books was an activity associated primarily with experts (ordinary people do not seem so ordinary if they are also published authors). Exceptions were permitted if producers wanted the guest badly enough, if the book was autobiographical rather than academic, and if the book was merely mentioned rather than foregrounded in the discussion.

When guests appear on shows that are more purely personal in nature, they have different motivations and are persuaded by different sorts of arguments. Those who respond directly to a solicitation or plug are essentially volunteering to participate; they tend to be more strongly invested in the topic and generally do not require much convincing. In fact, such guests sometimes make a sales pitch to the producer rather than the other way around. Tony, the aspiring actor, represents the extreme case since persuading producers to put him on TV became something of a part-time job for him. Other guests had more legitimate reasons for responding to plugs. Fran went on an *Oprah* show about con artists because she and her husband had been the victims of a scam. She was a "plaintiff," wanting to expose on national television the two men who had swindled her—both to keep them from victimizing others and to increase the chances that the police would apprehend them. Cora went on a *Diana* show titled "Secret Loves" because her husband had recently had an affair. Like many other *Diana* guests, she thought that her story might benefit others in the same boat; specifically, she wanted to let people know that an affair does not necessarily mean the end of a marriage. "I'm a Christian, God-fearing woman," she told me, "and there's so many marriages breakin' up over the least little thing. You know, he stepped on my shoe, so we's gettin' a divorce." Cora said that going on the show helped her regain a sense of humor and put the affair in perspective; she targeted *Diana* among all the other talk shows because she was a fan and wanted to meet the host in person.

By contrast, Anitra, a single mother living on welfare, responded to a *Jenny Jones* plug about family feuds and went on the show hoping to achieve closure on a long-standing conflict with her two sisters. The sisters believed her to be an incompetent mother, and one of them had repeatedly (although unsuccessfully) tried to obtain legal custody of Anitra's daughter after Anitra's boyfriend molested the girl. Anitra wanted her sisters to "butt out" of her life once and for all and was hoping that national attention to her case would scare them off. Nineteen-year-old Jordan called *Jerry Springer* in response to a plug about teen prostitution. On the streets since the age of thirteen, her motivation was to "make a clean start in life," and she believed that national media exposure (as well as the $100 stipend offered by producers) would help her achieve that goal. Barb, a self-described daredevil, went on *Randy* to confront her ex-boyfriend largely out of curiosity about the show and because she thought that appearing on national television would be an exciting and memorable experience. Wayne and Britanny went on a *Montel* show about hypnotism also largely out of curiosity (Wayne was, in fact, writing a paper about talk shows for a college class and wanted the inside scoop). Lori went on *Randy* to publicly humiliate her meddlesome sister-in-law, a trashy reason pure and simple, although, when she initially called the show, she never expected her sister-in-law to agree to participate. Joanne also went on *Randy* to confront and shame another woman, a guest whom she had seen on a previous *Randy* episode.

For topics involving romantic or family conflict, guests who respond to plugs then help producers secure other individuals connected to the story. These other individuals can be either easier or more difficult to persuade, depending on their relationship with the guest who initially phoned in, the nature of the topic, and what they hope to gain from participating. Jordan (the *Springer* guest) was particularly successful in her recruitment efforts. She convinced her mother, her uncle Casey, her sixty-four-year-old boyfriend (allegedly her pimp), and several other family members to accompany her on the show. The stated purpose was to stage a confrontation between the mother and the boyfriend and to encourage Jordan to get off the streets. Yet all those involved had their own reasons for going along. The mother, Sonny, knew that Jordan was "hell-bent on going" and needed supervision; she was also attracted by the free trip to Chicago. Sonny told me that Casey, a bisexual man known to work occasionally as a prostitute himself, saw the trip primarily as an opportunity to earn some extra money turning tricks. The elderly boyfriend—who, not surprisingly, got cold feet and skipped town the morning of the taping—reportedly went along to ensure that Jordan did not run off with somebody else. There was also something attractive about being on TV for both Sonny and Casey since they returned to Chicago a few months later for a second show about "love triangles."

Ramón, twenty-eight, and his legal ward, Cheri, fifteen, were likewise contacted by a family member: Cheri's mother, April, who had responded to a *Sally Jessy* plug about mother-daughter conflicts. As the temporary guardian waiting to be awarded permanent custody of Cheri, Ramón felt obligated to accompany the girl to the taping. Cheri watched talk shows regularly and had aspirations of being a model or an actress and, therefore, did not need much convincing to go on television, even though it seemed likely that her mother would be positioned as the victim in their stormy relationship (the show was titled "My Daughter's Out of Control!"). According to Ramón, producers made a point of emphasizing in their conversations with Cheri that many young women previously on the show had been noticed by agents and talent scouts and had gone on to successful modeling careers. Ramón himself was highly reluctant to let Cheri go. He and the mother were not on good terms, and he suspected that she would use the show to discredit publicly his bid for permanent guardianship by casting him as a pervert or pedophile—which, as it turned out, she attempted to do. For her part, April saw the trip to New York as a sort of "mother-daughter reunion" that Ramón's presence threatened to ruin. According to Ramón, "[April] was hoping the show would bring her and Cheri closer together because they can't be in the same room together for more than an hour without fighting."

Even very young children can be involved in the recruitment process, as when Pam and Len were persuaded to go on *Randy* by two of their children, aged eleven and six. The kids wanted to confront their mother about her lifestyle and persuade her to pursue counseling (they had seen siblings do a similar thing on *Montel*). Pam said that, despite her apprehensions, she ultimately agreed to do the show in order to prove to her children that she loved them and was serious about getting help. As Pam put it, "The [producer] kept telling me that it was important to my kids, so I went, even though I was scared to. I mean, everyone, *everyone* was telling me that I'm crazy for doing it." Pam admitted that the free trip was another attraction since she and her boyfriend had been wanting to take a vacation together but did not have the money. "We'd been talking about going somewhere for a long time, so the timing was perfect. I knew that it might be humiliating for me, but I was pretty excited about going." For Pam's ex-husband, Len, a shy, reserved man, the show served as a kind of ultimatum to Pam to "clean up her act." If she did not, he would revoke her visitation rights. "Like I explained to the kids, I don't ever want to cut their mamma's visitation off, but if I have to, to keep them from seein' violence and drugs, then that's what I'm going to do. So going on the show was kind of a last resort."

People thus have their reasons for going on a talk show, even when they have only vague knowledge about the topic, and even if they suspect that they will be subject to a potentially hostile or humiliating confrontation. In fact, as producers are well aware, the more acrimonious the underlying conflict, the greater the desire to participate. Happily married couples, sisters-in-law who get along, divorcing parents who negotiate amicable custody arrangements—such folks are not typically interested in appearing on a talk show, certainly not a trashy one like *Randy*. Nor are *Randy* producers particularly interested in having them on. Rather, producers are interested in guests like Winona, a recovering alcoholic whose two daughters had accused her of child abuse. Winona felt strongly that she had never received a fair hearing in the matter, so telling her side of the story was one motivation for participating. She also hoped that the show would lead to a reconciliation of sorts—despite the fact that she had had only negative contact with the two girls in recent years, that she had just reported the older daughter, Tiffany, to the police (ironically, alleging that Tiffany was abusing her own child), and that she was under court order not to see the other daughter at all. (It was Tiffany who played ringleader here, securing the participation of the others, and it was she, not the producer, who led Winona to believe that reconciliation was a possible outcome.) Not surprisingly, the two siblings had a very different agenda in mind for the show, and, as it turned out, their version of events held sway. So enthusiastic and venomous was their joint denunciation of Winona onstage that producers later decided to drop the other story in the lineup and devote the entire hour to the three women alone. (In theory, this other story should have been equally dramatic since it featured a confrontation between a mother and her oldest son, who had been convicted for sexually molesting his younger brother. But the performance lacked raw emotion. For one thing, a version of the story had been told before, when the entire family appeared on a different program two years earlier. Moreover, Jack, the child-molesting son, did not deny that he had done something wrong, and so his attitude was apologetic and conciliatory rather than antagonistic. In fact, he did the show primarily to placate his mother, who wanted very much to go on television.)

Claims to Fame

These examples reinforce several points made in earlier chapters. One is that producers are clearly intervening in some messy and intractable interpersonal conflicts. Legal battles seem especially well represented here, indicating both the general tendency of the media to emphasize dissension and the more specific tendency of guests to use talk shows as a secondary or default forum for airing, if not resolving, their disputes. A second, related, point is that, when booking conflict-based shows, producers get considerable help from the individual who calls in response to an on-air plug. This person can be more effective than producers are in recruiting other guests because he or she already shares a personal bond with them and may know better how to allay their fears or misgivings, play on their weaknesses or insecurities, or goad them into a confrontation (hence the policy among *Springer* producers of ditching a story immediately if the original caller is reluctant to help out).

Another, less obvious point is that, regardless of how guests are recruited, and regardless of whether they are motivated by a desire to educate the public or to seek revenge, it is difficult to know whether guests had certain motivations for participating prior to speaking with producers or whether guests *let* themselves be persuaded, adopting the reasons provided by producers (or other interested parties). Where did Pam get the idea that going on *Randy* to be confronted by her kids would prove to them that she loved them? Where did April get the notion that castigating her daughter on *Sally Jessy* would bring them closer together? How did Nancy come to conclude that she had an obligation to warn other women about the inequities of child-custody laws? Did Jordan really believe that a one-hour appearance on *Jerry Springer* would effectively end a life of prostitution? Why did Vince think that going on daytime talk shows would help rather than hurt his pending legal case?

My conversation with Vince illustrates particularly well the ways in which producers, sensing a guest's initial inclinations, come to articulate arguments that guests subsequently make their own. Vince, awaiting sentencing on charges of bigamy when he went on *Montel*, told me that he required half a dozen conversations with producers before finally agreeing to do the show. When I asked how producers successfully allayed his misgivings, he said, "The main incentive they had was the fact that I was facing trial, and this was an opportunity for me to spin a positive light on myself and maybe generate some public opinion in my favor, and hopefully it would fare well for me at the pending trial. That was the main carrot out there."

Vince then said that he chose *Montel* over other shows because one of the producers there came at him with "the brother angle," insisting that, because Montel was a black man like Vince, he would not allow Vince to be "lynched" onstage. Yet this was something that Vince himself had already considered, and "the brother angle" was why, when bombarded with dozens of phone calls from journalists and producers across the country, he phoned *Montel* producers back first.

At bottom, few guests who really do *not* want to go on television can be persuaded to do so, yet people need credible ways of explaining their desire. The creation of a justificatory framework for guests' participation does not necessarily originate with producers; producers also learn from guests which persuasive arguments work best and then use these arguments in subsequent interactions. This process of mutual elaboration was clearly at work in the way both producers and guests would insist that it was better to voice your problems and show your feelings than to keep them bottled up inside—a notion so taken for granted among guests that most could not explain to me why they believed it.

This belief in turn is related to an aspect of guests' participation that has consistently confounded critics: why people choose to reveal sensitive or potentially embarrassing information in a public rather than a private forum. I routinely overheard producers at *Randy* (and, less commonly, those at *Diana*) say to guests over the phone, "Trust me, it will be easier to tell so-and-so about such-and-such here than at home," and it was not an explanation that they conjured out of thin air. Guests would also say that they felt "safer" taking their personal conflicts on national television, that there was something about the public nature of the forum that they found comforting or attractive. As one *Diana* producer explained it, "I used to think, 'How can you do this on television?' But a lot of people say it's easier to do it in a public venue, it's easier because it's not as intimate, they're not sitting across the dining-room table from their husband, they're sitting next to him with Diana. You know, you argue with someone day after day over the same issue in the same room with the same sights and sounds and smells, and it goes nowhere. But, on a talk show, maybe there's more room for exchange." In addition to finding the public nature of the forum easier, some guests feel that it ensures that they follow through with a disclosure ("I'd never do it on my own, but now I'm getting forced to tell, and I needed that push") and at the same time provides a certain measure of safety in the event that the other party "flips out" or loses control.

There is no contesting the frequency with which guests (and pro-ducers) employ these sorts of arguments. But, after a year at *Diana* and three months at *Randy*, I came to view them with some skepticism. In fact, I came to view them as a kind of cover story to mask less "legitimate" mo-tivations. For one thing, there are obvious holes in the logic. No one ever mentions, for example, what happens to guests once they go back home. Guests might feel safer onstage, with the host and audience looking on, muscle-bound security guards in the wings, but their conflicts with other guests do not necessarily end with the show. The *Jenny Jones* murder is strong evidence of this. Nor does the injunction to tell all consider the fact that, if knowledge is a form of power, secrecy is not always bad or self-disclosure automatically liberating; depending on the circumstances, get-ting something off your chest might actually be a disempowering rather than an empowering move (see Tavris 1989; Heaton and Wilson 1995). Credible therapeutic practice aimed at catharsis or confrontation is quite different from what happens on daytime talk shows, for if productive ways of managing conflict and anger are not also part of the conversation, talk-ing about a problem can actually make it worse—an outcome that produc-ers and guests alike conveniently overlook. More generally, the model of therapeutic intervention promoted on daytime talk shows mistakenly pre-sumes that knowledge informs conduct, that simply disclosing a problem or providing information about it will make a positive difference in guests' lives (see Heaton and Wilson 1995).

The point here is not to second-guess people and suggest that their reasons for participating come from elsewhere and thus are not authentic or real. Nor is it to suggest that guests are particularly gullible individu-als, more vulnerable to the persuasive efforts of producers than people nor-mally ought to be. It is to suggest, however, that guests' motivations are not always or only their own, that guests may hold multiple motivations simul-taneously, and that, to the extent that justificatory frameworks are mutu-ally elaborated by producers and guests, both sets of players are invested in promoting (to themselves as well as to one another) explanations that ap-pear rational, sensible, or legitimate. In the case of serious topics that have potential educational value, guests tend to hold motivations—and have ways of talking about their motivations—that are by definition legitimate because they are comparable to those of professional experts. But what about the guest who is spiteful and seeks revenge, who responds to the lure of a paid vacation, or who is "moth-like" and simply wants to be seen on TV? When the desire for television exposure is partly what stigmatizes ordinary guests as trashy and debased, such guests may well learn—with or without the help of producers—to couch their desires in more acceptable terms. Consequently, while some guests surely believe that disclosure has therapeutic benefits and that taking your problems on television will help solve them, others—especially those on conflict-based shows—accept and use these explanations largely because they carry greater legitimacy than simply admitting, "I want to humiliate my mother-in-law," "I want a free vacation," or "I want to be on TV."

The degree to which wanting a free vacation or desiring media celebrity is perceived by guests to be a trashy motivation is evident in their tendency to attribute these motivations to other participants, particularly those they dislike or do not respect. Joanne, for example, had this to say about the woman she confronted on *Randy:* "I'll tell you why that woman went on. It was a free vacation for her and her kids. 'Cause she didn't have any money. I heard her talking to the other guests afterwards, you know, saying she couldn't afford to buy a drink on the plane, she wanted one but couldn't pay for it. The woman obviously has nothing." When I asked Lori why she thought that her sister-in-law agreed to go on *Randy* to be confronted, she replied, "Probably because it's television. She likes to be in the limelight. She likes to be the center of attention all the time. So it probably made her feel big." Likewise, Barb assumed that her ex-boyfriend was motivated to appear on *Randy* because "he's an attention getter." As she put it, "He wants to have everything focused on him. I found this out when I was dating him. All the attention has to be on him. And, by going on the show, the whole world was paying attention to him." When Vince and his wives appeared on *Montel,* he was asked repeatedly by the host and members of the studio audience why he married more than one woman at a time. Vince himself was evasive, but the wives were quick to point out that he did it largely for the celebrity: his arrest had garnered him a possible book deal and movie contract. Wife 2 actually called him a "media whore" at one point during the show. Talking with me later on the phone, Charlotte (Wife 3) compared Vince to superstar Michael Jackson because he got so much attention from the media: "He was always holdin' these press conferences, you know. He could snap his fingers, and they would run to him like he was Michael Jackson."

Although they may not always admit it, some guests clearly do desire free vacations or media attention—otherwise, these elements would not figure as prominently as they do in producers' repertoire of persuasive arguments. ("The vast majority of people who call in, I mean, we're lucky if they've ever been on a plane before, you know, so they're anxious to come here and stay in a hotel and all that.") Even *Diana* producers cited the travel and exposure as key motives for many of their guests. As one staffer there put it, "A lot of people don't have a lot of money. Life for them is going to the market and raising the kids. So it's just the plain old excitement of coming to a big city and being on TV." Guests give off subtle cues, both backstage and in phone conversations, that reveal their excitement about being on national television: they fuss over their clothes and makeup, they telephone producers two and three times a week wanting to know when their show will air, and, on the big day, they gather with friends and family members to watch. Talk shows afford people the opportunity to try on celebrity status, to travel in style, to explore previously untapped performative talent, even to fantasize about launching professional modeling or acting careers. This is most obvious in the case of struggling actors like Tony, but real ordinary guests welcome these opportunities as well.

Of all the real guests I interviewed, Charlotte was the most explicit about enjoying, and deliberately seeking, media celebrity—despite her contempt for Vince for exhibiting the very same desire. She justified this seeming inconsistency by noting that, whereas he broke the law in an attempt to garner notoriety, she was a victim simply trying to make the most of a bad situation. Once Vince was apprehended by police and his bigamous conduct became news, Charlotte found herself in the eye of a media storm. The story was covered by both tabloid and mainstream media, at both the local and the national levels. Her television appearances included *Inside Edition*, *Good Morning America*, *Geraldo*, *Montel*, and *Diana*, and she also gave interviews to the *National Enquirer*, *Good Housekeeping*, and *Marie Claire* as well as to dozens of local news outlets, print and television. She said that TV reporters even started showing up at the credit union where she worked: "It got to the point where all these media people were coming to my house and my job. My godmother was in the grocery store shoppin' with her daughter, and she sees me on the front cover of *Good Housekeeping*. It was all happening at one time, you know; the phone was ringin' off the hook. I'm gettin' bags under my eyes, I was flyin' here, flyin' there. . . . It was like Lorena Bobbitt," she added, referring to the woman who, some years back, made national headlines when she cut off her husband's penis with a kitchen knife.

Actually, in terms of her engagement with the media, Charlotte was more like John Wayne Bobbitt, Lorena's husband, who also went on the talk-show circuit in the hopes of profiting from his misfortune. (Lorena herself studiously avoided the media.) For Charlotte, as for John Bobbitt, financial gain was surely part of the attraction. Charlotte got paid handsomely for giving exclusives to *Inside Edition* and the *National Enquirer*, and she hinted that the daytime talk shows paid her as well. On top of that, of course, she flew first class, stayed in fancy hotels, and rode around in limousines. Money was only part of the story, however. Then twenty-four years old and still living in the same house in the same working-class black neighborhood where she was raised by her grandparents, she clearly found all the attention gratifying. "All the shows was after the story," she told me, a hint of nostalgia in her voice. "We got offers from everybody—except *Oprah*, 'cause she don't do those topics no more." At the height of the competition, producers from *Sally Jessy* sent all the wives roses in an effort to convince them to choose their show. Then, when the wives were finally in New York for the *Montel* taping, they were visited at the hotel by producers from a rival show, who tried to lure them away. *Montel* producers intervened and promptly whisked the women to a new hotel, registering them under false names. According to Charlotte, "It was quite an experience." At the time of our interview, she had plans to write a book and was hoping to secure a made-for-TV movie contract—an unlikely scenario given that Vince had already rejected the deal and none of the other women wanted to be involved.

Indeed, of all the wives, Charlotte was the only one to embrace her celebrity status. After the first group experience on *Montel*, she appeared on the other shows either alone or with Vince piped in via satellite. Her desire for celebrity eventually became a point of tension between her and her new boyfriend, who believed that talk shows are "low class" and that Charlotte was degrading herself by going on them. "He was always tellin' me, 'I don't want you going back on those shows, don't let me catch you on one of them shows.' Because I would go and not tell him, be really sneaky about it. My girlfriend is an actor, and I would call him from the airport and say, 'I'm going out of town with Patty for a couple of days to watch the filming.' When really I'd be going to do a show."

Charlotte's boyfriend is not the only one who thinks that seeking celebrity status on a talk show is degrading. Wanting media exposure is one of the key motivations attributed to guests by critics who disparage the genre.[2] Yet why shouldn't guests find the celebrity angle attractive, given

2. Consider one such example from the *New Yorker*. After noting that the traveling sideshow is still with us in the guise of daytime talk, the columnist writes, "What makes the new geek shows all the more unsettling is the American yearning for celebrity of any sort, at any cost." Celebrity has become a kind of currency, he suggests, one that will not buy food or shelter but will garner sexual attention or a taste of the limo life: "Talk-show guests aren't paid. They don't have to be. They long to be geeks. As they come onstage, the same sort of applause and clamorous music greets them that greets the movie stars and sports heroes on the *Tonight Show* and the *Late Show with David Letterman*" (Schiff 1995, 10).

that many of them would not otherwise get a taste of television stardom or a public hearing for their views? As mentioned earlier, celebrities in American culture constitute a special, elite class. Being a celebrity is a mark of distinction. To a lesser degree, so is knowing a celebrity, meeting a celebrity, and merely *seeing* a celebrity. (If you saw a major Hollywood star in an airport or a restaurant, wouldn't you consider that news to be shared with others?) Here, again, we find evidence of the ritual as opposed to transmission function of media. Some guests are less interested in transmitting messages or imparting specific information than in assuming a place in an imagined community, in this case, a community of celebrity elites.

The problem with this, from the perspective of critics, is that the celebrity of talk-show guests is not earned or achieved but rather manufactured and acquired. Moreover, these people must compromise their dignity to acquire their celebrity. Theirs is a pseudocelebrity based on transgression, tragedy, or personal hardship rather than on accomplishment, talent, or social contribution. To critics, talk-show guests symbolize, and are part of, a larger, disturbing trend toward the manufacture of celebrity for celebrity's sake, what Daniel Boorstin (1961, 57) long ago called the *human pseudoevent*, in which "the celebrity is a person who is known for his well-knownness." Talk-show guests—along with the participants on reality-based programs—are said to epitomize a culture that confuses notoriety with greatness, videation with validation. Talk-show guests are maligned above and beyond other pseudocelebrities, however, because in their case, wanting mere exposure violates not only the meritocratic assumptions that underpin traditional conceptions of celebrity but also deeply entrenched codes of public civility, codes that dictate that the more public the space, the more self-monitoring one's behavior. Unlike real celebrities, whose fame presumably has something to do with talent and whose aura of greatness depends on a persona carefully managed to reveal only occasional (and carefully packaged) glimpses of the authentic (i.e., private) self, the celebrity of talk-show guests depends on audiences having unfettered access—or at least the *perception* of unfettered access—to the private self. And, because emotions externalized are the most visible and dramatic signifier of this self, the guarantor of the real, on talk shows there is a kind of reversal of the code, where the more public the space, the less self-monitoring (i.e., the more emotional and dramatic) the behavior.

At the same time, and somewhat paradoxically, a too-obvious desire for celebrity on the part of ordinary guests compromises their authenticity from a production standpoint. It can act as a distancing mechanism, getting in the way of expressing real emotion, and keeping guests at a surface

Figure 9. "Maps to talk-show guests' homes." Original artwork by John O'Brien. First published in the *New Yorker,* 1995.

level of acting. (The casting director of the reality show *The Real World* faced exactly the same dilemma [see Marsh 2000].) For this reason, producers actually prefer guests who have some motivation for participating *other* than media exposure or for whom the trappings of celebrity status exist alongside other goals.

Being Ordinary, Performing Ordinariness

Whatever their motivations, and regardless of their stated reasons for participating, most guests understand at some level that they are expected to deliver an authentic, emotional performance. Guests who are talk-show viewers know about the money shot before having any direct contact with the show. ("You may not be completely cognizant, but, subliminally, viscerally, you know. You sense that you've gotta be a good talker, that you've gotta have a dramatic story, that you've gotta point fingers, express outrage, things of that sort.") Indeed, it was the transparency of the expectation that enabled Tony (the aspiring actor) to convince producers—on seven different occasions—to put him on TV. Tony knew how to leave the kind of phone message that would hook producers and ensure a return call: a message detailing an experience that was bizarre or unusual but not so far out as to be unbelievable, a message delivered in a voice that conveyed, as he so aptly put it, "the three Es—energy, enthusiasm, and emotion."

If real guests are not aware of the mandate for emotional expressiveness in advance, they get a sense of its importance during their initial conversations with producers or dur-

ing the fluffing sessions backstage if the topic precludes sustained prelimi-
nary contact. Katherine, the *Ricki Lake* guest, noted that producers spent a
great deal of time on the phone with her going over potential questions
that might come from audience members. Their main concern, Katherine
realized, "was that we not freeze up and become monosyllabic, or, worse,
uncommunicative, because, as they said to us when we got to the show, 'we
need *reaction.*'" Producers also specifically warned Katherine not to "go
easy" on her friend and fellow panelist Marie, who was representing the
other side of the story. "They were very explicit about that," Katherine recalled. "They said, 'We know you're friends, but don't coddle each other
when you get on camera. Mix it up! We need some controversy. You can be
friends later."

The mandate to produce emotional performances becomes even
more obvious to guests during the fluffing sessions backstage. Katherine
drew on the metaphor of the locker-room pep talk: "They basically whip
you up into—I won't say a frenzy, but definitely it reminded me of what
football teams must do. They prepped us to be a unified side, you know, to
believe we were in the right, so that you practically go out there yelling,
'Fight! Fight! Fight!'" Katherine knew that producers must have been doing the same thing with the women in the opposing camp and that the duality was clearly in the service of orchestrating drama. As she said with a
laugh, 'They don't want people to back down, you know. They don't want
people saying [with exaggerated politeness], 'Oh well, you've got a valid
point there!'"

Virtually every guest involved in a confrontational situation reported
a similar experience. Ramón, who was backstage with Cheri during her
fluffing session for the *Sally Jessy* show about mother-daughter conflicts,
recounted how producers first separated the two constituencies in different rooms and then encouraged the daughters to "band together against
the mothers" and "stick up for one another." Sonny likewise described
how her daughter Jordan and her stepbrother Casey went to the studio
ahead of all the other guests and came back to the hotel room "fighting
like cats and dogs." The producers had clearly done something to turn
them against each other, she said. As a consequence, when Jordan took the
stage, "she practically tried to kill [Casey]." Producers managed to get the
whole family going. According to Sonny, "Even my other brother, the
peacemaker of the family, even he was hittin' on Casey. And we don't normally do that. We're family; we don't *really* fight like that." Casey, in fact,
suffered two broken ribs during the taping and had to be rushed to the hospital. Minus the broken bones, the process was much the same for Winona

vis-à-vis her daughters at *Randy* and for Anitra vis-à-vis her two sisters at *Jenny Jones.*

Sharon, one of the *Randy* guests described in the opening pages of this book, actually felt that producers went overboard with their coaching and that their attempts to fluff her in the green room hurt rather than helped her performance, making her more nervous and self-conscious than she otherwise would have been. I remember thinking the same thing when I shadowed producers during the production of Sharon's show. Indeed, it seemed to me that, in many cases, fluffing was for the benefit of producers as well as guests and thus served a dual purpose, preparing those guests who needed the guidance while at the same time reassuring producers that they were doing everything in their power backstage to ensure a good performance onstage, short of actually going out there and telling the story themselves.

Fluffing translates into a genuine emotional performance, however, only if guests accept at some level the mandate to prioritize emotional expressiveness. Jordan was a good guest for *Jerry Springer* both because she was easily provoked and because she had no compunctions about losing her cool on television. She was, in her mother's words, "very wild tempered" and "willing to fight anyone for the drop of a dime." Which is why producers wanted her on the show so bad, as her mother made a point of telling me. It did not bother Jordan that she flew off the handle and attacked her uncle Casey or that Casey suffered two broken ribs as a result of the confrontation. "He deserved it," Jordan told me matter-of-factly. "I'm real with everybody, and he really did deserve it. He put his hands on my mom, and, if somebody puts their hands on your mom, you know, what are you going to do? You're going to kick their ass too, right? Or handle it any way you have to."

To be sure, *Springer* is exceptionally hard-core; most guests on most shows are not expected or encouraged to fight at the drop of a dime. Moreover, the same hot temper that made Jordan a good performer also made her difficult to work with behind the scenes, even for *Springer* producers. More ideal from a production standpoint are guests like Lori or Joanne, both of whom felt strongly about their topic, wanted to get their message across to others, and saw nothing wrong with expressing their emotions on television. Lori, an exotic dancer, went on *Randy* to tell her sister-in-law to butt out of her marriage because she was fed up with what she described as the sister-in-law's "childish interference." I was backstage assisting the mobile-camera operator for that particular show. I remember it clearly because the argument got very heated and at one point the two women left their chairs and lunged at each other, requiring bodyguards to intervene, although producers later edited the scene out.

According to Lori, "Nobody encouraged me [to fight]; that was just something that come out of me; that was just my anger and everything else." I ventured to suggest that fighting with your sister-in-law on national television is considered by some people to be undignified or inappropriate, to which Lori responded, "I'm not ashamed of anything that goes on in my life, you know. I'm not ashamed of what I do for a living. Everybody has problems, and there's nothing wrong with expressing them on television in front of other people."

Joanne, who went on a *Randy* show titled "I Want to Confront That Guest!" had a similar attitude and proved to be an even better guest than Lori. While at home recovering from back surgery, Joanne responded to a *Randy* plug inviting viewers to call in if they had ever been angered or upset by a former guest on the show. Not long before, Joanne had, in fact, been outraged by a woman on *Randy* who was dating a convicted child molester even though she was the mother of two young children. Joanne, now in her mid-fifties, had been molested herself as a girl and felt strongly that this woman's relationship was misguided and irresponsible because it put the children at risk of molestation. She insisted that she would have been willing to participate even if she had to pay her own transportation and hotel costs. "Never in a million years did I think I would go on a talk show," Joanne told me, laughing. "But I was so infuriated that [this woman] could do this to her children that it just sparked something in me that forced me to hit that redial button [on the telephone], I swear, a hundred times before I got through. I was determined to let the producers know, 'If you ever have that woman back on, I want to be there.'"

Joanne was adamant that she did not go on the show "to make a spectacle" or to be "part of a circus act" but rather to express her "heartfelt sympathy for the children." She admitted that many *Randy* shows *were* sensational, but she felt that, in this case, producers "were looking for genuine feeling compared to sensationalism." When I asked about a particular moment during the taping when the woman in question sat down next to her onstage and Joanne got up and moved her own chair so as to put more distance between them, Joanne replied, "The producers didn't tell me to do that. They never told me to do any theatrics. I did that because, to be honest, I don't want to breathe the same air as a woman like that. . . . I was 100 percent honest on that stage. . . . What came out of my mouth was my real gut natural feelings, and I do not regret the things I said to her." A guest like Joanne is a dream come true for producers. She is emotional, uninhibited, willing to speak her "real gut natural feelings," and voicing a position widely supported in the culture—that ex-sex offenders cannot be trusted around small children. Joanne proved an even more dynamic guest in person than over the phone; after her fluffing session backstage, producers decided to move her from third to first in the lineup so that her performance would kick off the show.

But not all guests so readily accept the mandate to deliver the money shot, even when they are deeply invested in the issue at hand, and even when they know that, by holding back, they are giving bad performances. Thus, while Katherine's friend Marie "really got into it" with the other guests on *Ricki Lake*, Katherine herself did not. "My heart was not in it," she said. "Personally, I hate to argue with people. It makes me physically ill. So, you know, basically I didn't have that much to contribute." Anitra gave a similarly subdued performance on *Jenny Jones*, although less out of a personal aversion to arguing than as a protective response to the hostile behavior of the other guests. Anitra's two sisters and daughter, who were anything but shy or reserved, grew increasingly confrontational as the show progressed. They accused her of being a bad mother, of mismanaging her financial affairs, and of failing to protect her daughter from abuse. Consequently, Anitra herself grew increasingly withdrawn, to the point where she simply could not comply when, during the commercial break, producers urged her to "jump in there and defend yourself."

As Anitra observed, "It was like they wanted a cockfight or, you know, a boxing match. Round 1. Round 2. And I'm just not that type of person. I'm not their favorite kind of guest because, if you watch the tape, you'll see that I was fairly passive. I just felt I couldn't speak up—every time I tried, someone would ridicule me and cut me off." The combative atmosphere took her by surprise, and by the end of the taping Anitra stopped trying to address or even make eye contact with her two sisters. It was only later, on the way home, that she let go of her emotions. "On the plane going back to California, I just sat there with tears streaming down my eyes," she told me. "It was horrible. I felt like a lamb who was thrown to the lions."

Vince, the man arrested for bigamy, was another guest who rejected the mandate for emotional expressiveness when he appeared via satellite on *Montel*. Given his recent arrest and the negative framing of his conduct established by his wives onstage before he himself was even allowed to speak, Vince decided that his best option was simply to disengage. "I didn't defend myself as they would normally expect," he said. "Nor did I make accusations towards the women. I just kind of ignored them. And I answered the questions from Montel as swiftly as possible; I did not embellish or

elaborate on much. And so they were really disappointed with my participation, I could tell." As with Anitra, Vince's passivity was largely a response
to the performances of the others guests involved, guests better able or
more willing to deliver the money shot. But, whereas Anitra wanted to
defend herself and could not, Vince's disengagement was more deliberate.
After assessing the situation, he chose not to get ruffled or riled and consequently was the kind of guest that producers generally like to avoid.

Guests thus recognize that producers want raw, real emotion, but not
all are able or willing to provide it, and, even among those who are, not all
have the same competence or performative ability. This fact, in combination with the mandate to produce sensational television, goes a long way
toward opening up a space for the successful infiltration of guests who give
excellent performances but who might be less than completely honest with
producers about their stories. As we saw in chapter 3, producers generally
do what they can to ensure that guests are real. They check facts; they talk
to witnesses or third parties; they make guests sign release forms guaranteeing authenticity (otherwise guests are liable for the production costs of
the show, upwards of $80,000). When I interviewed Len, Pam's husband,
he said that the producers at *Randy* grilled him at length about his motivations for participating: did he want to get back together with Pam, did he
want revenge on her, did he put his kids up to this, or did they call on their
own? On one occasion, I saw the executive producer cancel a show only
minutes before taping because one of the guests was found to be lying not
only about her name and identity but also about her age. She was not yet
sixteen, and had the producers allowed her on camera without parental
consent they could have been sued.

At the same time, truth is not an all-or-nothing matter, and there are
various degrees of faking. Katherine and Marie went on *Ricki Lake* as a
favor to one of the producers there. They were not exactly lying, but they
were not exactly telling the truth either. Darlene, one of the interns at
Diana, appeared on a makeover show with her roommate from college not
because the two women were in obvious need of a makeover (in fact, Darlene was always impeccably groomed) but because Darlene went to the
producer and begged to be a participant. Then again, who is to say that
Darlene did not need a makeover? Melissa, a part-time secretary and
screenwriter, appeared with a friend on *Geraldo* (and then again on *Montel*)
to talk about "sexual turnons" because she and the friend were writing a
book on the topic. The friend ran a sex club for men with large penises
called "The Hung Jury" and was promoting both the club and the book
on the talk-show circuit. He convinced Melissa to join him and play "the

Mistress of Measurement"—a made-up role that they invented solely to spice up the performance. And then there are Wayne and Brittany, who were chosen for a *Montel* show about hypnotism not because they proved particularly susceptible to hypnotism necessarily but because both had prior acting experience and performed being hypnotized in an animated way (three of the other guests on the show were full-time drama students). Britanny told me that it was difficult to know whether and to what degree she and Wayne did crazy things onstage because they were really hypnotized or because of their fluffing sessions backstage since producers made no effort to conceal the fact that they needed exaggerated reactions from guests.

When people make a habit of going on talk shows out of a desire to get on TV, they fall into the category *professional ordinary guest.*[3] Despite the fact that a too-obvious desire for media exposure can compromise the aura of authenticity that guests are supposed to convey, professional guests succeed in gaining entry to the genre because they know how to package and present themselves in ways that producers find difficult to resist. Professional guests provide producers with ready-made performances in much the same way that politicians and public-relations personnel provide journalists with ready-made news in the form of press releases: both admittedly compromise the integrity of professional media practice, but they are used anyway because they streamline the production process. Katherine made exactly this point when describing one of the other guests from the *Ricki Lake* show: "This woman was a professional. She'd been on six other shows, and she knew the producer by her first name. I mean, this was her area of expertise. She knew how to get the spotlight on her. She was going to break out. She was going to become very confrontational. That's what [the producers] wanted, you know. So she gave them what they wanted. And, by doing that, you get more camera time."

When professional guests are actors or pranksters whose stories are outright fabrications, they are considered bona fide fake guests, the talk-show equivalent of the freak-show gaff. Of all the guests I interviewed,

---

3. Arguably, Charlotte became something of a professional guest in that she was a repeat participant who went on multiple shows. But, unlike the sort of professional guest that producers say they like to avoid, Charlotte's entry into the talk-show circuit was less a function of personal initiative and more a natural consequence of the frenzy of coverage surrounding her story. Once inside, she found the celebrity attractive and took positive steps to prolong it. Charlotte was already news, so producers did not worry about the authenticity of her story, whereas professional guests often exaggerate, embellish, or lie about aspects of their stories.

Tony is the one who best fit this description. Like the woman on *Ricki Lake* that Katherine described, his goal was to be on TV, and he knew how to achieve it. Getting on TV was his "area of expertise." A young musician and aspiring actor, Tony lives in a tiny flat in West Hollywood with his girl-friend, Ingrid, who is also an aspiring actor. I spent an afternoon with them both one Sunday not long after they taped a show together at *Randy*. Two years previously, Tony made the first of several talk-show appearances on an episode of *Geraldo* about kids addicted to "crank" (a methamphetamine also known as crystal meth). He was recruited for the show by a friend and fellow addict, and, at the end of the taping, Geraldo offered to send all the panelists to a drug-rehabilitation center. Tony accepted the offer, went through the program, and has been drug free ever since. Out of a sense of obligation to the show, he later did an update episode titled "Where Are They Now?" (he was the success story on the panel, the guest who got clean and stayed clean—thanks to Geraldo).

Tony's first appearance, then, was authentic in the sense that he was playing a more or less accurate version of himself. He was, in fact, a teenage drug addict in need of help. After that, however, Tony and Ingrid appeared together on six other daytime talk shows, telling a different story every time. Tony said that their performance on *Sally Jessy* was so good that a clip was chosen for *Talk Soup*, a half-hour comedy program that features the week's most outrageous talk-show highlights. Invariably, the topics of Tony's shows revolved around sexual conflict since this was easy to perform and of greatest interest to producers. On *Sally Jessy*, for example, he played a cheating husband who bragged about his sexual exploits (the show was titled "He Cheated, Now I Can't Trust Him"). On *Randy*, Ingrid pretended to be having an affair with Tony's ex-wife. According to Tony, "We made up some story that I was engaged, and my alleged fiancée said she was hav-ing an affair with my ex-wife, and I pretended to freak out—it was all act-ing kind of stuff."

After the show taped, however, someone on staff recognized him from a rival show, and the producers became angry. "The producers came running into the dressing room and freaked out because they had rec-ognized me. These producers were, like, out of control, yelling at me in front of people and stuff, you know. It was an ugly, ugly scene. When I was leaving, one of them goes to me, 'You're not going to make *Talk Soup* this time, Tony!'"

I sought out Tony and his friends at the hotel across the street im-mediately after this encounter. Tony was incensed that producers had been angry with his deception rather than grateful for his crowd-pleasing performance, and when I interviewed him several weeks later he was still bitter about the experience. "I entertained their crowd," he said. "The audience was freaking out, loving it, you know. I gave them good television, which is what they want. I'm a ratings grabber." Producers don't care if you're faking, he insisted, they just care if someone else finds out about it. "They're such bullshitters."

"I guess they didn't like the fact that you were a ratings grabber for a bunch of other shows, too," I said. To this Tony replied, "Well, I'm in the entertainment business. I want to be an actor. You know, what am I going to do, start out as an 'extra'? Be in the background of some scene for, like, five seconds? Forget it."

Tony and Ingrid both emphasized that it was no easy matter to pull off a successful performance. The challenge was not so much displaying emotion but rather remembering the exact details of a story and keeping one person's version consistent with the other's. Ingrid also found it stressful to keep up appearances before audience members because the intense and sustained nature of the taping meant that there was no time when she could relax and "turn off." As she put it, "It's weird because the audience is so close to the stage and the people are just staring at you, checking you out, even during commercials. And so you've got to watch yourself 'cause you can't fall out of character. You really have to do a total transformation." Moreover, Ingrid said that the deception made her feel guilty when audience members expressed genuine sympathy for her situation (at the *Sally Jessy* taping, Tony had supposedly cheated on her thirteen times in five years and remained unrepentant). "People would come up to me afterwards, and tell me how sorry they were for me, you know, and wish me luck and everything." She felt even worse about playing the part of the wronged wife alongside other women whose stories were real. "Some of these women, they really did have assholes for husbands, and they were actually scared to say too much on the show because of what their husbands might do. And here I was just pretending to have these problems."

Tony had no such compunctions. Given his dream to become an actor, he was proud of the number of talk-show gigs that he had been able to secure. In this, he was not unlike the showmen of the nineteenth-century amusement world, men who thought nothing of "grifting" and "gaffing" the customer and for whom knowing the tricks of the trade was simply an important measure of success (Bogdan 1988). Tony even showed me the little black book he carries around containing the telephone numbers of all the talk shows currently on the air, his "conquests" boldly crossed out in red ink. At the time of my visit, he had just joined a casting agency and was using his talk-show appearances to compile a demo tape for his agent.

Tony's experience aside, aspiring actors are not as commonplace on daytime talk shows as critics tend to assume, at least not on the two shows where I worked. Producers did admit to being lied to by guests, and they also knew that guests were not always entirely truthful about every aspect of their stories. But, then, producers sometimes mislead guests and are not always entirely truthful about every detail of their shows. In between Tony, whose performance was an outright fabrication that deceived producers as well as viewers, and Joanne, whose performance expressed her real, gut feelings, lies everybody else, people who are more or less truthful, whose real self more or less matches their stage self, and who have more or less understandable (if not socially acceptable) reasons for participating.

The generic need for emotional expressiveness—in combination with the potential (and occasional actual) failure of guests to satisfy that need—not only opens up a space for the infiltration of fake guests, but increases the pressure on producers to ensure the money shot by means other than merely coaching and fluffing: targeting guests in conflict, orchestrating surprise encounters, focusing on only the most dramatic or sensational elements of a story, etc. For classy guests especially, such tactics are frustrating because they both create a performative space inhospitable to serious discussion and debate and undermine the "goodness of fit" between what they expect and what they get from their participation. Generally speaking, the greater the expectation that the genre is about something other or more than the money shot, the greater the sense of dissatisfaction can be.

Everybody has a skeleton in their closet. Everybody does. And unless you can bear the thought of your skeletons coming out of that closet and coming into the life of every relative, church person, every teller at the bank, unless you can deal with having the most personal, private part of your life being exposed to complete strangers or people that do matter—you know, ask yourself, do you want your grandfather to know that you had an affair? I mean, unless you can bear telling all these people, don't do it, don't go on a talk show. There's a lot of thinking to do before a person chooses to be on TV. It's a circus out there, and they want to make you the circus act.

—FRAN, guest on *Oprah* ("Casanova Con Men")

CHAPTER SIX

Inside the Fun House

Grievances and Complaints

Heaton and Wilson (1995, 176) argue that the experiences of talk-show guests are generally portrayed in a positive light, that "the public hears very little about what goes wrong for guests." I disagree, especially if the "the public" is getting its information from the establishment media. Talk shows tend to become news for much the same reasons that ordinary people become news—because they have done something extraordinary, deviant, or bizarre. Daytime talk shows were rarely in the headlines until the *Jenny Jones* murder, and, at that point, the coverage was anything but flattering. Guests who sue talk shows make the news, as do those who admit faking their stories. Otherwise, journalists and media critics rarely talk about talk-show guests except to put them down or to discuss the lamentable trend toward "manufactured celebrity" that guests supposedly represent.

What do guests themselves say about their experience of being on national television? Murders and lawsuits aside, the vast majority of guests I saw while interning at *Diana* appeared to enjoy their television debut, and this was true for a good many *Randy* guests as well. One of my jobs was to accompany guests to the waiting taxis or limousines after the taping was over, and I always made a point of asking how they felt the show had gone. The most common response was that it seemed unreal, like a movie or dream played in fast-forward—it was over almost before it had begun. Generally, they found the experience interesting and even exciting, and most believed that they had accomplished at least part of what they had set out to do. Guests like Charlotte, attracted to the trappings of stardom, enjoyed the special treatment, the attention, the public nature of the forum, and the opportunity to meet the celebrity host. Even certain guests who complained bitterly to me in interviews about a particular aspect of their experience indicated that they would, nonetheless, do it all again. Some, including Winona, Sonny, Sharon, Vince, and Bonnie, did, in fact, turn around and go on another show.

Nevertheless, guests had plenty of legitimate grievances, and they shared with me their complaints, partly because I asked them to, and partly because I deliberately sought out people who left the studio obviously displeased with what had transpired there—not to buttress the negative portrait of talk shows painted in the media, although that is always a possible reading, but to further illuminate the process by which ordinary people are made suitable for mass consumption in this context. This process reveals little about the evil intentions of producers or the stupidity of guests but much about the fact that the two sets of players occupy very different structural positions in the talk-show world. Whereas producers orient toward talk shows above all as work, with one show being much like any other, guests do not orient toward the genre this way unless they are actors faking their stories. When producers and guests come together, each with their own set of goals and expectations and with unequal amounts of power and influence, points of friction and moments of tension are inevitable.

Not surprisingly, what people complained about most were various forms of manipulation, sometimes a function of specific things that producers did to encourage conflict and drama, sometimes (as I discuss more thoroughly in the following section) a function of the codes and practices that characterize television production more generally. The nature and severity of the manipulation varied widely, from the trivial to the relatively egregious. For example, while it was not a major source of tension, guests were invariably surprised and put off by the short time span between having their first conversation with a producer and actually taping the show. Fran's situation going on *Oprah* was typical in that she got the initial phone call on Friday morning about a show that was taping three days later, on Monday afternoon. "And I had two kids to make arrangements for," she recalled. "I mean, it was very, very quick."

A number of guests reported tussles with producers and other staff members over wardrobe, hair, and makeup once they arrived at the studio and were being readied for their performance. Specifically, they mentioned being dissatisfied or uncomfortable with the efforts of staffers to change their appearance to make them more "camera friendly." Katherine got such a heavy makeup job that she ran back to the green room and wiped most of it off with tissue. "I couldn't believe it," she said. "They pile so much makeup on, you look like a 'ho." Pam's clash with the staff at *Randy* over this very issue so angered her that, at the last minute, she refused to go on the show and had to be coaxed back into appearing by the producer. The conflict started with clothes, then progressed to makeup and hair.

"I wore my own dress," Pam said, "but they tried their darndest to talk me out of it. They were bringing outfits in, asking me if I wanted this one or that one, and I said, 'No, no, no. I don't like any of them.' Then this lady who does the makeup, she started drawing eyebrows on me. And I told her, 'No, no, I don't have eyebrows, and you're not going to color them on. It looks stupid.'"

"They probably try to accentuate or exaggerate the way you look because it's for television," I observed.

"That's exactly what *she* said. But, you know, I wasn't worried about looking all glamorous. She said, 'You're supposed to be the star of the show,' and that was stupid too. I'm not a star in no show. I'm just there to listen to my kids. So, anyway, I wiped off my makeup, and then she started ratting my hair. And I said, 'Look, I'm not Phyllis Diller either; I don't rat my hair,' you know. So I combed my hair back out, and she started fussing with something else, so finally I said, 'That's it, forget it, I'm not doing the show! I look really stupid! I look like a slut! You guys have made me out to be something I'm not.'"

Clothes, hair, and makeup might seem trivial concerns, but appearances matter a great deal. Wearing clothes or makeup that alters one's image is particularly consequential on television, a medium where image is practically all there is. Guests play themselves, but in an exaggerated fashion, and producers want them to look the part. If the topic is "Homeless

Couples," the couple must look undeniably homeless. If the topic is "Promiscuous Teenage Daughters," the daughters must exude promiscuity in appearance and demeanor as well as in their talk and actions. Tattoos and piercings can be strategically covered or prominently displayed, depending on whether producers need audiences to be sympathetic or hostile toward guests. A guest's appearance must be consistent or harmonious not only with the topic but also with the general tenor and temper of the show. Consequently, clothing is never just clothing, nor makeup simply makeup; they are also costume.

Ramón and Cheri discovered this too late when they went on the *Sally Jessy Raphael* show about mother-daughter conflicts (featuring daughters who dress "too sexy" for their age). Producers told Cheri to wear something "really revealing" that would make her look "glamorous" on television, so she arrived at the studio wearing a strapless corset-style bodice with a short jacket and miniskirt. Producers were thrilled with the outfit, but they insisted that she wear the jacket thrown back off her shoulders, and they replaced her regular nylons with a garter belt and fishnet stockings. Not surprisingly, during the taping itself, which I attended, audience members consistently sided with the aggrieved mothers on the panel and accused the daughters of dressing like sluts. Eventually, the ridicule pushed Cheri to the breaking point. She leaped from her chair, marched to the edge of the stage, and shouted to the audience, "Do you know why I'm dressed like this? Because *they* told me to dress like this!" She pointed an accusing finger at the producers standing on the sidelines. "These aren't even my own stockings!" An awkward silence fell over the room, and I saw the red light on the camera go out. In an effort to initiate damage control, the senior producer took the microphone and testified that Cheri was wearing her own clothes, that all the girls on the panel were told to dress for the show "in the same clothes they normally wore." At that, Ramón, also onstage, snorted loudly. Eventually, Cheri sat down and the show resumed.

What they had learned, of course—as Ramón subsequently acknowledged during our interview—was that appearances play more than a minor role in establishing the interpretive framework for a guest's story and that the more sensational the story, the more over-the-top the appearance. In this particular case, producers were clearly aiming for hard-core drama. Toward the end of the taping, Cheri's mother accused Ramón (who is married) of being a pervert and a pedophile, seeking custody of fifteen-year-old Cheri so that he and his wife could seduce the girl into a ménage à trois. He later learned that producers had wanted to station a police officer in the audience just in case they could prove that he was having sexual relations with Cheri, but the mother had balked at taking things that far.

The scenario described here—especially the would-be arrest that producers hoped to spring on Ramón—recalls another major grievance expressed by guests: being surprised by something (or someone) on the air. Prior to the *Jenny Jones* murder, producers would routinely surprise guests, sometimes pleasantly, sometimes not. After the murder, producers continued the practice but grew more cautious about how they handled and prepared guests. When surprises are the explicit topic or focus of a show, guests are warned that they are coming on the program to be surprised, that someone they know wants to reveal a secret or make a confession, good or bad. Guests may be angry, hurt, or humiliated by the disclosure, but at least they know about it in advance. Indeed, producers can wind up giving guests more information than they would like in order to ensure that the taping will unfold as planned.[1]

It is actually guests on shows that do not revolve explicitly around surprises or confrontations (and thus do not entail specific warnings), who can feel the most hurt and betrayed because they can think that they are adequately prepared for a taping when, in fact, they are not. This happened to Nancy, who went on *Diana* to discuss athletes and domestic violence. Leery from the very beginning of going on television, she attached certain conditions to her participation. Not only did she refuse to talk about the details of the sexual assault itself (only the emotional and psychological effects), but, because she is white and her ex-boyfriend is black, she also made producers promise that they would not turn the matter of domestic violence into "a racial issue." (There were to be two other women on the panel with Nancy, also survivors of domestic violence, one white, one black; their

---

1. Pam was one guest who learned in advance what the show was about. She first got a message from a *Randy* producer telling her that "someone she knew" wanted to "talk to her on the show," but the producer could not say who because it was a surprise. The producer was vague about the topic, mentioning something about "divorced parents." At the same time, the producer kept asking about Pam's boyfriend, which made Pam suspicious and caused her to press for more information. As Pam described it, "She kept asking, didn't I have a boyfriend who wants to go with me so I don't have to travel by myself? And I said, 'Yeah, but he took off in a huff, and I don't know where he is, so I'll just go without him.' She said, 'No, we have to have him here.' And I was like, 'Why? what's he got do with it?' And a little bit more of the show came out. She said that my daughter called in, and she said, 'Your daughter's very smart, and she's very concerned about you—' And I was like, 'Oh, now I know what this is about.' Because my boyfriend and I, we're in this domestic-violence relationship, and my daughter's tired of the way we get along."

abusers were both high-profile male athletes, white and black, respectively. Nancy was thus the only panelist involved in an interracial relationship.) Despite having seen *Diana* on television many times before, despite multiple conversations with the producers over the phone, despite seeking advice from family members and friends and carefully weighing the costs and benefits of participating, and despite getting certain terms and conditions from the producers in writing, Nancy was still unpleasantly surprised during the taping when, during the third segment, out came "the opposition": the president of the Mike Tyson defender club, a black woman who insisted that there was no good excuse for well-educated women (like the three panelists) to stay in abusive relationships—if they did, they deserved whatever happened to them.

"I couldn't believe it!" Nancy said. "How could they bring someone like that on? I mean, what other 'side' is there to this issue? And the Mike Tyson angle! I mean, my God, he's a convicted rapist, I was raped by a professional athlete—you know, it was, like, *not* cool. I couldn't believe they had pulled this kind of bullshit. It totally threw us off." Nancy was so taken aback that she shut down, not saying another word the rest of the show.

While this surprise is mild compared to some, and while the host and audience members clearly took Nancy's side (as one woman asked, "How can having an education shield you from a fist in the face?"), Nancy nevertheless felt betrayed. She was angry, not so much because producers invited someone onstage with a different point of view, as because of "the way they did it, the fact that this woman knew all about us but we didn't know about her." The sense of betrayal was all the more acute both because of the rapport that Nancy had established with producers and because she had taken so many precautions before agreeing to participate. "I'm telling you, Laura, I really felt like I had done my homework, like I had asked a lot of questions and, you know, tried to protect myself." Farther along in the interview, Nancy likened the taping to a kind of second-order victimization, in that she knew that what was happening to her was wrong but felt inhibited by the public nature of the situation and could not speak out. "It was exactly how I felt in my abusive relationship. I wanted to stop it, but I felt suppressed because I was with someone who was in the public eye."

In Nancy's case, producers had introduced an element of conflict into what was otherwise a soft-core scenario, with the obvious intention of heightening the dramatic tension. I later learned that producers had not told Nancy and the other panelists about the surprise guest both because it was not clear until the eleventh hour that the woman would even go on and because they felt that, without her, the show would have lacked what little emotion it had.[2] As one of them told me, "These were classy ladies we were dealing with. It wasn't like they were going to burst into tears or break out fighting or whatever, so we had to think of some other way to bring in the emotion." He paused and then added, "I mean, what are we supposed to do? We're supposed to uphold this squeaky-clean image, but then, you know, the network is breathing down our necks about ratings. It's hard to have it both ways." This comment is telling, for producers at *Diana* did often feel that they were caught in a double bind: be nice, but get ratings; defy the trend toward conflict, but stay competitive. The result is a show like Nancy's, respectable overall, but with a mild element of conflict.

At times, however, even *Diana* crosses the line separating classy from trashy programming. Perhaps the best illustration of this is Bonnie's show about near-death experiences, which literally got reconstituted as a modern-day freak show. Producers did not initially frame it this way, but, after a series of production meetings in which higher-ups criticized producers for being "too soft" with the topic, they switched gears and took a different, more tabloid approach.

Bonnie, a homemaker and mother of two, was badly burned and scarred in a terrible plane crash. She then wrote a book describing the near-death experience that she had had while undergoing surgery following the crash as well as her heroic (and successful) efforts to save her neighbors from a house fire only days after leaving the hospital. Bonnie says that she originally wrote the book for the same reasons she went on the talk-show circuit: to "spread a message of hope and compassion" and to educate the public about the existence of the "world beyond," including human-spirit communication. She insisted that making money off the book was a secondary goal for wanting to appear on television. Like Nancy, she took precautions to have all the details spelled out in advance because she feared that the show would trivialize her topic. She was especially adamant about knowing in advance who would join her on the panel. "Other near-deathers," she was told, including a couple whom Bonnie already knew and liked.

But, several days before the taping, the couple phoned her with the

2. The guest who played the opposition was reluctant to go on the show because, while she was conscious of the disproportionate scrutiny that black men suffer in matters of sexual violence, especially when the violence is directed at white women, she was not comfortable confronting these particular panelists, one of whom was African American like herself. For their part, the producers were reluctant to tell the other panelists about this woman because they assumed that the knowledge would cause the panelists to withdraw, leaving them with potentially no guests at all.

news that they had been dropped from the lineup. Bonnie grew suspicious and, after repeated attempts to contact producers, eventually learned that, owing to "unforeseen problems," the format had radically changed. No longer was the show about spirituality and near-death experiences; it was now about odd and unusual phenomena. Bonnie pressed harder, demanding to know who the other guests would be. Reluctantly, the producer ran down the list: following Bonnie, there would be a body contortionist, then a human-combustion artist, then a hypnotist, and, finally, a hypnotherapist specializing in past-life regression.

"A body contortionist! A human-combustion artist! In other words," Bonnie said to me, her voice incredulous, "he was putting together a circus act! He wanted me to be part of a freak show!"

She then told the producer that he could forget it, that she would not "sacrifice [herself] for anybody's thrill," and that he could find himself another lead guest. She hung up and for the next twenty-four hours was besieged by phone calls from the producers and even Diana herself, begging her to reconsider. In the end, Bonnie agreed to participate if producers dropped the body contortionist, if they allowed her to bring her husband and mother along for support, and, most important, if they promised to advertise her book at least three times during the taping. She decided that promoting the book would take precedence over all else—if producers were going to profit from her performance, why shouldn't she? Yet, when the show aired two weeks later, all mention of the book had been edited out, as had much of Bonnie's own testimony (according to producers, Bonnie was "too talky," and they simply eliminated the parts that "lacked drama"). "They mentioned that I was an author," Bonnie told me, "but that was all. I was devastated. I just laid on my bed and cried, and I thought to myself, 'God, why did you put me through this?'"

As Bonnie's experience on *Diana* reveals, even "nice" talk shows can do some sleazy things. It also reveals that guests can be just as disappointed or upset by what does *not* transpire onstage as by what does. As I discuss in the following section, this disappointment is often a function of generic limitations and constraints, of the ways in which "talk" becomes "show" so as to preclude certain hoped-for outcomes (in Bonnie's case, having the issue of paranormal phenomena treated seriously). It can also be a function of more specific things that guests want to do or say on the air but cannot. Such restrictions are not always imposed in the interests of drama or because of generic constraints; they may also stem from unforeseen extrageneric developments. Thus, Jane went on *Diana* to talk about child-custody battles and to make an on-air plea for financial assistance to cover her legal expenses (a women's group at her university had started a fund for this purpose). Producers knew of her desire and were sympathetic to her plight, but, the morning of the taping, they were informed by the show's lawyer that such a plea might place the show at risk of a lawsuit initiated by the other party in the case. A similar thing happened to Fran when she went on *Oprah* to talk about losing thousands of dollars and the deed to her house in a marketing scam. Fran wanted more than anything to name the two con artists on national television, believing that the exposure would expedite their apprehension. It was her chief motivation for going on the show. But, backstage, moments before taping, she was told by producers that, while she could talk about being swindled, legal considerations precluded disclosure of any names. "I couldn't believe it," she exclaimed. "When I heard that, my jaw dropped, and I said, 'You're kidding me!' I mean, we were really disappointed."

Guests on conflict-based shows also complain about specific aspects of their experiences, expressing anger or frustration when the outcome of confrontation does not go their way or support their version of events. A variation on this theme occurs when guests do not get the rewards or compensation that they expect in exchange for engaging in a confrontation. Such was the case for Jordan, the teen prostitute on *Jerry Springer*. Jordan told me that she went on the show because producers promised that they would help "turn her life around." Specifically, Jordan said that they promised to help pay for counseling, get her into an apartment of her own, and forward any letters, gifts, or donations sent to her via the studio by viewers. According to Jordan, "They [the producers] said that they [would] do it all, you know, help you get off the street, pay for a lot of the stuff we need. But they didn't do shit. I didn't get nothin', except for two lousy letters." According to the producer in charge, Jordan didn't get anything because she failed to keep up her end of the bargain: first and last month's rent on an apartment was contingent on her securing a job and seeing a professional counselor. "That was the deal," the producer told me, "and it's a lot more than we offer most guests. We're a talk show, not a welfare service."

Jordan did get a job, clerking for minimum wage at the local 7-Eleven, but, with a one-year-old daughter at home and another baby on the way, she could not work enough hours to make ends meet. So she quit and went back to living with her sixty-four-year-old boyfriend. As for seeing a therapist, she told me that she had a list of people recommended by the producers but never made any calls. "I don't need no goddamn counselor," she said. She was disillusioned because she had a friend who went on *Jerry Springer* and he claimed that the show "helped him a lot," although she did not know just what *help* in his case entailed. At bottom, Jordan wanted more money and a better life, not therapy. "She [the producer] told me they were going to help me and my daughter. They didn't do a damn thing. As far as I'm concerned, that woman ain't nothin' but a lyin' bitch, excuse me." Whether producers intentionally misled Jordan is difficult to know. Jordan said contradictory things in our interview, and I had only a short phone conversation with one of the two producers in charge of her show. Regardless, it was clear that Jordan had certain expectations about how she ought to be compensated for participating, expectations that went unfulfilled.

Round Pegs in Square Holes

Guests clearly have many legitimate complaints about their participation and about their treatment at the hands of producers. Many disappointed guests, however, especially those on classy shows, do not (or do not only) complain about specific instances of deception at the hands of producers. They complain about the ways in which the stories that they tell producers on the phone become something different onstage or about the inability of the forum to meet their goals and aspirations. Like all forms of media (and as the work of producers behind the scenes attests), talk shows do not simply hold a mirror up to society, reflecting the world back to itself. Indeed, if there is any way in which the mass media can be said to reflect at all, it is, as Gitlin (1980) has noted, like mirrors in a fun house: by exaggerating, transfiguring, transforming. Like most other forms of media, talk shows emphasize deviance over normalcy, conflict over consensus, and the unusual or the extreme over the mundane and the mainstream. Guests without any media experience may go on a show expecting a faithful reproduction of their stories. They are then surprised to find themselves in the fun house, caught in the very act of mediation.

Producers tend to recognize that manipulation is built into the process, whereas guests, who do not have production experience, may not. Joe, a former producer at *Geraldo* and *Ricki Lake*, said that transforming ordinary people into extraordinary guests was like putting square pegs into round holes. The executive producer comes up with a title for the show, he explained, and then producers have to go forth and make that title real. "So you're putting these square pegs into round holes. And the story is almost there, but, to make it really happen, the manipulation has to take place. And so guests are like, 'Yeah, that was the story, but not exactly.'"[3]

This describes well the sentiment of guests from a wide range of shows. In Ramón's case, producers nearly succeeded in transforming a show about daughters who dress "too sexy" into "Girls Who Sleep with Their Guardians." Both Anitra and Winona went on television to counter charges of child abuse leveled by specific family members (sisters in one case, daughters in the other), but their shows might well have been titled "Child-Abusing Moms" because they did little more than reaffirm the accusations. Both women knew who would be on the show and what the point of conflict was, but they found that, once onstage, they could not control their own representation. Other guests reported milder instances of the same phenomenon. Katherine told me that her most vivid memory of the *Ricki Lake* taping was having the host rephrase on the air something that she had said in the preinterview, making it more inflammatory than she had intended. "It wasn't an outright twisting," she admitted. "Basically, minus a few hundred words, that was what I said, but I didn't mean it the way she made it sound." Likewise, Nancy was upset with *Diana* producers not only because they introduced an unexpected guest but because the host announced at one point during the taping that Nancy had been attacked by her boyfriend with a bottle when, in fact, he had only threatened to attack her. "All I told them was that he had raised up the bottle and said, 'If you try and leave, I'll bust you in the head.' He never hit me with the bottle."

Guests also resent the way talk shows decontextualize issues and events, focusing on only the most dramatic or sensational elements of a story. This process can be subtle, as in Nancy's case, or it can be quite extreme, as when Joe produced a show at *Geraldo* about young gang members who thought nothing of killing people they suspected of "disrespecting" them. Relatives of the victims were brought onstage to confront the gang members, yet, according to Joe, "The entire show focused on the hoodlums acting badass in front of the camera and talking tough, and virtually no time was given to the aggrieved relatives." Consequently, one woman

3. By way of illustration, Joe described a show that he once produced about models turned call girls. It featured young women who went starry-eyed to big cities—New York or Los Angeles or Miami—and discovered that making it as a model would be a long, tough haul, so they started working as escorts on the side. Maybe all they did was go on a couple of paid dates with a guy, Joe said, but, when they walked onstage, suddenly they were referred to as *prostitutes*. As he described it, "Suddenly the show was 'Runway Call Girls' instead of 'The Hard Road to Modeling.' You know, once guests get there, it starts to take a different course, and they find themselves in any arena they didn't anticipate being in."

broke down sobbing after the taping. "How could you celebrate these criminals and not let us tell our stories?" she asked Joe, tears streaming down her face. "I lost a fifteen-year-old son who's dead and buried, and you spent the whole hour talking about what does *dissing* mean in the inner city."

A less egregious version of this happened to Fran when she and her husband went on *Oprah* to talk about being conned. The couple felt that they had a very interesting story and, except for naming the two con men, believed that they would be able to tell it in its entirety—on the panel with the rest of the guests. But producers seated the couple in the front row of the audience and then during the taping asked only one question, zeroing in on what, for the producers, was the most sensational element of the story but, for Fran, was the most shameful: the fact that she had slept with one of the con artists in order to get the deed to her house back.

"We lost a lot of money in this scam," she told me, "but none of that got discussed; it was all left out. I was shocked at how [the producers] didn't take what we considered significant and make it significant. Instead, they asked me what I had done to get the house back. And, yes, I did sleep with a man to get the house back. But that was only a minute portion of the entire story. I was a single mom when I met my husband, and I worked seven and a half years at two jobs to get that house. So, I mean, there was a story behind the story in the fact that I couldn't let my house go. But none of that came out."

Fran realized that none of that came out because the other guests invited on the show were more glamorous-looking people with more sensational stories of injustice, and, in the end, most of the airtime was devoted to them. As Fran explained it, "These other people, the man looked like he walked out of *GQ*, and the women looked like they walked out of *Vogue*. They were dressed to the nines. And, uh, flamboyant. I felt they very much embellished their stories. I mean, this guy was talking about getting ripped off for hundreds of thousands of dollars. And these girls—they were twins—they supposedly had ripped off an old man for hundreds of thousands, too. So [the producers] wanted more than just a regular couple. See, my husband and I, we are very simple people. My husband's a plumber. We are the kind that wear blue jeans and sweatshirts, and we will work twelve hours a day to make a payment on a humble house."

Helen, like Fran, had a particular set of expectations about what she wanted to accomplish and how she would accomplish it; when her expectations were not realized, she, too, felt betrayed. For her, the problem was not so much the kind of personal story that the producers chose to prioritize—flamboyant versus run-of-the-mill—but the fact that the emphasis on personal experience edged out other types of discourse. Helen went on *Diana* to discuss date rape. She saw the show as a forum for educating people about the shortcomings of rape-prevention policies on college campuses—indeed, this was her main reason for going on the show; her personal experience mattered to her only insofar as it led to her activism. Producers, on the other hand, cared only about her personal experience; they did not want her discussing "boring" issues of policy at all. They had a different agenda—to produce good television by having real survivors of date rape tell their personal stories of abuse. They wanted body work rather than mind work, and this clash of agendas created a struggle between Helen and the producer, a struggle that Helen ultimately lost.

According to Helen, it started when she asked if she could take some notes onstage with her. "Notes?" the producer asked. "What are you talking about, notes? This is supposed to be a story from your heart. Don't you even know your own story?" Helen explained that of course she knew her own story, that the notes were not about the rape but about the new Victims' Bill of Rights that she intended to discuss on the panel. The following interaction then ensued, as described to me by Helen:

"We didn't invite you to be on the show to have an agenda," said the producer.

"Well, you're wrong," Helen replied, "because I do have an agenda and that's why I agreed to be on the show. There's no point for me to do this if I don't feel like I'm going to accomplish anything. It's not worth it to me."

"Well, don't you think that just talking about your experience is a big accomplishment?"

"No, it's not, not for me. Maybe it is for someone else, and that's fine, you know, but it's not for me. The important thing for me is getting this information out."

At that point, the producer left in a huff to discuss the problem with the host. She returned to say that the host agreed to ask one question where Helen could address the issue of victims' rights. But, during the taping itself, they ran out of time, so the producer promised to put the information in writing just before the closing credits by way of compensation. In other words, the information that Helen considered the most important got reduced to a one-page "fact sheet" flashed onscreen at the very end of the program. Needless to say, Helen was angry and disappointed. In particular, she was put off by the circus-like atmosphere of the taping, which made the kind of discourse that she desired nigh impossible. When I asked her whether she felt that the producers had deliberately misled her about what to expect, she said no, not really, but that there was manipulation involved nevertheless.

"I'm not a producer," she said, "but it seems to me like you don't have to have any high-tech education to know that six people on the panel plus the others in the audience is a bit too much for, you know, a forty-minute show on such a serious topic. Because, basically, there were just a bunch of weird statements being made, with no time for response or clarification. . . . I felt the *situation* was manipulated. It's entertainment is what it is. And they try and make it sound like it's not, and, you know, I bought into it for a while, but, once you get there, you realize they're settin' up a circus."

As Helen and other guests discovered, in the clash of agendas between producers and guests, guests often lose because there is a contradiction or lack of fit between their goals and what the forum will support or allow. Indeed, if there is a single, most-common complaint among guests, especially those with an agenda for advocacy or education, it is that the genre is too much show and too little talk, that guests have too little time to tell their stories as they feel they ought to be told—because there are so many competing voices onstage, because something unexpected takes the show in a different direction, because producers are trained to cut the exposition and get to the point, because the point left standing after all the exposition is gone invariably relates to the most sensational aspects of a story, and because the emphasis on personal experience seriously constrains what kind of story can be told.

Interestingly, guests on classy shows like *Diana* are just as, if not more, likely to complain about manipulation than are guests on *Randy*, despite the fact that *Randy* was by far the trashier show. This is partly because, as noted earlier, *Diana* guests are recruited via experts through established groups and organizations as well as plugs, while *Randy* guests are recruited almost exclusively through plugs. Consequently, *Randy* guests are usually talk-show viewers familiar with the genre, whereas many *Diana* guests do not watch talk shows on a regular basis, if at all. More significant, as Helen's case illustrates, guests at classy shows are more likely to desire and expect a level of discourse out of line with the realities of the medium. Many ordinary *Diana* guests, in fact, had expectations much like those of experts, who, at least among my pool of interviewees, were among the most dissatisfied guests of all. To the degree that talk shows are more about talking bodies than about talking heads, they are less accommodating to the goals of experts (and ordinary people who function as experts) than to those of guests with less noble aspirations. Thus, while Helen was annoyed with how producers at *Diana* handled her show about date rape, Jack—who went on *Randy* to be confronted by his mother for sexually molesting his young brother—had no complaints at all. In fact, when I interviewed him immediately after the taping in his hotel room, he seemed singularly unruffled by the experience, despite having been given very little information about the taping in advance, despite being positioned as the villain in the story, and despite the fact that he did not accomplish his stated goal—reconciliation with his family.

As Jack told me, "The producer wouldn't give me any information 'cause it's, like, I'm assuming there's gonna be this confrontation between my parents and me. You know, they flew us on separate flights, they put us in separate hotel rooms, we were in separate green rooms. She [the producer] doesn't want, you know, a heated thing to happen ahead of time because she wants it on the show. You know what I'm saying?"

"Right. Sure I do," I replied. "And that doesn't bother you, or . . . ?"

"No, because if I'm willing to go on the show . . . [*pause*] . . . How do I say this? If I'm willing to go on the show, then it's OK. I mean, they have to do what they have to do. They have a job, to produce ratings to keep their show on the air. They're out for the old advertising dollar. I understand this."

Jack understands this because he watches talk shows, and he watches *Randy* in particular. Although he was disappointed not to reconcile with his parents (in fact, the show made things worse), he did not feel manipulated or used because he knew that producers had a different goal: to attract advertisers through high ratings. Whatever his motivations, realized or not, there was a certain fit between expectation and outcome. As a talk-show fan, and as someone with prior talk-show experience, Jack had an "inside" knowledge of the fun house.

Resistance and Accommodation

Guests who are angered or upset by their experience on a talk show or by their treatment at the hands of producers have limited ways of registering their displeasure. Producers and guests together engineer a performance, but their relative contributions are hardly equal, for it is producers (and their superiors) who make the decisions that guests, for the most part, simply enact. Guests are not powerless or completely without recourse, but they are on foreign ground, having to operate according to rules and conditions that they did not create and do not always fully understand. When there is a clash of agendas between producers and guests—tension or disagreement over the framing and telling of stories, over wardrobe and makeup, over the terms of a guest's appearance—guests may engage in individual tactical maneuvers that prompt compensatory action from producers, but they rarely challenge the base syntax of the production process itself.

A number of producers mentioned the sense of power that they experience working in television, putting together programs that millions of people watch every day. Guests, too, have a certain kind of power in this context: the power to be watched by all those people. Indeed, without the guests and their stories, there would be no shows. Thus, one of the trump cards that guests hold is the threat to cancel or drop out, and the closer to show time, the more effective the card. As we have seen, Pam was one guest at *Randy* who threatened to back out when she became frustrated with the attempts of the staff to make her more presentable for television. Although, in the end, she did go through with the taping (wearing her own clothes and makeup), Pam's attitude was not unusual among *Randy* guests. Once when I asked a producer there if she thought that her guests were easier to manipulate or control because of their disadvantaged circumstances, she replied, "Not at all. In fact, a lot of them are tougher than I am. They're strong willed, you know. Most of the people that come on this show are pretty strong willed."

Even guests who do not consider themselves particularly strong willed have the option of backing down if they suspect foul play, as Bonnie threatened to do when she discovered that her show on near-death experiences was starting to resemble a circus act. Katherine actually followed through on her threat to cancel when she discovered that a producer at *Charles Perez* had not been forthright with her about the topic of the show. Katherine had already been on *Ricki Lake* with her friend Marie, each representing opposite sides of a staged controversy over whether women "needed" men. One of the producers there later moved to *Charles Perez*, taking her Rolodex of contacts with her. She called Katherine up, asking Katherine to reprise her role. The producer wanted to use the year-old preinterview, but Katherine insisted on doing a new one. The initial call came on a Wednesday, and the taping was scheduled for Friday. On Friday morning, Katherine began to get nervous because she still had not been interviewed. So she called and asked the producer, Don't you think it's time that we talk?

"Eventually, it came to light that the actual topic of the show was going to be something to the effect of 'Single Women are Pathetic,' or 'Single Women Are Suckers,' or something far more inflammatory than the *Ricki Lake* show was," Katherine told me. "And here I was about to play one of the single women!" She was not at all pleased and decided to cancel. The producer, not surprisingly, got upset. According to Katherine, they had the following exchange:

"I can't believe you're doing this on the day of the taping!" the producer yelled.

"I can't believe you were so unprofessional as to not do a preinterview with me and not tell me the truth about this show!" Katherine replied.

"Look. We get ratings through confrontation. We can't get ratings through people going on and being polite to each other. This is not a tea party. This is a talk show."

They argued back and forth for another few minutes, with the producer trying to shame Katherine into reconsidering. According to Katherine, "She tried to make it seem like I was having a sudden change of heart for some inexplicable reason, rather than what, you know, was actually the case, which was that I hadn't been told what direction this show was going to take."

Guests can play the cancellation card at various points along the way, but hours before taping is the most devastating from a production standpoint. Guests can also pull out midstream, so to speak, after taping has already begun. This is essentially what Margaret did, one of the *Diana* guests described in the opening pages of this book. Her rebellion was highly unusual; it was also highly effective, partly because producers did not intend to make her angry and were thus willing to renegotiate the terms of her appearance, and partly because Margaret defected prior to (not after) going onstage. Otherwise, walk-offs are not necessarily cause for alarm because they simply become part of the performance.

Another tactic employed by disgruntled guests is to minimize the drama, to grow quiet and reserved or stop talking altogether. In emotion-work terms, where the payoff for the emotional labor expended by producers is supposed to be the emotional performances of guests, this is essentially a form of nonpayment. Anitra did this more or less unconsciously on *Jenny Jones* when faced with a barrage of hostile accusations from her two sisters and her daughter. Nancy, too, found that she just naturally stopped talking when unexpectedly confronted with her adversary on *Diana*. Vince gave a deliberately subdued performance on *Montel*, realizing after the taping started that the best way to save face was to disengage from, rather than respond to, the accusations of his wives. Sonny also downplayed her emotions when she and her stepbrother Casey appeared for the second time on *Jerry Springer*. Of all these guests, Sonny was the most strategic and consciously oppositional about her decision to withhold the money shot. Because the first show about teen prostitution was so volatile, Sonny and Casey were asked to tape a second show about love triangles several months later (Casey was dating two women at the same time, and Sonny, as his older sister, was supposed to criticize his lifestyle and order him to make a choice). But, having learned a lesson, she made a pact with Casey not to get angry or fight.

As she explained it, "I said to Casey, 'No matter what they tell me to say about you, I'm not going to say nothin' bad.' I said, 'No matter what, me and you are not fighting this time.' So, when I got on that stage, I walked out there, and I said, 'Casey, you need to make a decision.' And that's all I said. I didn't say nothing else. And I know that made them mad."

"It made the producers mad?" I asked.

"Yeah, it made them mad. It ruined their show."

"You mean because you didn't get angry and fight like they wanted you to?"

"Uh-huh, and I wasn't going to. Why should I? I mean, the first time was bad enough; it done ruined everything because, any closeness there was, there is not anymore in this family."

Once a show has been taped, there is little that guests can do if they are unhappy with the outcome. They can telephone producers and complain, they can write a letter of protest (Nancy was one guest who did this), or, if their dissatisfaction is the result of fraud or willful deception, they can sue. Ramón, Jordan, and Bonnie all toyed with the idea of suing but, in the end, decided not to. Tony also wanted to sue, even though he had deceived producers rather than the other way around! (He felt that the producers overreacted when they discovered his ruse and that he suffered "emotional distress" as a result of their hostility.) On the rare occasions when talk-show guests have reportedly sued the owning network or syndication company, the charges have been for violations like breech of contract, fraud, and emotional harm, and such cases are typically settled out of court (see Heaton and Wilson 1995). A *Randy* producer told me that, on occasion, guests have also been known to sue one another.

Consequences and Effects

Given the range of experiences of guests, the types of frustrations and disappointments that they suffer, and the limited recourse available to them if things go badly, it is not surprising that guests felt differently and reported different consequences as the result of going on a talk show. Some guests—Barb, Cora, and Joanne among them—were entirely pleased with their participation and reported no adverse consequences at all. As Barb described her debut on *Randy*, "I had a ball!" They were glad that they participated and would do so again. Indeed, Cora had hopes of reappearing on *Diana* to renew her wedding vows. Tony's original appearance on *Geraldo* had far-reaching and dramatic consequences: the show sent him to a drug rehabilitation facility that helped him get clean. "It totally changed my life," he told me. "It was a very heavy experience." Less dramatic, but more typical, are the experiences of guests like Lori, Sharon, or Jane, who said that they had no strong feelings either way about the taping and were completely unaffected by the experience. As Jane told me, "My life is unchanged. I was disappointed I couldn't get help for my legal case, but not enormously. I mean, it wasn't like fifteen minutes of Andy Warhol fame."

Lori was also relatively indifferent after going on *Randy* to tell her sister-in-law to butt out of her marriage. The two women had actually come to blows during the taping, and I expected this to figure negatively in her assessment of the show. But, some weeks later on the phone, when I asked her if she felt that she had been treated fairly, Lori told me, "Oh yeah, everybody was really great. No complaints."

Like the guests in Priest's (1995) study, a number of those I spoke to said that they found it disconcerting but flattering to have total strangers recognize them from the show. Katherine reported that, after her experience on *Ricki Lake*, people would stop her and exclaim, "I saw you on *Ricki Lake!*" "So many people. People in my building who had never spoken to me before, friends whom I haven't seen in, like, a year, the guy in my deli, who has ever since given me extra pasta!"

Because her talk-show experience was unpleasant, Anitra was embarrassed when this happened to her. "People would, like, flag me down, 'Hey, I saw you on the *Jenny Jones* show!' Some drunk gets off at the bus, 'Oh, you were on *Jenny Jones!*'" Anitra's daughter, Rebecca, was equally embarrassed at having gone on the show and was teased about it by her classmates at school. According to Anitra, "Kids would come up to her and say stuff like, 'Your mom beat you? Your mom's a prostitute?' 'Cause that's what my sister said about me on the show." Despite having felt "like a lamb thrown to the lions," however, Anitra said that she would consider appearing again as long as the forum was not so confrontational. Not so Helen, who so regretted her participation on *Diana* that she forbade her family to tell anyone about it. She did not even want her free videotaped copy of the show. "I feel I shouldn't have been so easily swayed," she said. "I should have known better, and I'd rather just pretend I was never part of such a circus."

Sometimes, the consequences for guests are more severe than humiliation, embarrassment, or regret. Winona, for example, was under court order not to have any contact with her younger daughter when they appeared together on *Randy*. Her social worker saw the program when it aired, extended the terms of the court order to include the entire family, and doubled the penalty for violation. Relations between Jordan and her uncle Casey remained strained months after the *Jerry Springer* taping despite the fact that they had once been very close. Moreover, because she had admitted on television to working as a prostitute, Jordan could scarcely walk down the street in her hometown without attracting the attention of the police. Vince suffered a string of obscene phone calls from strangers who had seen him on TV, and he felt that, in the end, his talk-show appearances probably earned him a harsher sentence when he was actually tried for and convicted of bigamy than he might otherwise have gotten. Ramón is in the military, and, when his superior officer learned that Cheri's mother, April, had accused him on national television of statutory rape, he was formally reprimanded and told to forget about an expected promotion (he did get the promotion eventually). When April heard about the reprimand, she telephoned Ramón to apologize, saying that she had not expected things to get so out of hand. In fact, both April and Ramón had pleaded with producers not to air the program, but to no avail, even when April told them (falsely) that her was daughter was so devastated by the experience that she had become suicidal.

The formality of sanctions or consequences does not necessarily determine the strength of a guest's emotional response, however. Although Fran experienced no formal sanctions for her appearance on *Oprah*, of all the guests I spoke to she expressed the most anguish and regret, her feelings still very fresh even years later. She was angry with the producers for focusing on her adulterous behavior (she slept with one of the men who conned her) to the exclusion of all other aspects of her story. "I was absolutely humiliated when my sixty-eight-year-old aunt called and said, 'I saw you on *Oprah*.' I felt humiliated and like I was dirty. And I felt people looked at our marriage as different than what it really was because I'm a very loving and devoted housewife and I can tell you how I felt suicidal from doing something like that. And then to have it exposed on TV—I felt like I suffered terrible consequences because I'm not an idiot, and I'm not a cheat or an adulteress, and that's basically how I came across. And it hurts. My husband and I were hurt enough. We certainly didn't need an extra blow to us."

Not surprisingly, then, guests who have bad or unpleasant experiences on talk shows tend to regret their participation. Some may blame the producers for misleading them about the topic or the role that they were supposed to play, or they may blame themselves for not having learned more about the show before agreeing to be on it. For others, it is a matter not of placing blame anywhere in particular but of realizing, after the fact, that they misjudged the forum and the wisdom of performing in it. The immediate consequences that ensue—embarrassment, humiliation, strained personal relations, even legal sanctions—naturally enhance their feelings of anger or regret.

Consequences can be understood in broader terms as well, however, and it is worth broaching the matter here before leaving the subject of ordinary guests and moving on to experts. By and large, the consequences mentioned above affect guests in relatively concrete and tangible ways. Painful or embarrassing as they may be, such consequences are only part of the story, for there is also the question of what it means for guests to assume membership in a denigrated social category: that of *talk-show guest*. What are the larger social implications of participating in a discourse widely assumed to epitomize the degradation of American culture? Guests get a negative rap not just because they say and do things on national television that critics of the genre never would but because the willingness of people to "bare it all" on national television is said to reflect poorly on American society more generally. As we have seen, critics worry that talk shows blur the boundaries between information and entertainment, compromise the integrity of the public sphere by bringing into public discourse issues that ought to remain private, trivialize important social issues, normalize unusual or deviant behavior, foster a culture of victimhood and complaint, and generally erode standards of decency and good taste.

Of course, proof of such effects is difficult to come by, as it is for media effects more generally (see Livingstone 1996; McQuail 1991), and it is certainly possible to trot out contradictory evidence. Some studies suggest, for example, that watching talk shows helps people feel better about their own lives because viewers tend to engage in "downward social comparison" with guests (Frisby 1999; Kamrin 1999) and that, rather than trivializing social problems and desensitizing viewers, watching talk shows can actually heighten the importance of certain issues for viewers (Davis and Mares 1998; Rössler and Brosius 2001). Moreover, it can be argued that, far from encouraging moral laxity and depravity, even trashy shows like *Jerry Springer* exhibit a strong moral code in which wrongdoers are chastised for their sins and the put-upon vindicated (Shattuc 1997; Lowney 1999). This moral code is, for the most part, utterly conventional: infidelity is wrong, siblings should love one another, crime doesn't pay, do unto others as you would have them do unto you, and so forth. Consequently, critics who charge that talk shows normalize deviant behavior miss the point that such behavior is presented expressly to be condemned and that most viewers are unlikely to identify with, let alone imitate, it. Two recent studies of *Jerry Springer* viewers by and large confirm this observation (see Greenberg, Mastro, and Woods 1999; Kamrin 1999).[4]

Regardless of how effects are defined and measured, it seems safe to say that guests on the majority of talk shows tend to occupy a less than enviable position in life. It may assuage critics to know that viewers feel

---

4. Greenberg, Mastro, and Woods (1999) set out to test the notion that watching violent behavior on television encourages aggressive tendencies in viewers. This notion is derived from the general tenets of social-learning theory (Bandura 1973), which suggest that one of the ways individuals learn behavior is by observing it in others. However, whether the behavior is ultimately imitated or rejected depends on several factors, including the attractiveness of the model, the perceived consequences of the behavior, and whether the behavior itself is easily imitated (i.e., whether it is simple, distinct, salient, repeated, etc.). The authors found that college students failed to exhibit increased aggressive tendencies after watching *Springer* guests fight on the show, despite the fact that the violence on the show is simple, repetitive, and arousal provoking. This "failure" was due to the fact that other, more important, conditions for successful modeling were absent. Specifically, the authors suggest that college-student viewers are unlikely to imitate the behavior of guests on talk shows like *Jerry Springer* because (1) such guests are comparatively unattractive models (either physically, intellectually, or behaviorally), (2) they appear to get little, if any, reward for their aggressive behavior, (3) they typically fail to solve their problems and, in fact, often make them worse, and (4) their behaviors are portrayed as morally bankrupt and unjustifiably aggressive (Greenberg, Mastro, and Woods 1999, 13).

Of course, laboratory findings are not necessarily generalizable to the outside world, nor are college students representative of all viewers. But these findings do challenge the assumption that trashy talk shows are harmful to society because they encourage viewers to engage in the same aggressive or negative behaviors as guests. For her part, Kamrin (1999) wanted to know why relatively well-educated, middle-class viewers would choose to watch *Jerry Springer*, hypothesizing that watching the show allows viewers to feel superior to *Springer* guests and thus, indirectly, to feel better about themselves. Taking a three-pronged approach, she analyzed show content, solicited comments on-line from viewers, and administered a survey to college undergraduates. Overall, she found that, while only about half her respondents agreed that viewing the show made them feel better about themselves, there was very strong evidence in all three arenas to suggest that viewers feel superior to guests.

superior to guests and are therefore not easily influenced by their performances or that viewers are not developing a generalized tolerance for
deviant conduct, but these insights are not so flattering to the guests themselves. Even one of the most common arguments employed to defend the
genre—that it provides visibility for people and issues normally excluded
from television, reminding viewers of the ethnic, class, and sexual diversity
of American society—raises important questions about the precise nature
of this visibility and its effect on guests. The kind of visibility that leads
viewers to pity or denigrate participants might well be worse than no visibility at all.

This dilemma has implications for the larger generic category *ordinary guest*, but it has particular relevance for guests on trashy shows. Kamrin's (1999) study of *Jerry Springer* viewers is a dramatic illustration of this
point. "Making fun of guests" and "entertainment" came just after "passing the time" as the most frequently cited reasons for watching the show.
Asked to list the ways in which they themselves were similar or dissimilar
to *Springer* guests, respondents focused on the differences, writing things
like, "I'm educated," "I'm not a sexual deviant," "I don't take my problems
on television," "I have self-control," "I'm normal," and "I'm not white
trash." Viewers who submitted comments on-line were even more explicitly contemptuous. They described guests as "sewer rats," "vermin," and
"trailer trash" and admitted to watching the show (despite also being dis-
gusted by it) largely because the guests were so "pathetic" and "stupid" that
one could not help but be entertained by them.[5] Thus, another kind of effect to consider here is that of public opinion on guests, especially those of
marginal status, and whether one consequence of participating might be
further marginalization. The dilemma is potentially most serious for members of racial or sexual minority groups whose representation in the media
is limited and already less than ideal.

Not being sociologists or media critics, guests themselves tend not to
discuss consequences and effects in these terms, nor do they see themselves
as part of a denigrated group necessarily, although they are well aware of
the negative reputation of the genre overall and of the heightened stigma
attached to certain shows (it was this reputation that made guests wary of

---

5. One respondent, who identified as a visitor from Europe, read the show as an in-
dictment of American culture and implied that viewers were little different than guests: "I
never saw anybody so entertained by violence like Americans. For sure they live boring
lives, and all that can get their attention is violence. It is sick. They don't have real values in
their lives—at least most of them" (Kamrin 1999, 62; and see generally 26–41).

participating and that led them to voice many of the hesitations and concerns about participating discussed in the previous chapter). They do, however, see *other* people as part of that denigrated category *the talk-show guest*. This is not so surprising in the case of *Diana* guests, who had the luxury of distinguishing that show from other shows and themselves from "those other kinds of guests." Yet *Randy* participants were also critical of the genre and drew similar boundaries, despite *being* "that other kind of guest." Regardless of what show people went on or what the topic was, they rarely saw their own participation as subject to the same critical framework that they applied to others. They had specific criteria for judging acceptable public conduct but either exempted themselves from those criteria or employed such fine distinctions that they perceived a real difference between their behavior and that of the guests they criticized.

Thus, Vince, a con artist and bigamist, went on *Diana* and *Montel* to get soundly thrashed by four angry ex-wives but insisted that he would never go on *Jerry Springer* because of "all the transvestites that he has parading through there." Thus, Charlotte, Vince's ex-wife, willingly appeared in all the tabloid newsmagazines as well as on numerous daytime talk shows but said that she drew the line at *Randy* because those guests were crazy ("My brother's cousin's husband sleepin' with my aunt, I ate the dog for lunch, and all that kind of crazy stuff"). Thus, Joanne went on *Randy* to yell nasty things at another woman at the top of her lungs but at the same time told me that she couldn't understand why some people go on national television to air their dirty laundry: "Why would you get on there and air some of the filth you see nowadays? I mean, there are some secrets that you just don't air to millions of people." Joanne obviously saw a clear difference between what she did (give a woman who "deserved" it a piece of her mind) and what some other guests do (reveal personal secrets). Likewise, Fran said that she was appalled at how some people air their dirty laundry on talk shows, even though she revealed on *Oprah*, reluctantly to be sure, that she had cheated on her husband.

The level of specificity with which guests interpret their own actions and their reluctance to see themselves in categorical terms (as talk-show guests, with broad similarities to other guests) also preclude them from feeling as if they are reproducing negative stereotypes. For instance, none of the black guests I interviewed were concerned about the issue of stereotypes vis-à-vis African Americans. Vince, who was aware of the negative portrayal of black men in the media, especially in relation to crime, said that he was not worried about contributing to that negative imagery with his story because "there just aren't that many black bigamists out there." He acknowledged that his behavior might reflect badly on men in general, but even then he was less concerned about the image that he was projecting of the group than of the image that he was projecting of himself. "I'd like to take the high moral ground," he said, "but I wasn't concerned about that, you know. I was concerned about how long am I going to jail for?" Nor did the ex-wives I interviewed believe that their talk-show appearances reflected badly on African Americans, especially not black women. As one of them put it to me, "I thought about Vince, you know, us being black, that people might say, 'Look at that person, he's doin' this, he's doin' that.' But I didn't think about it as being negative, not on my part. Because *he* was the one who had done it all. I was just one of the people that got hurt behind it."

Jordan was the only guest I interviewed to acknowledge, indirectly, that her own performance on *Jerry Springer* might be conceived as conforming to a negative stereotype, perceived by others as trashy. Although both Jordan and her mother, Sonny, insisted that the basic facts of their family conflict were real (as Jordan put it, "Our show wasn't fake, you know, 'cause our whole family is a hell for real"), nevertheless, Jordan went around telling people that her story was fake, that she acted as she did simply to get on TV—thus revealing an implicit awareness of the negative stigma associated with being a guest on such a show. "That's what Jordan tells people when they ask her," Sonny informed me. "She'll say, 'None of it was true; I just did it to go on TV.'" Sonny believed this to be a common face-saving strategy among *Springer* guests and not one unique to her daughter. As she explained, "A lot of people on that show, you know, they get the free hotel, and the free vacation, and they go on TV, and then they come back and tell people that none of the stuff they said was true. When most of the time it is true. But you can lie and say it's all fake, you know?"

"And why would you do that?" I asked. "What's the purpose of lying?"

"So people can't call you trash. Because people think you're nothing but trash for going on that trashy show. Even the decent people that go on—there *is* some decent people, you know, it ain't only bad people that go on that show, but they [the producers] make 'em look bad anyway. My daughter, I know what she does is wrong and stuff, but she's—she's not trash."

Here we come back to the issue of authenticity with an interesting twist: not only do guests like Tony use fake stories to get on TV, claiming all the while that they are real, but guests like Jordan use real stories to get on TV and claim after the fact that they are fake. Both strategies speak to the same underlying desire—the desire for media exposure and the trappings of celebrity that go along with it—but the latter admits to the illegitimacy of this desire and to the illegitimacy of airing one's dirty laundry to fulfill it. Indeed, Jordan's disavowal of her own story suggests that it is more acceptable to fake your way on TV, *pretending* to air your dirty laundry, than to get on TV by airing your dirty laundry for real.

When it comes to experts, producers are looking for more than knowledge. It's not enough to know a lot about something; you also have to be able to say things in a concise way that's appealing to a large audience. It's entertainment, so you have to be able to perform. You have to be animated. So there are many wonderful scholars who just wouldn't make it on television because they would, you know, they'd be too high on the snore scale.

—JEREMY, expert guest

CHAPTER SEVEN

Will the Real Expert Please Stand Up?

Of Experts and Ordinary People: Reframing Expertise

So far, in discussing talk-show guests, I have been concerned mostly with so-called ordinary people, those who, by definition, are not professional experts or celebrities but are, nonetheless, the real stars and experts of the genre and, therefore, the main focus of production efforts. Here, I turn to that group or class of talk-show guests more peripheral to the genre: experts. Why do experts participate in a forum that often seems ill suited—even hostile—to rational discussion and debate? How is expertise packaged and sold for mass consumption? How does the clash of agendas between producers and guests play itself out when the guests are experts rather than ordinary people?

Experts—and particularly intellectuals—occupy a paradoxical position in American society. As Goldfarb (1998) notes, democracies need the specialized knowledge and creative capacities that intellectuals and other experts contribute because the democratic process requires an informed and critical citizenry, yet experts are still viewed with suspicion since hierarchy is questioned as a matter of fundamental principle. In the United States, this conflict dates back to the earliest years of colonial development, and it became more pronounced in the aftermath of the Industrial Revolution. According to Levine (1988), with industrialization and the rise of a new urban elite, both work and leisure became more fragmented, specialized, commodified, and, most significant, professionalized; as a result, during the nineteenth century, Americans learned to defer to experts in a wide range of activities that had previously been relatively open. At the same time, the tenets of republicanism remained strong, encouraging an undercurrent of persistent opposition to cultural authority, such that significant segments of the population remained at best ambivalent about, and at worse hostile toward, the categories and definitions of elite culture promoted by professional experts (Levine 1988, 195; see also Lasch 1978). This ambivalence has remained a core feature of American life, manifest in different ways and in a variety of political contexts, from the challenge posed to the conventional (male) medical establishment by the feminist health movement of the 1970s (Ehrenreich and English 1978), to the myriad self-help and recovery groups that offer alternative frameworks for understanding addiction and deviance (Lowney 1999; Simonds 1992).

Of all experts, intellectuals arguably feel the tension between expertise and egalitarianism most acutely since they tend to fall on the elite end of the expert spectrum. Americans seem to exhibit a special distrust of intellectualism. Studies of high school and college students, for example, show that these groups see intellectualism as unfriendly, "uppity," and undemocratic (Moffatt 1989). Lamont's (1992) cross-national research on the professional-managerial class in France and the United States reveals comparable attitudes among upper-class American men. Whereas French respondents placed considerable importance on intellectual growth, drew strong boundaries between elite and popular culture, and were quick to cite intellectuals as role models, Americans were more likely to mention business entrepreneurs as role models, had broader repertoires for what constituted legitimate cultural authority, and did not identify strongly with intellectualism (valuing instead *self-actualization*, defined as personal growth and individual career success). The two groups also had different standards for assessing intelligence. For the French, it meant literary and linguistic competence as well as the ability to develop complex, theoretical arguments based on abstract principles of analysis, while Americans read intelligence largely as the mastery of facts and practical knowledge and as task-oriented competence (the ability to get things done). Interestingly, the cross-national differences outlined here loosely parallel the differences between professional and lay expertise in the United States, with the former emphasizing theory and abstraction, the latter emphasizing more grounded, experiential ways of knowing.

In showcasing ordinary people, and in valuing personal experience over distanced or abstract modes of knowledge, daytime talk shows at once perpetuate and work against ordinary/expert distinctions. Sonia Livingstone and Peter Lunt (1994) view the historic growth of what they call *audience-discussion programs* in the United States and Britain as an important manifestation of the public anxiety about expert knowledge outlined above. According to Livingstone and Lunt, audience-discussion programs challenge the separation of expertise from ordinary understanding and signal a move from elite to more participatory social and political arrangements in which experts are increasingly contrasted with and held accountable to the laity, who are themselves constructed as the real experts. The construction of expertise here draws on two related oppositions: expert/lay and public/private. As experts are increasingly pressed to speak in lay terms and to use private individuals to illustrate public issues, ordinary people are encouraged to see personal experience as a legitimate form of evidence and to see themselves as experts on everyday life. Consequently, although television has traditionally been ambivalent about its respect for ordinary people, both promoting their visibility and contrasting them with the more privileged voices of professional experts, Livingstone and Lunt conclude that, as ordinary people gain visibility in the medium, and as experts themselves are shown to be in conflict over questions of policy and research, public discourse begins to change: expert knowledge is undermined and lay knowledge elevated.[1] The concept of expertise itself is not in question. At issue is what kind of expertise matters and who gets to own it.

1. Livingstone and Lunt's own research on talk-show audiences supports this observation: viewers consider hearing from ordinary people to be at least as valuable, if not more valuable, than hearing from experts, especially if they accept the public-sphere claims of the genre to provide a space for average people to come together and share their views (Livingstone and Lunt 1994). The authors found that, overall, viewers consider daytime talk shows (audience-discussion programs) to offer a "fair and valuable debate" and "a public sphere in which they [i.e., average people] can participate," with little difference between viewers in terms of age, sex, or class (Livingstone and Lunt 1994, 49). However, responses to television talk shows are complicated by the unstable and diverse expectations that audiences have

Consistent with their overall aesthetic, daytime talk shows illustrate the shifting balance of power between expert and ordinary knowledge in a heightened, exaggerated fashion. This is especially true of shows on the trashy end of the continuum, where "the degree-flashing expert is as eligible as anybody else, if not more so, to be 'schooled' by guests and audience members who know 'real life'" (Gamson 1998, 117; see also Carpignano et al. 1990; Masciarotte 1991; Munson 1993). Experts can and do make judgments, provide facts and statistical evidence, dispense advice, and generally critique the behavior of ordinary people, but whether anybody listens to them is quite another matter. Indeed, amid all the shouting, sobbing, and finger-pointing, it is experts rather than ordinary people who often appear bizarre and out of place. Just how marginal experts have become is well illustrated by a recent content analysis of the eleven top-rated shows, which found that experts accounted for only 3 percent of the total speaking turns on average, while audience members accounted for roughly 5 percent, hosts for 40 percent, and ordinary guests for 53 percent (Greenberg and Smith 1995). Experts fared best on classy shows like *Oprah* (with up to 10 percent of the total speaking turns) and worst on trashy shows like *Jenny Jones*, *Sally Jessy Raphael*, and *Ricki Lake*.

In addition to the marginality of experts, there is the related issue of the representation (and misrepresentation) of expertise itself. Just as talk shows render a cartoonish portrayal of ordinary people, they can present a cartoonish rendition of the expert. At the most extreme, this means allowing nonexperts to play the expert role, using generic titles such as *sex educator*, *communication specialist*, and *behavior therapist* to describe individuals who may have few or no professional qualifications. As with ordinary guests, the more sensational the topic or show, the greater the potential for misrepresentation or fraud. Mental-health professionals worry about this most, being the most ubiquitous type of expert guest.[2] Yet, even when

---

of such programs; what people think of daytime talk seems to depend largely on what kinds of information and/or representations they value. On the one hand, those respondents who valued hearing ordinary people's opinions over those of experts were more likely to believe that talk shows provide a fair forum for public discussion, that such a discussion has real-world consequences, and that the issues debated are personally and emotionally relevant to their own lives. On the other hand, respondents who valued the opinion of experts over those of ordinary people were more critical of talk shows, believing them to be at times crude, chaotic, out of control, and an invasion of privacy. These latter beliefs are stronger among male viewers and among viewers from higher social classes (Livingstone and Lunt 1994, 49–50).

2. The use of fake experts is typically a matter not of real experts deceiving producers by claiming qualifications that they do not actually possess but of producers knowingly

experts are real, and even when the venue is more or less respectable, a certain degradation of expertise is inevitable because of the media's inherent limitations in presenting complex arguments and scientific evidence. As Goldfarb (1998) notes, experts who seek to address the general public are caught in a double bind: they are dependent on the media to disseminate their works, but the media change the meaning of these works in one way or another, making it impossible for certain ideas to be articulated or even imagined. As Goldfarb puts it, "The logic of media communication dominates the logic of intellectual criticism" (10). Experts have media access because of who they are and what they know; their qualification to speak in the public domain is based on the authority granted them because of their specialist knowledge. But the specialist knowledge itself, untranslated, is not representable on television. Once on the media stage, once inside the fun house and subject to its rules, what experts know must be conveyed in nonspecialist, televisual terms.

Classifying Experts: Types, Motives, and Agendas

Rachel, an associate producer and my key informant at *Diana*, referred to the story of the three blind men and the elephant when I first broached the subject of expert guests with her: "Remember how the three blind men

---

allowing nonexperts to play the expert role—because it is too much work to find a real expert, because their original expert backed out, or because they could not persuade a credible expert to participate in the first place. Consider the *Ricki Lake* episode in which Katherine and her friend feigned disagreement about whether women "needed" men. Not only were most of the ordinary guests on this show personal friends of the producers, but, according to Katherine, the "relationship expert" was actually the fitness columnist for a men's magazine. Heaton and Wilson (1995) describe another *Ricki Lake* show, one about infidelity, in which the featured "therapist" was presented as an expert because she had written a popular self-help book advising women to train their wayward mates as they would train a dog—with firm commands followed by praise and pats on the head. On the show, the expert entertained the audience by demonstrating her techniques ("Sit!" "Stay!") with the couples onstage. Amusing as such performances may be, it is easy to see why they have raised the ire of legitimate professional experts.

As Heaton and Wilson (1995) note, talk TV is not just a powerful force in the entertainment world; as the primary public forum for discussing mental-health concerns, it undoubtedly holds sway over the general public's perception of the mental-health profession. In a more or less direct acknowledgment of this dilemma, the American Psychological Association has devoted entire conference panels to the "image problem" that talk shows have created for their members, while *Psychology Today* has published confessionals from former talk-show experts warning colleagues not to get involved (see Fischoff 1995).

come up to the elephant and touch a different part, and they each think it is something completely different? I think of that sometimes when I deal with experts—that their perspective, unless they have had a lot of media experience, is really different from what the producer's agenda is." This could not be more true, for, of all the guests I interviewed, experts were, in some ways, the most naive about the genre and the least prepared for its limitations and constraints.

According to Shattuc's (1997) content analysis of 260 hours of talk-show programming, the majority of experts on daytime talk shows are psychologists, psychiatrists, psychotherapists, social workers, and relationship counselors, followed by (in order of frequency) writers of self-help books, bureaucrats who manage social-welfare and health agencies, elected officials, academics, religious leaders, lawyers, and journalists. The expert guests I saw come and go as an intern at *Diana* and *Randy* covered a similar range, although, in my sample of interview subjects, therapists and other mental-health professionals were underrepresented and professional academics and community activists overrepresented, largely because my own occupation as a sociologist gave me disproportionate contact with these latter two groups.

In general, the expert guests I interviewed are best divided into two broad categories: *professional experts* and *organic experts*. Professional experts tend to be either *therapist experts*, psychologists and counselors of various kinds whose expertise derives from professional training and clinical practice, or *scholar experts*, academics or professionals whose expertise on subjects like crime, sexual assault, or teen pregnancy is based on research and teaching primarily within university settings. Therapist experts tend to be the lone voice of authority on any given show (aside from the host), while scholar experts more often share the stage with other kinds of experts, including organic experts. Organic experts are *activists* or *spokespersons* affiliated with community-service organizations, typically rape-crisis centers, battered women's shelters, gang-prevention or drug- and alcohol-rehabilitation programs, and HIV/AIDS-education and -support groups. Organic experts are essentially lay experts, differing from professional experts not only in terms of credentials and status but also in terms of having firsthand experience of the problem or issue that they are brought on the show to discuss.

Of course, these groupings are rough and not mutually exclusive. The difficulties that I faced in categorizing experts—and even in distinguishing an expert from an ordinary guest—partly reflect the genre's intentional blurring of the expert/ordinary distinction. This blurring was most obvious in the case of organic experts vis-à-vis ordinary people. Indeed, most of my organic experts had also made talk-show appearances at one time or another as an ordinary person—usually earlier in their media careers, as the typical trajectory is to move from ordinary to expert status rather than the other way around, with a commensurate decrease in air-time. This was true for Joyce, an African American woman falsely imprisoned for murder, now head of a nonprofit organization called MASS (Mothers for the Advancement of Social Systems) that helps people accused of crimes negotiate the legal system; for Lorna, another black woman who runs an antiviolence organization called Drive-By Agony because both her sons were murdered by gang members in South-Central Los Angeles; for Isaac, a Hispanic (his preferred term) man who joined the Prisoners' Rights Union because of the human-rights violations that he witnessed while incarcerated in a maximum-security prison; for Nathan, a white man in his early twenties who has been active in HIV/AIDS education and outreach in local high schools ever since contracting HIV at the age of nineteen; and for Abby, a white, male cross-dresser who founded the Renaissance Education Center in order to provide education and support to members of the transgender community.

The different categories of expert can be situated loosely along a continuum according to their distance from the problem or issue at hand, with academics who merely *study* the problem in question on one end and ordinary people turned experts who have *experienced* the problem on the other. An expert's placement on the continuum thus reflects his or her social distance from the ordinary guests sharing the stage: highly educated experts with multiple degrees working in elite institutions are mostly white and middle or upper class, whereas organic experts more closely approximate the class status of ordinary guests and are more ethnically diverse. The distinction that I draw between organic and professional experts is similar to the distinction that Robinson (1982, 373) makes between lay and professional experts in her early analysis of the *Donahue* show. She calls lay experts *insiders* and professional experts *outsiders* because the latter rarely discussed their personal experiences when presenting information on the air, while the former almost always did.

Expert guests on talk shows enter the production process either because of their affiliation with an established organization or institution or because they have been cited or quoted elsewhere in the media. Generally speaking, most of the experts I interviewed had some prior media exposure before going on a talk show, although this was more often the case for therapist experts and organic experts than for academics. Academics were also less likely to have had prior experience specifically on a daytime talk show than were these other groups. Thus, an expert's placement on the distance continuum also tends to reflect her level of familiarity with the genre: the closer an expert to the status of ordinary guest, the more experience she is likely to have had with daytime talk shows. The chief exceptions to this pattern in my sample were Rhoda, a therapist expert who had been on more than fifty different shows, and Jeremy, an academic expert and criminologist who studies (among other things) serial murder and hate crime. Like Rhoda, Jeremy had been on virtually every single talk show, some of them multiple times. Regardless of expert type, the key to continued media exposure was prior media exposure: once you enter the loop as an expert, and provided that you give a satisfactory performance, the calls from producers snowball.

General concerns about the trashy nature of the genre aside, the experts I interviewed tended not to have the misgivings and reservations about participating that ordinary guests did, or at least not to the same degree—perhaps because, regardless of the topic or the perceived quality of the show, playing expert does not carry the same potential for embarrassment or humiliation as does playing ordinary person. As Connie, an academic who studies domestic violence, put it, "I just figured, Oh well. It's an hour. You're up there, someone's going to ask your opinion, what do you care? Maybe it will help educate the public." This is not to say that experts were not sometimes wary of participating. Because Rebecca, the director of a university women's center, had never seen *Diana*, did not know its reputation, and did not want to be party to exploiting ordinary people ("'Cause that's what happens most of the time on those shows"), she initially tried to avoid appearing on the show, referring the producer to other experts. Not surprisingly, Abby was reluctant to appear on *Morton Downey Jr.* in the late 1980s since his role on the show was to defend the pleasures and legitimacy of cross-dressing. Grant, a writer and gay activist, had mixed feelings about playing the unenviable role of bad expert on *Donahue* since his job was to defend pornography against censorship. Jeremy, the criminologist with considerable media experience, also admitted to having mixed feelings about appearing on talk shows despite the frequency with which he did so. "I do have standards," he insisted, "but I hate to refuse when I know I'll get a chance to say something that I think is important, and to be able to say it to millions of people is quite a privilege."

Indeed, despite their hesitations and misgivings, experts are motivated to participate in the genre for the same reasons expressed by many serious ordinary guests: they want to proselytize, champion a cause, or educate the public. They adopt a transmission rather than a ritual orientation toward the media and discuss the attraction of talk shows largely in public-sphere terms. As Jeremy put it, "Talk shows give me a classroom of millions. A chance to educate people, a chance to bridge two cultures [elite and popular] by bringing my research into the public sphere. And that's something I not only enjoy doing but see as important."

Some experts were motivated by a specific desire to reframe an issue that they felt the media had misrepresented or to correct erroneous or incomplete information. This was the case for Richard, another academic expert, who was disturbed by the inaccurate reporting of crime statistics in the media. Some, like Abby, the cross-dressing expert, agreed to participate less to educate the general public (although this was also a goal) than to reach out to similarly stigmatized individuals. Thus, he was persuaded to go on *Morton Down Jr.* even though he knew that it would be "no day at the beach" because informing other cross-dressers about his organization outweighed whatever else would happen to him on the show (most probably, being positioned as a sideshow freak). Other organic experts also went on talk shows to garner support for their organization and its aims. This was true for Isaac, vice president of the Prisoners' Rights Union, Lorna, founder and director of Drive-By Agony, and Joyce, head of MASS. Grant, too, had activist aims and used his appearance on *Donahue* to discuss gay rights, AIDS education, and federal funding for the arts, all in addition to the scheduled topic of pornography and censorship. In his case, these goals existed in combination with the desire to have a little fun on the show. Grant had recently been crowned "International Mr. Leather" (the gay-male equivalent of Miss America), and he knew that the producers planned to screen a video clip of the contest, specifically of him walking down the ramp waving a bouquet of black-leather roses. As he told me, "I thought, sure, why not? There's a bit of media whore in most Americans, and I thought it could be fun."

As with ordinary guests, the reasons for participating are often mixed and may even be tangential to the topic at hand. Connie, for example, said that she did not give the matter much thought either way but that, in the end, she agreed to go on a *Randy* show about battered men because it meant that she could visit a friend who lived in the city where the show was taped. Rebecca says that she ultimately went on *Diana* after the other expert contacts that she gave the producer fell through because the producer demonstrated a feminist understanding of sexual violence and because the show offered to pay the women's center a substantial honorarium. As she put it, "It was the best I was ever paid for half a day's work." Increased book sales was another obvious incentive for expert guests, especially those writing for the general public. Lilian, one of the two therapist experts I interviewed, said that promoting her book was the primary reason that she agreed to go on *Montel.* The two experts who accompanied Grant on *Donahue* had written, and were promoting, books, as was Jeremy, at least for some portion of his many appearances.

On *Diana,* an expert who has made three or more appearances can command Screen Actors Guild wages because the show uses a unionized production crew. Rhoda, another therapist expert, was surprised and interested to hear this because, in fifty-odd talk-show appearances, she had never once been paid. She is the prototypical relationship expert brought out onstage in the last segment of a program in order to dispense thirty seconds of advice to the man who repeatedly cheats on his wife or the teenage girl whose sexual promiscuity is invariably deemed the result of low self-esteem. A Ph.D. and practicing psychologist for fifteen years, Rhoda said that she did talk shows initially because she wanted the opportunity to hone her media skills and thought that she might actually help a guest in distress. She quickly learned, however, that the expert role precluded the possibility of any real therapeutic intervention and, after that, redirected her efforts toward educating the audience. In her words, "As a therapist, there's very little you can do for the individual guest. It all happens so rapidly, you can't make an impact on them. You're really talking to the audience at large; that's your contribution."

Aside from Grant, who admitted having "a bit of media whore" in him, rarely did experts tell me that they were attracted to the trappings of celebrity or that they desired media exposure, except insofar as the exposure allowed them access to wider audiences for disseminating their expertise. Yet, for experts, whose identity is partly defined by their expert status and whose expertise can be written down in books and then advertised on the air, reaching wider audiences is almost by definition a form of self-promotion. For experts far more than for ordinary guests, commanding a mass audience is not mutually exclusive with making a contribution to society. In fact, the larger, more mass the audience, the bigger a contribution one potentially can make. In this way, experts who desire the media spotlight (whether for personal gratification or for selling books) have a built-in justification for their desire, for the pleasures and privileges of media exposure conveniently dovetail with their presumed educational mission.

This is lucky for experts because seeking celebrity for celebrity's sake is even less acceptable for them than it is for ordinary people. Indeed, the assumption that ordinary people are swayed by the glamour and excitement of being on TV (but that experts are not) is a point of distinction between ordinary and expert guests, one often made by experts themselves. Rhoda, for example, admitted going on talk shows because she enjoyed public speaking but nevertheless was dismissive of the ordinary guests she encountered for evincing much the same desire. "I've always been someone who enjoys a large audience," she said. "I've been a sex educator for years, and I'm used to being on a podium. So I thought the challenge [of going on talk shows] worthwhile." By contrast, she described ordinary guests as "people from small town USA" who are "easily seduced by the camera" and who think that, "by going on TV, they'll be somebody." Given that ordinary people by definition belong to the private rather than public domain, it is not surprising that some of them orient toward the genre this way. At some level, they are correct in assuming that being on television makes them somebody, insofar as it provides a point of entry into public discourse. The difference between ordinary people and experts here is *how* they become somebody and why.

Lending Credibility: Expert Roles, Functions, and Performances

Whatever the various motivations and agendas of experts, they are rarely the same as those of producers—hence Rachel's comment about the three blind men and the elephant. For producers, the elephant is an unwieldy, demanding, sometimes belligerent creature requiring careful coordination among many contradictory yet interdependent elements. The mandate to orchestrate the money shot under speedup conditions means that the expertise of experts, like the ordinariness of ordinary people, becomes objectified as an element of the production process. Although producers may care about educating the public on a personal level, this is not necessarily their professional priority. Producers want experts to put them in contact with ordinary people, take sides in a controversy, dispense advice to guests on the air, and, in general, lend an aura of credibility to the show. Rachel was very clear on this point. "The focal point of the show is obviously the guests who have personal stories, and that takes precedence over everything else," she said. "Really, producers could care less about experts. The expert is a sort of afterthought, brought in to cap off the discussion and to legitimate the discussion so you aren't just creating a bunch of titillating horror stories about people."

In legitimating the discussion, in giving ordinary people's personal stories the stamp of approval, expert guests also help elevate the genre and make it less vulnerable to censure and criticism. As talk shows have become trashier and the money shot more titillating, this legitimating function of experts becomes simultaneously more important (if the show wants to retain a veneer of dignity) and more expendable (if the show deliberately cultivates a trashy identity). Thus, shows like *Jenny Jones* and *Ricki Lake* now feature experts only occasionally, while *Jerry Springer* has done away with professional experts altogether. As a producer there told me, "Our show is about relationships and conflict, so you don't need an expert to come on and explain why these people act the way they do. I mean, they're pissed off because their mate is cheating on them or, you know, their girlfriend used to be a man!" Yet, even on *Springer*, the expert role has not been abandoned altogether. As the same producer remarked, "Our attempt at that expert voice is Jerry's 'Final Thought.' Jerry by no means claims to be a professional or anything, but he tries to put a little 'here's the moral of the story' at the end of the show. Because there is a moral a lot of the time to the story. And that moral is, Be honest, be honest to yourself, don't hurt other people, treat other people how you want to be treated."

Besides needing experts to legitimate a discussion or provide the moral voice of authority, producers also need experts to gain access to ordinary people, especially for serious, social-issue topics like sexual assault, gang violence, drug abuse, or teen pregnancy. The ordinary people who represent such topics may lie outside a producer's normal network of contacts and even beyond the reach of on-air plugs, with the result that experts—especially organic experts—become indispensable resources for locating guests. In this sense, experts fulfill a function similar to the stringers discussed in chapter 3, the difference being that experts do not get paid for their recruitment efforts. Every one of the organic experts I interviewed had helped producers recruit ordinary guests and considered the aid part of their activist agenda. Of the group, Lorna Hawkins was most frequently called on by producers for this purpose. Her organization provides information and support services to victims of gang-related violence and has a speakers bureau that sends people to inner-city high schools and prisons to educate at-risk youths about the consequences of gang involvement. As Lorna told me, "Producers are always asking if I can bring some guests with me, especially if they're looking for gang members. Matter of fact, I should be working for them! At one time they were calling me to death looking for guests, and, you know, I was like, 'I should be the producer!' Oh yes. *Geraldo,* they called me so much I said, 'Why don't you just hire me?'"

Of course, producers are not the only ones who benefit from such arrangements. As Gamson (1998) has noted, some experts are more than willing to serve as clearinghouses for producers in the search for guests because of the leverage that it gives them in controlling the representation of an issue. This is especially true for spokespersons of marginalized or stigmatized constituencies like ex-convicts, prostitutes, cross-dressers, transsexuals, lesbian mothers, or members of the lesbigay community more generally. In their capacity as stringers, experts can promote ordinary people who they know will be effective in countering damaging stereotypes and thus will cast the group or community in a positive light. (Of course, this same strategy can be used by stigmatized groups with very different political agendas. As I learned from working on *Randy,* Klan leaders were as angry with the representation of that organization on daytime talk shows as lesbigay activists were of the representation of homosexuality and had recently moved to restrict participation to certain "approved" members.) While convenient, using experts to recruit ordinary guests obviously poses certain risks to producers. Not only does it reduce their control over the representation of an issue, but it can jeopardize the show itself if they rely too heavily on an expert to book their panel and then discover that she cannot deliver the goods after all.[3]

---

3. Rachel learned the dangers of this practice the hard way. Her account is quite humorous, so I quote her here at length:

"Experts sometimes get wind of the fact that producers are looking for real-people stories and that they might be able to get themselves on TV by acting as agents for these people. So, to get on the show, a lot of experts spout off these promises—especially if they have a book they want to promote. Mostly it happens with therapists. They will say, 'Yeah, I'm a counselor, and, yeah, I have counseled couples with three heads, and I have five of [the couples], and they would make a great one-hour special for your program.' And, you know, the producer finds it enticing and bites the bait. Which is a big gamble because the show itself is contingent on the real guests with the stories and not the experts or their books or whatever. So [the producer] goes in, and they stick their neck out in a pitch meeting with their boss, and they sell the show—partly because they have been lured in by their own greed and because it's an easy show. They already have the expert and all the guests, and they can sit back and not be so stressed out. I fell for that a few times. So you happily call back the expert, and you say, 'OK, now let's talk about those guests, those first-person stories you were mentioning.'"

At this point, Rachel paused for breath before resuming, half laughing, half snorting in disgust—with herself or the expert, I couldn't tell:

"Well, now, suddenly it comes down to the fact that they don't really have five stories, they actually only have two, and then it turns out that, of those two, one of them

Helping recruit ordinary guests is a relatively invisible, backstage form of influence that experts exert on the genre, as are the long telephone conversations that they have with producers about the topic of the show. Many more experts than actually appear on talk shows exert this kind of influence. Those who go on to make an onstage contribution—helping legitimate the discussion, as mentioned above—find themselves subject to a set of performative criteria not unlike that governing the behavior of ordinary guests. The expert might be a supporting rather than a starring role, but it is a performance nonetheless, and it matters how the role is played. "It takes more than mere knowledge of a subject to get repeat calls from a national television program," Jeremy told me emphatically. Although we had met in person at a conference some weeks before, this conversation took place over the phone. "It's entertainment," he continued, "so you have to be able to perform, you have to be animated, you have to speak in sound bites." He drew a comparison to lecturing: "It takes the same skills to be on a television talk show as it takes to be a decent lecturer. You are being asked to give concise statements that can be easily understood by a mass audience, and that's exactly what it takes to do well in the classroom."

When experts have that skill, when they communicate their expertise with precision and dramatic flair, they may appear as regulars associated with a particular show or, like certain ordinary guests, travel the talk-show circuit. While Jeremy and several of the organic experts I interviewed made appearances on a wide range of shows, it is typically therapist experts like Rhoda who become regulars because their knowledge base is better suited to the personal focus of the genre. According to Shattuc (1997), relationship expert Gilda Carle has replaced Dr. Joyce Brothers as the star therapist of daytime TV, having made more than one hundred talk-show appearances. Unlike organic experts, who tend to collapse the ordinary/expert distinction, therapist experts more often blur the expert/celebrity distinction, and producers like working with star experts for the same reason they

---

doesn't really quite fit the topic. Then things get really quiet, and you don't hear back from the expert for a few days, and you are getting really nervous, and you tell your associate producer to start searching for guests, quick! Finally, you nail down the expert that has not been returning your calls, and it turns out that all the people they have promised you have backed out or have some kind of problem or special condition that would make it really unethical to bring them on television. And so you are left with a huge crisis and a real mess on your hands because you have to completely switch shows at the last minute, and you have literally two days to provide other guests, and you look like an idiot in front of your boss because you came in with all these claims and promises and now everything has unraveled and you have nothing to deliver."

like working with celebrities: they are media-savvy professionals who know how to perform and require little backstage preparation. Producers do not exhibit the same reluctance to recycle experts as they do ordinary guests because, unlike the ordinariness of ordinary people, the expertise of experts is enhanced rather than undermined by repeated exposure.

Inexperienced experts require more time and attention prior to taping than do experienced ones, although still considerably less than ordinary guests. In general, as with ordinary guests, initial preinterviews function as much as auditions as fact-finding missions. Richard, a criminologist, recognized this when he got the first of a series of calls from a producer at *Maury Povich* about doing a show on sex offenders.

"This producer calls me and says, 'We're thinking of doing a show'— they never say 'we're *doing* a show,' it's always 'we're *thinking* of doing a show—and we just wanted to get some background information from you.'" Richard leaned forward in his chair. "Now, see, I know exactly what they're doing. They're checking to see if I would make a good participant. To see how articulate I am, how I conduct myself. But of course they don't say anything about that. And they don't actually ask me to be on the show—yet."

In this audition, producers look for many of the same qualities that attract them to ordinary guests: Is the person energetic, articulate, concise (or at least trainable in this regard)? Most important, what is the likelihood that she will deliver the expert version of the money shot? For therapist experts, who rarely share the stage with other therapists, individual performative ability carries considerable weight. For scholar experts and organic experts, the potential for the money shot may be more a function of the external structure imposed on the show, of producers' success in bringing together opposing sides of an issue. Thus, producers often look for an expert who will espouse a view that they know the audience will challenge or for two experts who will disagree with one another and/or with the ordinary panelists. Getting experts to participate under these conditions is not easy. Indeed, persuading experts to assume an unpopular stance on volatile issues such as "what to do with sex offenders?" or "should pornography be censored?" is not unlike persuading ordinary guests to be confronted by a friend or family member over a betrayal or an injustice: in both cases, guests typically know that they are swimming against the tide.[4]

---

4. This explains the reticence of an expert I met during the production of a *Diana* show about Gulf War syndrome. She questioned the validity of the syndrome but was leery about saying so on television because the panel was filled primarily with victims (people

The Clash of Agendas: Struggles over Expertise

Not surprisingly, most of the professional experts I interviewed had serious complaints about their participation after the fact. They objected both to the marginal role allotted professional expertise and to the production practices that structure its parameters. Like ordinary guests, experts generally realize that they have to be articulate, direct, and concise, that producers are looking for energy and points of potential controversy. Yet these requirements can undermine the very expertise on which their participation itself depends. As discussed earlier, the expectation that experts should popularize their work and be accountable to the laity exists in tension with the fact that specialist knowledge cannot be communicated in a nonspecialist domain like television "without significant transformation and impoverishment" (Livingstone and Lunt 1994, 96; see also Goldfarb 1998). Of all the experts I interviewed, academic experts were the most frustrated by this tension. According to Jim, a sociologist invited on the *Shirley!* show to discuss teen pregnancy, "The dilemma is that you're almost always asked to be involved in complex issues but the opportunity to express your point of view is seldom more than five minutes. The other thing they want are definitive statements, not patterns or trends or probabilities. You know, what is good science and appropriate caution is a pain in the neck to the media people. If you are too cautious and too careful—some might say too responsible—about what you say, they're really not very interested in you."

Of course, an expert's options for making a contribution vary considerably from show to show and even from program to program within a given show. The first time Jeremy was on *Oprah*, he was the last panelist brought onstage and got to make only one statement. As he told me, "I really questioned whether it was worthwhile taking the time to go all the way to Chicago to ventilate my tonsils for three minutes." The next time around, however, he was onstage for the entire hour. "It's a mixed bag," he conceded. "You just never know. I guess, if it's your one and only time, and you get on for thirty seconds, you're going to be very upset about that."

Experts correctly perceive that the lack of airtime signals their low priority, a situation reinforced by the fact that they are often seated in the

---

who had fallen ill after serving in the Gulf) as well as two other experts whose views contradicted her own. As I recall, the woman almost backed out three or four times, causing the producer to complain bitterly to me that, on the one hand, he has a mandate to represent "both sides" of the issue but that, on the other hand, he has to "beg, borrow, and steal just to find an intelligent, interesting expert with an opposing view to come on the show."

studio audience and not on the panel at all—something that almost all the experts I interviewed remarked on with disfavor, and for good reason. According to Jeremy, not only does a seat in the audience make you a spectator-participant rather than a panelist-participant, it puts you at a structural disadvantage when countering arguments made by guests onstage because they are physically positioned above you, the focal point of attention. Under these circumstances, it becomes nearly impossible to intervene or interrupt spontaneously. To make matters worse, experts (and academics in particular) are rarely brought into the discussion until it is almost over. Producers aptly call the segment of the show in which experts typically appear *Siberia*. Aside from the lack of time, the main problem here is that, no matter what the issue or how it is framed, the frame is established long before the expert appears on the scene. Richard, the criminologist invited on *Maury Povich* to discuss sex offenders, made this point well: "The situation got totally defined before I ever had an opportunity to even appear, much less say anything," he said. "I was seated at the end, isolated from the other guests, and so the whole structure of the situation was, 'Here's the bad guy down at the end'—because what I had to say was not what the audience or the victims on the panel wanted to hear. No matter what I would have done, I could not have broken through that barrier."

Because the goodness of fit between professional expertise and the generic context is anything but good, and because experts play such peripheral (and predetermined) roles, experts have little room to maneuver when they disagree with how an issue has been scripted and framed. If they suspect a disagreeable situation in advance, they can threaten to drop out, but, given their marginal standing, this threat does not carry the same weight as it does coming from ordinary guests. Producers get annoyed if experts cancel at the last minute, but it rarely jeopardizes a show. Moreover, since experts have far less contact with producers prior to taping compared to ordinary guests, they may not know in advance just how well (or poorly) their own views fit with those of other participants or with the overall perspective of the show. If they find themselves in a bind once a taping is under way, their main option is to challenge the definition of the situation constructed by producers by attempting to assert their own. Both Connie and Jeremy had experiences in which they tried to do precisely that, with differing degrees of success.

Jeremy appeared on a *Sally Jessy Raphael* show titled "I Murdered My Girlfriend's Baby," based on a recent news story about a man who in fact killed his girlfriend's child. The girlfriend herself was on the show, although the man was not because he was in prison. Another couple was there as well to flesh out the panel, ostensibly because the man disliked his girlfriend's son, whom he thought was spoiled, but really because the producers intended to reframe his dislike as murderous desire. Jeremy is convinced that this couple did not know the real focus of the show. Consequently, Jeremy said, he watched in horror as "this illiterate, obscure, miserable couple from Chervil, Texas, got skinned alive on national television." And he was there to explain why the young man ostensibly wanted to murder his girlfriend's child. What he did instead, he told me, was make a big point of separating the theme of the show from the behavior of this particular couple: "I did exactly the opposite of what [the producers] wanted me to do." Chuckling, he added, "Maybe that's why they haven't called me back. That was the last time I was on!"

I asked whether it was clear to him before going onstage what role the producers wanted him to play.

"Yes," he replied. "I've noticed this; a lot of times they communicate quite explicitly, you know, in the green room, 'Here's what we want you to do.' The idea is to have experts play certain clearly defined roles. But that doesn't mean I have to go along with it, especially when they wait until the last minute to tell me."

Connie faced a similar situation on *Randy*, but, given her unfamiliarity with daytime talk shows and lack of prior media experience, the outcome was somewhat different. A sociologist specializing in domestic violence and wife abuse, Connie was invited on the show to be the expert voice on an episode devoted to "battered men." Her only preparation before arriving at the studio was a phone conversation with one of the producers several days earlier, during which Connie explained that, because of systemic gender inequality, very little heterosexual partner abuse is directed toward men. But you do agree that men can be battered? the producer asked. Connie said yes, it was possible, and, after some additional conversation, she agreed to participate because she wanted to visit a friend who lived in the city where the show is taped.

"And so you went without having seen the show or knowing anything about the show?" I asked her.

"Yes," Connie admitted. "I had never seen this show. In fact, I thought it was local. I only found out later it was national. I don't watch—that's not what I do in the afternoons, so how would I know? Afterward, though, I realized I had not checked into it at all."

Once at the studio, Connie got no further instructions from producers about her participation or about what would happen during the upcoming taping. She was kept isolated from the other guests and watched most of the show unfold on a television monitor in the green room, a notepad in her lap. The first two couples onstage were clearly working class, "a bit *Deliverance* looking," according to Connie. What she heard quickly convinced her that she was witnessing textbook cases of battered *women*, that while these women might hit their husbands, they did so in re-taliation for their husbands' violent actions, which included throwing them against walls and humiliating them in public. Yet the whole time no one had said a word to her backstage except, "Do you want a cup of coffee?" So, when she was finally escorted onto the panel and asked, "Dr. Foster, what sense do you make of this?" Connie gave a fifteen-minute lecture on gen-der inequality, explaining that what is important in a battering relationship is not necessarily the actual number of violent acts but the nature of the vi-olence and the gendered context of fear and domination in which it occurs. She concluded that the men on panel were not being battered but were, in fact, batterers.

Connie said that she thought that she had made quite a good presen-tation. But during the next commercial break the producer ran up to her and "read her the riot act." As Connie tells it, the following heated ex-change ensued:

"Dr. Foster, did you not understand that this show is on battered men and you've not said anything about battered men?" asked the pro-ducer, furious.

"Well, that's because you didn't give me any battered men to say any-thing about. These are not battered men," Connie replied.

"Now, in our interview, you agreed that there was such a thing, and we would like you to talk about that. Why do you think we are doing this show?"

"I don't know. I have no idea why you are doing this show. But it isn't what you told me it would be."

"Look, are there battered men or not?"

"Well, maybe 5 percent."

"Can't you just say—will you just be willing to make this statement on the air?"

"Well, if someone asks me, I'll make it."

Meanwhile, according to Connie, the camera person is counting down the time until the break is over—"*Ten! Nine! Eight! . . . Three! Two! One!*"—and then the producer suddenly disappears, and Connie is left sit-ting there "all frustrated and pissed off." "The whole thing was beyond ab-surd," she concluded.

Some weeks later, having missed the show when it aired on television,

Connie procured a copy of the tape. Without previewing it, she screened it in one of her college classes on family violence and discovered, much to her surprise, that the majority of what she had said during the taping had been edited from the final version. "They show my face, and once in a while they get a statement from me, but it never makes sense, it's never in the context of anything anybody's asked me," Connie told me ruefully. "They not only cut out the description of what battering is, or my little lecture there, they cut out all the data that supported it." As a result, both Connie and the ordinary women on the program looked quite foolish.

Straight from the Heart: Personal Experience as Expertise

Compared to professional experts, the aims and goals of organic experts are better suited to the genre and their expertise more amenable to televisual representation. Recall Richard's situation on *Maury Povich*, in which he was asked to give his expert opinion about sex offenders at the end of the program after the situation had already been defined by others. Since he spoke last, and since his perspective was unpopular, he was easily positioned as the bad guy on the panel. Isaac Cubillos found himself in a similar situation on *Diana* but got different results. As vice president of the Prisoners' Rights Union, he argued that, once released from prison, ex-cons (sex offenders included) have civil rights that should not be violated. Like Richard, he knew very well that, when it came to crime, sex offenders were the current hot button in the media and that his views would not be well received on a talk-show panel filled with victims and their supporters.

"Sexual predators being released from prison seems to be the emotional 'gut button' that sets people off," he told me. "And what happens is that all prisoners get characterized as child molesters and rapists. So, any time I go into any kind of public forum as an advocate for prisoners, I'm the bad guy, and I understand that."

What made Isaac's experience different than Richard's was both Isaac's more dramatic, confrontational style and his status as an ex-con with insider knowledge of the criminal-justice system.

As he explained, "The audience was already pumped up with the guests that were on prior to me. So I came on like gangbusters because one of the philosophies we have in the Prisoners' Rights Union is that we wear iron fists, and that's the way we fight our battles. We're not passive. We don't whine. We're going to be very, very confrontational. 'In your face' is the philosophy we take. That's something I learned from being in prison.

So, yeah, the audience was hostile at first, but by the end . . . [they were] starting to understand the dynamics of the situation, that there was another side to consider here—the side of the prisoner and the ex-con."

In a forum that privileges the authority of lived experience over that of professional expertise, Isaac's status as an ex-con, community activist, and organic expert gave him a certain edge that Richard, the academic, did not have. Not only are organic experts usually placed earlier in the lineup (sometimes right at the top) and allowed more time to speak, but the very basis of their expertise, and consequently their ways of articulating that expertise, better aligns them with the performative demands of the genre. Organic expert Joyce Ann Brown has been on every daytime talk show at least once, with the exception of *Oprah*, and says that she never felt at a disadvantage or had a negative experience because she draws on her personal experience and speaks "straight from the heart."

As she insisted in our interview, "When I go to a talk show, I'm coming straight from the heart. I never prepared for a talk show. I didn't have to sit down and study. 'Cause my experience with the system prepared me for talk shows. I knew that, whatever question was asked, I was going to bring it from the heart. It's experience, and, from experience, when the audience hears you, you can captivate that audience."

Joyce then recalled a particular taping in which both host and audience were reduced to tears by her personal testimony.

"When I did the *Bertice Berry* show, the audience was so captivated that we had to break—when we went on a break, you know how that person comes out and tries to keep the audience all jolly-jolly?"

"Yes, I know who you mean," I said, "the audience warm-up person."

"Well, they couldn't do that. They couldn't make the audience jolly-jolly. Because the audience was in tears, and the guy that usually comes out, he said that it would just, you know, he just didn't feel it was appropriate. And the host—she had to get herself together before we could start up again."

Producers, of course, are thrilled when guests can move audiences to tears with a dramatic personal narrative, as Joyce very well recognized. As she herself put it, "They get high ratings from it. So it's not all about, 'Oh, we love Joyce Brown, the way she expresses herself.' They love Joyce Brown because, if they get someone like me that can hold that audience attention and can tell that story, the other four or five or six guests, you know, is just something extra to add."

The role of personal testimony here is a complicated one, aside from its ability to garner high ratings. Historically, personal experience has been an important means by which white women, people of color, the working classes, and others denied expert status have asserted the reality of their lives, particularly the reality of their oppression and disadvantage. To paraphrase bell hooks (1989), the assertion of personal experience on the part of these groups can rescue them from negation and thus be a strategic response to domination and colonization. Such strategies reflect the struggles of oppressed peoples to have a standpoint on which to critique dominant structures. Consequently, critical pedagogies of liberation necessarily embrace experience, confession, and testimony as relevant ways of knowing and as vital dimensions of any learning experience. It could be argued, therefore, that daytime talk shows afford certain marginalized individuals the opportunity to share the reality of their lives in a manner closed to them elsewhere on television and thereby put a human face on stigmatized behaviors or identities.

On the other hand, without an understanding of how personal experience is shaped and informed by larger patterns of social inequality, the revelation of personal experience can become, to use Rachel's phrase, "just a bunch of titillating stories." And hooks (1989) makes this very point when she cautions that speaking of one's experience is only part of the process of politicization, that critical pedagogies involving confession and testimony must also be linked up to educational forums that teach about *structures* of domination and how these structures function. The absence of structural arguments on talk shows has led feminist scholars and critics to conclude that the genre undermines the feminist dictum *the personal is political* because it neglects the political side of the equation (see Steenland 1990; Kaminer 1993; Peck 1994; Heaton and Wilson 1995; Lowney 1999). Moreover, because invoking the authority of lived experience is not a strategy limited to marginalized groups, its use by dominant groups—white people, men, heterosexuals—can effectively neutralize opposition voices and reinscribe existing social hierarchies. Without recourse to how personal experience maps onto the larger institutional landscape, there is no overall framework within which to situate competing narratives, and one person's personal experience can simply trump or cancel out another's.

In combination with the media's tendency to focus on the most sensational or controversial aspects of an issue, the view that all personal experience is equally valid can lead to some pretty erroneous information. Thus it was that date rape got framed as an issue of "reverse discrimination" (i.e., discrimination against men) on the *Gabrielle Carteris Show* when producers encouraged young men in the audience to challenge the rape survivors on the panel with *their* personal experiences of being "victimized" by women sending mixed signals about sex. Likewise, the *Shirley!* episode on teen pregnancy concluded that teenage motherhood was not such a bad option for young girls after all—even when most research indicates otherwise, as the expert tried to explain—because a group of teenage mothers planted in the audience used their own first-person success stories to challenge the cautionary tales of the teenage mothers onstage. Interestingly, this frame got established despite the best intentions of the production staff. As Jim, the professional expert on the show, told me, "It is my strong belief that Shirley wanted to expose the difficulties of teen pregnancy. She wanted to have some controversy, yes, but she also wanted to end up with the message, 'This is not the best way to go in life.' Unfortunately, that's not the way it worked out because, in the last portion of the show, she lost control, and it became a free-for-all with these young women in the audience talking about how great it was to be a teenage mother."

The representation of personal experience on talk shows—especially the personal experience of disenfranchised groups—is fraught with contradictions. As Shattuc (1997) observes, in shifting the evidence of social justice from rational and distant forms of public discourse to a mélange of personal experience, physical evidence, and emotion, daytime talk reveals the influence of a diverse range of historical developments in the United States. The most important of these include the rise of identity politics stimulated by the civil-rights, feminist, and gay-rights movements of the 1960s and 1970s; the emphasis on testifying and witnessing popularized by the Southern black church; feminist challenges to the separation of public and private spheres and the exclusion of gender issues from the realm of legitimate politics; a belief in the therapeutic value of self-disclosure associated with American ego psychology and the rise of various twelve-step recovery programs; and the emphasis on building women's confidence and self-esteem advocated by various forms of feminist therapy.

Daytime talk shows draw on and reproduce these native discourses—especially therapeutic ones—not only in the topics that they pursue, but also in constructing a particular relation between ordinary and expert guests. As Livingstone and Lunt (1994, 101) observe, "Both kinds of guests are presented as interested parties, but as knowing different things in different ways." The media, they rightly insist, organize through particular rules and rhetoric what counts as a good argument, what evidence is required to ground claims, and what conclusions are valued. Following the modernist separation of expertise and common sense, television genres that draw on both kinds of knowledge have traditionally valorized experts over ordinary people by linking expertise with the first term in the following set of binary oppositions: objective/subjective, rational/emotional, general/particular, abstract/concrete, neutral/motivated, factual/supposi- tional, counterintuitive/obvious. These oppositions reflect the undermin- ing of the private life world and the triumph of the public system; they also construct a way of knowing that establishes experts as the more powerful group. Daytime talk shows, by contrast, challenge or subvert this way of knowing by laying claim to a different epistemology. Talk shows reject crit- icisms of the ordinary person as incompetent or ignorant, question the def- erence traditionally paid experts, and assert instead the worth of common opinion—thus offering an alternative set of binary oppositions that asso- ciate experts with the second, negative term in each pair: authentic/alien- ated, narrative/fragmented, hot/cold, relevant/irrelevant, grounded/un- grounded, practical/useless, real/artificial (see Livingstone and Lunt 1994, 102). This alternative construction does not challenge the binary organi- zation of expertise per se but reproduces its logic by substituting new terms for the old.

Not only does this series of inversions revalue (and devalue) the ex- pertise of experts, but it also creates an environment in which experts are increasingly pushed to personalize issues themselves. As Heaton and Wil- son (1995) note, when experts are questioned, the questions are often per- sonal: Are you a rape survivor? Are you a battered woman? Are you in re- covery? For organic experts with activist aims, such questions do not necessarily pose a problem, but, for professional academic experts, they can since their expertise is based on more distanced or disembodied criteria. Professional experts generally aim to distinguish between personal experi- ence or opinion and professional observations. The pressure on experts to personalize their expertise was one of Robinson's (1982) main concerns in her analysis of family experts on *Donahue* and was mentioned by a number of psychologists interviewed by Livingstone and Lunt (1994) as well. As one man in Livingstone and Lunt's study put it, "It was very difficult be- cause all they were interested in was my personal experience, and in a sense that was the reason they were there, to talk about their personal experience, and so why shouldn't I talk about mine? . . . It was an ambiguous situation [because] I felt I was there as the expert and yet my expertise was being un- dermined" (101, 110).

There is also the difficulty involved in applying general research per- spectives to individual cases. As the professional experts I interviewed were quick to point out, personal experience does not necessarily provide repre- sentative or generalizable information about a problem or an issue—a pri- mary goal for conducting research in the first place. On a daytime talk show, the best that an expert might be able to do is point to an ordinary guest and say, "This is a typical situation because . . . ," or, conversely, "This is *not* a typical situation because . . . ," for, unless it is connected with other evidence, personal experience alone renders at best a partial and at worse a false or misleading picture of the world. This is true of both the personal experience of ordinary guests, who gain entry expressly because they have an *extra*ordinary story to share, and the personal experience of therapist experts in clinical contexts, whose client base is also likely to consist of people unlike the population as whole and even unlike the subpopulation of individuals with similar problems.[5] Yet, if only scientific research can provide a representative or accurate view of a social problem, and if only professional experts are capable of conducting such research and discussing it on television, once again we have banished ordinary people from the arena of media discourse and public debate.

There are at least two issues compounding the tension between expert and ordinary knowledge. One is that academic experts and ordinary guests share little common ground, especially on the newer, more conflict-oriented shows. They have different goals and expectations, different risks and concerns, different ways of knowing the world, and different ways of expressing what they know. Producers also place different performative demands on each. Yet the two groups are thrown together on the same stage in the same forum, part of the same eclectic mix of brash confrontation and serious debate. Not surprisingly, then, the clash of agendas that characterizes relations between producers and guests also characterizes the relations between expert and ordinary guests and even between different kinds of

5. This point was made best by Jim, the *Shirley!* expert on teen pregnancy and an epidemiologist specializing in mental health. "There's a phenomenon called *the clinician's illusion*," he explained to me, as we sat together in his living room, the tape recorder on the coffee table between us. "It's complicated to describe, but, basically, it can be demonstrated that the likelihood of being in any clinical sample is directly a function of how big your problems are, how intense your sickness is, and how long you've been ill—in other words, who a clinician sees would be remarkably more chronic and at greater risk than the population as a whole. And the problem is that, in the experience of that clinician, the patient sample is the entire sample. Take cocaine use," he said, by way of illustration. "A clinician will tell you with 100 percent certainty that, if you use cocaine, you'll be addicted. That's because 100 percent of the people they see are addicted. We know from community studies of course that that's not true. Some people never become addicted. The same thing happens with schizophrenia. A psychiatrist will tell you schizophrenics don't get better, but they don't see everyone diagnosed with the disorder. If they did, they would know that about one-third never experience another psychotic break. So, when people are speaking from their personal experience to an audience about the nature of a social problem, you know, the instant red flag is 'circumstances'—what are the limits of the circumstances?"

*"This one says, 'I think I would have learned a lot more if the
course had been conducted in talk-show format.'"*

Figure 10. Cartoon by Mischa Richter and Harald Bakken. Originally published in the
Chronicle of Higher Education, 1997. Courtesy Marjorie Bakken.

experts. Disseminating representative or generalizable information is not
necessarily the goal of an ordinary guest. Rather, her goal might be to convey the message, "This happened to me; it was painful; it pissed me off;
watch out, it could happen to you." The other issue is that both academics
and ordinary people are marginal to media discourse and see talk shows as
one of the few opportunities for media exposure. Here, ironically, academic
experts and ordinary guests are more alike than different, for, although experts in general have greater (and more routinized) access to television than
ordinary people, most are politicians and government officials, not academics (Sigal 1973, 1986; Gans 1979). Thus, the kind of structural arguments about social problems that sociologists and other intellectuals strive
to promote are rarely seen or heard or read *anywhere* in the American media, and this exclusion can make the perceived inadequacies of daytime talk
all the more disappointing.

Experts, Activism, and the Media

Given the generic emphasis on emotion and personal experience, organic experts play a particularly important role in the genre. In key ways, they are not unlike Antonio Gramsci's notion of the *organic intellectual.* Gramsci considered the opposition between bourgeois intellectual and working-class nonintellectual to be untenable because there is always an intellectual or abstract component to the social and material relations of class subordination; not only do working-class people assume a particular place in the sphere of production, but they also understand the ways in which their everyday lives are circumscribed by that sphere. Moreover, the working classes include individuals—teachers, industrial workers, and organizers—who are aware of, and self-conscious about, their place in the economic, social, and political order. In Gramsci's words, "Every group . . . creates together with itself, organically, one or more strata of intellectuals which give it homogeneity and an awareness of its own function not only in the economic but also in the social and political fields" (1971, 5). This stratum is part of, not separate from, the particular community or constituency that it represents: "The mode of new intellectuals can no longer consist of eloquence, which is an exterior and momentary mover of feelings and passions . . . rather, it participates actively in practical life as constructor, organizer, and 'permanent persuader'" (10). Consequently, Gramsci called for the nomination of working-class thought as an organic form of "primitive and unqualified" intellectualism, one constructed through the personal experiences and material circumstances of working-class life.

Shattuc (1997) also uses the notion of organic intellectual in her work on talk shows, although more specifically in relation to African American scholars and experts. She suggests that black scholars like Cornel West, Henry Louis Gates Jr., and Maya Angelou are examples of organic intellectuals who use commercial media to reach both their own communities and the dominant white society. They remain firmly grounded in African American traditions and the nuances of its popular culture while at the same time working alongside European models of intellectualism. Despite leaving their communities of origin and returning as top-down authorities, black intellectuals remain viable spokespersons because of their shared experience of racial oppression. "This is the daytime talk show version of the organic intellectual: an urbane, middle-class spokesperson who can approach or analyze a social issue from the vantage point of his or her own experience" (Shattuc 1997, 107).

The organic intellectuals discussed by Shattuc represent a particular subset of professional experts: scholars and writers both in and outside the academy whose expertise is constituted through engaged, intellectual inquiry. They are public intellectuals and a rarity on daytime talk shows, as are intellectuals more generally. By contrast, the guests I call *organic experts* participate with greater frequency. They do not move in intellectual circles, have academic credentials, or hold academic appointments. Indeed, except for Grant, the organic experts I interviewed did not consider themselves *intellectuals* at all, at least not in the conventional sense of that term. Nevertheless, organic experts clearly exhibit the "primitive and unqualified" form of intellectualism outlined by Gramsci in that they strive to emphasize the connection between personal experience and larger patterns of social inequality. They use their stories strategically as a tool or wedge to discuss how their own lives connect with those of others in similar circumstances and with the larger social structures circumscribing them.

Joyce, for example, spent nine years, five months, and twenty-four days in prison for a crime that she did not commit and knew firsthand that many other innocent people—most of them African American and Latino—were going to jail. She now works for the Dallas County Commissioner as a legal assistant in addition to her work with MASS. "My responsibility, as I see it," she said, "is standing and speaking for those that can't speak for themselves. I feel a responsibility for speaking for those that's crying in the wilderness, that underdog who everybody wants to cast out once they've been labeled a criminal."

Isaac Cubillos gave a similar explanation for his involvement in the Prisoners' Rights Union and his decision to use talk shows as a forum for advancing that organization's goals. "I use [the genre] as a medium to illustrate the other side of the coin about prisoners' rights," he told me, "meaning their constitutional rights, their civil rights, and their human rights, all of which are being violated. Because we're talking about a million families in the state of California alone who have loved ones in prison or on parole." Isaac said he joined the union in May 1993, the very afternoon he was released from Folsom Prison. "I saw what was occurring in the prison system, and now, as a free citizen and a person who would eventually be paying taxes, I could not tolerate the abuses that were occurring there. And this is not like me, to join an organization. But, that afternoon, I took the trolley from Folsom Prison directly to the door of the Prisoners' Rights Union. And I've been involved with them ever since."

Although their specific circumstances were different, Lorna, Nathan, Grant, and Abby all had the same general goal—using talk shows for activist purposes. Lorna described the mission of her organization, Drive-By Agony, as promoting awareness about gang-related violence and the effects that it has on families. Like Joyce and Isaac, she had no doubt that talk shows helped her realize that mission and more. "I knew that television would be the medium for me to spread my word," she told me. "I can see the impact that I've made here in Los Angeles. The peace marches that I started? In their seventh year. And people are branchin' out, startin' their own organizations in other cities. A good idea has spread all over the place, in other words."

Lorna said that having "insiders" educate the public about the causes and consequences of gang-related violence was especially crucial because, until recently, there existed what she called *a cloak of silence* about the issue within the mostly poor, mostly black and Latino communities where the impact of gangs is most devastating. This silence gave politicians and law-enforcement officials disproportionate influence in shaping public perception about gangs in the media and also allowed gang activity to proliferate unchecked. As she put it, "[This issue] needs to be brought out full-blown and addressed, you know what I'm sayin'? Because it is part of society, and it has been for a very long time. These kids [gang members and potential recruits] are hurting, and they're angry. They're very, very angry. Somebody has to try and reach them, let them know there's another way."

Lorna said that she's been characterized in the media as "a South-Central Oprah Winfrey" and that she would, in fact, like to have her own TV show someday. Initially, she did the talk-show circuit as an ordinary guest but eventually graduated to expert status. Lorna herself was quick to note that her expertise was not of the conventional sort because she had no official credentials. In her view, this was not a shortcoming, however, since people with official credentials had done little to stem gang violence. She noted that, in contrast to those personally affected by gangs, producers do not really care about the issue except insofar as it garners high ratings, just as politicians do not care about it except insofar as getting tough on crime improves their standing in the polls. "It's all a game to those people," she said. "No wonder the kids of the world are so fucked up. But that's the way it is. That's the way it is, and so I've learned to waltz."

Learning to waltz here means "learning to play the game," learning to use the media for your own purposes and political agendas, just as media professionals and politicians use you for theirs. This theme of mutual exploitation—one that all the organic experts I interviewed more or less explicitly addressed—emerged most forcefully in my interviews with Grant and Abby, both leaders in lesbigay/transgender rights organizations.

Grant, a gay writer and activist, described getting involved with the media as "making a pact with the devil." He had done some local television and radio talk shows before going on *Donahue*, and, although not fond of the genre overall, he believed that it had a place in the activist agenda. He oriented toward the media much as he did toward political activism, seeing the former as a vehicle for accomplishing the latter, and seeing both as requiring, inevitably, a certain degree of compromise.

"The moment you do politics, by definition, you're no saint," he said. "You get your hands dirty. You can't be a purist. And I remember, after I agreed to go on *Donahue*, I wrote in my diary that it was a pact with the devil. I still feel that way. But I don't regret having gone on the show."

The *Donahue* taping focused on the issue of pornography and censorship. For AIDS activists, the censorship of sexually explicit material had become a life-or-death issue because politicians were leading congressional campaigns against the dissemination of safe-sex and health-care information under the guise of protecting people from pornography. Going on *Donahue* was one more way for Grant to go public about this issue. At the same time, he insisted, social change does not happen on *Donahue*. "I mean, the guy couldn't be more square without growing corners. Social change doesn't happen on *any* talk show. It happens elsewhere. What [talk shows] do, if you're lucky, is give you a forum."

Grant admitted that it would be nicer for experts if the forum "were more sophisticated about the substance of the debates" and if talk shows did not rely so heavily on a "nuts-and-sluts" formula. As Grant recalled, "It was pretty clear to me that I was supposed to play the role of slut. I was being scripted as the extremist, the sexual libertine, namely, the person who had been International Mr. Leather, and the person who opposed the censorship of pornography." The idea was to pit Grant against another expert guest who favored censorship, while a third expert assumed the position of moderate. But even the nuts-and-sluts formula can—within limits—be used as a strategy for getting heard. Grant did not object to producers showing the video clip of him winning the International Mr. Leather contest, and he wore an outfit—leather pants, bright turquoise shirt, biker boots—consistent with his Mr. Leather persona.

"I made a decision that I was not going to look like a guy in a suit, which is what [the other two experts] looked like. And that was probably a good visual for the show, but it was also a statement I wanted to make. About difference, my difference from them, in both a visual sense and a political sense."

Grant knew he was "something of an alien" in this context. Indeed, it was his alien status that earned him a hearing in the first place: "Would there have been any place for me on *Donahue* if I hadn't also been International Mr. Leather is an interesting question. Because I'm also a writer, I have ideas. But, if [being International Mr. Leather] is the hook I have to use to get in, I will use it. My view is, if you are a visitor from another planet, you might as well speak up."

Arguably, speaking up on *Donahue* was a good bit easier than speaking up on some other talk shows. During its twenty-six-year run on the air, *Donahue* was widely recognized as the most serious show of the genre and, not coincidentally, one in which expert guests played a substantial role. Despite being so square that he could grow corners, Phil Donahue was also well-known for his liberal stance on social issues, particularly women's and gay rights. Thus, Grant was willing to do *Donahue* but, two years earlier, had simply hung up on producers from *Morton Downey Jr.* (considered an early forerunner of *Jerry Springer*) when they called to invite him on a show about violence against gays. As he said with a snort, "I didn't have a ton of media experience, but I knew the difference between *Donahue* and *Downey*." Indeed, unless seriously disengaged from popular culture, most people knew the difference between *Donahue* and *Downey*, just as most people today know the difference between *Diana* and *Randy*.

Nevertheless, some activists *are* willing to brave appearances on *Randy*-like shows located at the trashy end of the continuum. Abby, a white-male cross-dresser and cofounder of the Renaissance Education Foundation, did, in fact, go on *Morton Downey Jr.* in the late 1980s and then on *Charles Perez* and *Shirley!* nearly a decade later. As with many of the "sexually deviant" talk-show guests interviewed by Priest (1995), he participated not because he expected to be treated with compassion or respect but because he wanted to reach out to other similarly stigmatized individuals. As Abby explained, "For cross-dressers, the biggest thing is just letting them know about other people like themselves because they immediately go, 'Oh, wow, I am not alone. I am not the only weirdo like this in the world.' We did *Downey* because we knew there were transgendered people out there who would be watching."

Abby admits that he would never have agreed to go on *Morton Downey* if it had not been for the extended pretaping negotiations with producers, which lasted nearly a month. The hook for him was that the show agreed to publicize the name and telephone number of his organization, which provides information and support services to transgendered people and their supporters. "My primary goal was to get publicity. If you get publicity, then it's worth whatever they do to you." Indeed, going on national television that first time gave Abby's organization the biggest membership boost of its history. "Our outreach director, who was also on the show, was really depressed afterwards because the audience had attacked us. It was not until the show aired and our answering machine was jammed with people calling for information that it really sunk in what we had accomplished."

Yet there are limits to what expert activists like Abby will do to push their political agendas, especially as their organizations grow and gain legitimacy. As a group or community moves from relative invisibility to visibility, the concerns of spokespersons shift from obtaining visibility at any cost to controlling the kind of visibility obtained. At the time of our interview, for example, Abby had just refused an opportunity to appear on *Jerry Springer*, despite its huge audience and high ratings. His decision was partly a function of his last talk-show experience on *Charles Perez*, which he described as "little more than a scream fest," and partly a function of a wider moratorium on *Springer* appearances imposed by leaders of the lesbigay/transgender community. The consensus about *Springer* was that no amount of publicity was worth the cost of participating because the treatment of gay and transgender guests was so derogatory. As Abby put it, "My attitude now is, well, yeah, talk shows are still a way to reach people, but I think that, as the transgendered community becomes more organized and gains strength, we have other needs that have to be considered, and talk shows are not the only route to go."

At the same time, Abby expressed concern over the moratorium, and his own decision to abide by it, because it effectively limited the kind of guest that producers put onstage. When respectable spokespersons decline to participate, it leaves the door open to others whose agendas may be less noble and whose behavior may further compromise the already-tenuous reputation of the group. In Abby's words, "It leaves us with a situation where the only people appearing are total idiots, who are just doing it for the fifteen minutes of fame." He was not so much bothered by the theatrical or circus-like atmosphere of *Springer* and some other shows. ("Don't get me wrong. I'm all for theatricality," he assured me. "I'm an actor, and I have a performing side, so I love to go onstage.") Rather, he was bothered by the "low-life, trash aspect," by guests who were "loud and out of control" and who represented only the "fringe element" of the transgender community. He was bothered by guests like Reno, a female-to-male transsexual well-known on *Jerry Springer* and someone I met in 1998 when we were both invited to do a radio interview on the subject of talk shows. Then twenty-three years old, Reno said that he went on *Springer* because he liked the attention and the fame but also because he wanted visibility for all transgendered people. Abby, however, did not appreciate the kind of visibility that Reno provided, Reno having confessed on the air to his "unsuspecting" girlfriend that he used to be a she—thus fostering the negative (and false) perception that transgender relationships always involve deception.[6]

The tension between legitimate and illegitimate spokespersons is something that Gamson (1998) discusses at some length in his study of talk shows. As the vulgar head of the genre took off and the class (and age) profile of guests started to shift, middle-class activists and their mainstreaming political agendas gradually got pushed out. Those who took center stage—often "flamboyant, unaffiliated, untrained in political agendas, and of lower education, economic, and social status" (185–86)—make good talk-show guests, but they do not necessarily make the best representatives of a movement fighting for tolerance, acceptance, and rights. In Gamson's words, the opposition of many gay activists to the trashy talk-show guest "is primarily a pragmatic position (we can ill afford such images right now) but one also often tinged with animosity (these people don't know how to behave in public), and the confidence that comes from having long felt entitled to call the shots" (191).

Gay activists and experts are right, of course, that talk shows currently provide a narrow and, therefore, distorted view of gay life. But, as Gamson points out, the image was no less distorted (only more socially acceptable) when it prioritized white, middle-class movement leaders. In other words, the queer guests on *Jerry Springer* might be unrepresentative and stereotypical, but, in a different way, so were the queer guests on *Donahue*. The transition from respectable to vulgar spokespersons, which mirrors the larger tabloid shift in the genre, has effectively magnified class differences within the lesbigay community, just as it has within the culture at

---

6. I learned more about the particular show that Reno went on from Stephen Hocking, a graduate student at the University of Pennsylvania who is conducting dissertation research on talk shows and the transgender community. Hocking has twice interviewed Reno. As it turns out, the surprise element of Reno's show was fabricated by the producers since the girlfriend already knew of Reno's transgender status at the time of the taping. She agreed to pretend otherwise because, like Reno, she wanted to be on TV. She was also reluctant to have her parents and employer know about her relationship with Reno. So, rather than admit to being in a consensual relationship with a man who used to be, biologically speaking, a woman, she played the role of heterosexual woman tricked into having sexual relations with a transsexual. This sort of deception narrative is common on talk shows when it comes to transgender relationships, and it functions to mask the fact that the vast majority of such relationships are honest and consensual.

large. Yet, while middle-class folks of all stripes decry the shift from classy to trashy representation and the primacy of place granted guests who come from the wrong side of the tracks, the shift is especially troubling for middle-class gays because of their own marginalized status. Because lesbian, gay, bisexual, and transgendered people have been rendered largely invisible in media and popular culture, every individual image carries the burden of representing the group in a way that images of heterosexuals, however poor or disenfranchised, do not. Straight guests do and say some pretty outrageous things to get on television, but the repertoire of available imagery for contextualizing their behavior is vastly greater than is that for contextualizing the behavior of queer guests who do the same. For marginalized individuals, participating in the media therefore always involves a risk: their marginality may be the very thing that grants them visibility, but the *nature* of the visibility may end up reproducing their marginality.

The Whole World Is Watching: Concluding Thoughts on Media Activism

A bisexual activist interviewed by Gamson (1998) compared going on a talk show to lobbing little nuggets of information through a tiny window that keeps opening and closing. You have important things to say, and, as the window opens, you try and get them through as quickly as possible because that window can shut at any moment. This describes well the experience of experts on daytime talk shows. Even more than ordinary guests, experts have agendas (and preferred ways of articulating those agendas) that are at odds with how the genre's "windows" function. At the same time, media exposure is highly desirable for experts, and the more invested one is in reaching large audiences, the more desirable this exposure becomes. Thus, for social-movement activists looking to build organizations and win constituencies, the issue is not so much, "Should I go on television?" as, "What price am I willing to pay? How to exploit them before they exploit me?" Media and movements have long been considered interacting systems (Gamson and Wolsfeld 1993; see also Wolsfeld 1984; Gitlin 1980; Molotch 1979). As Molotch (1979) notes, the media contribute both to the attainment of an organization's goals and to activists' sense that what they do matters in the world. But movement leaders confront serious challenges in attempting to deal with the media because the media are not concerned with the issues important to the movement itself and because the things that *do* preoccupy the media (deviance, conflict, pathology) lead to patterns of coverage that, more often than not, work against social-movement aims.

Confronted with this situation, activists can move in one of two directions, according to Molotch. They can secure coverage by engaging in protest actions that are newsworthy (because extraordinary) yet easily incorporated into the existing beat structure, then use these actions as a wedge to generate serious discussion. It is not the kind of coverage that they would ideally like to have, but it is better than being ignored. This was the preferred strategy of early civil-rights activists in the 1960s, and it is roughly comparable to the way some organic experts get on talk shows. By contrast, activists can dispense altogether with any appearance of rationality and present themselves as anarchists, unresponsive to the normative order of things. The Yippies of the 1960s are the obvious historical example here, and at some level their talk-show correlates are trashy ordinary guests like Reno, who eschew any pretense of decorum or restraint and who have only the most tenuous of links to any organized movement agenda. In effect, Reno is to the lesbigay community today what Yippie leader Jerry Rubin was to the New Left in the 1960s: a rogue performer simultaneously rejected by movement leaders and embraced by the media. In Gitlin's (1980) view, the danger of this embrace is that the medium can become the movement—the media's endorsement of extravagant, expressive action can fashion the movement into something that is focused more and more on developing such action.

The larger issue at stake for organic experts and movement activists is the nature of the mediated public discourse that they must negotiate in order to reach broader audiences. This is the principle concern for professional experts as well. If professional experts are only indirectly invested in the attainment of an organization's goals (promoting their professions, e.g.) or in winning followers (potential clients for one's clinical practice or readers for one's book), they are very much invested in the public-sphere potential of the genre—the ability of daytime talk shows to provide a forum for public discussion and debate. Academics and intellectuals in particular are concerned about this. They agree to go on talk shows in part because they desire, and feel obliged, to be part of a larger dialogue about issues and events, to disseminate their expertise more widely, and to share their knowledge with others so that it might influence public opinion and policy. The potential for creating such a public sphere is said to exist whenever people come together to negotiate a political consensus through the free and rational exchange of views (see Habermas 1989).[7]

Yet talk shows typically fall short of this ideal, as the experiences of the experts discussed in this chapter attest. At best, talk shows can be considered a plebeian rather than a bourgeois public sphere, providing audiences with surface exposure to a broad range of topics rather than in-depth understanding of specifically sociopolitical issues. Being more therapeutic than cognitive, talk shows are less a balance of viewpoints than a serial association of testimonies in which issues are rarely resolved. As Polan (1990, 260) observes, the very call for "open" public discussion is closed by the structural demands of the media in which the discussion takes place: "One watches really more for the excitement, the good fight, than for the enunciation of reasoned positions within the society." At the same time, the public sphere as conceived by Habermas has its limitations, too, for it both excludes many so-called private issues from the realm of public debate and places a heavy premium on political consensus, thus ignoring the democratic possibilities of *multiple* public spheres in which groups with diverse and even conflicting ideologies participate (Fraser 1990; Garnham 1994). Of course, all public forums have limitations and constraints; talk shows are not unique in this regard. Like ordinary people, experts orient toward talk shows strategically, as a resource for achieving certain goals, but find the goals themselves inevitably altered by the forum in which they speak.

7. To elaborate, the public sphere is a space outside the family that mediates between state and society, where private citizens come together to discuss public matters. Habermas concedes that the public sphere today exists more as a promise than as a reality, having been undermined by the expansion of an interventionist state, a loss of public meeting places, and the growth of centralized corporate and media monopolies that produce an ever narrower and more uniform range of views. Mass media and party politics have contributed to a "refeudalization" of the public sphere, where image and representation are said to outweigh rational debate and *the public* is largely transformed into *public opinion*—a nonparticipatory mass. In this view, a heavy premium is placed on dialogue and a free and equal exchange of views through rational debate, which is supposed to generate political consensus. Political action is largely whatever people do in the public sphere in order to affect public-policy decisions and challenge established state authority.

Those who point fingers at talk shows are trying to cover up. It's interesting that politicians like William Bennett or, you know, Bob Dole are the ones to take up the cry, for, frankly, a Bob Dole is more responsible, having been in the Senate and a political leader for the last twenty years, for the decay and decline of the country than any talk show. If anything, I would say that what I see on Sally Jessy Raphael *would lead me to vote* against *Bob Dole because it is his policies and his vision of America that has led to the guests who appear on* Sally Jessy Raphael.

—SAUL FELDMAN, former television executive and
talk-show producer

I don't like this reality television. Real people should not be on television. It's for special people like us, people who have trained and studied to appear to be real.

—ACTOR GARY SHANDLING,
hosting the 2000 Emmy Awards

CHAPTER EIGHT

Trash, Class, and Cultural Hierarchy

Part of the larger trend toward reality programming, daytime talk shows have proved to be one of the most controversial television genres of our times. When friends and acquaintances first learned that I was conducting this research, they responded with a predictable mixture of fascination and distaste—it was as if I had infiltrated a cult or an underground drug ring. And most took for granted that I would approach talk shows much as one might approach a cult or an underground drug ring: as a social problem in need of a solution.

I have not done that in this book. Instead, I have been concerned with the ways in which talk shows make stars and experts out of ordinary people and, in the process, produce ordinariness as something both similar to yet distinct from conventional stardom and expertise. I have been interested less in the question of how specific topics and issues are represented on talk shows, or in who watches them and why, than in the work that producers do in translating taken-for-granted, class-based assumptions about ordinary people into extraordinary performances onstage. Key to this translation is the assumption that ordinariness is associated with emotion (the body) and with the private life world of personal relations, while expertness is associated with rationality (the mind) and the public realm of social relations. At the same time, talk shows trouble these distinctions, elevating laypeople to expert status, and prioritizing forms of expertise that are themselves rooted in personal experience to varying degrees.

In many ways, the work of producing a talk show has much in common with other forms of media production. Like journalists, producers have beat territories that they cover on a regular basis, deadlines that they have to meet, and routine channels for securing participants. They must orient simultaneously to the constraints of the media organization (the need for certain kinds of stories told in certain kinds of ways) and to the constraints of the outside world (the availability, willingness, and performative competence of guests, ordinary and expert alike). Like the producers of late-night celebrity talk, producers of daytime talk must generate lively interaction among participants in order to deliver good television. This is partly a function of the topic itself, partly a function of the strategic juxtaposition of panelists, and partly a function of backstage preparation and coaching. At the same time, because of what ordinariness signifies, lively interaction looks somewhat different on daytime talk shows than it does elsewhere on television, and its orchestration poses some unique challenges to producers behind the scenes. Significantly, the things that they do to elicit a dramatic money shot—targeting people experiencing a conflict or crisis, orchestrating surprises and confrontations—can lead to a volatile production context and exacerbate the tension between scriptedness and spontaneity that producers love to hate.

As we have seen, producing the money shot requires a certain amount of emotional labor from producers. As Hochschild (1983) observes, the commodification of emotion occurs whenever feelings enter the marketplace and are bought and sold as an aspect of labor power. In effect, producers are buying the emotional performances of guests with their own commodified displays of sympathy and friendship, in combination with more tangible rewards like television exposure and free vacations. Sometimes these displays are genuinely felt, but often they are not since the conditions of workplace speedup tend to foster a disjuncture between display and feeling—what Hochschild calls *emotive dissonance*. Speedup demands that workers "make personal human contact at an inhuman speed" (Hoch-schild 1983, 126), and producers respond by falling back on surface acting, relying on situations in which underlying conflict is already built into the topic, and foregrounding the material benefits of participating in their in-teractions with guests. Emotive dissonance is further encouraged by the cultural and socioeconomic distance between producers and guests, espe-cially at trashy shows like *Randy*. As the profile of guests shifted from mid-dle to lower class, and as the money shot consequently grew more hard-core, it became increasingly difficult for producers to empathize with guests, both for personal and for professional reasons.

For Hochschild, emotion management in commercial contexts is largely a middle-class phenomenon, most prevalent in quasi-professional occupations (nursing, social work, bill collecting, insurance, sales, etc.) that require extended personal contact with the public and that involve the pro-duction of a particular emotional state in others.[1] Middle-class women tend to dominate these occupations, according to Hochschild, because they are taught from a young age to be more cooperative and to adapt to the needs of others and because the general economic subordination of women means that women often make a special resource out of feeling, both on and off the job. For women, deep acting has high "secondary gains," and thus, as with others of low status, it is in women's interests to be good ac-tors (Hochschild 1983, 167). But men do institutionalized emotion work, too, albeit of a different sort. Whereas women often manage feeling in the service of "making nice," men are more likely to manage feeling in order to

---

1. As Hochschild notes, a great many jobs place emotional burdens on workers, re-gardless of class (which is one reason why *work* is defined as work and not play). For exam-ple, when work is boring and deskilled, as it is for the data processor or the factory seam-stress, one may have to suppress feelings of anger, boredom, or frustration. But, while this is an emotional burden, it is not in itself emotional labor, for what is made into a commodity or resource is one's physical rather than one's emotional capacity. This is not to suggest that emotional labor is exclusively middle class. Consider, for example, the work of the personal servant, the prostitute, the Park Avenue doorman, or the waitress. These people, too, must do emotion work as a routine part of the job, especially when their clients or customers have greater status than they themselves do. Yet Hochschild is most concerned with forms of emotion work that have been removed from the private domain and placed in the public arena, where feeling is processed, standardized, and subject to hierarchic control by institu-tional mechanisms. And most jobs of this sort, she insists, tend to be filled by members of the middle class. Hochschild suggests a connection here to class differences in socialization since middle-class parents tend to discipline their children via appeals to feeling and to managing feeling, whereas working-class parents tend to focus more on controlling behav-ior—differences in socialization that amount to different degrees of training for the com-modification of emotion in commercial contexts (see Hochschild 1983, 156–61; see also Kohn 1963; Bernstein 1974).

persuade, enforce rules, or secure compliance (see Hochschild 1983, 162–98). By any of these criteria, talk-show producers, women and men alike, are emotional laborers par excellence. They simply reverse the normal functioning of the work, which is to discourage rather than to encourage "a scene."

If managing emotion is construed as a largely middle-class phenomenon, one in which women play a central role, the work of performing or embodying emotion is presented on daytime talk shows as a largely working- or lower-class phenomenon, also one in which women play a central—although increasingly a less central—role. In contrast to the performances of experts, who are understood to be more distanced and dignified participants, it falls to "just folks" to display the feeling that producers so carefully cultivate, to deliver the scene that in everyday (nontelevised) life emotional labor is supposed to diffuse or prevent. The link between class and the particular type of emotional expressiveness that talk shows promote is clear enough in the way the genre changed over time and in the current distinction between classy and trashy variants. Classy shows like *Diana*, featuring more serious topics, are devoted to a more or less tasteful version of the money shot. They bear the imprint of the self-help recovery movement and the rise of popular psychology as well as of mainstream feminism and other identity-based social movements of the 1960s and 1970s. Trashy shows like *Randy*, on the other hand, which prioritize conflict and confrontation, overlay these same influences with a distinctly tabloid brand of emotional display, one that is perceived by critics to be excessive, transgressive, and out of control. Trashy shows produce a hardcore version of the money shot, and they garner high ratings because they "shock and amaze," much like the nineteenth-century freak show. They shock and amaze not so much because they exhibit anomalous bodies, however. When friends tell me that they cannot believe that real people actually get up there and do those things on national television, they are marveling at the transgression of taken-for-granted codes governing normative public conduct. Part of what I have tried to do in this book, then, is examine how producers normalize and make routine that transgression.

I also examine why real people do in fact get up there and do those things on national television, what happens to them along the way, and how they think about their participation. Guests are by no means uniformly pleased with their experience or with the strategies employed by producers to elicit from them the right sort of performance. Just as the circus sideshow raised important ethical questions about the exploitation of human freaks, talk shows raise similar questions about the manipulation and exploitation of guests. Even when guests have no specific complaints about their experience, there is a larger question about the nature of their representation and how that representation is received by others. In the course of my research, I worried about the ethical dimensions of producers' work (and, by implication, my own). I still worry, for the issues involved are complicated and, to my thinking, not easily resolved. But, since this chapter is the final segment of this particular "show" and it's time for the "host" to wrap things up, it is to the matter of exploitation that I now turn.

Generally speaking, there have been two intertwined concerns about daytime talk shows as voiced by critics in the media: the specific ways in which guests are manipulated and deceived by producers and the more generalized exploitation assumed to inhere in the act of airing one's dirty laundry in public—the former most strongly emphasized in the immediate aftermath of the *Jenny Jones* murder, the latter a more diffuse and long-standing concern that grew in direct proportion to the genre's increasing levels of sensationalism. Critics are right when they suggest that producers have an instrumental stance toward guests and their problems, that, as much as hosts or producers might stress educational, informational, or therapeutic goals, talk shows are making entertainment out of ordinary people's lives, using their transgressions and hardships to garner ratings. Critics are also right when they point out that, for the most part, ordinary guests are drawn from trailer parks and tenements rather than country clubs or penthouse suites. As Barbara Ehrenreich (1995) has observed, you will not find investment bankers bickering on *Ricki Lake* or see Montel Williams recommending therapy to sobbing professors. But whether this is "class exploitation pure and simple," as she concludes, is a rather more complicated question. By what right do scholars and critics sit in judgment of the guest who bickers with her in-laws, admits to cheating on her spouse, or discloses the details of her acrimonious divorce on national television? More to the point, is it possible to separate a concern with exploitation from middle-class notions of appropriate conduct and good taste?

Manipulation and Mass Mediation

The issue of manipulation on talk shows is far from simple or clear-cut. Manipulation occurs at both the individual and the structural levels, and, while some forms are relatively easy to identify and condemn, others are not. A certain amount of manipulation or deception is inherent in talk-show production since part of what producers do is convince people to tell their stories on television and then package those stories in ways that enhance their dramatic, unusual, or spectacular effect. Every phase of the process involves the transformation of an old reality into a new one. As a producer once said to me, "Asking a producer to describe manipulation is like asking a fish to describe the aquarium." Certainly, it is unethical for producers to lie to guests, make promises that they have no intention of keeping, or lure guests onto a show under false pretenses. Such tactics have drawn considerable fire from critics in and outside the industry and made potential guests wary of participating. Producers, not surprisingly, deny these practices and insist that honesty is not only good ethics but good producing as well since it ensures a stronger bond with guests and, therefore, greater compliance. Nevertheless, producers can avoid outright deception and still not be completely forthright with guests or adequately prepare them for their performance.

The *Jenny Jones* murder was an indirect warning signal to the industry about the acceptable limits of deception in the service of obtaining a dramatic money shot. At the same time, the failure to adequately inform guests is not always or necessarily deliberate since the genre is predicated on spontaneity and live-audience participation (and hence may involve unanticipated events) and since producers themselves may not know in advance all the details of a show. Even when they do know, the pace of production prevents them from reviewing every element with each and every guest—in fact, producers are trained *not* to "overrehearse" guests. Moreover, as we have seen, whether guests feel manipulated or deceived can have less to do with what actually happens to them onstage, objectively speaking, and more to do with a goodness of fit between expectation and outcome.[2] For producers and guests alike, there is a fine line between being informed and being uninformed, between honesty and deception, between exaggeration and outright distortion. Producers who encourage guests to exaggerate their emotions or prioritize the more sensational aspects of their stories do so in the name not of deception but of producing good television; this *requires* a certain level of manipulation. For their part, some guests exaggerate their emotions or embellish their stories with little

---

2. Complicating this scenario is the fact that, when guests *do* feel manipulated because they have been unexpectedly humiliated or ridiculed, producers are often not the only ones responsible, at least from an ethical standpoint, for producers could never orchestrate a surprise confrontation without the complicity of the person who wants to do the confronting.

or no encouragement from producers because they, too, know what constitutes good television within the parameters of the genre and are eager to prove their performative competence. Carried to an extreme, this can lead to deception of another sort: the deception of audiences by fake guests, which may or may not involve the complicity of producers.

There are many manipulative aspects to the production of daytime talk shows. As Gamson (1996) notes, talk shows can be a dangerous place to speak and a difficult place to get heard. But focusing on extreme instances of manipulation, as critics are wont to do, both reproduces the sensationalism that critics despise and ignores the ways in which manipulation is systemic, built into the routines and practices of the production process. It also masks the degree to which manipulation and mediation are fundamentally intertwined. The media do not simply reflect reality "out there." By definition, they mediate, even when, or perhaps especially when, it is real life that is purportedly being revealed. The ways in which talk shows mediate the experiences of ordinary people are not random or haphazard but systematic and patterned; talk shows institutionalize certain kinds of manipulation. In doing so, however, they have much in common with other forms of media—in particular the news. Paul Willis (1994, 38) has noted the sense of "colossal misinterpretation" often felt by people who find themselves or their experiences the subject of news reports. From the outside, the news may appear to have a certain "straightforward reasonableness," he writes, "but for those involved in the real events being reported, there is a characteristic, if muted, sense of colossal misinterpretation. The continuity of real events has been sacrificed in the media to the continuity of much larger myths about the real."

The news media construct these myths in much the same way talk shows do: by decontextualizing issues and events, privileging individual solutions to complex, social problems, creating drama by juxtaposing opposing viewpoints, and emphasizing deviance, conflict, and violence over normal consensual relations.[3] Both talk shows and news media also require participants to speak in sound bites, perhaps the biggest point of frustration for the guests I interviewed, ordinary and expert alike. One industry veteran estimated, in fact, that the pressure to "cut the exposition and get to the sound bite" accounts for upwards of 80 percent of the manipulation on talk shows. Guests complain that the genre is too much show and too

3. These patterns have been documented by, among others, Cohen and Young (1973), Tuchman (1978), Gans (1979), Gitlin (1980), Hartley (1982), and Manoff and Schudson (1986).

little talk, that the format precludes them from telling their stories as they feel their stories deserve to be told. They are right about this, but the problem is not unique to talk shows and is arguably much worse in the news. As one of my expert guests observed, he has greater opportunity to articulate and explain his point of view on talk shows, limited as the opportunity might be, than he does on the CBS evening news. "I could be on a national network news program for fifteen to twenty seconds," he said, "and I've been on [a talk show] for an hour! So which one is tabloid, which one is ethical? Well, from my point of view, I'd rather be on [a talk show]."

Like daytime talk, other forms of media are self-referential or "incestuous," recycling ideas, information, sources, and contacts. Almost all mass-media organizations seek to maximize profits, and most media professionals believe that a dramatic personal narrative will affect audiences in a way that abstract generalizations and statistical data cannot. It is for this reason that virtually all media texts—especially televisual ones—deliver their own particular versions of the money shot. All good television is built around moments of dramatic revelation. All television, from news and documentary to soap opera and sports, aims to stimulate people visually, give people a look, let people see for themselves—hence the importance of slow motion and the close-up. Indeed, to the extent that television is itself a visual discourse better suited to expressive than to informational content, devoted to making public and visible what would otherwise remain private and invisible (see Meyrowitz 1985), it can be seen as a kind of machine for producing the money shot. How else to explain the incessant news coverage of President Clinton's affair with Monica Lewinsky? Not since the coverage of John Wayne Bobbitt have I heard so much public discussion about a man's penis. There were moments when the biggest difference between *Larry King Live* and *Jerry Springer* was the fact that all the guests on King's show were white men with perfect teeth.

Desire for the money shot was the driving force behind the long-running *Candid Camera*, which deliberately placed ordinary people in extraordinary situations in order to provoke them into losing their cool, and it is the reason why shows like *The Real World* and *Survivor* do not just throw together a random collection of participants but carefully select a particular mix that will yield maximum dramatic potential (see Marsh 2000; Zurawik 2000). Desire for the money shot is what prompts Barbara Walters to ask, regardless of topic or interview subject, "So how does that make you *feel?*" and it is also what compels reporters to interrogate people immediately after they have experienced a terrible shock or tragedy—a form of ambushing if ever there was one. Randy himself made this point in our interview: "For ten years, I used to anchor the news, and every day we would jam a microphone in the face of someone who didn't ask to be on the air—someone coming out of the courthouse, out of a scandal—or you go into their homes, and you ask them a question. Sometimes they're humiliated, sometimes you embarrass their families, but you do it anyway—and we say it's OK because it's the news."

Critics are also concerned that talk shows blur the boundary between fact and fiction, that they deceive audiences and compromise truth for the sake of ratings. This is a charge to which industry insiders are particularly sensitive, especially when it comes to the matter of fake guests—after all, real stories told by ordinary people are the bedrock of the genre. Over and over, I witnessed staffers at both *Diana* and *Randy* deliberately reject people who appeared overly eager to get on TV, whose lives seemed to fit every topic under the sun, or whose stories kept changing from one day to the next. At the same time, the structural demands of the workplace can mitigate *against* authenticity. Producers desire real guests with real problems, people who are not slick or practiced, who express genuine emotion, who are not media savvy, and who have never been on a talk show before. But these are also the guests who, in some ways, pose the greatest challenge to producers, for the very qualities that make them real make them more difficult to manage in routine ways. The pressure of deadlines, the nature of the topics, and the performances required of guests can push producers toward people who *are* media savvy, have had prior talk-show experience, and may even be actors faking their stories. Thus, the blurring of fact and fiction has structural causes and is not a conspiracy but a practicality.

At the same time, even the "realest" of guests are inserted into a theatrical context that fictionalizes their performances to some degree, and fictionalizing of this sort occurs in news, documentary, and reality programming, too—in the selection and juxtaposition of images, the choice of music and narration, the presence of cutaways and reaction shots, the artful shaping of story lines, and the things people say (and possibly lie about) on camera. As Randy said about news reporting, "When I did the news, how many times did people lie to me? Every day if I interviewed a politician." Likewise, a former cast member of *The Real World* admits that he was not "entirely himself" on the set and that neither were the other participants. Even if they had been, the final portrait might well have conveyed something else. According to Marsh (2000), the amount of raw footage shot on *The Real World* is so vast that each twenty-two-minute episode takes an entire month to assemble. She describes the show as "a cut and paste version of reality" exhibiting a "surprising degree of manipulation." "[They get] the footage they need for the ends they want" (76), one cast member told her. Former participants on *Big Brother* have lodged similar complaints in the press, claiming that they were "manipulated into stereotypes" and had become "pawns in a game" (McCann 2000). These charges would no doubt sound familiar to vérité filmmaker Craig Gilbert, as they are remarkably like those of the family members featured in his PBS documentary series *An American Family*, on which *The Real World* is based (see Gilbert 1988a, 1988b).[4]

The most significant feature that talk shows share with other media, however, is the tendency to deny ordinary people routine access unless they engage in exceptional behavior. Talk shows are by no means alone in this regard. Because ordinary people exist largely outside the official channels and established routines of newsmaking and the entertainment industry, they must do and say *extra*ordinary things to gain entry. Gans (1979) noted long ago that experts and officials constitute between 70 and 80 percent of all individuals appearing in the U.S. domestic news media, both print and electronic, while ordinary people obtain about a fifth of the available time or space. Aside from a small percentage who are voters or survey respondents, these ordinary people are newsworthy precisely because they are disruptive or deviant. Not being naturally newsworthy for *who they are* (as is the case with celebrities and other elites), ordinary people gain access to media more because of *what they do*, and notions of unusualness, disruptiveness, and deviance play a crucial role in determining this access (see also Hall et al. 1978; Sigal 1986; Langer 1998). Thus, the tendency of media critics to distance daytime talk as the "other"—as if talk shows were the only discourse "othering" ordinary people—is more than a little disingenuous. Talk shows simply exaggerate or throw into high relief the manipulative practices of other media forms.[5] News coverage of daytime talk shows—focused almost exclusively on murder, deception, and fraud— is itself good evidence of their common ground. Talk shows are es

4. Gilbert wanted to document the "typical" American family in their natural setting in order to explore, as he put it to the Louds, both the ordinariness and the universality of their everyday lives. The cameras rolled every day, all day, for seven months, and the footage was assembled into twelve one-hour segments for broadcast on public television. Not only did the family agree to participate, but they approved a rough cut of each episode. But the press following the broadcast was largely negative, characterizing the Louds as shallow and dysfunctional, and the family blamed Gilbert for "setting them up" (see Gilbert 1988a, 1988b).

5. Langer (1992, 1998) makes much the same point about the similarities between the serious and the tabloid ("unworthy") news, arguing that they are different in degree, not in kind. As he writes, "The unworthy news may get its bad name, not because of its

pecially maligned, however, because their strategies of manipulation are particularly visible, because they sometimes take manipulation to unacceptable levels, and, most important, because of the kind of ordinary people they target and the nature of the performances that these people are asked to give.

Ethics and Exploitation

The kind of ordinary people that talk shows target and the nature of the performances that they are asked to give bring me to the second ethical concern mentioned earlier: the issue of class exploitation. For some critics, the problem with daytime talk shows is not so much that producers deceive or manipulate guests but that they go after the most vulnerable and disenfranchised, making entertainment out of lives distorted by poverty and hardship. According to Ehrenreich (1995, 92), "[Guests] are so needy—of social support, of education, of material resources and self-esteem—that they mistake being the center of attention for being actually loved and respected." While this characterization is clearly biased toward shows on the trashy end of the continuum, it is true that such shows do not attract just anybody. I once heard the executive producer of *Jerry Springer* say that his guests represent a "cross section of the American public." This is absurd, for the guests on *Springer* are no more a cross section of the American public than are the guests on *Nightline*.[6] Certain groups of people are more vulnerable to experiencing the kinds of problems that trashy talk shows capitalize on, and certain groups of people are more willing to bring these problems on national television.

The case of Sonny and her daughter, Jordan, is illustrative. They appeared on a *Springer* show about teen prostitution, along with several other family members. Jordan is nineteen, has a baby daughter, is pregnant with a second child, and has been working intermittently as a prostitute since

---

popularity or shameless persistence in bulletins, but because it is unruly, more openly acknowledging and flaunting devices and constructions which the serious news suppresses and hides. Perhaps, in the end, this is why the lament is so harsh on this kind of news, because it is what news is, only more so" (1992, 128).

6. A study of *Nightline* by Hoynes and Croteau (1989) showed that, in the late 1980s, 90 percent of *Nightline* guests were men and 83 percent were white. Professionals, government officials, and corporate representatives together accounted for 80 percent of all guests, while public-interest representatives, labor leaders, and racial/ethnic leaders together accounted for only 6 percent of all guests.

the age of thirteen. She is currently living with her sixty-four-year-old boyfriend, who provides her with expensive cars, clothes, and whatever else she wants, including (so family members claim) drugs and clients. It was Jordan who first contacted producers in response to a plug. Initially, the show was supposed to feature a confrontation between the elderly boyfriend and Sonny, the mom. Sonny was to accuse the boyfriend of being a pedophile and a pimp and to tell him to "get the hell out of my daughter's life" or risk arrest for solicitation. But the boyfriend got cold feet and disappeared from his hotel room the morning of the taping. So producers quickly reframed the confrontation, substituting Jordan's uncle Casey (Sonny's stepbrother) for the other man. Bisexual, addicted to crack, and allegedly a prostitute himself, Casey told producers that his very first girlfriend—a call girl murdered by a serial killer—actually helped Jordan secure her first trick. He admitted that he, too, introduced his niece to "trustworthy" clients on occasion, but only to save her a fate like the girlfriend's. He claimed that Sonny, the mom, secured Jordan tricks for the same reason. So the conflict was between Sonny and her stepbrother, Casey, each accusing the other of prostituting Jordan.

Ehrenreich's assertion that talk shows take lives distorted by poverty and hold them up as entertaining exhibits rings painfully true here. Yet the show itself represents but the tip of the iceberg when it comes to the hardships that some guests face. Now thirty-seven and on permanent disability because of multiple sclerosis, Sonny never knew her biological father and was raised by her alcoholic mother and stepfather. A white woman, Sonny says she was raped at the age of seventeen by a black man and conceived Jordan as a result, but, because she refused to give the child up for adoption, her family accused her of being a "nigger lover" and disowned her. Stepbrother Casey was the only one who stood by her. Sonny then entered a bad marriage with an abusive white husband, whose sister was also a prostitute. Sonny is currently divorced, living with her mother, and, before going on disability, worked as a housekeeper in a large hotel. She says that she did her best raising Jordan but has never been able to control the girl. As she put it, "Sometimes you have choices of where you live, and how your kids are raised, and what they're raised around. I had no choices because this family is into drugs, and prostitution, and everything else—that's what Jordan's had to get around."

The lives of certain other guests were no less difficult. Winona, who went on *Randy* to be confronted by her two daughters for child abuse, was adopted as an infant and raised in a well-to-do but strict religious home. As a teenager, she was sent away to boarding school, where she was gang-raped, became pregnant as a result, and was forced to give the baby up for adoption. She later married an abusive man and became severely depressed and alcoholic. Now in her late forties, Winona lives in the rural South; she has no steady income and no telephone. For her part, Anitra went on *Jenny Jones* to confront her siblings, who accused her of being a bad mother because her only daughter had been molested by her boyfriend and subsequently placed in foster care. Anitra describes her own childhood as "traumatic." Her mother was an exotic dancer, and the two were constantly on the road, living mostly out of cheap hotels.

Is it ethical for producers to put such individuals onstage? Does it matter if they are consenting adults, willing participants, regular talk-show viewers? If they have prior talk-show experience? To paraphrase a former *Geraldo* producer, tricking guests into going on a talk show is like tricking people into swimming: if they've ever seen water, they know that they are going to get wet. The particular circumstances surrounding a guest matter, of course. People who are, say, suffering from psychiatric disorders are probably not in the best position to make a decision about whether to appear on national television, regardless of how much or how little they watch talk shows. The same goes for those normal guests whose experience of loss, betrayal, victimization, or abuse is acute, recent, or overwhelming. For producers (or, worse yet, these guests' friends and family members) to capitalize on their vulnerability seems clearly unethical and exploitative.

But what about guests who are more or less mentally stable or whose conflicts and problems are not fresh or raw but ongoing and long-standing? What about guests who, in the absence of being duped or deceived by producers, *choose* to air their dirty laundry on television? What about guests who are simply poor or lower class? Are they, too, atypically vulnerable such that we can speak of their participation on talk shows as exploitative? What if guests themselves do not see it this way? In an essay about the ethics of nineteenth-century freak shows, Gerber (1996) asks by what right we sit in judgment of such people as the fat lady who displays herself for profit. The same question obviously applies to certain guests on trashy talk shows. In both cases, as Gerber points out, one runs the risk of condescension.

In the case of freak-show exhibits, people with physical anomalies faced extreme ostracism and stigmatization, which effectively limited their opportunities for work and social interaction. This larger context of oppression leads Gerber to conclude that choice on the part of human exhibits was so constrained that freak shows can never be seen as anything but exploitative. Is this how we should think about the choices of Sonny or

Winona? Even individuals who have everything going for them often make poor choices, and *Randy* guests could hardly be said to have everything going for them. Nor does a person need to experience exploitation consciously in order for it to exist. Whether one considers talk shows exploitative might depend not only on the attitude or motivation of specific guests but on the attitude of audience members toward the genre as a whole. On the other hand, unlike sideshow freaks, talk-show guests do not earn a living from their performances, and, if a guest wants to participate and has not been coerced by producers, what right do critics have to insist that she is being exploited, regardless of what audiences think? How paternalistic are we willing to be? Talk shows are not some special arena of victimization here. Choice can never be other than a relative concept, for, in a society characterized by structural inequality, the choices of those at the bottom are never as free as the choices of those at the top.

There are no right answers to these questions. Some producers I interviewed actually insisted that putting stories of conflict and abuse on television was a positive thing for society. Tyler, formerly with *Jerry Springer*, said that television had an ethical responsibility to portray all kinds of reality, not just the reality represented by *Leave It to Beaver* or *Ozzie and Harriet*.

"Is everything in life good?" she asked me. "No. The reality is most people are miserable. This is not an Ozzie-and-Harriet world, and any talk show that tries to make life look like *Ozzie and Harriet* is being irresponsible. Because there are both sides. There are the happinesses, the joys, the overcoming tremendous odds, that sort of thing. But there's also the misery and the conflict and the hatred that is such a big part of humanity. And I think it would be extremely irresponsible of television to portray only the happy side of life."

Saul Feldman made a similar point when he compared daytime talk shows to the sitcom *Friends*, suggesting that the latter was as exploitative as any talk show. At least a talk show is relatively honest in its portrayal, he said. "The people are not attractive necessarily; they are not well dressed; they're not wealthy; they're maybe not even very literate or thoughtful." By contrast, *Friends* is full of beautiful people leading beautiful lives, people who never seem to work yet always have plenty of money, people whose biggest worry is, in Feldman's words, "getting laid." And *Friends* has millions more viewers than even the top-rated talk show. "Now, what kind of influence does that have on all these viewers, week after week after week, to see those images of wealth and privilege?"

Of course, *no* television show presents life as it really is, talk shows no less than sitcoms. The problem with such arguments is that a show like *Randy* does not simply portray life's hardships. It portrays a narrow range of hardships (mostly sexual and family conflict) represented by a narrow range of people (mostly poor or working class) who perform these conflicts in narrow, predictable ways—ways that rarely foster an empathetic response from audiences. The experiences of guests are too decontextualized for empathy. *Randy* producers tend to "cut the exposition and get to the sound bite" in such a way as to preclude most everything but a brief spurt of trashy behavior. As a result, it is difficult to relate to guests and their problems; there seems to be no sensible way of responding save to laugh or feel contempt. Thus, even if we agree that the media should portray the bad as well as the good in life, it is important to ask what kind of badness gets represented, who represents it, how, and with what consequences. At the same time, it is important to reiterate that producing the money shot is not a deliberate act of class exploitation on the part of producers necessarily but is mandated and made possible by a variety of institutional and generic needs as well as by a more general media structure that excludes many populations from public visibility and, therefore, feeds them willingly, if ambivalently, into a genre that exaggerates their lower status.[7]

As Seen on TV

Talk shows appear especially exploitative if one does not see media exposure (particularly *that* kind of media exposure) as a fair trade-off for whatever consequences guests incur by participating. People often wonder why guests do it, why they are seemingly complicit in their own degradation. This wonderment is clearly directed more toward guests on the *Randy* end of the continuum since classy shows typically are not degrading (at least not in the same way or to the same degree) and the motivations of their guests are easier to understand. Guests on trashy shows tend to have less legitimate motivations: they may have an ax to grind, a secret to reveal, or a score to settle; they may have acting or modeling aspirations, enjoy the trappings of celebrity, want a free vacation, or just want to be seen on TV. Of all these reasons, it is the desire for television exposure that most confounds critics. Unlike the participants on the primetime reality-based shows *The Real World*, *Road Rules*, or *Survivor*, talk-show guests raise not only the question

---

7. Thanks to Joshua Gamson (personal communication, July 1997) for helping clarify this point.

of why ordinary people want media celebrity but also the question of why they are willing to accept it on such unflattering terms.

As with the issue of exploitation, there are both individual and structural explanations to consider. One answer, implied in the discussion presented above, is that guests are so poor or needy or screwed up that they mistake media attention for compassion and respect. Another possibility is that some guests do not see anything wrong with discussing their personal lives or expressing their emotions on television. "Everybody has problems," Lori, a *Randy* guest, told me, "and there's nothing wrong with expressing them on television in front of other people." Moreover, guests understand at some level that they are playing roles and thus can distance themselves from their own trashy behavior, displacing it onto the larger theatrical context. Even Joanne, a *Randy* guest who went on the show to express her "real, natural, gut feelings" toward a woman she despised, was playing a role and a stock one at that: the *genuinely outraged guest*. She knew that producers wanted her to express raw emotion onstage, and she complied. Generally speaking, the degree to which guests are self-conscious about their role-playing appears to increase as the characters they play grow more melodramatic or cartoonish; guests seem to have an easier time dissociating self from role when the level of exaggeration is high.

But the most obvious explanation, and one that does not by definition exclude the rest, is that guests who desire television exposure want to leave a mark on the world, however small or fleeting or disdained. Guests do not say this in so many words, but I believe it to be true and not so difficult to understand. Most people want to feel that who they are and what they do matter to others. They want to be noticed; they want recognition or validation; they want to be part of something larger than themselves. The desire to leave a mark is surely common to all classes and strata of society, even if the specific avenues for fulfilling it are not. Professors write books; politicians author laws; athletes win medals; directors make films; artists make art; activists effect social change. Some ways of making one's mark on the world are clearly more prestigious and far-reaching than others. The elite or truly gifted leave entire legacies and dynasties behind them. Their actions become part of the "official" historical record, their names memorialized on monuments and museums, buildings and street signs, parks, rivers, and towns.

Most ordinary guests on daytime talk shows have more modest aims and arenas of influence. Those on a show like *Randy* do not hold official titles or professional jobs. They have little connection to, or experience with, the production of official knowledge, whether in the realm of science, art, politics, or law. Universities, Wall Street, Congress—these institutions are not necessarily perceived as relevant to, or part of, their everyday lives. But television is. Television is a discourse that they know. Many of them, in fact, know it quite intimately, at least as consumers, for television viewing is inversely correlated with social class. Writing a book or authoring a law is not really on the map for most *Randy* guests. But starring in a talk show is. And, at some level, it does not much matter that the role is a negative or unflattering one, for the larger goal is simply to participate in the discourse and be part of the scene. As with many of the audience members I saw asking questions at tapings, and in contrast to experts, such guests could be said to exemplify a ritual as opposed to a transmission model of communication (see Carey 1989), where the mere act of conveying a message is more important than what, specifically, gets said.

It is very likely that guests on *Randy, Ricki Lake,* or *Jenny Jones* would prefer media exposure on more dignified terms. Guests, even those who respond to plugs, need a lot of persuasion. The better part of producers' emotional labor at *Randy* is spent convincing people to do the show or to follow through with their initial impulse to volunteer. No doubt, such folks would prefer starring roles in *The Real World, Road Rules,* or *Survivor.* But most talk-show guests are not hip and attractive enough for these shows. Moreover, they would have to compete with thousands of other people and do much more than make a telephone call to apply. Despite the less prestigious nature of talk shows, guests allow themselves to be persuaded to go on them because they want to be part of television and because, unless they break the law and appear on *Cops*, they see few other options for fulfilling this desire.

Talk-show guests are clearly not the only ordinary people seeking television exposure these days. Thirty-five thousand eager applicants submitted audition tapes to MTV in 1999, hoping to get on *The Real World.* Since its debut in 1992, the show has chronicled forty-five months in the lives of sixty-three young adults, capturing a marriage, an abortion, a gay commitment ceremony, a drunk-driving episode, a physical assault, and "thousands of bitchy spats" (Marsh 2000, 71). As one former participant told Marsh, "Everyone in my cast wanted to go into entertainment, and they were all using the show as a springboard" (76). Likewise, it is not for the prize money alone that people agree to be stranded together in remote locations, suffer physical exhaustion, and engage in a wilderness version of smarmy office politics, as they are in *Survivor.* Nor was it just greed that compelled Darva Conger to compete with fifty other women for the privilege of marrying a total stranger on FOX's *Who Wants to Marry a Multi-Millionaire*—and then attempt to reclaim her dignity by giving dozens of television interviews and posing nude in *Playboy*, all the while pleading to be left alone (as she put it in her interview on *Good Morning America*, "I'm a private person, and I just want my life back"). Twenty-three million viewers tuned in to watch the TV marriage, while the final *Survivor* episode clocked a record 58 million, the most-watched program of 2000 next to the Superbowl. (More people watched *Survivor* than even the Academy Awards—which some commentators took as proof that viewers prefer watching ordinary people compete for money rather than celebrities compete for Oscars.) Of course, once an ordinary person stars in a primetime series and is watched by 58 million viewers, the line between ordinariness and stardom begins to break down. Cast members from the middlebrow reality shows appear routinely on morning and late-night talk shows, grace the covers of mass-circulation magazines, do commercial endorsements, travel the college lecture circuit, and are represented by agents and publicists. (In Britain, where *Big Brother* was a hit, the show's best-known contestant is said to be worth £1 million in endorsements annually.)[8] So great is the media attention paid to the participants on reality shows that I would not be surprised if celebrities start passing themselves off as ordinary people in order to get on TV rather than the other way around.

Media coverage or exposure is a powerful form of validation in our culture, for ordinary people no less than celebrities, experts, politicians, and activists of various sorts. As Larry Gross (1994, 143) puts it, "Representation in the mediated 'reality' of our mass culture is in itself power . . . [and] those who are at the bottom of the various hierarchies will be kept in their place in part through their relative invisibility." Yet, when people do gain visibility, it is only by submitting to the implicit rules of the media industry, by conforming to journalistic notions of what constitutes a good story, a dramatic event, or a compelling performance. This submission is required of all media participants, not just ordinary people on daytime talk shows. How many experts on *Nightline* actually *like* debating international politics in thirty-second sound bites? How many black actors on television *prefer* stereotypical bit parts as sidekicks or comic relief? How many white women *opt* to play the passive love interest rather than the take-charge protagonist in the latest Hollywood film? Clearly, even experts and celebrities

---

8. This estimate comes from an article in the *London Daily Telegraph* (see Leonard 2000).

are manipulated and constrained by media discourse in systematic—and unequal—ways. To paraphrase Gamson (1996), seizing the microphone is a complicated sort of power in a media culture because the voice that emerges is never only yours: if you speak, you must prepare to be used. To this I would add that not all ways of being used are equal and that, the more invisible within mainstream media—by virtue of one's political activities and convictions, physical attractiveness, education/credentials, occupation, age, class status, sexuality, race, or gender—the "higher" the price of admission is likely to be.

When a category of people without a lot of power and resources suddenly gains visibility in popular discourse after having been largely ignored, the resulting portrait is rarely multifaceted or complex—at least initially. We have seen this principle at work with carnival freak shows, but there are other examples as well. Kano (2001) documents how, when women were first admitted to the kabuki theater in Japan, they had to enact ultrastereotypical versions of femininity in order to convey the notion of femaleness, which, up to that point, had been the purview of male actors. Ironically, when real women took over, their biological status was not enough; they had to play exaggerated, male-defined versions of themselves.

Minstrel shows provide another clear example in relation to racialized representations of African Americans. One of the earliest points of entry of black culture into American popular entertainment, minstrel performances—which initially featured white actors performing in blackface—were hardly an accurate representation of blackness. With few exceptions, and in both comic and sentimental variants, minstrel shows were stereotypically racist, positioning African Americans as inferior to whites. Even when African American actors became part of the minstrel tradition, their physiognomic status as *racial other* apparently was not "other" enough, for their roles were no less stereotypical, and they too performed in blackface (see Lott 1993; Lhamon 1998). The parallel here to the participation of the lower classes on trashy daytime talk shows is clear: when real nonexpert, noncelebrity people play the role of ordinary guest, their actual ordinariness cannot stand on its own and be presented as such but must be re-presented as a stereotypical facsimile of lower-class life. Indeed, talk shows are often compared to freak shows, but they are also like modern-day minstrel shows, with guests performing in "poorface."

Consequently, the issue of realness and authenticity in relation to guests on daytime talk shows is not strictly limited to the case of the aspiring actor faking her story *but rather extends to the real ordinary guest as well.*

Figure 11. Guests deliver the money shot on *Jerry Springer.* Photograph by Larry Fink. Originally published in *Rolling Stone,* 1998.

In the world of daytime talk shows, excessive emotional and bodily displays operate implicitly as markers of class difference, not because they come naturally to guests necessarily (if they did, producers would not spend so much time preparing guests for their roles), but because they are consistent with existing cultural stereotypes and thus are actively constituted as such through the backstage activities of the production process. Only by conforming to these markers do ordinary people have routine access to national television in the first place. Far from being neutral, then, the representation of "just folks" on daytime talk shows is shaped by their larger invisibility in media discourse as well as by the implicit rules and practices of the discourse itself. Talk shows are not and never have been a forum for expressing the interests and urgencies of ordinary people *as* ordinary people since the very conditions that subtend their entry into television transform them into something else.

Trash, Class, and Distinction

In the case of trashy shows, the existing cultural stereotype to which guests are made to conform—that something else that they become—is perhaps best summed up by the pejorative label *white trash*. Of all people without a lot of power and resources in our culture, few are disparaged with quite the same sense of impunity as white trash. As Jim Goad (1997) puts it, "White trash are open game. The trailer park has become the media's cultural toilet, the only acceptable place to dump one's racist inclinations." From *The Beverly Hillbillies* to *Deliverance*, white trash have been stereotyped as stupid, lazy, shiftless, licentious, alcoholic, and prone to violence and inbreeding. Such stereotypes are uniquely American, the result of a complex racial history as well as the general failure to recognize social class as a central category of identity and consciousness outside the extremes of rich and poor.

On the one hand, as Bettie (1995, 140) notes, the phrase *poor white trash* upholds the existing racial hierarchy by suggesting that color, poverty, and degenerate lifestyle go together so naturally that, when white folks behave this way, "their whiteness needs to be named." White trash are traitors to their race because they are not "doing whiteness" properly. On the other hand, in bringing together two attributes normally separated in popular discourse—whiteness and poverty—the term foregrounds the class diversity among whites (reminding us that, while class privilege is associated with whiteness, it is not essential to it) and *belies* the ideology of white supremacy: if whites are naturally so superior, then how do you explain white trash (Wray and Newitz 1997)? *White trash* thus challenges the presumed superiority of whiteness, as well as the myth of upward mobility that goes with it, by making explicit the existence of class difference, and the operation of class inequality, per se.

In both cases, the primary function of invoking the term *white trash* is to solidify for the middle and upper classes a sense of cultural and intellectual superiority. According to Wray and Newitz (1997), white-trash stereotypes both serve as a useful way of blaming the poor for being poor and help distance middle- and upper-class whites from their guilt and animosity toward racial minorities by substituting a safe target believed to embody many of the same racist assumptions. *White trash* creates a new racial other, which, like racial others of old, is linked to notions of uncivilized savagery and thus occupies the primitive side of the primitive/civilized divide (see Newitz 1997; Torgovnik 1991).[9] As such, as Hartigan (1997, 51) points out, *white trash* is not simply a stereotype or a false preconception; rather, "it delineates a discourse of difference whereby class identities are relationally formulated." The white middle classes rely on the attributes embodied by *white trash* to distinguish themselves from the lower orders, in effect saying, *We are not that.* Like *primitive* and *civilized*, *trashy* and *classy* are oppositional and relational, helping define and reinforce one another.

For all these reasons, *trashy* as used in the talk-show context is not just about class, nor is it coterminous with the term *poor white*. While the latter denotes a specific socioeconomic status, *trashy* connotes an interlocking set of despised behavioral, cultural, and aesthetic qualities that can be applied to a broader spectrum of individuals—within a limited degree across color and, as the case of *The Beverly Hillbillies* proves, despite actual material circumstances. Recall the description of *Randy* guests provided by Brian, a *Diana* producer: "White trash, black trash, Hispanic—any kind of, like, low-caliber people. Physical violence is such a routine part of their lives. . . . It's, like, they fight all the time, and they're half drunk, I don't think you'd even need to offer them money to do it." Indeed, any guests who look, talk, or behave a certain way can be labeled *white trash* or *trailer trash* regardless of whether they are poor, white, or living in a trailer park because the term *white trash* contains such an excess of meanings, functioning to mark symbolic boundaries between groups rather than simply differences of race or class per se. As we know from Durkheim (1965), symbolic boundaries

9. Here, again, we have significant parallels to black minstrelsy, for, if *white trash* represents a discourse about class inflected with racial overtones, minstrel shows represented a discourse of race inflected with class overtones. According to Lott (1993, 68), "Blackface in a real if partial sense, *figured* class. Its languages of race so invoked ideas about class as to provide displaced maps or representations of working-classness." Lott suggests that there was a historical logic in glossing working-class whites as black, given the degree to which large portions of both groups shared a common culture in the North, and given that many popular racial slurs (*coon, buck*) referred to whites as well as to blacks. In Lott's words, "Blackface quickly became a sort of useful shorthand in referring to working men." This was true in England as well, where American minstrel shows gained wide popularity. As Lott writes, quoting F. C. Wemyss, a historian of the period, "It is said of T. D. Rice's English tour that his burlesque skits were 'vulgar even to grossness,' and captivated 'the chimney sweeps and apprentice boys of London, who wheeled about and turned about and jumped Jim Crow, from morning until night, to the annoyance of their masters, but the great delight of the cockneys.'"

presuppose both inclusion ("us," desirable) and exclusion ("them," undesirable), and they survive only if they are repeatedly defended by members of the more powerful group. Of course, most *Randy* guests *are* in fact lower- or working-class whites, but, in and of itself, this is not what makes them trashy, and this is not why critics object to their performances.

It is certainly a problem that a show like *Randy* makes white trash out of ordinary people, that it produces a cartoonish version of lower class-ness cut from the cloth of *The Beverly Hillbillies* rather than, say, *The Waltons*. Yet it is not just a concern with negative stereotyping that prompts critics to disparage the genre. Indeed, the vast majority of critics in the mainstream media rarely mention stereotyping at all, instead, like producers, reading the trashy performances of guests as authentic expressions of their natural inclinations. Nor are the majority of critics concerned about the potential manipulation of guests (although some are) or even about class exploitation (although, again, some are). Barbara Ehrenreich notwithstanding, the denigration of daytime talk shows appears to be motivated less by a concern with the material circumstances of guests than by a concern to enforce symbolic boundaries, a sense of distinction, what Bourdieu (1984) calls the *aesthetic disposition*—the separation of culture from nature such that the *nature* against which *culture* is constructed is whatever is deemed low, vulgar, coarse, common, generic, easy, etc. Bourdieu argues that culture is used to distinguish among social classes, but the political dimensions of this function are naturalized as matters of aesthetics or taste. Tastes are a practical affirmation of seemingly inevitable (because seemingly natural) cultural difference, which is why aesthetic intolerance can be, and often is, quite strong.

Talk shows undoubtedly got trashier as they got more personal and emotionally expressive, and they undoubtedly linked these qualities with lower-class folks in stereotypical and derogatory ways. In the binary organization that opposes mind to matter, culture to nature, and textuality to orality, *the body* is the domain in which the lower classes—and other others—have been allowed and encouraged to operate. Like women generally, blacks and white ethnic groups have been considered creatures of feeling, naturally inclined toward emotional display.[10] On the other hand, why should emotional and bodily displays be considered trashy? Concepts of

---

10. Women are said to be more "embodied" than men not only because of their presumed greater emotionality but also because of their historic role in the reproduction and maintenance of bodies (bearing, feeding, washing, clothing, and sheltering bodies), their connection to private, domestic space (where the reproduction of bodies occurs), and

aesthetic merit and appropriate conduct are *not* natural or universal; they reflect dominant class interests. The outcry against *Jerry Springer* is good evidence of this, and the fact that lots of lower-class people probably hate the show does not change the fundamentally class-based nature of the response.

For Bourdieu, the body is the most indisputable materialization of class taste as well as its most explicit battleground. Biological or physical differences are underlined and symbolically accentuated by differences in bearing, gesture, and behavior that express a whole relation to the social world. Culturally legitimate bodies reflect the bourgeois aesthetic that privileges restraint, control, distance, and discipline over excess, impulse, and sensuality, and certain bodies—those that defy social norms of proper size, dress, manner, speech, etc.—are by definition in violation of that aesthetic. At the same time, the signs that constitute the body and its distance from nature themselves appear grounded in nature so that "the legitimate use of the body is perceived as an index of moral uprightness, while its opposite, a 'natural' body, is seen as an index of 'letting oneself go,' a culpable surrender to facility" (Bourdieu 1984, 193).[11]

What is at stake in the struggle for distinction, then, as Bourdieu so aptly demonstrates, is the ability to establish a perceived distance from, and

---

the larger cultural tendency to define women in sexual rather than intellectual or cognitive terms. For different but related reasons, this same presumed lack of emotional control and "rootedness in the body" has been attributed to people of color (see chapter 1).

11. In the contemporary moment, this "surrender to facility" is linked strongly to fatness, which in turn is linked explicitly and implicitly to the lower classes. In her brilliant 1996 essay "Life in the Fat Lane," Laura Kipnis suggests that our culture treats fat people with an unparalleled viciousness that generally goes unchallenged because the "index of moral uprightness" signified by fat bodies appears so natural and universal. Body type, Kipnis argues, is linked both factually and stereotypically to social class, with fatness—and the discriminatory behavior that accompanies it—increasing as one goes down the economic scale. Fat people are less likely to be hired, less likely to be promoted if hired, and less likely to marry up socially or economically—and this is especially true for fat women. According to Kipnis, psychological studies of body image suggest that fat is linked to a range of things that people fear and despise, including loss of control, infantile regression, failure, self-loathing, laziness, sloth, and passivity. She writes, "Substitute 'welfare class' for 'fat' here and you start to see that the phobia of fat and the phobia of the poor are heavily cross-coded" (1996, 101). The irony in this is not only that we live in a culture that encourages overconsumption while punishing all bodily evidence of it but that fat people (read poor people) come to stand as its privileged signifier. "The burden of fat is not only of pounds," Kipnis concludes. "It's the sorry fate of being trapped in a body that conveys such an excess of meanings" (102). The equation between fatness and social class appears to be borne out on daytime talk shows, which is one of the few places on television where fat people are given representation.

mastery over, the body and its material existence. The association of the lower classes with the body is both an embodied manifestation of class difference, grounded in historical-material reality, and the ideological means by which difference as hierarchy is justified. Middle-class disgust with daytime talk shows helps reproduce the hierarchy when it confuses the characterization of talk shows as overly emotional and excessive with a negative, moral evaluation of those characteristics.[12]

The taste-class nexus is, in turn, connected to the separation of public from private space. Like the aesthetic disposition, *the private*—a product of history, culture, and ideology—is defined naturally in moral terms. The private is constructed as sacred, inviolable, and exclusive. It is the space of bodily processes, intimate functions, the backstage preparation of self. So, when private matters spill out into public discourse—especially those private matters branded shameful, dirty, or polluting—it is perceived as a moral breech. The immorality lies not so much in the specific contents of private life as in the violation of the public/private boundary itself, the intrusion of the contents of one sphere into the space of the other. (As Bourdieu [1984, 56] puts it, "The most intolerable thing for those who regard themselves as the possessors of legitimate culture is the sacrilegious reuniting of tastes which taste dictates shall be separated.") Like the aesthetic dimensions of taste, the moral dimensions of privacy work to naturalize social and material privilege. In the United States, privacy and access to privacy—including, especially, private goods and services—are connected explicitly to wealth. Many poor people in this country know that when you depend for your existence on public assistance, there is no aspect of your private life—including your sexual and reproductive life—that is off-limits to public scrutiny, public surveillance, and public control. Ehrenreich (1995, 92) herself recognizes this when she observes, "It is easy enough for those who can afford spacious homes and private therapy to sneer at their financial inferiors and label their pathetic moments of stardom vulgar." If she had a talk show, she says, it would feature a different cast of characters and a different category of crimes: "CEOs who rake in millions while their employees get downsized" and "senators who voted for welfare and Medicaid cuts." This is a great idea, but booking guests would be quite a challenge since the ability to keep one's "private" affairs off-limits to public scrutiny is partly what constitutes the eliteness of elites to begin with.

12. Fiske (1989, 103–27) makes a similar observation about the highbrow criticism of supermarket tabloids.

Like distinctions between public and private space, class distinctions between culture and nature did not arise in a historical vacuum. Norms of emotional control and bodily discipline, so fundamental to bourgeois sensibility, emerged in the United States alongside larger social, economic, and cultural transformations during the latter half of the nineteenth century. During this period, massive immigration and a lack of established social traditions—in combination with the rise of a new monied class eager to distinguish itself from those below—made civility nothing less than a moral imperative (see Kasson 1990; Levine 1988). And, because industrialization and urbanization created sharp discontinuities between public and private life, drawing together in intimate proximity strangers of diverse backgrounds, one's personal conduct *in public* was of special concern. As etiquette manuals exhorted tact and respect for privacy, individuals attempted to be as inconspicuous and self-effacing in public as possible. This was especially true for upper-class white women, whose participation in public life was precarious, and for whom the stakes of transgression were high. According to Kasson (1990), laughing, loud or boisterous talk, demonstrations of affection, or expressions of anger were branded vulgar and indecent, considered proof of one's inferior breeding, as were staring, bodily contact, and other expressions of familiarity or overinvolvement in the affairs of others. Underlying these exhortations was an increasingly instrumental stance toward feeling, consistent with the greater demands for emotional control and the growing disgust for bodily functions evident in Western societies from the fifteenth century on (Elias 1994).

In the United States, the segmentation of the individual epitomized by rising standards of emotional control and the separation of private from public space paralleled the increasing segmentation of society, including a more rigid separation of elite from popular culture. In the antebellum period, the boundaries between different forms of art, entertainment, and performance were relatively fluid: minstrel shows shared the stage with Shakespearean drama, and mastodon bones were exhibited alongside paintings and sculpture (Levine 1988). But all this changed as culture underwent a process that Levine calls *sacrilization*, whereby certain forms of high art, music, and performance were removed from their popular origins (in effect, rescued from the marketplace) and enshrined in official institutions controlled by wealthy patrons (see also DiMaggio 1982a, 1982b). Sacrilization had profound implications not only for the content of cultural forms but also for venue, clientele, the reasons audiences attended, and the ways audiences were expected to behave: as people mounted the scale to high or refined art, they were expected to behave in a more refined (i.e., restrained) manner themselves. Sacrilization thus changed the norms of engagement between actor and spectator, increasing the distance and hierarchy between them, and eroding "a communal and amateur spirit of participation in which the lower classes played a vital role" (Kasson 1990, 255). Eventually, the rules of middle-class gentility became the norm of public conduct for everyone, and even the popular entertainments such as cabaret and vaudeville were similarly transformed. This was but one aspect of a more general process of professionalization in the late nineteenth century in which the systems of taste and canons of behavior embraced by elites— legal, political, economic, medical, and scientific as well as artistic and cultural—were increasingly separated from and elevated above the tastes and behaviors of the masses.[13]

Laura's Final Thought

Generally speaking, the commercialization of leisure that occurred at the turn of the twentieth century and the full-scale mass mediation of culture that followed had a leveling effect on distinctions between high and low culture (see Crane 1992). As a result, our notions of cultural hierarchy are more fluid today than they were in the past. Yet cultural hierarchy per se has not disappeared, and the struggle for distinction continues to be played out within the realm of mass culture itself in the ongoing debates between the serious and the tabloid media. Whereas the former have aligned themselves with the framework and trappings of science, the latter are excessive, sensational, and contradictory and draw heavily on the codes of melodrama. The tabloid media are focused on the personal and the proverbial, evoking a world in which notions of general morality are shared by all human beings regardless of social position and in which emotions play a deep and fundamental role (see Gripsrud 1992; Fiske 1992). This reflects in mediated form the character of working-class knowledge itself, which is said

---

13. Moreover, at a time when the ranks of the masses were more and more made up of recent immigrants and migrant blacks, the emerging ideology separating elite from popular culture began to assume ethnic and racial dimensions. Levine reminds us that the terms *highbrow* and *lowbrow* have their origins in the nineteenth-century practice of craniometry, a "science" that purported to distinguish intelligence levels on the basis of racial classifications: the closer to Western and Northern Europe a people's origins were, the higher their brows and thus the more intelligent they were said to be. Adjectives such as *high, low, legitimate,* and *vulgar* thus cluster around a set of values that not only define and distinguish culture vertically but also are inseparable from other social hierarchies.

to focus on the immediacies of home, family, and neighborhood and emphasize concreteness, subjectivity, and orality (see Hoggart 1957). By contrast, the serious media emphasize knowledge that is abstract, rational, and impersonal. They traffic in public, not private, affairs, focus mostly on the doings of officials and other elites, and speak in the language of "truth," "fact," and "objectivity" (see Schudson 1978; Campbell 1991). Within the terms of this discourse, the print media have generally had a superior claim to scientific adequacy and are associated with literacy, whereas the visual image has been generally characterized as "soft" and linked with femininity or with the illiteracy of marginalized classes (Campbell 1991).

Historically, daytime talk shows have existed somewhere between the two forms, both reinscribing and blurring the boundaries between expert and ordinary, reason and emotion, public and private, serious and tabloid. Over time, as talk shows as a whole grew more sensational, a trashy/classy distinction developed internal to the genre itself, one that reproduced on a smaller scale many of the same boundaries. This "tabloid turn" is part and parcel of a more general popularization of the media landscape, in which even the serious media are said increasingly to resemble a daytime talk show. Some scholars and critics see this as a threat to democracy and civilization, symptomatic of a deep and possibly irreparable cultural failing (see Postman 1985; Mitroff and Bennis 1989; Ewen 1989). Randy remarked to me that more Americans know the words to the *Brady Bunch* theme song than to the national anthem. Kipnis (1996) notes that more people watch daytime talk shows than vote. If these things are true, then perhaps we really are "amusing ourselves to death," as Postman (1985) laments.

But, if more people watch daytime talk shows than vote, presumably this also has something to with the meanings that the genre makes available and with the meanings attached to the act of watching itself. In the case of *Randy*, this may involve little more than the gawk factor said to characterize the nineteenth-century freak show, where witnessing the difference of others serves to reassure spectators of their own superiority. But, on other shows, as Kipnis (1996) points out, underneath the marital sniping and tales of injustice are some serious questions: How do you act ethically when your desires conflict with someone else's? What is the personal price of conformity versus the social violence exacted on nonconformity? Is human nature at bottom selfish or benevolent? Such questions have a general relevance to viewers' lives, even if the particular circumstances or experiences of guests do not. Producers at *Diana* had a mandate to provide information that viewers could relate to and use, and perhaps they did this. At the same time, like the tabloid media more generally, talk shows are less about dispensing information in the classic town-hall sense and more about drawing moral boundaries through stories of hardship, transgression, and conflict. Like ritual, the stories can be valued as much for the sameness of the responses that they elicit as for the quality or variety of information that they yield; the repetition allows audiences and guests alike to "enter into the game" using a familiar formula or code (Bourdieu 1984; Bird 1992). For this reason, the specific talk that occurs is subordinate to the larger performative context in which the talk is embedded, something that guests themselves, especially professional experts, do not always understand (not surprisingly since experts by definition have been trained to operate according to the logic of a different code). According to Meyrowitz (1985), the emphasis of television on expressive over informational content reflects the inherent bias of electronic versus print-based media, a bias that talk shows throw into high relief. In Meyrowitz's words, "Talk shows do not succeed because of talk . . . the 'learning' in these programs comes from the 'truth' and 'reality' inherent in human behavior and experience" (103).[14]

If more people watch talk shows than vote, I would also venture to guess that more people volunteer to be on talk shows—and other forms of television—than volunteer to get involved in their own communities or in official party politics. But to say that the mass media create apathy and lead people away from traditional forms of civic engagement is to miss an important point. People, especially the young and the poor, are not necessarily apathetic about politics because they watch too much television or because the "unreality" promoted by the media has become "our primary mode of reference" (Mitroff and Bennis 1989, 10). They are apathetic because they see official party politics as an insider game that has little direct relevance to their lives. Bourdieu and others have noted that one's investment in, and ability to influence the destiny of, an institution varies

14. This is exactly what Randy meant when he told me that his was not an informational show, "other than what you learn by seeing how people relate to one another." Indeed, for Meyrowitz, *all* television programs that depict the behavior of people are about the same thing: "human gesture, feeling, and emotion" (1985, 108). And, while the bias toward expressive content clearly renders television less effective than print-based media in conveying complex ideas and critical analysis (a core concern for critics), the bias has also democratized media consumption. Meyrowitz (1985, 107–8) observes that groups of people who are excluded from the public forum created by print (and now the Internet) because they lack the requisite entry skills can nevertheless participate in the public arena created by television. In contrast to reading and writing, television viewing involves an access code that is barely a code at all: the expressive quality of television makes almost any program accessible to the average viewer.

according to one's status within it. To explain the relation between status and political involvement, one must consider more than the objective capacity to understand or produce political discourse. One must also consider the subjective (and socially encouraged) sense of being entitled to be concerned with politics in the first place, of being authorized to talk politics, and of feeling at home with, *even caring to have*, this authorization. Not surprisingly, political participation in the United States is higher among men than among women, among older people than among younger, and among the upper classes than among the lower.

What is interesting about daytime talk shows is that they *do* afford a certain kind of political engagement with the world, but on popular rather than elite terms. The discourse of talk shows is not the discourse of the *New York Times*, for the popular aesthetic demands that its cultural forms have a local relevance and use, a certain perceived continuity with everyday life. I was reminded of this recently when I attended a rally protesting sexual violence against women. During the open-mike portion of the program in which survivors of sexual assault share their experiences of victimization with the audience, a woman in her mid-fifties revealed that she had been molested by her father as a child. Back then, she told the crowd, no one ever spoke of matters like incest; it was as if they did not exist. She first learned about incest from watching daytime talk shows. As she put it, "It was not until I heard those women talking on television did I understand that I was not alone or that there was a name for what had happened to me." To be sure, the emphasis of the media here on the private and the personal can be read as tabloidization, but it can also be read as bringing issues of import into the life worlds of ordinary people.[15] Of course, the meanings and messages of popular culture are not always or only progressive, and they may just as easily perpetuate as challenge oppressive social arrangements. Popular culture is not simply a space outside elite discourse for celebrating the culture of the masses or paying homage to a romanticized notion of class resistance. Rather, to paraphrase Bird (1992), popular culture is the symbolic order within which subordinate classes live their subordination.

There are serious problems with talk shows, as I have tried to docu-

---

15. The same point is made by Bird (2000) in discussing the trend toward "personalization" in the tabloid media. At the same time, she warns against personalization as the only way to engage audiences, especially if the personal is disconnected from a larger social or political context. For a discussion of the role of the personal story in informing audiences about global issues, see Tomlinson (1997). For a discussion of tabloid media more generally, see Sparks and Tulloch (2000).

ment in this book. They give ordinary people a voice, but only a certain kind of voice, only under certain conditions, and only according to certain rules. In Foucauldian terms, they extend the visibility of marginalized groups, but the nature of this visibility simultaneously creates fresh opportunities for marginalization. At the same time, the critical condemnation of the genre as trashy and debased is not any less classifying than the genre's initial stereotypical association of emotional and physical expressiveness with ordinary people. However much a matter of consensus, this condemnation further contributes to the marginalization of guests when it confuses middle-class notions of civility with morality and when it takes for granted a set of cultural codes in which divisions of taste mask and reinforce divisions of class. There are serious problems with talk shows, but there are serious problems with the "respectable" media, too, and even more serious problems with society at large. It is therefore important not to scapegoat talk shows for the activities and practices common to the media more generally or to use talk shows (or the media more generally) as a way of *not* talking about society's most pressing social problems. Certain talk shows might take advantage of people in poverty or distress, but they do not create out of whole cloth the conditions of hardship under which many guests live. Indeed, it is telling that those who *do* bear some responsibility for these conditions—politicians who oppose increased spending for welfare and public education, for instance—are among the genre's most ardent critics, as if to suggest that the real problem is the cartoonish display of poverty on television rather than the actual fact of poverty itself. There is no one factor responsible for the perceived decline of American culture, but, if I believed in such a decline and wanted someone or something to blame, talk shows are not the first place I would look.

EPILOGUE

Airing Another Kind of Dirty Laundry:
Confessions of a Feminist Fieldworker

Above all else, this has been a book about production, the production of a particular cultural form. I have detailed how talk-show producers go about their work and how they transform the personal experiences of ordinary people (and the expertise of experts) into mass entertainment. But there is another kind of production at stake here, one that closely parallels the first. I speak, of course, of the production of this book. Historically, it has not been common practice among ethnographers to discuss the exact nature of the fieldwork process, especially its personal and emotional dimensions. While this has changed somewhat in recent years and "confessional tales" are now standard reading in many fieldwork courses at the graduate level,[1] such tales are still typically segregated in appendices or turned into separate works altogether. In part, this reflects the marginal position of fieldwork itself within the social sciences; exposing the seams of the production process, including one's failures as well as one's successes, is to render an already soft form of knowledge even more vulnerable

1. See Van Maanen (1988); Lareau (1989); Shaffir and Stebbins (1991); Brettell (1993); Ellis (1995); Jackson and Ives (1996); and Duneier (1999).

to criticism. It is, in effect, to air the dirty laundry of the ethnographic enterprise.

Yet ethnography has never been a pure or purely scientific discourse. Like daytime talk, it is the offspring of mixed parentage. It is both art and science, both a matter of collecting data and a matter of telling stories about the world in which we live. The entry of confessional tales into the fieldwork canon is part of a larger cultural moment in which disciplinary canons of all sorts are being challenged and in which truth and knowledge are taken as historically situated, partial, and incomplete. As Clifford (1988, 2) has noted, the "historical predicament" of ethnography is that it is always caught up in the invention, not just the representation, of cultures.

This epilogue, then, is my confessional tale, and I write it not only because I wish to share with others my insights about the limits of my work but also because, in my case, the *how* of my observing cannot be disentangled from what I came to see: that daytime talk as a genre shares common ground with sociology as a discipline (distasteful as that might seem to sociologists) and that, more important, the methods and practices of talk-show production in many ways mirror the methods and practices of fieldwork (distasteful as that might seem to ethnographers). Despite the many differences—not the least of which is the fact that talk shows are trashy texts that critics despise while ethnographies are classy texts with more limited but positive reception—I understood the work of producers and guests, the relations between them, the choices that they faced, and the decisions that they made all the better because I encountered similar relations, dilemmas, and choices of my own.

Field Relations: Self and Other

Participant observation has a long tradition in the social sciences (see Wax 1971; Lofland and Lofland 1984) even if confessional tales have not. Through their engagement with others, ethnographers strive to understand a universe of meanings given through language, culture, and forms of social organization. Because it is typically exploratory or investigative in nature, fieldwork often results in an overwhelming amount and variety of material, with no definitive rules or guidelines about what to include, how best to frame what is in fact included, or even when to stop collecting data. Recall Rachel's comparison between producing a talk show and working a giant siphon or funnel: you start off with an enormous amount of material and then sift, refine, and distill until you extract the basic elements that will make for a compelling show. You end up with a lot of waste, she acknowledged, because only a tiny portion of what you start with actually gets used—"but you have to have that huge pool of resources to get those nuggets." The funnel metaphor has been used widely within ethnography as well (Agar 1996).

In my case, I collected more than a year's worth of fieldnotes, roughly eighty in-depth interviews with producers and guests, a dozen large binders full of paperwork related to the production process—booking sheets, memos, scripts, air-date schedules, fan mail, and production notes—and a small library of press clippings about daytime talk shows published over the five-year period between 1995 and 2000. Despite having "foreshadowed problems" (Malinowski 1922) in mind when entering the field, it was a constant struggle to clarify my intellectual goals and agenda. As Lareau (1989, 189) observes, "Using qualitative methods means learning to live with uncertainty, ambiguity, and confusion, sometimes for weeks at a time. It also means carving a path by making many decisions, with only the vaguest guide posts." As did Lareau, I sometimes wished for a rigid template to impose, a singular path to follow, a specific formula to apply (such as the one used by producers: preexisting conflict equals intense emotions on-stage equals the money shot). I would have welcomed the very constraints and generic conventions about which producers complained. This is not to suggest that I was free from conventions or constraints, only that they were disciplinary rather than generic, less routinized, and a good deal less formulaic.

Differing degrees of routinization aside, "working the funnel" involves a certain amount of emotional labor, and herein lies another important similarity between talk-show production and fieldwork. Indeed, at the same time I was learning how to do emotional labor vis-à-vis guests, I was engaged in emotion work of a different sort vis-à-vis producers and other staff members. Fieldwork depends, in a deep and fundamental way, on establishing a rapport with and forming personal attachments to one's research subjects, just as producing a talk show depends fundamentally on the formation of emotional bonds between producers and guests. The chief difference here is that, with fieldwork, one's emotional investment is on-going and long-standing, entails greater levels of reciprocity, and cannot easily be sustained with surface levels of acting. Many ethnographers live and work among those they study for months and years at a time; they share meals, moments of relaxation and play, the subtle textures and nuances of everyday life. Fieldwork experiences can form the basis of friendships that last well beyond the period of fieldwork itself, in some cases for life. Nevertheless, as with the production of a talk show, at some point the research is over, and the fieldworker packs up and goes home. "They share so much of themselves with you," a *Diana* producer said of her guests, "it's weird how you develop a personal relationship so close to somebody and then it's just gone." Ending relations in the field can be similarly disconcerting, for both researcher and researched alike.

But leave fieldworkers do, for at bottom their relations with subjects, like producers' relations with guests, are instrumental as well as personal. Their emotional labor, whatever its meaning for the fieldworker personally, is always also in the service of something else. Like producers, who must simultaneously empathize with and yet distance themselves from guests in order to elicit the right sort of performance and survive the emotional exigencies of their work, ethnographers, too, walk a fine line between intimacy and detachment in their efforts to learn "the native" point of view. Fieldworkers who immerse themselves in a community for extended periods of time are both stranger and friend, part of, and separate from, the people among whom they live. There is a hyphenated quality to their vision since they experience things from within while simultaneously maintaining an outside perspective as a scholar. This duality is indicated in the very term *participant observer.* Thus, even while striving to assume a native perspective, the ethnographer will not see exactly the same world that insiders see and will not write an account that says exactly what an insider would say. The difference can then lead research subjects to feel deceived or betrayed, just as talk-show guests sometimes feel deceived or betrayed by what transpires onstage. This, in turn, can prompt additional, less pleasant forms of emotional labor on the part of fieldworkers (see Brettell 1993; Ellis 1995), just as it does for producers.

Another important link between fieldwork and talk shows has to do with the direction of study—the people and issues targeted as data. Any history of fieldwork will reveal that sociologists have often studied "down," meaning that they focus on people or groups with less status, power, and privilege than they themselves have.[2] According to Shils (1980), the first large-scale inquiries based on interview data in the United States focused

2. I am aware that to use terms like *up, down,* and *sideways* (or *across*) is to reproduce and artificially reify problematic assumptions about the relative status (and perhaps, by implication, worth) of dominant and marginalized groups and their unique cultures. For example, one might very well believe that Native American perspectives on land use and environmental protection are superior to those of European Americans and, therefore, that to study

on immigrants, the urban poor, African Americans, and persons with dubious moral standards such as "fallen women" and "unadjusted girls." Likewise, during the 1920s and 1930s, the first generation of sociologists conducting fieldwork in the United States focused on, among other things, the hobo, the ghetto, and the gang (see Wax 1971; Van Maanen 1988)—topics that continue to garner considerable attention today. And, while the motivations of sociologists might differ from those of producers—sociologists typically want social justice and a better understanding of society, while producers just want to make money—the penchant for marginal or deviant subject matter in both cases is partly structural. The rich and powerful do not often go on daytime talk shows or let themselves be studied; conversely, marginalized groups may have few other options for public representation.[3]

Personally, I wrestled with these questions of power and struggled to pin down my own social location in the field. In focusing on daytime television talk shows, I was studying an aspect of my own culture, not a foreign one. Moreover, it was an aspect to which I had had some prior exposure since I have an advanced degree in broadcast journalism and have worked on various film and video projects. Thus, I was not the privileged Western

---

tribal land use is to study "up." It is important to recognize, however, that terms like *up* and *down* as used in critiques of fieldwork and ethnography typically refer to a group's *structural* position within a culture, society, or global system characterized by systemic inequality, not to the way the researcher personally regards the group or its beliefs.

3. Anthropologists engage in their own form of studying down when they focus on exotic, remote, preliterate cultures, bracketing the relations of domination that make such fieldwork possible. Even as they attempted to apprehend other cultural practices and moralities from the inside so that they might appear intelligible and rational from the outside, ethnographers assumed the power to define and represent other cultural groups without challenge from those groups, their own position as researchers largely taken for granted and invisible. It was not until much later that the "respectable" classes came under the scrutiny of sociologists or that anthropologists began to study closer to home, in terms of both geography and social distance.

The direction of study (up, down, across) has implications for policy as well as epistemology. Using crime as an example, Nader (1972) points out that, by virtue of our concentration on some crimes over others, we have aided in the public definition of the "law-and-order problem" in terms of working-class or street crimes so that this type of crime has become practically synonymous with *crime* itself (and, as a result, taxpayers are more aware of, and more likely to support policies that target, street crime rather than corporate or white-collar crime). In a more general sense, focusing on racial and sexual minorities, women, or the poor rather than whites, heterosexuals, or the affluent in the context of studying *social problems* helps render the latter unmarked and invisible—and therefore helps perpetuate their privileged status. Of course, if ethnography were built on studying up, then, as Nader points out, ethnographers would sooner or later need to study down as well, for it is not an either/or proposition but a matter of widening perspectives.

subject taking as my object the quaint rituals and practices of an exotic other, although I may have been privileged and my methods objectifying in other ways. At the same time, because talk shows have been criticized for othering or pathologizing the so-called ordinary people who participate as guests, as a part of the production apparatus (and as someone who was closer in social status to producers than to guests), I was inevitably implicated in this othering. The direction of study posed similar contradictions. Initially, I felt that, by immersing myself in the American television industry—one of the most powerful institutions in the world—I was studying up, but, if one accepts popular opinion about talk shows, I was also studying down.

Of course, *up, down, high,* and *low* are relative, not absolute, terms. I came to realize that my status as researcher was unstable because the field site gave me access to very different categories of people and placed me at the crossroads of multiple hierarchies. As a member of an academic community that typically dismisses mass culture as trivial and debased, I was above talk-show producers, but, as one who studies mass culture and does not consider it trivial and debased, I was often at odds with other intellectuals. As a participant in the world of daytime talk shows, I was below those who worked in primetime television and even other forms of daytime programming but above academics, considered by media professionals to be out of touch with reality and inconsequential to the workings of society. As a production assistant and intern, my status was so low that I was practically invisible. Yet even interns were in some ways above the ordinary guests because we were inside the entertainment industry and they were not—with the exception of their fleeting appearance on the show. Thus, the nature and the degree of my relative privilege (or subordination) were constantly in flux, contingent on location and circumstance as well as the prevailing attitude toward talk shows circulating in society at large.

Disclosure and Deception

I struggled with questions of power not only in terms of my positioning above or below producers and guests but also in terms of my decision to enter the field somewhat covertly, without fully disclosing my true identity or purpose until I had established a position there. Without doubt, this was the most emotionally difficult aspect of the fieldwork for me, one that required considerable emotional labor to negotiate. If one is going to study some group or phenomenon firsthand, one must gain access to a research site. Even under the best of circumstances, however, access can be a delicate negotiation. In my case, the problem of access was compounded by the fact that an industry devoted to revealing the intimate details of people's private lives on national television proved to be very tightlipped about its own activities and practices. More than anything I wanted total honesty in my field relations, not just for ethical reasons, or because the majority of writers on the topic of covert research oppose the practice, but because deception seriously compromises the type and quality of data collected. If participant observation is a means of knowing others through oneself (and vice versa), the research can be only as good as one's relations with informants.[4] The same is true for producers and their relations with guests. Like fieldworkers who insist that honesty ensures continued access to the site, greater cooperation from informants, and more reliable data, many producers say that being forthright with guests is not only good ethics but also good producing for exactly the same reasons. More than anything, then, I wanted to be like Todd Gitlin (1983), who, having decided to study

4. Shils (1980, 436), e.g., insists that any observation of private behavior without the explicit and fully informed permission of the persons observed must be regarded as utterly reprehensible, justifiable only as an emergency measure necessary for the maintenance of public order or the protection of the society as a whole. The growth of sociological, anthropological, and psychological knowledge, he says, scarcely falls into this class of emergencies. Both Wax (1971) and Jackson (1987) suggest not only that lying about what you are doing is bad ethics but that it might also be bad fieldwork because, if people suspect the truth, they may find subtle ways to take revenge. Similarly, Richardson (1991) reminds readers that gaining initial permission and approval from leaders or authority figures will likely lead to greater cooperation from other group members and that covert research severely limits access to information and interactions with informants, including the types of questions that can be asked, the range of people that can be addressed, and the kinds of attachments that can be formed. Richardson also suggests that deceit on the part of one fieldworker will likely ruin the site for future fieldworkers.

Of course, sociologists sometimes deceive the people they observe anyway and claim that the knowledge gained is worth the deception. Indeed, it seems that abstract discussions of research ethics mandate rigid standards of honesty, but firsthand accounts from the field often suggest otherwise. For example, Dan Rose conducted covert research in order to write his *Black American Street Life* (1987). He lived and worked with welfare and working-class African Americans without disclosing his identity as an ethnographer who was documenting their lives, believing that this approach would reveal far more than could be discovered simply by hanging out or using questionnaires. In her field study of black domestic workers and their employers, Rollins (1985) fabricated reference letters and posed as a domestic, never revealing to her informants her true identity or purpose. While Rollins acknowledges that deception is an ethical issue that exacts a personal and social price each time it is used, she decided that the ends justified the means because her project allowed her to explore the intersection of race, class, and gender oppression in a manner that would have been unavailable to her had she used alternative methods.

primetime television and armed only with Berkeley letterhead and the
names of a few friends, simply showed up at the offices of network executives and was granted nearly unlimited time and access to key players in the
industry: vice presidents gave five-hour interviews, and producers let him
hang around the set for weeks.

But I was not so lucky or well connected, nor was I a professor at
Berkeley. Because my research agenda was relatively unformulated and I
considered the fieldwork exploratory, because I had never done fieldwork
before and did not think of myself as an ethnographer, and because a formal internship program between the television industry and the academy
was already in place at both *Diana* and *Randy*, I downplayed my role as a
scholar and entered the field as an intern "interested in learning and writing about talk shows." My coworkers knew that I was a doctoral candidate
writing about my experiences on the show—and other interns were doing
the same thing at the undergraduate level—but I did not request formal
permission from a gatekeeper to be there outside the bounds of the internship program. I felt that I had to get in and establish myself before such
a request could be heard and taken seriously. Consequently, in the early
stages of the work, uncertainty coupled with fear of rejection led to a certain amount of deception (and subsequent feelings of guilt) on my part. I
also recognized the irony of the situation in that my own actions paralleled
those of the producers I observed: we were both using the real-life experiences of other people as the basis for a story and employing varying degrees
of deception to ensure that the story was a good one.

Eventually, of course, I did come to emphasize my academic role, and,
at both shows, the longer I was there, the more I revealed, depending on
the level of others' interest in me and in conjunction with my own emerging identity as an ethnographer. My "coming out" was thus not a single,
discrete event but a gradual process cushioned by the formal and informal
relations that I had established with producers and executives. Like the actual process of coming out for many gay men and lesbians, my initial disclosures were selective, limited to those I trusted most and had the most
contact with, but included everyone I interviewed. In general, the closer I
worked with people, the more they knew about me, and vice versa. To my
surprise, the disclosure that caused me so much emotional anguish caused
barely a ripple in my working relations; staffers were singularly uncon-
cerned about my researcher status. Ironically, then, the person most affected by my identity shift was me.

I will never know whether a more forthright approach would have
yielded better results, although an experience that I had at a *Sally Jessy*

taping—in which I was accused of being a spy—makes me doubt it.[5] In hindsight, I believe that my method of entry was the right one, and it worked not just because of the reasons listed above but because it allowed me to continue being "just an intern" in the eyes of my coworkers even while I was also clearly something more. Of course, being just an intern was trying at times. It meant always having to defer to others, accept unquestioningly any task no matter how small or menial, tolerate assumptions about one's worth, intellect, or capability, and never show anger when people canceled or refused meetings or interviews. The very lack of status that advantaged me in certain ways also meant sacrificing whatever opportunities might have come my way had I emphasized the more prestigious, official role of researcher. As it was, at *Diana*, it took me six months to get an interview with the supervising producer of the show, another six months to secure a ten-minute phone conversation with the head of daytime programming for the licensing network, and more than a year of persistent inquiry to speak off the record with the host herself. On the other hand, as just an intern, I became integrated into the production sphere in a way that someone identified as an official researcher from the outset likely never would. Since interns are available to virtually everyone else on staff, I per-

---

5. I was sitting in the audience of *Sally Jessy Raphael* and, having grown complacent being out as a researcher, was taking notes during the warm-up routine before the show. Suddenly, the warm-up lady was beside me, demanding in front of two hundred people to know what I was doing. She shoved the microphone in my face. Too surprised and flustered to invent an excuse, I told the truth: I was conducting fieldwork for a research project on talk shows. Apparently, that was not the answer she wanted. "Who gave you permission to be here?" she snapped. Irritated, I told her I did not need permission, that this taping was in the public domain (all of this said into the microphone with the entire audience listening). Wrong answer again. She insisted that I follow her backstage to speak with the executive producer. After handing me over to him like a criminal to the police, she returned to the stage. Through the thin walls of the set, I heard her joke to the audience, "Don't worry, everything's under control—she's just a spy for *Ricki Lake*." I told the executive producer who I was and what I was doing. I said that I knew better than to take notes while the cameras were rolling. I told him that I had attended three other talk shows in the last four days without this kind of harassment and that I was not a spy for Ricki Lake or anyone else. Eventually, he allowed me to slink back to my seat. I swore that I would never take notes in public again. Once the humiliation wore off, however, I began to appreciate what I had unwittingly learned by being out as a researcher: for whatever reasons, employees of this show were not at all comfortable being observed. This discomfort was not shared by those at other shows necessarily. For example, when the staff at *Donahue* saw me taking notes and photographs as well), they actually offered me a seat with a better view. This experience reinforced for me the fact that, regardless of your intentions, when you are an outsider to an organization of dubious reputation, you may have little choice but to get in and establish trust first before you can study that organization. It also taught me that how people respond to the presence of a researcher is as informative as any other kind of behavior.

formed an astonishingly wide range of duties and tasks. (I suspect that, after interning for more than a year on two different shows, I had a broader-
based knowledge of the production process than many producers.) As a result, by the end of my stint at *Diana*, I was invited to help produce several
shows and thus gained entry to the inner sanctum of the production
process. This unique opportunity reinforced for me the insight that research access is not merely granted or withheld at one particular point in
time but an ongoing issue, for people at different levels and in different positions within an organization can provide very different kinds of information (see Shaffir and Stebbins 1991).

On a more general level, I came to realize that deception and disclosure are more complicated matters than I had at first assumed, matters not
resolved simply by stating up front who you are and what you intend to do.
As my experience of gaining access attests, fieldwork is not a discrete, static
event but an ongoing process, typically accomplished over long periods
of time. The same holds true for the process by which a researcher comes
to understand her project and reveal that understanding to others, for,
while ethnographers often enter a situation with a problem or question
in mind, the specific details of an inquiry are almost always worked out in
the field. As with producers and their shows, ethnographers can rarely say
with certainty at the outset, "This is where my project is going to go," because changes are inevitable in fieldwork—indeed, the fieldwork process
actively *encourages* growth and change. Even if the aims and scope of a project *are* certain, questions of deception may arise if the scholar discusses
some aspects of the work more thoroughly than others or gives some informants more information than others. Deception is an issue even for the
scholar who has a clear agenda, sticks closely to that agenda, and discusses
every detail of the research with each and every member of the culture or
community in question—if only because she will write an account from
a scholarly perspective that may be foreign to, and therefore at odds with,
informants' understanding of themselves (Daniels 1983, 196; see also Borland 1991; Brettell 1993). As we have seen, producers face comparable
dilemmas, for the reality that they depict on television is not always something that guests can anticipate, no matter how much or how little they
are told.

Secrecy is not an all-or-nothing matter clearly distinct from honest
behavior, and fieldwork typically involves a wide range of behaviors involving elements and moments of deception, however small, unwitting, or pro-
visional. This recognition does not justify lying or elide the ethical considerations associated with field research. But it does situate deception and

disclosure on a continuum and contribute to our understanding of the is-sues involved when we make decisions about our work. It also reminds us that traditional formulations of informed consent—originally designed to protect patients from medical abuses in clinical contexts—are inappropri-ate to the ethnographic context because they fail to account for either the dynamic or the personal nature of field relations (see Thorne 1980; Galli-her 1980; Wax 1980). Informed consent is a complicated matter that varies over time and from setting to setting. At early stages of research, getting the written consent of subjects may be enough. But, as relationships deepen and intensify over time, and as fieldworkers learn more about their own re-search goals, this legalistic notion of consent may prove inadequate. In-deed, for talk-show producers, legal consent actually enabled deception be-cause, whatever happened during the taping of a show, good or bad, they could always claim that guests had consented to it. More developmental than contractual, the understandings between observer and observed are better conceptualized as an ongoing series of *research bargains* (Hughes 1974) that have to be negotiated on a continual basis rather than decided once and for all in advance. The question then is at what point the field-worker stops being accountable to subjects since the reception of the final text (and not just its production) can significantly influence, *after the fact*, a participant's sense of having been adequately informed.[6]

Feminism and Fieldwork

None of the concerns that I have outlined here became real for me until I dealt with them for myself. How-to accounts of ethnography are helpful and necessary but not sufficient because so much depends on context. This

---

6. Craig Gilbert's experience filming *An American Family* with the Louds of Santa Barbara provides a dramatic illustration of this point. As noted in the previous chapter, Gil-bert wanted to document the typical American family in their natural setting. Not only did the family agree to participate, but they also approved a rough cut of each episode. After the negative press following the broadcast, however, the Louds blamed Gilbert for deliberately portraying them in a negative light. In his own defense, Gilbert (1988b, 292) writes: "Unless you are doing an investigative report, it is hard to explain, with absolute truth, what your documentary is about. If what you are doing is concerned with an 'issue,' it is easy and accu-rate to say, 'I am making a film about the dangers of nuclear energy,' or 'I am making a film about how nursing homes mistreat old people.' . . . But if what you are doing is concerned with more general questions of human behavior, it is a good deal more difficult to give a specific and satisfactory answer without either misleading or antagonizing the subjects of your film and in the process endangering the life of the project."

is why discussions of research ethics invariably mandate very specific codes of conduct but firsthand accounts from the field often suggest a more nuanced understanding of these codes. The difference between me and producers here is not so much that I was willing to admit to deception and they were not, or that I was personally troubled by its use and they were not, or even that academic institutions frown on deception and the television industry does not. The difference was that my backdoor method of entry and the gradual nature of my coming out deeply upset my feminist sensibilities and that, at some point, I began to connect my anxiety over these issues specifically with my identity as a feminist.

Sensitive to abuses of interpretive authority, feminist scholars have been particularly mindful of the moral and ethical dimensions of fieldwork.[7] This is true despite—or perhaps because of—the common ground between feminist research practices and ethnographic inquiry.[8] Knowing the feminist critiques of fieldwork and identifying as a feminist myself put me in an awkward position when I first started working at *Diana* and *Randy*. Feminists and other intellectuals outside the mainstream tend to be well aware of the relations of domination that have characterized much traditional ethnography and want to avoid replicating power inequalities between researchers and informants. Many feminists want the research process to be more egalitarian and collaborative. Stacey (1988), for example, turned to ethnography from more positivist methods precisely out of a desire for this kind of power sharing and collaboration. But now she wonders whether the intense engagement between ethnographer and informant masks a deeper, more troublesome form of exploitation in that it transforms personal relationships into *use value* (as research) and leaves subjects at greater risk of manipulation and betrayal. This is, of course, what talk-show producers are accused of doing to guests.

Other feminists, however, worry that such discussions can construct an unattainable moral standard that works to undermine feminist

7. See Stacey (1988); Gordon (1988); Abu-Lughod (1990); Clough (1992); Behar and Gordon (1995); and Wolf (1996).

8. Ethnographers strive to view the world from the perspective of others (particularly the socially marginal or the oppressed), which aligns fieldwork with feminist-standpoint theory (see Hartsock 1987; Smith 1987). Like feminist research, ethnography emphasizes interaction with, and empathy for, the subjects of analysis, and it takes experience as an important source of knowledge about the world. Feminism and fieldwork both emphasize the dialectic between experience and interpretation, local events and global structures, so that the personal is understood within a larger social and political context ("the personal is political"). Finally, because of all these qualities, both ethnography and feminist studies have been dismissed as biased and subjective, inappropriate to real social science.

authority and obviate feminist claims (see DeVault 1996; Wheatley 1994). Indeed, some of the informal mandates of feminist scholarship seem to replicate the very gender-based stereotypes that feminists have been at pains to challenge: the notion that women are especially ethical and caring, that women should place the thoughts and feelings of others first, or that women are uncomfortable exercising interpretive power on their own and others' behalf. As Behar (1995, 6) notes, "It is tiring to have to be so responsive; that is so often the role that women play in our society." In the abstract, I supported power sharing between researchers and informants. At the same time, I did not feel particularly powerful, nor was I so sure that I wanted to cede interpretive authority to television executives and producers in order to collaborate on the meaning of what I observed. Wanting to make the research process more egalitarian and collaborative is an admirable goal, but that goal is often difficult to achieve in actual practice, and it is one that works better for feminists who study people they like or want to help rather than people they want to challenge or expose.

These issues are additionally complicated by the fact that concern about potential harm to informants can border on paternalism and reinforce stereotypes about some subjects as childlike and naive. As Wolf (1992, 134) observes, "In our concern over our colonial luggage, we tend to forget the complex power negotiations that also go on among individuals. Even the most arrogant neocolonialist soon discovers that one cannot order rural people to reveal important thoughts about their culture." To be sure, scholars affiliated with formal institutions have a certain kind of authority and privilege regardless of research topic or setting. Preexisting social inequalities of race, class, gender, and so forth may very well translate into unequal relations in the field. But, just as talk-show guests are rarely powerless in their interactions with producers, informants are rarely powerless in their interactions with researchers. In fact, as Van Maanen (1991, 31) points out, while the ethnographer observes other people and their activities, often *they* simultaneously observe the ethnographer and *her* activities; thus, the success of any fieldwork endeavor can depend on the results of both kinds of study. Successful fieldwork is always and inevitably collaborative in this sense.

Ultimately, the moral quandaries engaging feminist ethnographers are better framed as questions of epistemology and representation that *any* writer confronts in her work, not just the ethnographer, questions that undoubtedly have moral dimensions but that cannot be solved by ceding interpretive authority. When Stacey (1988) insists that elements of inequality, exploitation, and even betrayal are endemic to ethnography, it is important to remember that inequality, exploitation, and even betrayal are endemic to *any* discourse or method of inquiry in which the researcher has more power than respondents to frame the issues, gather data, interpret the results, and then author an account. It is also important to remember that the very closeness between researcher and subject that foregrounds these issues in the case of ethnography and potentially exposes informants to greater harm simultaneously has the capacity to challenge and undermine conventional research hierarchies and to include informants in the research process in ways that they might actually enjoy and find meaningful. When it comes to exploitation, then, ethnography has the double-edged potential to be both better and worse than more distanced or objective methods. This is exactly the relation of daytime talk shows to other forms of more respectable media, where the more extended and intimate interaction between producers and guests on talk shows can either minimize or exacerbate the manipulative practices endemic to all mass-media discourse. Neither ethnographers nor producers have a monopoly on using personal relationships for professional purposes. One might argue, in fact, that all relationships have use value. The larger issue at stake in all this is not *whether* power is operating but *what kind* of power is operating, how it is wielded, and to what use it is put.

In the end, I directed my feminist sensibilities not toward sharing authorial control of the ethnographic text but toward recognizing the similarities between myself and the others of my analysis. Consequently, I came to see sameness where it is perhaps more natural for a scholar to see difference. I came to see that the production of daytime talk shows is like the methods and practices of fieldwork in interesting, if limited, ways. Perhaps most important is the fact that both ethnography and daytime talk shows are means of representation and that representation is always enmeshed in questions of power and responsibility. The nature and gravity of these questions will vary across contexts, of course, but they will never disappear, regardless of whether one studies up or down, or at home or abroad, and regardless of whether one's findings are published in books or broadcast on television. Power and privilege, honesty and deceit, trust and consent— these are matters for all individuals who take as the object of their research or the aim of their production efforts other human beings.

REFERENCES

Abt, Vicki, and Leonard Mustazza. 1997. *Coming after Oprah: Cultural Fallout in the Age of the TV Talk Show.* Bowling Green, Ohio: Bowling Green State University Press.

Abt, Vicki, and Mel Seesholtz. 1994. "The Shameless World of Phil, Sally, and Oprah: Television Talk Shows and the Deconstruction of Society." *Journal of Popular Culture* 28, no. 1 (summer): 171–91.

Abu-Lughod, Lila. 1990. "Can There Be a Feminist Ethnography?" *Women and Performance: A Journal of Feminist Theory* 5, no. 1:7–27.

Acland, Charles. 1995. "Crisis and Display: The Nature of Evidence on the Daytime Television Talk Show." In *Youth, Murder, Spectacle: The Cultural Politics of "Youth in Crisis,"* 97–114. Boulder, Colo.: Westview.

Agar, Michael. 1996. *The Professional Stranger: An Informal Introduction to Ethnography.* 2d ed. New York: Academic.

Andersen, Kurt. 1993. "Oprah and JoJo the Dog-Faced Boy." *Time,* 11 October, 94.

Bacon-Smith, Camille. 1992. *Enterprising Women: Television Fandom and the Creation of Popular Myth.* Philadelphia: University of Pennsylvania Press.

Bandura, A. 1973. *Aggression: A Social Learning Analysis.* Englewood Cliffs, N.J.: Prentice-Hall.

Becker, Howard. 1982. *Art Worlds.* Berkeley and Los Angeles: University of California Press.

Behar, Ruth. 1995. "Introduction: Out of Exile." In *Women Writing Culture,* ed. Ruth Behar and

Deborah Gordon, 1–29. Berkeley and Los Angeles: University of California Press.

Behar, Ruth, and Deborah Gordon, eds. 1995. *Women Writing Culture*. Berkeley and Los Angeles: University of California Press.

Belcher, Walt. 1995. "Group Springs Worthy Dupe on Host." *Tampa Tribune*, 11 February, A6.

Bennett, William. 1996. "In Civilized Society, Shame Has Its Place." *Los Angeles Times*, 26 January, B9.

Berkman, Meredith. 1995. "Daytime Talk Shows Are Fraud-Casters." *New York Post*, 4 December, E1.

Bernstein, Basil. 1974. *Class, Codes, and Control*. London: Routledge & Kegan Paul.

Bettie, Julie. 1995. "Class Dismissed? Roseanne and the Changing Face of Working-Class Iconography." *Social Text* 45 (winter): 125–49.

———. 2000. "Women without Class: Chicas, Cholas, Trash, and the Presence/Absence of Class Identity." *Signs: Journal of Women in Culture and Society* 26, no. 1 (autumn): 1–35.

Bird, Elizabeth. 1992. *For Enquiring Minds: A Cultural Study of Supermarket Tabloids*. Knoxville: University of Tennessee Press.

———. 2000. "Audience Demands in a Murderous Market: Tabloidization in US Television News." In *Tabloid Tales: Global Debates over Media Standards*, ed. Colin Sparks and John Tulloch, 213–28. New York: Rowman & Littlefield.

Bogdan, Robert. 1988. *Freak Show: Presenting Human Oddities for Amusement and Profit*. Chicago: University of Chicago Press.

———. 1996. "The Social Construction of Freaks." In *Freakery: Cultural Spectacles of the Extraordinary Body*, ed. Rosemarie Garland Thomson, 23–37. New York: New York University Press.

Boorstin, Daniel J. 1961. *The Image: A Guide to Pseudo-Events in America*. New York: Harper & Row.

Borland, Katherine. 1991. "'That's Not What I Said': Interpretive Conflict in Oral Narrative Research." In *Women's Words: The Feminist Practice of Oral History*, ed. Sherna Berger Gluck and Daphne Patai, 63–75. New York: Routledge.

Bourdieu, Pierre. 1984. *Distinction: A Social Critique of the Judgment of Taste*. Cambridge: Harvard University Press.

Brettell, Caroline, ed. 1993. *When They Read What We Write: The Politics of Ethnography*. Westport, Conn.: Bergin & Garvey.

Butsch, Richard. 1992. "Class and Gender in Four Decades of Television Situation Comedy: Plus ca Change. . . ." *Critical Studies in Mass Communication* 9 (December): 387–99.

Campbell, Richard. 1991. "Word vs. Image: Elitism, Popularity, and TV News." *Television Quarterly* 25, no. 2:73–81.

Carbaugh, Donal. 1988. *Talking American: Cultural Discourses on "Donahue."* Norwood, N.J.: Ablex.

Carey, James. 1989. *Communication as Culture*. New York: Unwin Hyman.

Carpignano, Paolo, Robin Anderson, Stanley Aronowitz, and William Difazio. 1990. "Chatter in the Age of Electronic Reproduction: Talk Television and the 'Public Mind.'" *Social Text* 25/26:33–55.

Clifford, James. 1988. *The Predicament of Culture: Twentieth-Century Ethnography, Literature, and Art.* Cambridge: Harvard University Press.

Clough, Patricia. 1992. *The End(s) of Ethnography: From Realism to Social Criticism.* Newbury Park, Calif.: Sage.

Cohen, Stanley, and Jock Young. 1973. *The Manufacture of News.* Beverly Hills, Calif.: Sage.

Crane, Diana. 1992. "High Culture versus Popular Culture Revisited: A Reconceptualization of Recorded Cultures." In *Cultivating Differences: Symbolic Boundaries and the Making of Inequality,* ed. Michele Lamont and Marcel Fournier, 58–74. Chicago: University of Chicago Press.

Cruz, Jon. 1990. "Moralizing Resentment: *The Morton Downey Jr. Show* and Conservative Populism." In *Marginal Conventions: Popular Culture, Mass Media, and Social Deviance,* ed. Clinton Sanders, 155–80. Bowling Green, Ohio: Bowling Green State University Popular Press.

Daniels, Arlene Kaplan. 1983. "Self-Deception and Self-Discovery in Fieldwork." *Qualitative Sociology* 6, no. 3 (fall): 195–214.

Davis, Stacy, and Marie-Louise Mares. 1998. "Effects of Talk Show Viewing on Adolescents." *Journal of Communication* 48, no. 3 (summer): 69–86.

de Certeau, Michel. 1984. *The Practice of Everyday Life.* Berkeley and Los Angeles: University of California Press.

DeMott, Benjamin. 1990. *The Imperial Middle: Why Americans Can't Think Straight about Class.* New York: Morrow.

Dennett, Andrea Stulman. 1996. "The Dime Museum Freak Show Reconfigured as Talk Show." In *Freakery: Cultural Spectacles of the Extraordinary Body,* ed. Rosemarie Garland Thomson, 315–26. New York: New York University Press.

DeVault, Marjorie L. 1996. "Talking Back to Sociology: Distinctive Contributions of Feminist Methodology." *Annual Review of Sociology* 22:29–50.

DiMaggio, Paul. 1982a. "Cultural Entrepreneurship in Nineteenth-Century Boston, Part I: The Creation of an Organizational Base for High Culture in America." *Media, Culture, and Society* 4:33–50.

———. 1982b. "Cultural Entrepreneurship in Nineteenth-Century Boston, Part II: The Classification and Framing of American Art." *Media, Culture, and Society* 4:303–22.

Donahue, Phil, & Co. 1979. *Donahue: My Own Story.* New York: Simon & Schuster.

Downes, Lilli. 2000. "Quasi-Utopian Fantasies of Blame and Penance: Working-Class Females and the True Confession Magazine, 1964–1995." Paper presented at the annual meeting of the American Sociological Association, Washington, D.C., 12–16 August.

Duneier, Mitchell. 1999. *Sidewalk.* New York: Farrar, Straus and Giroux.

Durkheim, Emile. 1965. *The Elementary Forms of Religious Life.* Translated by Joseph Ward Swain. New York: Free Press.

Ehrenreich, Barbara. 1995. "In Defense of Talk Shows." *Time*, 4 December, 92.

Ehrenreich, Barbara, and Deirdre English. 1978. *For Her Own Good: 150 Years of the Experts' Advice to Women.* Garden City, N.Y.: Anchor/Doubleday.

Ehrenreich, Barbara, Elizabeth Hess, and Gloria Jacobs. 1992. "Beatlemania: Girls Just Want to Have Fun." In *The Adoring Audience: Fan Culture and Popular Media,* ed. Lisa A. Lewis, 84–106. London: Routledge.

Elias, Norbert. 1994. *The Civilizing Process.* Translated by Edmund Jephcott. Cambridge, Mass.: Blackwell.

Ellis, Carolyn. 1995. "Emotional and Ethical Quagmires in Returning to the Field." *Journal of Contemporary Ethnography* 24, no. 1 (April): 68–98.

Ewen, Stuart. 1989. *All Consuming Images: The Politics of Style in Contemporary Culture.* New York: Basic.

Faludi, Susan. 1995. "The Money Shot." *New Yorker,* 30 October, 64–87.

Fischoff, Stuart. 1995. "Confessions of a TV Talk-Show Shrink." *Psychology Today* 28, no. 5: 38–45.

Fishman, Mark. 1980. *Manufacturing the News.* Austin: University of Texas Press.

Fiske, John. 1989. *Understanding Popular Culture.* Boston: Unwin Hyman.

———. 1992. "Popularity and the Politics of Information." In *Journalism and Popular Culture,* ed. Peter Dahlgren and Colin Sparks, 45–63. Newbury Park, Calif.: Sage.

Fraser, Nancy. 1990. "Rethinking the Public Sphere: A Contribution to the Critique of Actually Existing Democracy." *Social Text* 25/26:56–80.

Frisby, Cynthia. 1999. "When Bad Things Happen to Bad People: Motivations for Viewing TV Talk Shows." Paper presented at the annual convention of the Association for Education in Journalism and Mass Communication, New Orleans, 4–7 August.

Galliher, John. 1980. "Social Scientists' Ethical Responsibilities to Superordinates: Looking Upward Meekly." *Social Problems* 27, no. 3 (February): 298–308.

Gamson, Joshua. 1994. *Claims to Fame: Celebrity in Contemporary America.* Berkeley and Los Angeles: University of California Press.

———. 1996. "Do Ask, Do Tell." *Utne Reader,* January/February, 79–83.

———. 1998. *Freaks Talk Back: Tabloid Talk Shows and Sexual Nonconformity.* Chicago: University of Chicago Press.

Gamson, William, and Gadi Wolsfeld. 1993. "Movements and Media as Interacting Systems." *Annals of the American Association of Political and Social Sciences,* no. 528 (July): 114–25.

Gans, Herbert. 1979. *Deciding What's News.* New York: Pantheon.

Garnham, Nicholas. 1994. "The Media and the Public Sphere." In *Capitalism and Communication: Global Culture and the Economics of Information,* ed. Fred Inglis, 104–14. Newbury Park, Calif.: Sage.

Geertz, Clifford. 1973. *The Interpretation of Culture.* New York: Basic.

Gerber, David. 1996. "The Careers of People Exhibited in Freak Shows: The Problem of Volition and Valorization." In *Freakery: Cultural Spectacles of the Extraordinary*

Body, ed. Rosemarie Garland Thomson, 38–54. New York: New York University Press.

Gilbert, Craig. 1988a. "Reflections on an American Family I." In *New Challenges for Documentary*, ed. Alan Rosenthal, 191–201. Berkeley and Los Angeles: University of California Press.

———. 1988b. "Reflections on an American Family II." In *New Challenges for Documentary*, ed. Alan Rosenthal, 289–307. Berkeley and Los Angeles: University of California Press.

Gitlin, Todd. 1980. *The Whole World Is Watching: Mass Media in the Making and Unmaking of the New Left*. Berkeley and Los Angeles: University of California Press.

———. 1983. *Inside Prime Time*. New York: Pantheon.

Goad, Jim. 1997. *The Redneck Manifesto: How Hillbillies, Hicks, and White Trash Became America's Scapegoats*. New York: Simon & Schuster.

Goffman, Erving. 1959. *The Presentation of Self in Everyday Life*. Garden City, N.Y.: Anchor Books.

Goldberg, David Theo. 1993. *Racist Culture: Philosophy and the Politics of Meaning*. Oxford: Blackwell.

Goldfarb, Jeffrey C. 1998. *Civility and Subversion: The Intellectual in Democratic Society*. New York: Cambridge University Press.

Gordon, Deborah. 1988. "Writing Culture, Writing Feminism: The Poetics and Politics of Experimental Ethnography." *Inscriptions* 3/4:7–26.

Gramsci, Antonio. 1971. *Selections from the Prison Notebooks*. Translated and edited by Quintin Hoare and Geoffrey Nowell Smith. New York: International.

Greenberg, Bradley, Dana Mastro, and Mark Woods. 1999. "Aggression Responses to Physical and Verbal Violence on *The Jerry Springer Show*." Paper presented at the annual meeting of the International Communication Association, San Francisco, 27–30 May.

Greenberg, Bradley, and Sandi Smith. 1995. "The Content of Television Talk Shows: Topics, Guests, and Interactions." Report prepared for the Henry J. Kaiser Family Foundation by the Departments of Communication and Telecommunication, Michigan State University.

Gripsrud, Jostein. 1992. "The Aesthetics and Politics of Melodrama." In *Journalism and Popular Culture*, ed. Peter Dahlgren and Colin Sparks, 84–95. Newbury Park, Calif.: Sage.

Gross, Larry. 1994. "What's Wrong with This Picture?" In *Queer Words, Queer Images: Communication and the Construction of Homosexuality*, ed. R. Jeffrey Ringer, 143–156. New York: New York University Press.

Habermas, Jurgen. 1989. *The Structural Transformation of the Public Sphere: An Inquiry Into a Category of Bourgeois Society*. Translated by Thomas Burger. Cambridge: MIT Press.

Hall, Stuart. 1981. "Notes on Deconstructing the Popular." In *People's History and Socialist Theory*, ed. R. Samuel, 227–40. London: Routledge & Kegan Paul.

Hall, Stuart, Chas Critcher, Tony Jefferson, John Clarke, and Brian Roberts. 1978. *Policing the Crisis*. New York: Holmes & Meier.

Hallin, Daniel. 1994. *We Keep America on Top of the World: Television Journalism and the Public Sphere*. New York: Routledge.

Hartigan, John. 1997. "Name Calling: Objectifying 'Poor Whites' and 'White Trash' in Detroit." In *White Trash: Race and Class in America*, ed. Matt Wray and Annalee Newitz, 41–56. New York: Routledge.

Hartley, John. 1982. *Understanding News*. London: Methuen.

Hartsock, Nancy. 1987. "The Feminist Standpoint." In *Feminism and Methodology*, ed. Sandra Harding, 157–80. Bloomington: Indiana University Press.

Heaton, Jean Albronda, and Nona Leigh Wilson. 1995. *Tuning in Trouble: Talk TV's Destructive Impact on Mental Health*. San Francisco: Jossey-Bass.

Hebdige, Dick. 1979. *Subculture: The Meaning of Style*. London: Methuen.

Herbst, Susan. 1995. "On Electronic Public Space: Talk Shows in Theoretical Perspective." *Political Communication* 12:263–74.

Hochschild, Arlie Russell. 1983. *The Managed Heart: Commercialization of Human Feeling*. Berkeley and Los Angeles: University of California Press.

Hoggart, Richard. 1957. *The Uses of Literacy*. New York: Oxford University Press.

hooks, bell. 1989. *Talking Back*. Boston: South End.

Hoynes, William, and David Croteau. 1989. *Are You on the* Nightline *Guest List? An Analysis of 40 Months of* Nightline *Programming*. A special report prepared for Fairness and Accuracy in Reporting.

Hughes, Everett. 1974. "Who Studies Whom?" *Human Organization* 33:209–15.

Jackson, Bruce. 1987. *Fieldwork*. Urbana: University of Illinois Press.

Jackson, Bruce, and Edward Ives. 1996. *Reflections on the Fieldwork Process*. Urbana: University of Illinois Press.

Jarvis, Jeff. 1994. "Ricki Lake." *TV Guide*, 2 July, 7.

Jhally, Sut, and Justin Lewis. 1992. *Enlightened Racism: The Cosby Show, Audiences, and the Myth of the American Dream*. Boulder, Colo.: Westview.

Kaminer, Wendy. 1993. *I'm Dysfunctional, You're Dysfunctional: The Recovery Movement and Other Self-Help Fashions*. New York: Random House.

Kamrin, Kacey. 1999. "And Today's Topic: I Am Middle-Upper Class and I Love the Jerry Springer Show!" Senior honors thesis, Department of Sociology, University of California, Davis.

Kano, Ayako. 2001. *Acting Like a Woman in Modern Japan: Theater, Gender, and Nationalism*. New York: Palgrave.

Kaplan, Janice. 1995. "Are Talk Shows out of Control?" *TV Guide*, 1 April, 10–15.

Kasson, John. 1990. *Rudeness and Civility: Manners in Nineteenth Century Urban America*. New York: Hill & Wang.

Kipnis, Laura. 1996. *Bound and Gagged: Pornography and the Politics of Fantasy in America*. New York: Grove.

Kohn, Melvin. 1963. "Social Class and the Exercise of Parental Authority." In *Person-*

ality and Social Systems, ed. Neil Smelser and William Smelser, 297–313. New York: Wiley.

Kurtz, Howard. 1996. *Hot Air: All Talk, All the Time.* New York: Times Books.

Lamont, Michele. 1992. *Money, Morals, and Manners: The Culture of the French and the American Upper-Middle Class.* Chicago: University of Chicago Press.

Langer, John. 1992. "Truly Awful News on Television." In *Journalism and Popular Culture,* ed. Peter Dahlgren and Colin Sparks, 113–29. Newbury Park, Calif.: Sage.

———. 1998. *Tabloid Television: Popular Journalism and the "Other News."* London: Routledge.

Lareau, Annette. 1989. "Appendix: Common Problems in Field Work: A Personal Essay." In *Home Advantage,* 187–223. New York: Falmer.

Lasch, Christopher. 1978. *The Culture of Narcissism.* New York: Norton.

Leonard, Tom. 2000. "Why the Tabloids Are Turning." *London Daily Telegraph,* 7 September, 21.

Levine, Lawrence. 1988. *Highbrow Lowbrow: The Emergence of Cultural Hierarchy in America.* Cambridge: Harvard University Press.

Lhamon, W. T., Jr. 1998. *Raising Cain: Blackface Performance from Jim Crow to Hip Hop.* Cambridge: Harvard University Press.

Livingstone, Sonia. 1996. "On the Continuing Problem of Media Effects." In *Mass Media and Society* (2d ed.), ed. James Curran and Michael Gurevitch, 305–24. New York: St. Martin's.

Livingstone, Sonia, and Peter Lunt. 1994. *Talk on Television: Audience Participation and Public Debate.* London: Routledge.

Lofland, John, and Lyn Lofland. 1984. *Analyzing Social Settings: A Guide to Qualitative Observation and Analysis.* Belmont, Calif.: Wadsworth.

"A Look at the Week Ahead; on 'Jerry': Movies That Sleep with TV." 1998. *Los Angeles Times,* 23 November, on-line edition.

Lott, Eric. 1993. *Love and Theft: Blackface Minstrelsy and the American Working Class.* New York: Oxford University Press.

Lowney, Kathleen. 1999. *Baring Our Souls: TV Talk Shows and the Religion of Recovery.* New York: Aldine de Gruyter.

Malinowski, Bronislaw. 1922. *Argonauts of the Western Pacific.* London: Routledge & Kegan Paul.

Manoff, Karl, and Michael Schudson, eds. 1986. *Reading the News.* New York: Pantheon.

Marsh, Katherine. 2000. "What Is Real? Deep behind the Scenes of the New Season of MTV's *The Real World.*" *Rolling Stone,* June, 71–79, 141.

Masciarotte, Gloria-Jean. 1991. "C'mon Girl: Oprah Winfrey and the Discourse of Feminine Talk." *Genders* 11 (fall): 81–110.

McCann, Paul (2000) "Stars of Real-Life TV Attack 'Distorted' Footage." *Times* (London), 13 November, on-line edition.

McQuail, Dennis. 1991. "Reflections on Uses and Gratifications Research." In *Criti-*

cal Perspectives on Media and Society, ed. Robert Avery and David Eason, 9–27. New York: Guilford.

Mellencamp, Patricia. 1992. *High Anxiety: Catastrophe, Scandal, Age and Comedy*. Bloomington: Indiana University Press.

Meyrowitz, Joshua. 1985. *No Sense of Place: The Impact of Electronic Media on Social Behavior*. New York: Oxford University Press.

Mitroff, Ian, and Warren Bennis. 1989. *The Unreality Industry: The Deliberate Manufacturing of Falsehood and What It Is Doing to Our Lives*. New York: Carol Publishing Group.

Modleski, Tania. 1982. *Loving with a Vengeance: Mass-Produced Fantasies for Women*. New York: Methuen.

Moffatt, Michael. 1989. *Coming of Age in New Jersey: College and American Culture*. New Brunswick, N.J.: Rutgers University Press.

Molotch, Harvey. 1979. "Media and Movements." In *The Dynamics of Social Movements: Resource Mobilization, Social Control, and Tactics*, ed. Mayer Zald and John McCarthy, 71–93. Cambridge, Mass.: Winthrop.

Molotch, Harvey, and Marilyn Lester. 1974. "News as Purposive Behavior: On the Strategic Use of Routine Events, Accidents, and Scandals." *American Sociological Review* 39 (February): 101–12.

Munson, Wayne. 1993. *All Talk: The Talk Show in Media Culture*. Philadelphia: Temple University Press.

Nader, Laura. 1972. "Up the Anthropologist—Perspectives Gained from Studying Up." In *Reinventing Anthropology*, ed. Dell Hymes, 284–311. New York: Pantheon.

Nelson, Adie, and B. W. Robinson. 1994. "'Reality Talk' or 'Telling Tales': The Social Construction of Sexual and Gender Deviance on a Television Talk Show." *Journal of Contemporary Ethnography* 23, no. 1 (April): 51–78.

Newitz, Annalee. 1997. "White Savagery and Humiliation; or, A New Racial Consciousness in the Media." In *White Trash: Race and Class in America*, ed. Matt Wray and Annalee Newitz, 131–54. New York: Routledge.

Omi, Michael, and Howard Winant. 1995. *Racial Formation in the United States*, 2d ed. New York: Routledge.

Pakulski, Jan, and Malcolm Waters. 1996. *The Death of Class*. Thousand Oaks, Calif.: Sage.

Peck, Janice. 1994. "Talk about Race: Framing a Popular Discourse of Race on *Oprah Winfrey*." *Cultural Critique* 27 (spring): 89–126.

———. 1995. "TV Talk Shows as Therapeutic Discourse: The Ideological Labor of the Televised Talking Cure." *Communication Theory* 5, no. 1 (February): 58–81.

Peiss, Kathy. 1986. *Cheap Amusements: Working Women and Leisure in Turn-of-the-Century New York*. Philadelphia: Temple University Press.

Petro, Patrice. 1986. "Mass Culture and the Feminine: The 'Place' of Television in Film Studies." *Cinema Journal* 25, no. 3: 5–21.

Polan, Dana. 1990. "The Public's Fear, or Media as Monster in Habermas, Negt, and Kluge." *Social Text* 25/26: 260–66.

Postman, Neil. 1985. *Amusing Ourselves to Death: Public Discourse in the Age of Show-business.* New York: Penguin.

Powdermaker, Hortense. 1951. *Hollywood, the Dream Factory: An Anthropologist Looks at the Movie-Makers.* London: Secker & Warburg.

Priest, Patricia. 1995. *Public Intimacies: Talk Show Participants and Tell-All TV.* Creskill, N.J.: Hampton.

Priest, Patricia, and Joseph R. Dominick. 1994. "Pulp Pulpits: Self-Disclosure on *Donahue*." *Journal of Communication* 44, no. 4 (autumn): 74–97.

Radway, Janice. 1988. "Reception Study: Ethnography and the Problems of Dispersed Audiences and Nomadic Subjects." *Cultural Studies* 2, no. 3 (October): 359–76.

Raphael, Chad. 1997. "The Political Economy of Reality-Based Television." *Jump Cut* 41:102–9.

Richardson, James. 1991. "Experiencing Research on New Religions and Cults: Practical and Ethical Considerations." In *Experiencing Fieldwork: An Inside View of Qualitative Research*, ed. William Shaffir and Robert Stebbins, 62–71. Newbury Park, Calif.: Sage.

Robinson, Beatrice. 1982. "Family Experts on Television Talk Shows: Facts, Values, and Half-Truths." *Family Relations* 31 (July): 369–78.

Rollins, Judith. 1985. *Between Women: Domestics and Their Employers.* Philadelphia: Temple University Press.

Rose, Brian. 1985. "The Talk Show." In *TV Genres*, ed. Brian Rose, 329–52. Westport, Conn.: Greenwood.

Rose, Dan. 1987. *Black American Street Life: South Philadelphia, 1969–1971.* Philadelphia: University of Pennsylvania Press.

Ross, Andrew. 1989. "Candid Camera." In *No Respect: Intellectuals and Popular Culture*, 102–34. New York: Routledge.

Rössler, Patrick, and Hans-Bernd Brosius. 2001. "Do Talk Shows Cultivate Adolescents' Views of the World? A Prolonged Exposure Experiment." *Journal of Communication* 51, no. 1 (March): 143–63.

Scheff, Thomas. 1977. "The Distancing of Emotion in Ritual." *Current Anthropology* 18, no. 3 (September): 483–90.

Schiff, Steven. 1995. "Geek Shows." *New Yorker*, 6 November, 9–10.

Schone, Mark. 1996. "Talked Out." *Spin*, May, 66–75, 118.

Schudson, Michael. 1978. *Discovering the News: A Social History of American Newspapers.* New York: Basic.

Shaffir, William, and Robert Stebbins. 1991. *Experiencing Fieldwork: An Inside View of Qualitative Research.* Newbury Park, Calif.: Sage.

Shattuc, Jane. 1997. *The Talking Cure: TV Talk Shows and Women.* New York: Routledge.

Shils, Edward. 1980. "Social Inquiry and the Autonomy of the Private Sphere." In *The Calling of Sociology and Other Essays on the Pursuit of Learning*, 421–51. Chicago: University of Chicago Press.

Sigal, Leon. 1973. *Reporters and Officials.* Lexington, Mass.: Heath.

————. 1986. "Who? Sources Make the News." In *Reading the News*, ed. Karl Manoff and Michael Schudson. New York: Pantheon.

Simonds, Wendy. 1992. *Women and Self-Help Culture: Reading Between the Lines.* New Brunswick, N.J.: Rutgers University Press.

Smith, Dorothy. 1987. *The Everyday World as Problematic: A Feminist Sociology.* Boston: Northeastern University Press.

Sparks, Colin, and John Tulloch, eds. 2000. *Tabloid Tales: Global Debates over Media Standards.* New York: Rowman & Littlefield.

Squire, Corinne. 1994. "Empowering Women? *The Oprah Winfrey Show.*" *Feminism and Psychology* 4, no. 1:63–79.

Stacey, Judith. 1988. "Can There Be a Feminist Ethnography?" *Women's Studies International Forum* 11:21–27.

Stasio, Marilyn. 1995. "When Talk Shows Become Horror Shows." *Cosmopolitan*, October, 250–53.

Steenland, Sally. 1990. "Those Daytime Talk Shows." *Television Quarterly* 24, no. 4:5–12.

Tavris, Carol. 1989. *Anger: The Misunderstood Emotion.* New York: Touchstone.

Thomson, Rosemarie Garland. 1996. "Introduction: From Wonder to Error—a Genealogy of Freak Discourse in Modernity." In *Freakery: Cultural Spectacles of the Extraordinary Body*, ed. Rosemarie Garland Thomson, 1–22. New York: New York University Press.

Thorne, Barrie. 1980. "'You Still Takin' Notes?' Fieldwork and Problems of Informed Consent." *Social Problems* 27, no. 3 (February): 284–97.

Tomlinson, John. 1997. "'And Besides, the Wench Is Dead': Media Scandals and the Globalization of Communication." In *Media Scandals: Morality and Desire in the Popular Culture Marketplace*, ed. James Lull and Stephen Hinerman, 65–84. London: Polity.

Torgovnik, Marianna. 1991. *Gone Primitive.* Chicago: University of Chicago Press.

Tuchman, Gaye. 1973. "Making News by Doing Work: Routinizing the Unexpected." *American Journal of Sociology* 79, no. 1:110–31.

————. 1974. "Assembling a Network Talk-Show." In *The TV Establishment: Programming for Power and Profit*, ed. Gaye Tuchman, 119–35. Englewood Cliffs, N.J.: Prentice-Hall.

————. 1978. *Making News: A Study in the Construction of Reality.* London: Free Press.

Van Maanen, John. 1988. *Tales of the Field: On Writing Ethnography.* Chicago: University of Chicago Press.

————. 1991. "Playing Back the Tape: Early Days in the Field." In *Experiencing Fieldwork: An Inside View of Qualitative Research*, ed. William Shaffir and Robert Stebbins, 31–42. Newbury Park, Calif.: Sage.

Wax, Murray. 1980. "Paradoxes of 'Consent' to the Practice of Fieldwork." *Social Problems* 27, no. 3 (February): 272–83.

Wax, Rosalie. 1971. *Doing Fieldwork: Warnings and Advice.* Chicago: University of Chicago Press.

Wheatley, Elizabeth. 1994. "How Can We Engender Ethnography with a Feminist Imagination?" *Women's Studies International Forum* 17, no. 4:403–16.

White, Harrison. 1993. *Careers and Creativity: Social Forces in the Arts.* Boulder, Colo.: Westview.

Willis, Paul. 1994. "Women in Sport in Ideology." In *Women, Sport, and Culture,* ed. Susan Birrell and Cheryl Cole, 31–46. Champaign, Ill.: Human Kinetics.

Wolf, Diane. 1996. "Situating Feminist Dilemmas in Fieldwork." In *Feminist Dilemmas in Fieldwork,* ed. Diane Wolf, 1–55. Boulder, Colo.: Westview.

Wolf, Margery. 1992. *A Thrice-Told Tale: Feminism, Postmodernism, and Ethnographic Responsibility.* Stanford, Calif.: Stanford University Press.

Wolsfeld, Gadi. 1984. "The Symbiosis of Press and Protest: An Exchange Analysis." *Journalism Quarterly* 61:550–56.

Wray, Matt, and Annalee Newitz, eds. 1997. *White Trash: Race and Class in America.* New York: Routledge.

Zurakwik, David. 2000. "We Become the Watchful Big Brother, Big Sister: From 'Survivors' on a Tropical Island to a British Family Living without Running Water and McDonald's, 'Reality Television' Gives Us the Chance to Test Our Voyeuristic Sensibilities." *Baltimore Sun,* 31 May, 1E.

Page numbers in italics refer to figures.

confessional style, 28
confrontalk, concept of, 52
confrontational style: after *Jenny Jones* murder, 117; audiences' encouragement of, 67; booking guests and, 103, 105, 107; emergence of, 50–53; emotion work and, 133; ethical issues and, 140–41; of expert guest, 224–25; guests' grievances/disappointments in, 185–86; guests' satisfaction with, 191; postperformance atmosphere and, 131–32; prepping guests for, 125–26, 167–68; producer/guest relationships and, 110–11; production challenges of, 77–78, 95–96; rejection of, 57–59, 170–71, 194; selecting topics for, 85; success of, 60; theatrical enactment of, 53–54n. 6. *See also* sensationalism; trashy talk shows
Conger, Darva, 260
Connie (pseud., expert guest): on attempts to redefine issue, 221, 222–23; motivation of, 212, 213; postshow disappointment of, 224
Cora (pseud., guest), 152, 155, 195
craniometry, 269n. 13
credibility, expert guests' role in, 215–16. *See also* authenticity and truth
crime, study of, 279n. 3
Croteau, David, 253n. 6
Cruz, Jon, 52
Cubillos, Isaac: activist goal of, 232–33; background of, 211; on being confrontational, 224–25; motivation of, 213
cultural hierarchies: academy's place in, 34; class and, 29–33, 266–67; experts in, 206; fluidity but persistence of, 269–70; inversion of, 20–21; in journalism, 26–28; of race, 263. *See also* stereotypes
culture: assumptions in, 278–79n. 2; decline of, 273; fatness in, 266n. 11; fragmentation of, 206, 268–69; heterogeneity and, 68n. 16; high vs. low, 20, 31, 34, 53–54, 68–69, 269n. 13; mass mediation of, 269–70; nature vs., 20, 31–32, 265, 266–68; production of, 34–35, 275–76; sacralization of, 268–69

Dallas County Commissioner, 232
Danny (talk show), 37
Darlene (pseud., intern), 171
daytime talk shows: behind-the-scenes footage of, 124; benefits of watching, 198; changes in, 50–54; characteristics of, 18–21, 23n. 2, 186; as circus, 190; classy/trashy binarism in, 26–27; compared to other media, 252–53; conflicts embedded in, 30–31; criticism of, 21–24, *25, 26,* 164–65, *166,* 197, 226, 251, 253, 265; defense of, 24–25; denigration of, 197, 265–66; as entertainment, 199, 247; fact/fiction blurred in, 251–52; as forum for discussion, 234–35; legal grievances aired on, 159; mental health discussions on, 208–9n. 2; news coverage of, 177–78; origins of, 27–29, 47, 48–50, 54–56; as performative, 126–27, 132, 218–19, 248–49; personal conflict aired on, 160–61; as political engagement, 272; as public sphere, 240; respectability and, 202; scriptedness vs. spontaneity in, 38–39, 78, 100–101, 128–29, 244; shortcomings of, 272–73; sociology's link to, 276, 288; structural position of guests in, 178, 191–92, 220–21, 224. *See also* audiences (general); bodily and emotional expression; classy talk shows; fieldwork; guests (ordinary); producers; show topics; trashy talk shows
deception: fieldwork and, 280–85; guests and, 97–98, 120, 142, 251–52; producers and, 106, 251–52. *See also* ethics; fake guests
de Certeau, Michel, 33
Deliverance (film), 263
Diana (pseud., host), 3–4
Diana (pseud., talk show): airing personal conflict on, 160–61; audiences of, 64–65, 121–22; authenticity of, 98, 171; celebrities on, 74, 75n. 17; class and race issues at, 145; as classy, 7–8, 26–27, 58–59, 143, 246; criteria for booking guests on, 95, 96; description of, 36–37; diversity of, 102; dropout guests of, 109;